READINGS IN SOCIAL PSYCHOLOGY
The Art and Science of Research

Steven Fein
Williams College

Steven Spencer
University of Waterloo

HOUGHTON MIFFLIN COMPANY   BOSTON   NEW YORK

Sponsoring Editor: Rebecca J. Dudley
Senior Associate Editor: Jane Knetzger
Senior Project Editor: Carol Newman
Production Coordinator: Debora Frydman
Senior Manufacturing Coordinator: Priscilla Bailey
Marketing Manager: Pamela Shaffer

Printed in the U.S.A.

ISBN: 0-395-95127-5

789-VG- 05 04 03 02 01

CONTENTS

INTRODUCTION

THE PURPOSE OF THIS BOOK

One of the most rewarding aspects of teaching social psychology is that most students are interested in social psychological issues. Most of us—students as well as instructors—are interested in explaining the causes of others' behaviors, in predicting how people will react in various situations, and in understanding the attraction or hostility between people. But this interest can also present an important challenge to instructors. When people learn social psychological theories or findings that are at odds with their own intuition or personal observations, they may be too quick to dismiss these theories or findings as wrong or unrepresentative. Then when they learn other theories or findings that are consistent with their own intuition or personal observations, they may disparage the first theories and findings as mere common sense.

The difference between the discipline of social psychology and people's intuitions and observations is empirical research. Intuition and common sense can be frustratingly accommodating. One can, for example, cite, "Absence makes the heart grow fonder," to explain the continued success of a romantic relationship after the couple has been forced to spend some time apart from each other, and yet also cite, "Out of sight, out of mind," to explain the failure of a different couple to endure a similar amount of time apart. Social psychology, in contrast, cannot have it so easy. Social psychological theories must be more rigorous, and they must be supported by the results of systematic, methodically sound research. To fully understand and appreciate social psychology, therefore, one must understand and appreciate the research on which the field of social psychology has been, and will continue to be, based. Your textbook, the Third Edition of *Social Psychology* by Sharon Brehm and Saul Kassin, explains much of this research clearly, concretely, and compellingly. The authors have made it a point to make this research come alive to students, to give students enough information so that they can imagine what it would be like to be a subject in many of these studies.

This book of readings was designed to take this emphasis a step further by presenting a diverse sample of important, unabridged, original research articles. Whereas a textbook and class lectures can offer summaries of a number of studies, only a sample of representative studies can give valuable insight into the *process* as well as the *content* of social psychology. The goal is to encourage students not only to learn the important theories and principles of the field, but also to think critically about them—to see where they came from, how they have been supported, *why* they have been supported, and what their potential flaws are. This kind of critical thinking not only makes the material more interesting and compelling but also leads to a deeper understanding of the material.

Another goal of this book of readings is to illustrate the creativity involved in designing studies to test one's hypotheses. In this process, social psychologists often are challenged to combine elements of theater and science. Their experiments must be controlled and precise; procedures should be identical across conditions, with the exception of the manipulated independent variable(s); and potential alternative explanations should be anticipated and ruled out. Within these constraints, however, researchers often need to create an artificial but very real world for their subjects. They need to anticipate the thoughts, feelings, and reactions of the people who participate in their studies, and they must create situations that are realistic and meaningful. "Doing" social psychology, therefore, often involves acting like a playwright; in conducting research, the social psychologist often must create characters, dialogue, and interactions among characters, must place these characters into various situations, and must create a setting, all with the intention of drawing the participants into this fabricated reality so that their reactions and responses are real and spontaneous.

Not all social psychological experiments require this level of creativity. Some studies are, by necessity, simple, whereas others are quite elaborate. Some involve a great deal of deception; others involve no deception. Some elicit strong emotional reaction; others are quite mundane. Some are conducted in a laboratory; others are conducted in the field. But whatever the level of complexity, the process that begins with a set of hypotheses and proceeds through the execution of a study to test these hypotheses is creative and enjoyable. We hope that the enjoyment of this process will become evident to the reader in this set of articles.

THE SELECTION OF ARTICLES

In keeping with the goals outlined above, we have selected readings that we, along with the authors of the textbook, feel will help (1) inspire critical thinking about several of the most important issues raised in the textbook, (2) produce a better understanding of various important social psychological principles and findings, and (3) illustrate the creativity of the science of conducting social psychological research. Thus these readings not only present important findings, but they also describe interesting designs, procedures, or settings. We chose psychology journal articles that were written well and concisely and that can be understood and appreciated by people not familiar with all of the literature cited or details given. This is particularly significant because we wanted to present these readings in their entirety, unabridged, as the original authors wrote them. We emphasize this for a number of reasons. We feel there is no substitute for reading these important works firsthand, without the articles being diluted or filtered by anyone else. These are, after all, papers that have helped change the field of social psychology. In addition, an entire article can meet a variety of needs. Readers who want only the gist of the article and readers who want to study and learn the details of the research—such as exactly how some construct was measured or exactly why the researchers believed their results supported their hypothesis—can get what they want from the articles presented in this book. Perhaps most importantly, all students who read these articles must organize and synthesize the information for themselves—whether this means abstracting out the gist or outlining all of the important points and procedures—and this is an excellent way to improve understanding and retention of the information.

These articles include both classic articles that have withstood the test of time and contributed to the development of social psychology, and contemporary articles concerning research that has already made important contributions to the field and that is likely to inspire the research that will help reshape social psychology for years to come. The selection of both classic and contemporary articles can give students a sense of how the field has changed, and continues to change. For example, contemporary articles tend to feature more sophisticated methods and statistical analyses. Another difference is the language used in these articles. Some of the classic articles contain language that would be considered sexist by today's standards, whereas contemporary articles must conform to the American Psychological Association's guidelines for nonsexist language. Yet another example concerns the ethics of the research. Research today must be approved by a review board, and social psychologists today are more sensitive to the needs of those who participate in their research than they were in the past.

This is by no means an exhaustive set of the most important articles in social psychology. Rather, it is a sample of important classic and contemporary articles that report original, empirical research and that are readable and interesting. Moreover, these articles concern the variety of topics covered in Brehm and Kassin's *Social Psychology*. Like the text, they are divided into four parts: Social Perception, Social Interaction, Social Influence, and Applying Social Psychology. These readings concern issues raised in every chapter of the textbook.

We have briefly introduced each article to set the article in its proper context, including the sections in the textbook to which the article is most relevant. At the end of each article we have added some critical thinking questions, designed to suggest *some* of the questions or thoughts that are raised by the research. These questions should trigger other questions and thoughts, which should help the reader think about the important issues and implications as well as provide some ideas for interesting class discussions.

Previous Edition Chapter Correlation Guide
Brehm/Kassin/Fein, *Social Psychology,* 5/e

If you are using the Fourth or Fifth edition of Brehm/Kassin/Fein, *Social Psychology,* please refer to the following guide when you encounter chapter references in *Readings in Social Psychology.*

Brehm/Kassin, *Social Psychology,* 3/e	Brehm/Kassin/Fein, *Social Psychology,* 4/e, 5/e
Chapter 1: Introduction to Social Psychology	Chapter 1: Introduction
Chapter 2: The Social Self	Chapter 2: Doing Social Psychology Research
Chapter 3: Perceiving Persons	Chapter 3: The Social Self
Chapter 4: Perceiving Groups	Chapter 4: Perceiving Persons
Chapter 5: Interpersonal Attraction	Chapter 5: Perceiving Groups
Chapter 6: Intimate Relationships	Chapter 6: Attitudes
Chapter 7: Helping Others	Chapter 7: Conformity
Chapter 8: Aggression	Chapter 8: Group Processes
Chapter 9: Conformity	Chapter 9: Attraction and Close Relationships
Chapter 10: Attitudes	Chapter 10: Helping Others
Chapter 11: Group Processes	Chapter 11: Aggression
Chapter 12: Law	Chapter 12: Law
Chapter 13: Business	Chapter 13: Business
Chapter 14: Health	Chapter 14: Health

NOTE TO STUDENTS:
HOW TO READ THE READINGS

Several of the readings in this book were written in a style with which you are likely to be unfamiliar. They were written for psychology journals that have a particular format and set of norms. When approaching these readings, therefore, DO NOT BE INTIMIDATED. We selected articles that even those unfamiliar with the literature cited, jargon used, and statistical analyses reported should be able to understand without much trouble. The key is to know how to read these articles, such as what to read carefully and what to skim. Unless your instructor indicates otherwise, you don't need to understand all of the details.

THE FOUR MAJOR SECTIONS OF MANY ARTICLES

Many, but not all, of these articles share a particular structure. They begin with an Introduction, followed by a Method section, followed by a Results section, followed by a Discussion section. Articles that describe more than one study begin with a general Introduction and conclude with a General Discussion section; in between, each study reported is introduced with its own brief Introduction, has its own Method and Results sections, and may have its own Discussion section. The complete references of the literature cited in each article are listed at the very end of the article. Many of these articles also have a brief abstract, or summary of the entire article, before the Introduction.

In the Introduction, the purpose of the research is explained and placed into a general context, and hypotheses are developed. By the end of the Introduction, the research that was conducted to begin to test these hypotheses is explained in rather broad detail. The Method section presents the specific details of how the research was conducted. The purpose of this section is to allow the readers to see exactly how the research was done so that they can evaluate the validity of the research and, if they so desire, try to replicate the study themselves. The Results section usually is the most detailed section. It reports the results of the statistical analyses that were used to determine to what extent the data collected were consistent or inconsistent with the hypotheses. The Discussion section summarizes these results and discusses such things as *why* the research found what it did, what the implications of the research may be, and what questions remain unanswered.

These articles can be described as having an hourglass shape: they start out relatively broad, usually by making general statements about a particular problem, then become more and more focused as they introduce the specific research conducted and results found, and then become more and more broad again as the Discussion section first summarizes the results and then discusses the broader implications of these results.

A SUGGESTED ORDER IN WHICH TO READ THE
MORE DIFFICULT ARTICLES

To the extent, then, that some of these articles include details that are difficult to understand, how should you read them? First of all, you should be sure to have read Chapter 1 in your textbook carefully, particularly the sections concerning hypothesis, theory, basic research, and applied research; correlations; the essential features of experiments; the language of research, including independent variables, dependent variables, statistical significance, main effect, and interaction; and evaluating research.

Although you should check with your instructor, the way we suggest reading the more difficult (or less "user friendly") articles is to first read the sections that set the context and summarize the research most clearly, and then read the sections that provide more details. Thus, if the article begins with a brief abstract, or summary, begin by reading this carefully. Because of the jargon used, it is sometimes necessary to reread the abstract a few times until you understand the general purpose and findings of the research. Then read the Introduction. If the Introduction ends with a description of the research design and hypotheses, read this description carefully. Next, you may want to skip to the first few paragraphs of the Discussion section toward the end of the paper (this might be called the General Discussion section if there are multiple studies reported). The first paragraphs usually summarize the main points of the research findings. Once you understand these principal findings, you have the context needed to go back and read the rest of the article.

Next, read the Method section. As you read this section, it's often a good idea to jot down notes so you can keep track of the conditions of the study. Try to imagine yourself as a subject in this study. What would you be experiencing? What would you be thinking? Also, imagine yourself as the experimenter. What would you be saying to subjects? How would you be observing or measuring their responses? If you come across jargon or references that you don't understand, don't worry about it. You may want to make a note of it and ask your instructor about it, but if you read ahead you should be able to understand the central idea. After you read the Method section, think about the predictions or hypotheses stated in the Introduction. Anticipate how subjects will react differently in the different conditions of the study. You may want to go back to the end of the Introduction section where the hypotheses or predictions were stated and explained.

READING THE RESULTS SECTION

Skim the Results section as best you can. Remember to familiarize yourself with each of the following from Chapter 1 of your textbook: correlations, independent variables, dependent variables, statistical significance, main effects, and interactions. In some of these articles, a number of statistical analyses will be reported that will be difficult, if not impossible, to understand. We'll give you a few guidelines in the following paragraphs to help you with these, but if you can't understand the Results section, you shouldn't be too concerned because you should be able to understand the most important results by reading the Discussion section and, if available, the Abstract.

As you read the results, go slowly and keep in mind the different conditions of the study and the hypotheses for these different conditions. Researchers are often interested in measuring the "average" response of subjects in each condition. Suppose 20 subjects in one condition were asked to rate how attractive some other person was, and 20 subjects in another condition were asked the same thing. The researchers are interested in determining if the *average* rating given by the 20 subjects in one condition was different than the *average* rating given by the 20 subjects in the other condition. Whenever differences between conditions are reported, try to get a sense of the averages for each condition. The averages for each condition may be depicted in a table or figure, or they may be reported in parentheses, as in ($M = 3.47$), which should be read as "the mean, or average, of this condition is 3.47."

The next thing to look for is whether the differences between the averages of the various conditions are significant. As Chapter 1 indicates, the convention in psychology is to say that a difference between two conditions is statistically significant if the analyses suggest that the probability that this difference could have occurred by chance alone is less than 5 out of 100.

For example, if you toss a coin 100 times, you may find that the coin landed on heads 53 times and tails 47 times. Is this difference significant? It is not significant because there is a very high likelihood that the difference reflects nothing more than a random outcome. What if you divide people into different conditions and have each of them rate something on a 100-point scale, and you find that the average response is 53 for the subjects in one condition and 47 for the subjects in the other condition? Is this significant? There is no way to determine whether this difference is significant without performing some statistical analyses.

The probability that a difference occurred by chance alone is usually reported as a number that comes after the phrase $p <$, where p means the probability. Thus, if $p < .05$, the probability that this difference occurred by chance is less than .05, or 5 out of 100, and so the difference is considered significant. Whenever differences between conditions are reported, you should try to get a sense of the averages for each group, and then see if the p level is less than .05.

When there is more than one independent variable in a study, researchers are interested not only in whether the average of one condition differs from that of another, but also in whether the independent variables interact with each other to create different patterns of results. Be sure to reread the section on interactions in Chapter 1.

In addition to differences between conditions, correlations also can be statistically significant or not. A correlation is an association between two variables that vary in quantity. It is positive when both variables increase or decrease together; it is negative when one variable increases as the other variable decreases. Chapter 1 explains and gives various examples of correlations. A correlation can occur by chance alone, such as if you flip a coin and roll some dice at the same time and find that rolling higher numbers with the dice was correlated with the coin landing on tails. This most likely was just a fluke. What if there is an association between watching a lot of television and being very aggressive? Is this a significant correlation? To the extent that the association between these two variables is a reliable one, it is more likely to be considered statistically significant. But if the probability that this association occurred by chance is less than .05, or 5 out of 100, it is considered statistically significant.

Again, it is important to keep in mind that if you begin to get lost in the details of the results, step back and gain perspective by rereading the Abstract and the beginning of the Discussion section.

PART I
Social Perception

READING 1

This article by Rosenthal and Jacobson is an appropriate selection for the first reading because it is concerned with important issues that are raised in the first four chapters of your textbook. It also shows that situational influences, which can be very subtle, can profoundly affect how people see themselves, other people, their behaviors, and ultimately their lives. The idea of self-fulfilling prophecies makes this point very well.

In Chapter 3 of the textbook, a self-fulfilling prophecy is defined as the process by which a perceiver's expectations about a person eventually lead that person to confirm those expectations. Rosenthal and Jacobson's study is one of the first and most important demonstrations of this process. After giving teachers false expectations about the intellectual potential of particular students (who, in fact, were selected at random by the researchers), Rosenthal and Jacobson found that these expectations created their own reality. The teachers' expectations influenced their behaviors toward the children, which in turn influenced the children's performance. That is, not only did the false expectations cause the teachers to *perceive* that these expectations were confirmed, but they also caused the children to actually *behave* in ways consistent with the expectations.

As already stated, this reading is relevant to each of the first four chapters of the textbook. Rosenthal and Jacobson's research, along with other research by Rosenthal discussed in this reading, demonstrates the potential power of expectations. This idea relates to the discussion in Chapter 1 on experimenter expectancy effects and to the discussion in Chapter 3 on confirmatory hypothesis testing and self-fulfilling prophecies. The issue of the effects of teachers' expectations on their students is also relevant to the issues raised in Chapter 2 concerning the social factors that influence the development of one's self-concept. Finally, Rosenthal and Jacobson point out frequently that teachers have expectations about their students based on ethnic, cultural, and economic issues, and that these expectations may lead to self-fulfilling prophecies. This idea clearly is quite relevant to Chapter 4's focus on stereotypes.

Teacher Expectations for the Disadvantaged

Robert Rosenthal and Lenore F. Jacobson

It is widely believed that poor children lag in school because they are members of a disadvantaged group. Experiments in a school suggest that they may also do so because that is what their teachers expect.

One of the central problems of American society lies in the fact that certain children suffer a handicap in their education which then persists throughout life. The "disadvantaged" child is a Negro American, a Mexican American, a Puerto Rican or any other child who lives in conditions of poverty. He is a lower-class child who performs poorly in an educational system that is staffed almost entirely by middle-class teachers.

The reason usually given for the poor performance of the disadvantaged child is simply that the child is a member of a disadvantaged group. There may well be another rea-

son. It is that the child does poorly in school because that is what is expected of him. In other words, his shortcomings may originate not in his different ethnic, cultural and economic background but in his teachers' response to that background.

If there is any substance to this hypothesis, educators are confronted with some major questions. Have these children, who account for most of the academic failures in the U.S., shaped the expectations that their teachers have for them? Have the schools failed the children by anticipating their poor performance and thus in effect teaching them to fail? Are the massive public programs of educational assistance to such children reinforcing the assumption that they are likely to fail? Would the children do appreciably better if their teachers could be induced to expect more of them?

We have explored the effect of teacher expectations with experiments in which teachers were led to believe at the beginning of a school year that certain of their pupils could be expected to show considerable academic improvement during the year. The teachers thought the predictions were based on tests that had been administered to the student body toward the end of the preceding school year. In actuality the children designated as potential "spurters" had been chosen at random and not on the basis of testing. Nonetheless, intelligence tests given after the experiment had been in progress for several months indicated that on the whole the randomly chosen children had improved more than the rest.

The central concept behind our investigation was that of the "self-fulfilling prophecy." The essence of this concept is that one person's prediction of another person's behavior somehow comes to be realized. The prediction may, of course, be realized only in the perception of the predictor. It is also possible, however, that the predictor's expectation is communicated to the other person, perhaps in quite subtle and unintended ways, and so has an influence on his actual behavior.

An experimenter cannot be sure that he is dealing with a self-fulfilling prophecy until he has taken steps to make certain that a prediction is not based on behavior that has already been observed. If schoolchildren who perform

Verbal ability of children in kindergarten and first grade was tested with questions of this type in the Flanagan Tests of General Ability. In the drawings at top the children were asked to cross out the thing that can be eaten; in the bottom drawings the task was to mark "the thing that is used to hit a ball." The tests are published by Science Research Associates, Inc. of Chicago.

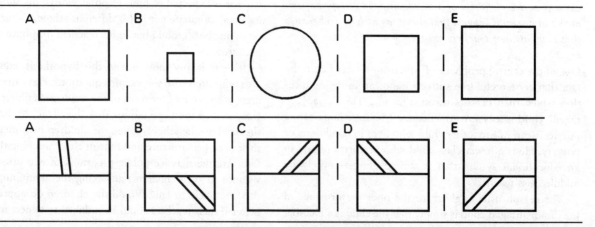

Reasoning ability of children in kindergarten and first grade was tested with abstract drawings. The children were told that four of the drawings in each example followed the same rule and one did not. The task was to mark the exception. In the drawings at top the exception is the circle; at bottom all the drawings except the first one have parallel lines that terminate at a corner.

poorly are those expected by their teachers to perform poorly, one cannot say in the normal school situation whether the teacher's expectation was the cause of the performance or whether she simply made an accurate prognosis based on her knowledge of past performance by the particular children involved. To test for the existence of self-fulfilling prophecy the experimenter must establish conditions in which an expectation is uncontaminated by the past behavior of the subject whose performance is being predicted.

It is easy to establish such conditions in the psychological laboratory by presenting an experimenter with a group of laboratory animals and telling him what kind of behavior he can expect from them. One of us (Rosenthal) has carried out a number of experiments along this line using rats that were said to be either bright or dull. In one experiment 12 students in psychology were each given five laboratory rats of the same strain. Six of the students were told that their rats had been bred for brightness in running a maze; the other six students were told that their rats could be expected for genetic reasons to be poor at running a maze. The assignment given the students was to teach the rats to run the maze.

From the outset the rats believed to have the higher potential proved to be the better performers. The rats thought to be dull made poor progress and sometimes would not

Advanced tests were given to children in second and third grades and grades four through six. Two examples from the test of verbal reasoning for grades four through six appear here. In the example at top the children were asked to "find the beverage." In the bottom example the instruction that the pupils received from the teacher was "Find the one you are most likely to see in the city."

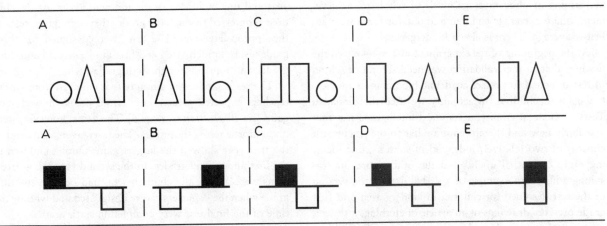

Reasoning test for children in grades four through six was based on the same principles as the test for younger children but used more sophisticated examples. At top the exception is *C*, which has no triangle. In the example at bottom the exception is *E*, because in all the other drawings the black and white squares are not aligned vertically. The tests were used to measure pupils' progress.

even budge from the starting position in the maze. A questionnaire given after the experiment showed that the students with the allegedly brighter rats ranked their subjects as brighter, more pleasant and more likable than did the students who had the allegedly duller rats. Asked about their methods of dealing with the rats, the students with the "bright" group turned out to have been friendlier, more enthusiastic and less talkative with the animals than the students with the "dull" group had been. The students with the "bright" rats also said they handled their animals more, as well as more gently, than the students expecting poor performances did.

Our task was to establish similar conditions in a classroom situation. We wanted to create expectations that were based only on what teachers had been told, so that we could preclude the possibility of judgments based on previous observations of the children involved. It was with this objective that we set up our experiment in what we shall call Oak School, an elementary school in the South San Francisco Unified School District. To avoid the dangers of letting it be thought that some children could be expected to perform poorly we established only the expectation that certain pupils might show superior performance. Our experiments had the financial support of the National Science Foundation and the cooperation of Paul Nielsen, the superintendent of the school district.

Oak School is in an established and somewhat run-down section of a middle-sized city. The school draws some students from middle-class families but more from lower-class families. Included in the latter category are children from families receiving welfare payments, from low-income families and from Mexican-American families. The school has six grades, each organized into three classes—one for children performing at above-average levels of scholastic achievement, one for average children and one for those who are below average. There is also a kindergarten.

At the beginning of the experiment in 1964 we told the teachers that further validation was needed for a new kind of test designed to predict academic blooming or intellectual gain in children. In actuality we used the Flanagan Tests of General Ability, a standard intelligence test that was fairly new and therefore unfamiliar to the teachers. It consists of two relatively independent subtests, one focusing more on verbal ability and the other more on reasoning ability. An example of a verbal item in the version of the test designed for children in kindergarten and first grade presents drawings of an article of clothing, a flower, an envelope, an apple and a glass of water; the children are asked to mark with a crayon "the thing that you can eat." In the reasoning subtest a typical item consists of

drawings of five abstractions, such as four squares and a circle; the pupils are asked to cross out the one that differs from the others.

We had special covers printed for the test; they bore the high-sounding title "Test of Inflected Acquisition." The teachers were told that the testing was part of an undertaking being carried out by investigators from Harvard University and that the test would be given several times in the future. The tests were to be sent to Harvard for scoring and for addition to the data being compiled for validation. In May, 1964, the teachers administered the test to all the children then in kindergarten and grades one through five. The children in sixth grade were not tested because they would be in junior high school the next year.

Before Oak School opened the following September about 20 percent of the children were designated as potential academic spurters. There were about five such children in each classroom. The manner of conveying their names to the teachers was deliberately made rather casual: the subject was brought up at the end of the first staff meeting with the remark, "By the way, in case you're interested in who did what in those tests we're doing for Harvard. . . ."

The names of the "spurters" had been chosen by means of a table of random numbers. The experimental treatment of the children involved nothing more than giving their names to their new teachers as children who could be expected to show unusual intellectual gains in the year ahead. The difference, then, between these children and the undesignated children who constituted a control group was entirely in the minds of the teachers.

All the children were given the same test again four months after school had started, at the end of that school year and finally in May of the following year. As the children progressed through the grades they were given tests of the appropriate level. The tests were designed for three grade levels: kindergarten and first grade, second and third grades and fourth through sixth grades.

The results indicated strongly that children from whom teachers expected greater intellectual gains showed such gains [*see illustration on page 6*]. The gains, however, were not uniform across the grades. The tests given at the end of the first year showed the largest gains among children in the first and second grades. In the second year the greatest gains were among the children who had been in the fifth grade when the "spurters" were designated and who by the time of the final test were completing sixth grade.

At the end of the academic year 1964–1965 the teachers were asked to describe the classroom behavior of their pupils. The children from whom intellectual growth was

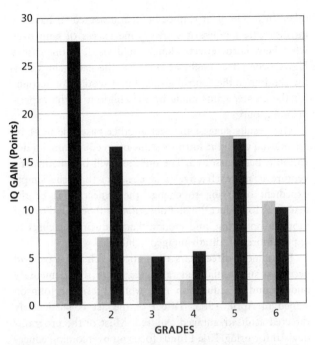

Gains in intelligence were shown by children by the end of the academic year in which the experiment was conducted in an elementary school in the San Francisco area. Children in the experimental group (*dark bars*) are the ones the teachers had been told could be expected to show intellectual gains. In fact their names were chosen randomly. Control-group children (*light bars*), of whom nothing special was said, also showed gains.

expected were described as having a better chance of being successful in later life and as being happier, more curious and more interesting than the other children. There was also a tendency for the designated children to be seen as more appealing, better adjusted and more affectionate, and as less in need of social approval. In short, the children for whom intellectual growth was expected became more alive and autonomous intellectually, or at least were so perceived by their teachers. These findings were particularly striking among the children in the first grade.

An interesting contrast became apparent when teachers were asked to rate the undesignated children. Many of these children had also gained in I.Q. during the year. The more they gained, the less favorably they were rated.

From these results it seems evident that when children who are expected to gain intellectually do gain, they may be benefited in other ways. As "personalities" they go up in the estimation of their teachers. The opposite is true of children who gain intellectually when improvement is not expected of them. They are looked on as showing undesirable behavior. It would seem that there are hazards in unpredicted intellectual growth.

A closer examination revealed that the most unfavorable ratings were given to the children in low-ability classrooms who gained the most intellectually. When these "slow track" children were in the control group, where little intellectual gain was expected of them, they were rated more unfavorably by their teachers if they did show gains in I.Q. The more they gained, the more unfavorably they were rated. Even when the slow-track children were in the experimental group, where greater intellectual gains were expected of them, they were not rated as favorably with respect to their control-group peers as were the children of the high track and the medium track. Evidently it is likely to be difficult for a slow-track child, even if his I.Q. is rising, to be seen by his teacher as well adjusted and as a potentially successful student.

How is one to account for the fact that the children who were expected to gain did gain? The first answer that comes to mind is that the teachers must have spent more time with them than with the children of whom nothing was said. This hypothesis seems to be wrong, judging not only from some questions we asked the teachers about the time they spent with their pupils but also from the fact that in a given classroom the more the "spurters" gained in I.Q., the more the other children gained.

Another bit of evidence that the hypothesis is wrong appears in the pattern of the test results. If teachers had talked to the designated children more, which would be the most likely way of investing more time in work with them, one might expect to see the largest gains in verbal intelligence. In actuality the largest gains were in reasoning intelligence.

It would seem that the explanation we are seeking lies in a subtler feature of the interaction of the teacher and her pupils. Her tone of voice, facial expression, touch and posture may be the means by which—probably quite unwittingly—she communicates her expectations to the pupils. Such communication might help the child by changing his conception of himself, his anticipation of his own behavior, his motivation or his cognitive skills. This is an area in which further research is clearly needed.

Why was the effect of teacher expectations most pronounced in the lower grades? It is difficult to be sure, but several hypotheses can be advanced. Younger children may be easier to change than older ones are. They are likely to have less well-established reputations in the school. It may be that they are more sensitive to the processes by which teachers communicate their expectations to pupils.

It is also difficult to be certain why the older children showed the best performance in the follow-up year. Perhaps

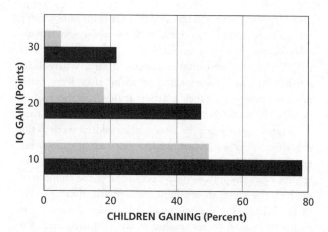

Children in lower grades showed the most dramatic gains. The chart shows the percent of children in the first and second grades by amount of their gains in I.Q. points. Again dark bars represent experimental-group children, light bars control-group children. Two lower sets of bars include children from higher groups, so that *lowest set sums results.*

the younger children, who by then had different teachers, needed continued contract with the teachers who had influenced them in order to maintain their improved performance. The older children who were harder to influence at first, may have been better able to maintain an improved performance autonomously once they had achieved it.

In considering our results, particularly the substantial gains shown by the children in the control group, one must take into account the possibility that what is called the Hawthorne effect might have been involved. The name comes from the Western Electric Company's Hawthorne Works in Chicago. In the 1920's the plant was the scene of an intensive series of experiments designed to determine what effect various changes in working conditions would have on the performance of female workers. Some of the experiments, for example, involved changes in lighting. It soon became evident that the significant thing was not whether the worker had more or less light but merely that she was the subject of attention. Any changes that involved her, and even actions that she only thought were changes, were likely to improve her performance.

In the Oak School experiment the fact that university researchers, supported by Federal funds, were interested in the school may have led to a general improvement of morale and effort on the part of the teachers. In any case, the possibility of a Hawthorne effect cannot be ruled out either in this experiment or in other studies of educational practices. Whenever a new educational practice is under-

taken in a school, it cannot be demonstrated to have an intrinsic effect unless it shows some excess of gain over what Hawthorne effects alone would yield. In our case a Hawthorne effect might account for the gains shown by the children in the control group, but it would not account for the greater gains made by the children in the experimental group.

Our results suggest that yet another base line must be introduced when the intrinsic value of an educational innovation is being assessed. The question will be whether the venture is more effective (and cheaper) than the simple expedient of trying to change the expectations of the teacher. Most educational innovations will be found to cost more in both time and money than inducing teachers to expect more of "disadvantaged" children.

For almost three years the nation's schools have had access to substantial Federal funds under the Elementary and Secondary Education Act, which President Johnson signed in April, 1965. Title I of the act is particularly directed at disadvantaged children. Most of the programs devised for using Title I funds focus on overcoming educational handicaps by acting on the child—through remedial instruction, cultural enrichment and the like. The premise seems to be that the deficiencies are all in the child and in the environment from which he comes.

Our experiment rested on the premise that at least some of the deficiencies—and therefore at least some of the remedies—might be in the schools, and particularly in the attitudes of teachers toward disadvantaged children. In our experiment nothing was done directly for the child. There was no crash program to improve his reading ability, no extra time for tutoring, no program of trips to museums and art galleries. The only people affected directly were the teachers, the effect on the children was indirect.

It is interesting to note that one "total push" program of the kind devised under Title I led in three years to a 10-point gain in I.Q. by 38 percent of the children and a 20-point gain by 12 percent. The gains were dramatic, but they did not even match the ones achieved by the control-group children in the first and second grades of Oak School. They were far smaller than the gains made by the children in our experimental group.

Perhaps, then, more attention in educational research should be focused on the teacher. If it could be learned how she is able to bring about dramatic improvement in the performance of her pupils without formal changes in her methods of teaching, other teachers could be taught to do the same. If further research shows that it is possible to find teachers whose untrained educational style does for their pupils what our teachers did for the special children,

the prospect would arise that a combination of sophisticated selection of teachers and suitable training of teachers
would give all children a boost toward getting as much as
they possibly can out of their schooling.

CRITICAL THINKING QUESTIONS

1. Rosenthal and Jacobson wrote that even when schoolchildren seem to confirm the expec-
    tations that their teachers have of them, it is usually impossible to tell if this reflects a
    self-fulfilling prophecy. Why is this impossible under most circumstances, and why did
    Rosenthal and Jacobson think that their study demonstrated the self-fulfilling prophecy?
2. This reading describes an earlier study by Rosenthal concerning psychology students'
    expectations about laboratory rats that they were training. How are the results of Rosen-
    thal and Jacobson's study consistent with this earlier research?
3. Chapter 2 in your textbook discusses the classic theories of Cooley (1902) and Mead
    (1934) concerning the role of other people in the development of one's self-concept.
    Discuss how Rosenthal and Jacobson's findings may be consistent with these early theories
    about the self.
4. Even the control subjects (students about whom no expectation was manipulated) showed
    important gains in I.Q. What interpretation of this result is suggested by Rosenthal and
    Jacobson? What other possible interpretations can you think of? What other conditions
    or control groups do you think should have been added to this study, if any?
5. The title of this article is "Teacher Expectations for the Disadvantaged," and yet the
    expectations that were manipulated in this study did not concern disadvantaged children.
    Why? How well do you think these results apply to the effects of teacher expectations for
    the disadvantaged? Why?
6. Considering the research discussed in Chapter 3 on self-fulfilling prophecies and in Chap-
    ter 4 on stereotypes, what factors do you think would make self-fulfilling prophecies based
    on teachers' expectations less likely to happen? How could the environments in which
    children learn be made less susceptible to negative expectations?

READING 2

Like Rosenthal and Jacobson (1968), the authors of the previous reading, Lepper, Greene, and Nisbett also conducted research on an issue of great importance to education. They investigated whether giving rewards to children for engaging in some activity could undermine the students' interest in that activity. Chapter 2 of the textbook distinguishes between intrinsic and extrinsic motivation, and discusses how rewards can have paradoxical effects on people's interests and behaviors. Social psychologists first began to understand these effects largely because of this article by Lepper and his colleagues.

Lepper, Greene, and Nisbett's research was also one of the most important applications of Daryl Bem's self-perception theory, discussed in Chapter 2. According to Bem's theory, in many situations people make inferences about themselves in the same way they would make inferences about anyone else. Just as we observe someone else's behavior and try to attribute that behavior to personal or situational causes (see the discussion of attribution theory in Chapter 3 of the textbook), we also observe our own behavior and try to attribute it to personal or situational causes. Lepper and his colleagues reasoned that when someone engages in a behavior and expects to be rewarded for the behavior, this person will infer that he or she may have done it for situational reasons (that is, to get the reward) rather than for personal reasons (that is, a personal interest in the behavior). If, on the other hand, the person engages in the behavior and does not expect to receive any reward, there is no clear, strong situational factor that could account for the behavior, so this person should infer that he or she did this behavior for personal reasons, such as being intrinsically interested in the behavior.

To better understand this prediction, imagine that you were observing some children drawing with magic markers. Would you be more likely to think that the children had a genuine interest in drawing with the magic markers if you knew that the children expected to win a prize for doing this, or if you knew that the children did not expect to win anything for doing this? According to attribution theory discussed in Chapter 3, you should be more confident that the children were drawing with the markers because of genuine interest if you thought the children did *not* expect to receive a reward. If self-perception theory is correct, then, the children should make the same kind of inference about themselves (although not necessarily consciously). That is, if they had not expected to receive a reward, they should infer that they were drawing with the marker because they genuinely enjoy drawing with markers; if they had expected to receive a reward, they should infer that they were drawing with the marker at least partly because they were going to receive a reward for it. Lepper and his colleagues designed this simple but ingenious study to test this and related hypotheses.

As you read this article, think about the important implications that this research has for education (as well as for sports, extracurricular hobbies, careers, and other activities).

Undermining Children's Intrinsic Interest with Extrinsic Reward: A Test of the "Overjustification" Hypothesis

Mark R. Lepper and David Greene
Stanford University

Richard E. Nisbett
University of Michigan

A field experiment was conducted with children to test the "overjustification" hypothesis suggested by self-perception theory—the proposition that a person's intrinsic interest

in an activity may be decreased by inducing him to engage in that activity as an explicit means to some extrinsic goal. Children showing intrinsic interest in a target activity

SOURCE: "Undermining Children's Intrinsic Interest with Extrinsic Reward: A Test of the 'Overjustification' Hypothesis" by Mark R. Lepper, David Greene, and Richard E. Nisbett, *Journal of Personality and Social Psychology* 1973, Vol. 28, No. 1, 129–137. Copyright © 1973 by the American Psychological Association. Reprinted with permission.

during base-line observations were exposed to one of three conditions: In the expected-award condition, subjects agreed to engage in the target activity in order to obtain an extrinsic reward; in the unexpected-award condition, subjects had no knowledge of the reward until after they had finished with the activity; and in the no-award condition, subjects neither expected nor received the reward. The results support the prediction that subjects in the expected-award condition would show less subsequent intrinsic interest in the target activity than subjects in either of the other two conditions.

The process by which man seeks to understand his environment—to discern the causes of events which surround him and explain the behavior of others toward him—has been of central concern to social psychology for many years (e.g., Brunswik, 1934; Heider, 1958; Michotte, 1946); but only in the past few years have psychologists concerned themselves with the process by which man explains and understands his own actions and their causes (Bem, 1965, 1967, 1972; Jones & Davis, 1965; Jones, Kanouse, Kelley, Nisbett, Valins, & Weiner, 1972; Kelley, 1967). Recently, theoretical analyses of the process of self-perception or self-attribution by Bem (1965, 1967) and by Kelley (1967) have suggested that processes of self-perception have a common ground with those of other-perception.

When an individual observes another person engaging in some activity, he infers that the other is intrinsically motivated to engage in that activity to the extent that he does not perceive salient, unambiguous, and sufficient extrinsic contingencies to which to attribute the other's behavior. Self-perception theory proposes that a person engages in similar processes of inference about his own behavior and its meaning. To the extent that the external reinforcement contingencies controlling his behavior are salient, unambiguous, and sufficient to explain it, the person attributes his behavior to these controlling circumstances. But if external contingencies are not perceived, or if they are unclear, invisible, and psychologically insufficient to account for his actions, the person attributes his behavior to his own dispositions, interests, and desires.

Originally, self-perception theory was proposed as an alternative explanation of the large dissonance literature on "insufficient justification" (cf. Aronson, 1966), where subjects are induced to engage in unpleasant or attitudinally inconsistent behavior under conditions of either clearly sufficient or psychologically inadequate external justification. Typically, these studies have demonstrated that subjects given little extrinsic justification for the behavior they have been induced to perform come to believe that their actions were intrinsically motivated. In a self-perception analysis, this outcome is simply the result of a self-directed inference process. In the low-justification conditions, the subject infers from his behavior and the lack of apparent external pressure that he must have wished to act as he did; while in the high-justification conditions, the subject infers that his behavior was determined by the external pressures in the situation.

Besides its application to many classic dissonance paradigms, self-perception theory has a number of heuristic implications, one of the most intriguing of which could be termed the "overjustification" hypothesis—the proposition that a person's intrinsic interest in an activity may be undermined by inducing him to engage in that activity as an explicit means to some extrinsic goal. If the external justification provided to induce a person to engage in an activity is unnecessarily high and psychologically "oversufficient," the person might come to infer that his actions were basically motivated by the external contingencies of the situation, rather than by any intrinsic interest in the activity itself. In short, a person induced to undertake an inherently desirable activity as a means to some ulterior end should cease to see the activity as an end in itself.

While the existence of such an overjustification effect has been postulated by a number of authors (DeCharms, 1968; Deci, 1971; Kruglanski, Friedman, & Zeevi, 1971; Lepper, 1973; Nisbett & Valins, 1971), this proposition has received virtually no experimental examination. Nisbett and Valins (1971) reviewed several studies which, on reinterpretation, provided evidence consistent with this proposition, but the first study to intentionally pursue a directly related hypothesis was that of Deci (1971).

Specifically, Deci hypothesized that rewarding subjects with money and "closely related tangible rewards" for engaging in an intrinsically interesting task would decrease their subsequent interest in that task in the absence of such external rewards. To test this proposition, Deci asked college subjects to solve a number of inherently interesting puzzles during three experimental sessions. Following an initial base-line session for all subjects, one group of subjects was paid for solving a second series of puzzles, while a second group was not paid. In a third session neither group was paid. During a break in each session, subjects were left alone for a few minutes to do whatever they wished, including continuing work on the puzzles. During this time, the subjects' behavior was observed and recorded from behind a one-way mirror. Subjects who had been paid during the second session tended to show a greater decrease in intrinsic interest from the first to the third session than subjects who had not been paid. This result was consistent with the overjustification hypothesis, but unfortunately this finding was of only marginal statistical significance and depended as much on differences between the groups during the base-line session as during the final sessions.

Deci (1971) couched his hypothesis in terms of monetary or other material rewards. As an implication of self-perception theory, however, the overjustification hypothesis is formulated in terms of the perception of oneself as having undertaken an activity *in order to obtain some extrinsic goal.* The nature of the extrinsic goal should be of little consequence. Thus, an overjustification effect is predicted for any situation which results in an extrinsic attribution where previously intrinsic interest was the only salient attribution. Contracting explicitly to engage in an activity for a reward should undermine interest in the activity even when the reward is insubstantial or merely symbolic. Conversely, receipt of an unforeseen, unexpected reward *after* engaging in an activity should have little or no detrimental effect, even when the reward is a highly prized material one.

This analysis suggests two features necessary for an unequivocal test of the overjustification hypothesis: (*a*) a subject population intrinsically motivated to engage in a target activity and (*b*) a comparison of two experimental treatments—one in which subjects are asked to engage in this activity as a means to some extrinsic goal and one in which subjects are asked to engage in the activity for its own sake but subsequently receive the same extrinsic reward. Subjects who expect a reward should show less subsequent intrinsic interest in the target activity than subjects who do not. An appropriate test of this hypothesis requires a dependent measure taken some time after the experimental sessions and in a situation as different as possible from that in which the rewards were administered. Thus, in this study the rewards were delivered in an experimental room, while the dependent measure of intrinsic interest was obtained in a naturalistic field setting.

The present experiment was conducted with children in an educational setting in order to test the overjustification hypothesis in a context where its practical implications may be greatest. The notion of overjustification immediately raises issues relevant to two widespread "contractual" techniques—one old and one new—of controlling the behavior of school children. The long-established practice of giving grades, gold stars, and similar awards to children is, in the present terms, a contractual one likely to induce the cognition, "I am doing this [arithmetic, drawing, reading] *in order to....*" The newly developed "token economies," in which children are offered redeemable tokens for desirable behavior, seem quite likely to produce the same cognition. The overjustification hypothesis implies that such contractual techniques may backfire for at least those children initially interested in the activities presented in such a context. Demonstrating an overjustification effect in an educational setting, therefore, would suggest the need for greater attention to the possible side effects and long-term consequences of powerful systems of extrinsic rewards.

METHOD

Overview

Preschool children showing initial intrinsic interest in a drawing activity during base-line observations in their classrooms were selected as subjects for the experiment. These subjects were blocked by degree of initial interest in the activity and assigned randomly to one of three treatment conditions: In the expected-award condition, subjects agreed to engage in the drawing activity in order to obtain an extrinsic reward—a certificate with a gold seal and ribbon. In the unexpected-award condition, subjects engaged in the same activity and received the same reward, but had no knowledge of the reward until after they had finished the activity. In the no-award control condition, subjects neither expected nor received the reward, but otherwise duplicated the experience of the subjects in the other two conditions. These experimental sessions were conducted individually in a room apart from the subjects' classrooms. The target-drawing activity was again introduced into the children's classrooms 1–2 weeks after the experimental sessions. Measures of subsequent intrinsic interest were obtained unobtrusively by covert observation of the classrooms from behind a one-way mirror.

Subject Population

Subjects were selected from the student population at the Bing Nursery School, located on the Stanford University Campus. These children, ranging in age from 40 to 64 months, were of predominantly white, middle-class backgrounds and of average or above-average intelligence. Three black children who would otherwise have been included in the experiment were arbitrarily excluded from the subject pool in order to increase the precision with which the population could be defined.

Observational Setting

The nursery school's facilities included three classrooms in which independent programs were run simultaneously. In each classroom, three different classes, each consisting of about 35 children and four to five teachers, met for either 2 or 3 half-days per week. The present study was conducted with four of these classes in the two classrooms equipped with one-way mirrors and sound equipment for observational purposes.

The program in these classrooms was such that with the exception of a single 15-minute "juice" break, children were free throughout the day to choose among a variety of activities. Some activities (such as building blocks, easels, housekeeping equipment, and outdoor activities) were available to them continuously; others (such as collage materials, "play dough," and drawing materials) were made available periodically by their teachers. Typically, at the beginning of each class session, children took note of the "periodic" activities, which had been set out for the day on each of three tables located near the center of the classroom.

For the purposes of the present study, the arrangement provided an opportunity to introduce a novel "target" activity into the ongoing nursery school program on a periodic basis. Moreover, the activity could easily be integrated into the normal classroom routine without the experimenters having to be present. It was thus possible to obtain an unobtrusive measure of the children's intrinsic interest in the target activity in a situation in which the activity was not associated with the experimenters or any extrinsic reward.

Experimental Activity

The experimental activity was chosen to meet three criteria: (a) sufficient similarity to other typical periodic activities so as not to appear out of place, (b) sufficient attractiveness to ensure that most children would express at least some initial interest, and (c) amenability of the activity to some objective definition of interest. These criteria were met handily by the opportunity to draw freely with multicolored felt-tipped drawing pens ("magic markers") not normally available in the children's classrooms.

Measurement of Intrinsic Interest

Base-line data on initial interest were collected during the first hour of 3 consecutive class days. On days when data were to be collected, a few minutes before the class began, the teachers placed a set of magic markers and a sheaf of fine white artist's drawing paper on a hexagonal table located directly in front of the observational mirror. After the first hour of class, these materials were replaced with some other table activity. Thus the target activity was

available to a child from the time he arrived until the end of the first hour of class and was presented by the teachers as simply another activity with which the children might choose to play.

During this hour, two observers were stationed behind the one-way mirror, each equipped with a Rustrak eight-track continuous event recorder. The first six channels on both recorders were numbered to correspond to the six positions around the hexagonal target table. One observer was responsible for recording children's actions at Positions 1 through 4; the other was responsible for Positions 4 through 6 and Position 1. The data recorded on Channels 1 and 4 were used to test agreement between observers. For each observer, two additional channels (Channels 7 and 8 of each recorder) were available for recording behavior not clearly tied to one of the six positions at the table. Hence, the two observers were equipped to record data on up to 10 children at a time.

A child was defined as "interested" in the target activity whenever he either sat down in one of the six chairs at the target table or put his hand on a marker; he was considered no longer interested when he was neither sitting at the table nor in possession of a marker. In practice, typically, the first discrimination which had to be made by the observer was when the child should be considered "sitting." It was decided to regard the target table as a system with six regular inputs, such that whenever a child was effectively occupying one of these inputs to the practical exclusion of another child, he or she was considered to be sitting. This criterion was felt to be a more valid indication of interest than a "fanny-touching-seat" criterion and was only slightly more difficult to discriminate reliably. When a child reached for a marker before sitting down or got up from his seat to draw on the floor or somewhere else, his behavior was recorded by one of the observers on Channel 7 or 8.

The measurement procedure was highly reliable. A product-moment correlation of the records of the two observers for the 47 children who appeared on either Channel 1 or 4 proved close to unity ($r = .99$). To further ensure that this method of measurement would be as sensitive and accurate as possible, three slight modifications of standard classroom procedure were introduced. First, since the mere presence of an adult at any of the activity tables was highly correlated with the presence of several children, teachers and other adults were asked to defer all requests from children to sit at the table until the experimental activity had been removed. Second, highly similar materials (e.g., crayons, scissors, other paper, etc.) were made inaccessible to the children while the target materials were available in order to avoid forcing observers to make unnecessarily difficult judgments. Third, teachers recorded not only absences but also time of arrival for any children who arrived late on days of data collection. These data allowed the calculation for each child of a more precise index of interest, namely, the percentage of time that he chose to play with the experimental activity out of the total time that he was present while the materials were available.

At least some play was recorded during base-line periods for 102 of the 139 children who appeared in their respective rooms at any time during the 3 hours of measurement. All children whose total playing time exceeded 4 minutes of play with the target activity were blocked by class and sex within class and ranked in order of total playing time. Each of the eight class-sex blocks was divided into as many groups of 3 as possible, with extra children discarded from the bottom of the rankings. This procedure yielded a potential subject population of 24 boys and 45 girls. Within groups of 3, a table of random permutations was used to assign subjects to treatment conditions.

Experimental Procedure

Following the third hour of base-line observations in each class, the experimental materials were removed from the classroom until they were needed again for postexperimental observations. Experimental sessions began within 2 weeks after the baseline period and were completed for each class on 3 consecutive school days.

Two persons conducted each experimental session: The first experimenter brought the child to and from his classroom and administered the experimental manipulation; the second experimenter stayed with the child while he was in the experimental room and administered the reward. Two (male) experimenters each played the role of the first experimenter for subjects from two of the four classes, and four (two males and two females) assistants each played the role of the second experimenter for subjects from one of the classes.

Potential subjects were approached by the first experimenter in their classrooms, engaged in play and/or conversation, and then asked if they would like to come to the "surprise room" with him. Twelve of 45 girls and 2 of 24 boys refused to come to the experimental room on three separate occasions and hence were lost from the experiment. Thus, 55 subjects actually participated in the experiment (19 each in the expected- and unexpected-award conditions, 17 in the no-award control group).

Each subject was brought individually to the experimental room by the first experimenter. The subject was seated at a child-sized table containing a set of magic markers and a sheaf of paper. At this point, the first experimenter had in his possession a sample "Good Player Award," the extrinsic reward employed in this study. These Good Player Awards—colored 3×5 inch cards with the words "Good Player Award" and spaces for the child's name and school engraved on the front next to a large gold star and a red ribbon—have proved effective rewards in previous studies (e.g., Harter & Zigler, 1972).

Presenting the drawing materials to the subject, the first experimenter said,

Do you remember these magic markers that you played with back in your room? Well, there's a man [lady] who's come to the nursery school for a few days to see what kinds of pictures boys and girls like to draw with magic markers.

For subjects in the unexpected-award and the no-award groups, the first experimenter continued,

Would you like to draw some pictures for him?

For subjects in the expected-award condition, the first experimenter produced the sample Good Player Award and continued instead,

And he's brought along a few of these Good Player Awards to give to boys and girls who will help him out by drawing some pictures for him. See? It's got a big gold star and a bright red ribbon, and there's a place here for your name and your school. Would you like to win one of these Good Player Awards?

Each subject indicated assent to the first experimenter's final question, typically with considerable enthusiasm. For all subjects the first experimenter concluded,

Good. He should be right outside. I'll go get him.

The first experimenter introduced the second experimenter to the subject and then excused himself, leaving the second experimenter alone with the subject. The second experimenter sat down across the table from the subject, started a stopwatch, and asked the subject, "What would you like to draw first?" Most of the time the subject began to draw a picture immediately; when he did not, a little coaxing was always sufficient to get him started. During the session, the second experimenter was friendly but not overly responsive to the subject. Generally, he attempted to show interest in, rather than explicit approval of, the subject's performance.

Each subject was allowed 6 minutes to draw pictures. If the second experimenter felt that an interruption after precisely 6 minutes was inopportune, up to 30 seconds more was provided. This procedure was designed to control against confounding of the classroom measure by satiation effects. The drawings made by each child were kept to allow an examination of the child's performance, during experimental sessions, along both quantitative and qualitative dimensions. Ratings of these drawings on a number of descriptive indexes were made by judges blind to the subject's condition.

The second experimenter was completely blind to the subject's condition for the first 5 minutes of the session. At the end of 5 minutes, the second experimenter casually looked inside a manila folder which had been left on the table by the first experimenter to determine whether the subject was to receive an award or not. After this point, the second experimenter knew only whether the subject was in one of the two award conditions as opposed to the no-award control condition.

One minute later, the second experimenter looked conspicuously at his stopwatch and said,

Well, it looks like our time is up. Thank you very much for helping me out by drawing these pictures for me. You really did a good job.

For subjects who were to receive an award, the second experimenter continued as follows:

In fact, you have been such a big help to me that I have something very special to give you. [The second experimenter rose, got a Good Player Award and a black pen, and returned to the table.] I'm going to give you one of my Good Player Awards, with your name and school on it. [The second experimenter showed the award to the subject and wrote the subject's name and school on the award with a flourish.] Now turn around and let me show you our special Honor Roll board where you can put your award so that everyone will know what a good player you are! [The second experimenter stood as he spoke, walked to the corner of the room, and pulled back a standing slat screen to expose a bulletin board. This board was decorated with the title "Honor Roll" and contained a standard display of several Good Player Awards. The second experimenter escorted the subject to the bulletin board and placed a push pin through the top of his award.] You can put your Good Player Award anywhere you want on the Honor Roll Board. That looks very nice.

Then, for all subjects, the second experimenter said,

Now, let's see if we can find [the first experimenter] to take you back to your room.

As the second experimenter opened the door, the first experimenter entered and returned the subject to his classroom.

Postexperimental Observations

The observational setting and data collection procedure were the same as during the base-line periods. Observers were blind to the conditions of the subjects. Data collection began 7 to 14 days after the last subject had been run in a given class and was completed over no more than 4 consecutive school days for each class. In three of the classes, one of the first three class meetings had to be skipped for reasons ranging from the unanticipated arrival of a goat in the classroom to equipment failure. Four subjects were lost during these sessions: Three were never in class during the three observational sessions; a fourth was present for only 10 out of a possible 180 minutes and was discarded, although inclusion of his data would not have affected the significance or pattern of the data reported. The final sample, then, consisted of 51 children—19 males and 32 females. There were 18 subjects in both the expected-award and the unexpected-award conditions and 15 subjects in the no-award condition.

RESULTS

The overjustification hypothesis led to the anticipation that subjects in the expected-award condition would show less subsequent intrinsic interest in the target activity than subjects in the unexpected-award and no-award conditions. The data relevant to this proposition—the mean proportion of time that children chose to play with the target activity in the postexperimental sessions—are presented in Table 1.

It may be seen that as predicted, children in the expected-award condition spent less time playing with the drawing materials than children in the other conditions. Preliminary analysis of the data by sex of child revealed no significant sex difference and no interaction of sex of child with experimental condition. The data were therefore collapsed across this dimension for purposes of analysis. Since the variances of the treatment groups were significantly different ($F_{max} = 5.39$, $df = 3/17$, $p < .01$) and the standard deviations of the groups were proportional to the means, a

TABLE 1 Mean Percentage of Free-Choice Time That Subjects Chose to Play with the Target Activity, by Treatments

Experimental condition	n	%
Expected award	18	8.59
No award	15	16.73
Unexpected award	18	18.09

TABLE 2   Analysis of Variance on Transformed Proportions of Time Spent with Target Activity

Source	df	MS	F
Between	2	3.96	3.25*
Contrast	1	7.55	6.19**
Residual	1	.37	< 1
Within	48	1.22	

*$p < .05$.
**$p < .025$.

log transformation $[Y' = 1n\ (Y + 1)]$ was performed on the data to produce homogenous treatment variances (Winer, 1962, p. 221). These transformed data were submitted to a one-way unweighted-means analysis of variance, which is presented in Table 2. This analysis yielded a significant effect of experimental treatments on subsequent intrinsic interest in the experimental materials ($F = 3.25$, $df = 2/48$, $p < .05$). To clarify the precise nature of this effect, a contrast was performed to test the specific prediction of the study. This contrast proved highly significant ($F = 6.19$, $df = 1/48$, $p < .025$), accounting for most of the systematic variance and indicating that subjects in the expected-award condition chose to spend a smaller proportion of their time playing with the target materials than subjects in either the unexpected-award ($t = 2.32$, $p < .025$) or the no-award ($t = 2.05$, $p < .025$) conditions.[1]

In addition, although blocking subjects on initial interest in the target activity of course eliminated any between-groups differences in this variable, it is of some interest to compare postexperimental interest with original interest within each treatment condition. Subjects in both the un-expected-award and no-award conditions showed very slight and non-significant (both $ts < 1$) increases in interest from preexperimental to postexperimental measurement sessions. Subjects in the expected-award condition, however, manifested a significant decrease in interest in the target materials from base-line to postexperimental sessions ($t = 2.61$, $p < .02$).

Some readers may find it surprising that receipt of the award did not increase the interest of children in the un-expected-award group. It should be recalled, however, that subjects were selected on the basis of their relatively great initial interest in the drawing activity. There would be little reason to expect that the award would have had much effect on the behavior of children for whom the drawing activity was already highly salient and pleasurable. On the other hand, the range of initial interest was fairly large, and

it might be expected that the award would have had some effect among those children in the present sample with relatively little interest. This was apparently the case. Each experimental group was divided into two groups on the basis of initial interest in the drawing activity. Of the resulting six groups, only the children in the unexpected-award group who were below the median in degree of initial interest showed a substantial increase in interest following the experimental manipulation ($t = 2.35$, $p < .05$). Children above the median in initial interest in the unexpected-award group showed a trivial decrease in interest, and children in the control (no-award) group, whether above or below the median, showed a trivial increase in interest.

It would be of some theoretical interest to know whether the expected-award treatment had a different effect on children high in initial interest than on children low in initial interest. Unfortunately, the data do not allow a clear answer to this question. Both the high group and the low group declined in interest in the drawing activity. The high group declined more than the low group, but this could have occurred either because the manipulation was more effective for the high group or simply because there was a "floor effect" for the group already relatively low in interest. It would be interesting to repeat the present experiment in a context avoiding such an artificial restriction of movement.

Finally, it is important to note that the award manipulation also had an immediate effect on children's performance during the experimental sessions. The pictures drawn by the children for the experimenter were rated on overall quality by three blind judges on a scale from 1 (very poor) to 5 (very good). Although the three conditions did not differ in the number of pictures drawn (2.61 for the expected-award, 2.44 for the unexpected-award, and 2.33 for the no-award children), the quality of pictures drawn in the expected-award condition was lower than in the other groups. The average quality ratings for the expected-award group (2.18) differed significantly from both the unexpected-award (2.85) and no-award (2.69) groups ($t = 3.01$, $p < .01$, and $t = 2.08$, $p < .05$, respectively). Thus the detrimental effects of the expected-award manipulation were apparent during the experimental sessions, as well as later in the classroom setting.

DISCUSSION

The present results indicate that it is possible to produce an overjustification effect. In the expected-award condition, children showed decreased interest in the drawing activity after having undertaken it in order to obtain a goal which was extrinsic to the pleasures and satisfaction of drawing in its own right. In the unexpected-award condition, on the other hand, children receiving the same extrinsic reward showed undiminished or increased interest in the activity. This detrimental effect of the expected-award procedure was manifest both in quality of performance during the experimental sessions and in subsequent unobtrusive measures of intrinsic interest in the classroom setting.

As an empirical proposition, the present findings have important practical implications for situations in which extrinsic incentives are used to enhance or maintain children's interest in activities of some initial interest to the child. Such situations, we would suggest, occur frequently in traditional classrooms where systems of extrinsic rewards—whether grades, gold stars, or the awarding of special privileges—are applied as a matter of course to an entire class of children.

Many of the activities we ask children to attempt in school, in fact, are of intrinsic interest to at least some of the children; one effect of presenting these activities within a system of extrinsic incentives, the present study suggests, is to undermine the intrinsic interest in these activities of at least those children who had some interest to begin with. The quite limited manipulation employed in this study, involving a symbolic reward not unlike those routinely employed in the classroom, was sufficient to produce significant differences in the children's subsequent behavior in a natural preschool classroom. This is consistent with the complaint, from Dewey (1900) and Whitehead (1929) up to the time of Holt (1964) and Silberman (1970), that a central problem with our educational system is its inability to preserve the intrinsic interest in learning and exploration that the child seems to possess when he first enters school. Instead, these authors have suggested, the schooling process seems almost to undermine children's spontaneous interest in the process of learning itself.

At the same time, because the implications of this point of view for social control and socialization are potentially so great, it is important to point immediately to the hazards of overgeneralization from the present experiment. Certainly there is nothing in the present line of reasoning or the present data to suggest that contracting to engage in an activity for an extrinsic reward will always, or even usually, result in a decrement in intrinsic interest in the activity. The present experiment was carefully designed to allow a demonstration of the overjustification effect. The target activity was deliberately chosen to be highly attractive, and subjects were all children who actually manifested some intrinsic interest in the activity. Extrinsic incentives were superfluous. Under such circumstances, there is every

reason to believe that it should be relatively easy to manipulate loss of interest and difficult to increase it above its already fairly high level.

The present experiment does not speak to situations which depart very greatly from the present situation. There is considerable evidence from studies of token-economy programs (Fargo, Behrns, & Nolen, 1970; O'Leary & Drabman, 1971) supporting the proposition that extrinsic incentives may often be used effectively to increase interest in certain broad classes of activities. On the present line of reasoning, this proposition should be particularly true when (a) the level of initial intrinsic interest in the activity is very low and some extrinsic device is essential for producing involvement with the activity; or (b) the activity is one whose attractiveness becomes apparent only through engaging in it for a long time or only after some minimal level of mastery has been attained. In fact, such conditions characterize the prototypical token-economy program in that tangible extrinsic rewards are *necessary* to elicit the desired behavior. Hence, it would be a mistaken overgeneralization from the present study to proscribe broadly the use of token-economy programs to modify children's behavior.

It has already been recommended by some thoughtful proponents of token economies that their use be limited to circumstances in which less powerful techniques have been tried and found inadequate (O'Leary, Poulos, & Devine, 1972)—in other words, only when they are necessary. It has also been stressed that in any case, the successful implementation of powerful reinforcement systems demands considerable sensitivity as well as ingenuity on the part of the practitioner (Bandura, 1969). The present study provides empirical evidence of an undesirable consequence of the unnecessary use of extrinsic rewards, supporting the case for the exercise of discretion in their application (O'Leary & Drabman, 1971).

REFERENCES

Aronson, E. The psychology of insufficient justification: An analysis of some conflicting data. In S. Feldman (Ed.), *Cognitive consistency.* New York: Academic Press, 1966.

Bandura, A. *Principles of behavior modification.* New York: Holt, Rinehart & Winston, 1969.

Bem, D. J. An experimental analysis of self-persuasion. *Journal of Experimental Social Psychology,* 1965, 1, 199–218.

Bem, D. J. Self-perception: An alternative interpretation of cognitive dissonance phenomena. *Psychological Review,* 1967, 74, 183–200.

Bem, D. J. Self-perception theory. In L. Berkowitz (Ed.), *Advances in experimental social psychology.* Vol. 6. New York: Academic Press, 1972.

Brunswik, E. *Perception and the object world.* Leipzig: Deuticke, 1934.

DeCharms, R. *Personal causation.* New York: Academic Press, 1968.

Deci, E. L. Effects of externally mediated rewards on intrinsic motivation. *Journal of Personality and Social Psychology,* 1971, 18, 105–115.

Dewey, J. *The school and society.* Chicago: University of Chicago Press, 1900.

Fargo, G. A., Behrns, C., & Nolen, P. *Behavior modification in the classroom.* Belmont, Calif.: Wadsworth, 1970.

Harter, S., & Zigler, E. Effectance motivation in normal and retarded children. Unpublished manuscript, Yale University, 1972.

Heider, F. *The psychology of interpersonal relations.* New York: Wiley, 1958.

Holt, J. *How children fail.* New York: Dell, 1964.

Jones, E. E., & Davis, K. E. From acts to dispositions: The attribution process in person perception. In L. Berkowitz (Ed.), *Advances in experimental social psychology.* Vol. 2. New York: Academic Press, 1965.

Jones, E. E., Kanouse, D. E., Kelley, H. H., Nisbett, R. E., Valins, S., & Weiner, B. *Attribution: Perceiving the causes of behavior.* New York: General Learning Press, 1972.

Kelley, H. H. Attribution theory in social psychology. In D. Levine (Ed.), *Nebraska symposium on motivation: 1967.* Lincoln: University of Nebraska Press, 1967.

Kruglanski, A. W., Friedman, I., & Zeevi, G. The effects of extrinsic incentive on some qualitative aspects of task performance. *Journal of Personality,* 1971, 39, 606–617.

Lepper, M. R. Dissonance, self-perception, and honesty in children. *Journal of Personality and Social Psychology,* 1973, 25, 63–74.

Michotte, A. E. *The perception of causality.* Paris: Vrin, 1946.

Nisbett, R. E., & Valins, S. *Perceiving the causes of one's own behavior.* New York: General Learning Press, 1971.

O'Leary, K. D., & Drabman, R. Token reinforcement programs in the classroom: A review. *Psychological Bulletin,* 1971, 75, 379–398.

O'Leary, K. D., Poulos, R. W., & Devine, V. T. Tangible reinforcers: Bonuses or bribes? *Journal of Consulting and Clinical Psychology,* 1972, 38, 1–8.

Silberman, C. *Crisis in the classroom.* New York: Random House, 1970.

Whitehead, A. N. *The aims of education.* New York: Mentor, 1929.

Winer, B. J. *Statistical principles in experimental design.* New York: McGraw-Hill, 1962.

NOTES

1. All p values reported in this article are based on two-tailed tests of significance.

(Received April 10, 1972)

CRITICAL THINKING QUESTIONS

1. As discussed in Chapter 2, behaviorists such as B. F. Skinner emphasized how rewards increased people's likelihood of performing a behavior. Lepper, Greene, and Nisbett's research suggests that rewards can make people *less* likely to engage in a behavior. How can one explain these different effects?

2. Using self-perception theory, explain why the subjects who received an unexpected reward did not show a decrease in intrinsic motivation whereas the subjects who expected to receive a reward did show a decrease in motivation.

3. Lepper and his colleagues selected children for their study only if they showed an intrinsic interest in the activity the researchers would be observing. Why did they select only these children? What effects would the rewards have had if the children had shown very little interest in the activity initially? Why?

4. Why were two experimenters used for each child? Discuss this in relation to experimenter expectancy effects, explained in Chapter 1.

5. Chapter 3 of your textbook explains Jones's correspondent inference theory. On the basis of this theory, explain why perceivers should be more likely to infer that children are intrinsically interested in drawing if they see the children drawing with no expectation of a reward than if they see them drawing with the expectation of a reward.

6. What are the implications of this research for education? What recommendations, if any, would you make for nursery schools and elementary schools to help maintain children's interest in learning and exploration? What recommendations would you make to college professors or administrators, coaches, or employers to help maintain their students', players', or employees' levels of interest?

READING 3 _____

Like the first two readings, this article also deals with educational issues and with how people interpret and understand their academic performance. This third article discusses how students report and understand their performance on the Scholastic Aptitude Test (SAT). It finds that students, especially those who did not do as well as they would have liked on the SAT, tend to inflate their performance when reporting their score. The article suggests that this false reporting is partly due to a desire to manage the impression of other people, but it is also partly an effort to repair self-esteem.

Chapter 2 in the textbook describes self-enhancing motives as an important aspect of self-esteem. This article examines one way that such self-enhancing motives can affect people's estimations and descriptions of their academic performance. It also discusses impression management theory, which is treated in detail in Chapter 10.

We also like this study for the elegance and simplicity of the methods. The basic procedure is simply to ask subjects what score they got on the SAT, whether this score was an accurate reflection of their ability, and what score would be an accurate reflection of their ability. In social psychology, often the simplest methodologies produce the best evidence. However, this article is also somewhat complex in that it reports three similar studies, a common practice in social psychological journals. When presenting a scientific argument it is often crucial to not only demonstrate one's own position and present evidence that supports one's theory, but also to conduct additional experiments that test that theory against other theories and that rule out alterative explanations of one's results.

Student Derogation of the Scholastic Aptitude Test: Biases in Perceptions and Presentations of College Board Scores

James A. Shepperd
University of Florida

A consistent finding in laboratory research is that individuals are quite adept at dismissing and disavowing unfavorable feedback. Three studies extend this research to a nonlaboratory setting by examining how students who receive relatively low scores on the Scholastic Aptitude Test (SAT) respond to this "failure" feedback. Studies 1 and 2 revealed biases in both perceptions and presentations of test scores. Students with lower SAT scores regarded their score as invalid and also believed that a higher score would be more accurate. This was true even though actual SAT scores significantly predicted current college grade-point average (GPA), whereas the scores subjects estimated would be accurate did not. In addition, when reporting their SAT scores, students systematically inflated them, reporting scores higher than those they actually received. Study 3 suggests that the misreporting of SAT

scores is attributable partly, but not entirely, to impression management.

Over the last several decades, hundreds of studies have examined how individuals respond to unfavorable feedback and how they dismiss the self-implications of such feedback. Most research on responses to unfavorable feedback has been conducted in the psychology laboratory. In the typical study, individuals receive negative feedback on some ego-relevant task, such as an intelligence test, and are then given an opportunity to explain their poor performance. The reliance on the psychology laboratory is not surprising; it offers greater experimental control, permitting greater confidence in inferences regarding cause and effect. Moreover, providing unfavorable feedback, such as a poor test performance, outside the laboratory (and, hence, without

SOURCE: "Student Derogation of the Scholastic Aptitude Test: Biases in Perceptions and Presentations of College Board Scores" by James A. Shepperd from *Basic and Applied Social Psychology*, 1993, 14(4), 455–473. Reprinted with permission.

informed consent, the opportunity for subjects to withdraw, and a detailed debriefing) raises serious ethical concerns. Nevertheless, outside the laboratory a test exists that is highly ego-relevant, that is taken by roughly 1 million people each year (Grandy, 1989), and for which many people regard their performance as poor—the Scholastic Aptitude Test (SAT). This article investigates responses to unfavorable feedback outside the psychology laboratory by examining how people perceive and present their SAT scores.

PERCEPTIONS OF THE SAT

Although designed to predict college academic performance (Morgan, 1989), the SAT has acquired the mystique of being an accurate, reliable indicator of an individual's competence, ability, and intellectual potential. Many students, parents, and faculty regard the SAT score as an immutable measure of a student's intelligence. This over-interpretation of the test has created an immense concern with College Board scores and has generated a thriving business for entrepreneurs promising they can raise students' scores. There also are numerous reports of schools "teaching to the test" and of school districts and state education departments inflating reports of their students' performances (Morganthau, 1990). Many college-bound students take the test repeatedly in hopes of raising their scores. For students with high scores, the test becomes an affirmation of their intellectual excellence; for students with low scores, the test becomes a declaration of academic inferiority. Indeed, the SAT seems to be regarded as an indicator of the upper limits of academic ability—a statement of intellectual worth.

But what of students who do not achieve high SAT scores? Do they conclude that they are intellectually deficient? Do they abandon their aspirations of obtaining good grades in the classroom or of entering medical, law, or graduate school? The answer seems to be no. Many students with modest SAT scores maintain high scholastic ambitions. In light of the pervasive perception of the predictive breadth of the SAT, how do students with modest SAT scores continue to hold high intellectual aspirations?

Perhaps students who perform poorly on the test perceive their scores as inaccurate and as unrepresentative of their intellectual acumen. Evidence from laboratory research reveals that individuals tend to characterize unfavorable feedback in ways that are not identity threatening. For example, there is substantial laboratory research demonstrating a pervasive tendency for individuals (particularly those high in self-esteem) to attribute their poor performance externally (i.e., the self-serving bias; Bradley, 1978) as

well as to unstable and uncontrollable causes (Weiner, 1985). Other research has shown that individuals make excuse-like attributions for unfavorable outcomes, claiming high consensus, low consistency, and high distinctiveness (Shepperd, Arkin, & Slaughter, 1993; Snyder & Higgins, 1988; Snyder, Higgins, & Stucky, 1983; Whitehead & Smith, 1990). Still other research has shown that individuals disparage the validity of the source of unfavorable feedback (Shepperd et al., 1993) or define the task itself as unimportant to their self-definition (Tesser, 1988; Tesser & Campbell, 1983). The present research investigated whether similar processes occur when students contemplate their SAT scores. Studies 1 and 2 examined factors influencing the perception of SAT scores, whereas Studies 2 and 3 examined biases in the presentation of SAT scores.

STUDY 1: A PILOT STUDY

A pilot study examined perceptions of the SAT. In line with laboratory research examining response to negative feedback, it was predicted that students with low SAT scores would be more likely than students with high SAT scores to perceive their score as inaccurate. It also was predicted that, when asked to estimate a more accurate score, persons receiving low scores would "boost" their score more than would persons receiving high scores. Specifically, among subjects reporting their score as inaccurate, the difference between the reported score and estimated score would be greater for low scorers than for high scorers.

Method

Subjects were 164 introductory psychology students at a small liberal arts college who completed a three-item anonymous questionnaire as part of a class project. Data from 9 subjects were omitted from analyses because they could not remember their SAT score or because they did not supply a response. The first item asked subjects to supply their total (Verbal plus Math) SAT score, the second item asked subjects to indicate (yes or no) whether they believed that their SAT score accurately reflected their aptitude or ability, and the third item, directed only at those students who answered "no" to the second question, asked subjects to estimate the SAT score they believed would accurately reflect their aptitude or ability.

Results and Discussion

Were students with lower SAT scores more likely to perceive their score as inaccurate? The results suggest they were. Subjects ($n = 89$) who believed their SAT score was inaccurate reported having a lower score ($M = 1169.1$) than did subjects ($n = 66$) who believed their SAT score was accurate ($M = 1254.8$), $t(153) = 5.21$, $p < .0001$.

Admittedly, examining accuracy reports is potentially misleading; the reports do not reveal whether subjects viewed their scores as inaccurately low or inaccurately high. Consequently, subjects were divided into four groups: (a) those reporting that their SAT score was accurate, (b) those reporting that their SAT score was inaccurate and estimating that a higher score would be more accurate, (c) those reporting that their SAT score was inaccurate and estimating that a lower score would be more accurate, and (d) those reporting that their SAT score was inaccurate yet refusing to estimate a score that would be more accurate. A one-way, unequal-n analysis of variance (ANOVA) comparing the self-reported SAT scores of these four groups revealed a significant difference between groups, $F(3, 151) = 17.67$, $p < .0001$. As evident in Table 1, subjects who estimated that a lower SAT score would be more accurate reported a score that was markedly higher on average than that of subjects who reported that their SAT score was accurate. Subjects who believed that their SAT score was accurate in turn reported a score that was markedly higher on average than that of subjects who either estimated a higher score to be more accurate or refused to estimate a score that would be more accurate.

Importantly, an alternative way to address the question of whether low scorers were more likely to perceive their score as inaccurate is to examine the proportion of high and low scorers who reported their score was too low. Subjects thus were divided into high and low scorers based on a median split of reported SAT scores. Consistent with predictions, more low scores (73%) than high scores (30%) estimated that a higher score would be more accurate, $\chi^2(1, N = 140) = 25.5$, $p < .0001$.

A second prediction of the pilot study was directed at the 80 subjects who believed their SAT score was inaccurate (including those subjects who regarded their score as too high) and who supplied an estimate of the score they believed would be more accurate. Among these subjects, it was predicted that the lower a subject's SAT score, the greater increase he or she would believe was necessary before the score was accurate. This prediction was supported by a significant negative correlation between reported SAT score and the amount of change subjects estimated was necessary before their score was accurate, $r = -.67$, $p < .0001$. Of interest, the mean estimated SAT score of the 80 subjects who regarded their score as inaccurate was 1273.4, 104.2 points higher than their mean reported SAT score, $t(78) = 8.08$, $p < .0001$. Apparently, these subjects not only viewed their SAT score as inaccurate, but also perceived that it was off by over 100 points.

Of course, given the 1600 ceiling on SAT scores, the significant negative correlation between reporting SAT score and estimated accurate score may be attributable to students with lower SAT scores having more room to boost their scores. To examine this possibility, the proportional change in SAT scores was calculated by dividing the magnitude of change estimated (estimated accurate SAT score minus reported SAT score) by the magnitude of change possible (1600 minus the estimated SAT score). The correlation between this quotient and subjects' reported SAT

TABLE 1   Reported SAT Scores From Studies 1, 2, and 3 as a Function of Perceptions of Score Accuracy

Subject Perception	Study 1			Study 2			Study 3		
	n	*M*	*SD*	*n*	*M*	*SD*	*n*	*M*	*SD*
Reported that their score was too high	6	1356.7$_a$	(70.3)	0	—	—	0	—	—
Reported that their score was accurate	66	1254.8$_b$	(91.5)	52	1243.9$_a$	(78.3)	58	1055.0$_a$	(100.1)
Reported that their score was too low	74	1154.1$_c$	(99.6)	39	1104.9$_c$	(103.6)	27	941.1$_b$	(113.5)
Reported that their score was inaccurate, yet refused to say how	9	1167.8$_c$	(136.7)	10	1243.9$_b$	(111.7)	7	1042.9$_a$	(157.6)

Note: Means within columns with different subscripts differ at $p < .05$.

score was significant, $r(80) = -.050$, $p < .0001$, indicating that low scorers boosted their SAT scores proportionately more than did high scorers.

In summary, the pilot study was designed to examine the extent to which subjects perceived their SAT scores as accurate. Consistent with predictions, students with low SAT scores were more likely than students with high SAT scores to perceive their scores as inaccurate. In addition, when asked to estimate a more accurate SAT score, subjects with lower SAT scores boosted their scores more than subjects with higher SAT scores.

STUDY 2

Why did students who received a low SAT score perceive the test as inaccurate? Self-enhancement theory would argue that these students were motivated to derogate the SAT because a low score on a highly ego-relevant test is esteem threatening. Accordingly, these students perceived the test as invalid to deflect the personal implications of a poor performance. It is also possible, however, that the perception that the score is inaccurate results from an objective appraisal of relevant academic information and does not reflect a motivated bias. Specifically, students receiving a low score may have found their score inconsistent with their expectations or with past experience. These students may have expected to receive a high SAT score because they normally perform well in academic settings. When the score was lower than expected, they assumed that the score, rather than their expectation or past experience, was in error. Alternatively, students receiving a low score may have initially perceived their score as accurate. However, they later derogated the SAT because their score was inconsistent with their college grade-point average (GPA). That is, because the SAT was designed to predict college GPA, students with low scores may have judged their score as erroneous because they are performing better in their college classes than their SAT score would predict.

Admittedly, it is exceedingly difficult to provide a crucial test of cognitive versus motivational explanations for self-serving cognitions and behaviors. Short of assessing students' expectations prior to taking the SAT, it would be difficult to determine whether students with low SAT scores derogate the test to protect self-esteem or because the score is inconsistent with their expectations. In addition, without knowing students' perceptions of the SAT immediately after receiving their score, it is difficult to know when (immediately vs. after acquiring a college GPA) students receiving low scores come to perceive their score as

erroneous. Nevertheless, by correlating students' SAT score with their current GPA, it is possible to test whether students derogate the SAT, at least in part, because their score is inconsistent with their college GPA. Presumably, if the perception of inaccuracy results from the score being inconsistent with college GPA, then for students who derogate their SAT score, college GPA should correlate more highly with the estimated SAT score than with the actual SAT score.

Study 2 also examined whether individuals receiving low scores perceive the SAT in general to be invalid or whether they merely regard their own score as invalid. Students with low SAT scores may believe in the veracity of the test as a measure of intellectual aptitude yet perceive that their own test score does not accurately portray these qualities in themselves. To examine this possibility, subjects in Study 2 made judgments about hypothetical students with high and low SAT scores. If subjects believe that the SAT in general is invalid, then their judgments regarding hypothetical students should be unaffected by the SAT scores of these students. Conversely, if subjects believe that the test is valid, then they should judge hypothetical high scorers more favorably than hypothetical low scorers.

A third purpose of Study 2 was to examine how people present their SAT scores. Given the importance placed on having a high score, students may be motivated to misreport, claiming a score higher than the one they actually received. By so doing, they can enjoy the praise and admiration often bestowed on those reporting high SAT scores with little risk, for few people outside of college selection committees seek official verification of self-reported scores. Moreover, there is preliminary evidence that students do exaggerate their SAT scores. Specifically, Pryor, Gibbons, Wicklund, Fazio, and Hood (1977) found misreporting in a sample of male college students, with students scoring below the median exaggerating more than students scoring above the median. In light of this preliminary evidence, it was predicted that students in the present study would misreport their SAT scores, reporting a higher score than they actually received. It also was predicted that students who received a low score would exaggerate their score more than would students receiving a high SAT score.

Method

Subjects Subjects were 101 undergraduate students enrolled in psychology courses at a small liberal arts college in New England and participating in the study as part of a classroom project.

Procedure   Subjects completed a two-part questionnaire. In the first part, subjects imagined that they were part of an admissions committee at a small, selective liberal arts college. Subjects were presented with a brief description of several hypothetical applicants and rated the likelihood that they would recommend admission of each applicant along a 7-point scale ranging from *very unlikely* (1) to *very likely* (7). Applicants were presented as having an SAT score of 700, 900, 1100, 1300, or 1500. Fully crossed with the manipulation of SAT score was a manipulation of applicants' class rank. Half the applicants were described as being in the top 10% of their graduating class and half the applicants were described as being in the top 40% (but not the top 30%) of their graduating class. Thus, each subject evaluated 10 different applicants presented in random order. To control for sex-of-target effects, half the subjects evaluated only male applicants and half the subjects evaluated only female applicants.

In the second part of the questionnaire, subjects responded to three items designed to assess judgments of the validity of the SAT in general. Specifically, subjects indicated whether they believed that the SAT in general (a) is a valid predictor of academic success, (b) is a good measure of aptitude or ability, and (c) provides a valid measure of intelligence. All responses were made on a 7-point Likert scale ranging from *strongly disagree* (1) to *strongly agree* (7). Responses to these three items were added to provide a single measure. Next, subjects responded to the three items from Study 1 assessing their perceptions of their own SAT score. Finally, permission was solicited to examine subjects' academic transcripts.

Results and Discussion

Study 2 examined three questions: (a) Do students misreport their SAT scores, reporting scores higher than those they actually received? (b) Is the perception that one's own SAT score is invalid attributable to the score being inconsistent with college GPA? (c) Do students with low scores regard the SAT in general as invalid or merely their own score as erroneous? Before addressing these questions, let us examine whether Study 2 replicates the findings of Study 1.

Self-reported SAT scores   Preliminary analyses revealed that the findings from Study 1 were replicated. Similar to Study 1, subjects ($n = 49$) who believed their SAT score to be inaccurate reported having a lower score ($M = 119.8$) than did subjects ($n = 52$) who believed their SAT score to be accurate ($M = 1243.9$), $t(99) = 6.54$, $p < .0001$.

As in Study 1, subjects were divided into groups: (a) those reporting their SAT score was accurate, (b) those reporting that a higher SAT score would be more accurate, and (c) those reporting that their SAT score was inaccurate yet refusing to estimate a score that would be more accurate. Unlike Study 1, no subject reported that a lower SAT score would be more accurate. A one-way unequal-n ANOVA comparing the self-reported SAT scores of these three groups revealed a significant difference between groups, $F(2,98) = 25.60$, $p < .0001$. As is evident in Table 1, subjects who regarded their SAT score as accurate reported a score that was markedly higher on average than that of subjects who either estimated that a higher score would be more accurate or refused to estimate a score that would be more accurate.

Finally, examination of the 39 subjects who believed their SAT score was inaccurate revealed that subjects with low scores boosted their score more than subjects with high scores, $r(39) = -.31$, $p < .06$. Consistent with Study 1, the mean estimated SAT score of the 39 subjects in Study 2 who regarded their score as inaccurate was 1279.5, 175.4 points higher than their mean reported SAT score, $t(38) = 14.50$, $p < .0001$. Once again, these subjects not only viewed their SAT score as inaccurate, they viewed it as substantially inaccurate.

In sum, these findings replicate Study 1. Students with low SAT scores were more likely than students with high SAT scores to perceive their score as inaccurate. In addition, when asked to estimate a more accurate SAT score, students with lower SAT scores boosted their score more than did students with higher SAT scores.

Veracity of self-reports   Do students report their SAT scores accurately? To examine this question, permission was solicited from subjects to examine their academic files. Eighty-three of 101 subjects granted permission. Because students took the SAT an average of 2 times each (range = 1 to 4), two sets of analyses were conducted: one examining the highest combined (Verbal plus Math) test score subjects received within a single administration of the test, and another examining the average of the combined test scores received across test administrations.

Examining the highest combined SAT score revealed that subjects did misreport their score, with 51% reporting a score higher than the highest score found in their academic file, 36% reporting a score equal to the highest score found in their academic files, and 13% reporting a score lower than the highest score found in the files. A comparison of the SAT score subjects reported receiving ($M = 1193.6$) and the highest SAT score recorded in subjects' academic files (M = 1175.8) revealed that the two were significantly different, $t(82)$ = 3.81, p < .0003. When the analyses were repeated on the average combined test score received across test administrations (M = 1145.3), the discrepancy was more pronounced: 87% of the sample reported an SAT score higher than the average combined score reported in the academic files. A dependent t test of the 48.3-point difference between self-reported and average recorded test score was highly significant, $t(82)$ = 9.55, p < .0001.[1]

A final analysis examined whether low scorers were more likely than high scorers to misreport their score. As expected, subjects who misreported their score (i.e., reported a score different from the highest combined test score received within a test period) scored lower on the SAT (M = 1137.7) than did subjects who accurately reported their score (M = 1243.0), $t(81)$ = 4.41, p < .0001.

The significant difference between the self-reported SAT score and the average and highest SAT scores recorded in subjects' academic files suggests that subjects were not merely misremembering their test score. Instead, they were systematically inflating their score, reporting a score higher than the average combined SAT scores received and higher than the highest SAT score actually achieved. Moreover, as expected, low scorers were more likely than high scorers to inflate their SAT scores.

SAT scores and college GPA   The next analysis examined whether the perception that one's SAT score is invalid is attributable to the score being inconsistent with college GPA. That is, students who derogate the SAT may do so because their college GPA is higher than would be predicted by their SAT score. To examine this possibility, the current GPA of subjects who regarded their SAT score as inaccurate was correlated with (a) the self-reported SAT score, (b) the SAT score that subjects estimated was more accurate, (c) the highest SAT score received within a given

test period, and (d) the average of all SAT scores received across test administrations. The results suggest that subjects were not derogating their SAT score because it was inconsistent with their college GPA. As evident in Table 2, the test score that predicted least well was the score that subjects estimated would be most accurate; the test score that predicted best was the average of all SAT scores reported by the Educational Testing Service. Importantly, owing to the small sample size (complete data were available for only 31 subjects), only (a) the correlation between the average recorded SAT score and GPA and (b) the correlation between the estimated SAT score and GPA differed from one another, $t(28)$ = 2.04, p < .06. Finally, it is noteworthy in the lower half of Table 2 that the standard deviations corresponding to the various methods for reporting SAT scores are comparable. This suggests that the lower correlation associated with the estimated SAT score is not attributable to a restriction in the range of scores.

Two final analyses examined the accuracy with which estimated SAT scores and average SAT scores predicted college GPA. In the first analysis, college GPA was regressed on the average SAT score to obtain parameter estimates (i.e., a slope and intercept). Predicted GPA was then calculated twice for each subject: once using the average SAT scores and once using the estimated SAT score. A dependent t test revealed that the predicted GPA was consistently and significantly higher (on average, .36 points higher) when the estimated SAT score rather than the average SAT score was used as the predictor, $t(30)$ = 12.32, p < .0001. In the second analysis, the discrepancy between predicted GPA and actual GPA was calculated twice: once when the estimated SAT score was used to predict GPA and once when the average SAT score was used to predict GPA. As expected, a dependent t test revealed that the discrepancy between predicted GPA and actual GPA was greater when the estimated SAT score was the predictor, $t(30)$ = 1.83, p < .05, one-tailed. Taken together these

TABLE 2   Correlations Between College GPA and SAT Scores (With Means and Standard Deviation for Each Score Type)

	Average Score Reported by ETS	Highest Score Reported by ETS	Self-Reported SAT Score	Estimated SAT Score
GPA	.40**	.34*	.29	.20
M	1052.2	1077.4	1099.4	1273.2
SD	134.0	135.9	105.6	107.4

Note: ETS = Educational Testing Service.
*Significant at p < .07.
**Significant at p < .05.

analyses revealed that the average SAT score was a more accurate predictor of college GPA than was the estimated SAT score.[2]

Perceptions of SAT Validity   Finally, do individuals who derogate the SAT regard the test in general to be invalid or merely their own score to be invalid? To address this question, responses to the three items asking subjects whether they regarded the SAT in general to be valid were added. The summed responses ranged from 3 to 20 ($M = 10.0$, $SD = 4.0$) with higher values indicating a stronger belief in the validity of the SAT. A Pearson correlation revealed that subjects who regarded their own score as inaccurate (coded as 0; accurate was coded as 1) were more likely to perceive the test in general to be invalid, $r(101) = .45$.

An alternative, more subtle way to investigate whether subjects regard the test in general as valid is to examine whether subjects will use the test in making decisions about others. To this end, subjects were asked to make admission decisions about hypothetical college applicants. For ease of presentation, a median split of the SAT validity measure was used to separate subjects who were more versus less likely to regard the SAT in general to be valid.

The means presented in Figure 1 indicate that, regardless of whether they believed the SAT in general to be valid, all subjects used the SAT scores of hypothetical applicants in making admission decisions. A 2 (Rating of SAT Validity) × 2 (Applicant's High-School Rank) × 5 (Applicant's SAT Score) ANOVA supported this conclusion in that hypothetical applicants were more likely to be recommended for admission the higher their SAT score, $F(4, 396) = 368.30$, $p < .0001$. The main effect of applicant's SAT score was qualified by a relatively modest interaction of SAT score and perceptions of accuracy, $F(4, 396) = 3.21, p < .05$. Subsequent analyses revealed that the interaction was attributable solely to a greater likelihood of accepting a student with a score of 900 or below by subjects who viewed the SAT as invalid. In short, subjects who believed the SAT to be invalid used the SAT less than did subjects who believed it to be valid. This difference notwithstanding, the fact that the mean ratings for these applicants fell below the 4.0 midpoint indicates that all subjects were generally opposed to accepting a student with an SAT score of 900 or lower.

Of note, analysis also revealed a significant effect of high-school rank on admission decisions, $F(1, 99) = 495.50$, $p < .0001$; higher ranked applicants ($M = 5.44$) were more likely to be recommended for admission than were lower ranked applicants ($M = 3.86$). This latter finding indicates that subjects were willing to use other criteria beside SAT score in making decisions about others.

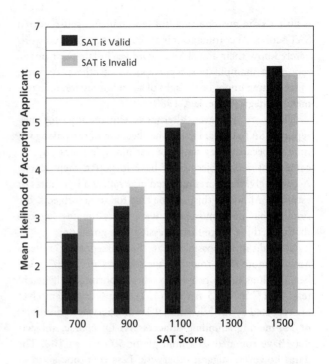

FIGURE 1   Ratings of hypothetical college applicants as a function of applicant's SAT score and rater's perception of SAT validity.

Summary   In addition to replicating Study 1, the results from Study 2 confirm the hypotheses regarding perceptions and presentations of SAT scores. First, the perception that one's own SAT score is invalid does not appear to be attributable to the score being inconsistent with college GPA. Subjects' average and highest recorded SAT scores correlated significantly with current GPA, whereas subjects' estimated SAT score did not. In addition, the estimated SAT score was less accurate than the average SAT score in predicting college GPA. Second, the results of the admissions part of the questionnaire suggest that subjects will use scores from the SAT in making decisions that affect others even though they may regard the test itself to be invalid. Third, the difference between self-reported and actual SAT scores suggests that students (low scorers in particular) do not merely misremember their test score but instead systematically inflate their score, reporting a score higher than the one they actually received.

STUDY 3

Why do individuals inflate their reported SAT scores? It was hypothesized initially that individuals inflate their scores to receive the praise and admiration often bestowed on those reporting high scores. It was also noted that there is little risk in misreporting, for few challenge self-reported SAT scores. According to this explanation, individuals privately know their actual SAT score yet inflate their public reports to manipulate the perceptions of others. As such, misreporting might be thought of as an impression management strategy (Schlenker, 1980).

There are, however, alternative explanations for misreported SAT scores. First, either because of the passage of time or because they took the test multiple times and became confused, subjects may have forgotten their scores. Accordingly, the scores reported may reflect a best guess or estimate. Although this may be true for some subjects, the finding that most misreports were overestimates suggests that something more than guessing was going on.

Second, it is possible that the misreporting reflects nothing more than rounding the score to an "even" number, much as many people do when reporting their height (e.g., 5 ft 7 in. vs. 5 ft 6½ in.). Yet the scores themselves are reported by the Educational Testing Service in multiples of 10, making rounding unnecessary. Of course, subjects may have rounded to a multiple of 50 or even 100. The data, however, suggest otherwise. Less than one sixth of those subjects misreporting their scores rounded up to the nearest multiple of 50 and far fewer rounded up to the nearest multiple of 100. Thus, misreporting is not attributable to rounding.

The most compelling alternative explanation for the inflated SAT reports is that the misreporting in Study 2 was done without awareness and may even represent a form of self-deception (Goleman, 1985; Lockard & Paulhus, 1988; Martin, 1985). Perhaps, subjects initially misreported their SAT scores for impression management reasons, but after repeated misreporting, they eventually came to believe the false reports themselves. Or perhaps the SAT score subjects received was inconsistent with the score expected or desired, creating dissonance (Festinger & Carlsmith, 1959). Subjects subsequently reduced the dissonance by "remembering" a score more in line with their expectations or desires. Finally, it is possible that the score received was inconsistent with subjects' self-schema and that the memory distortion represents a simple error in the direction of greater schema congruity (Greenwald, 1980). Regardless of the cause, according to this alternative explanation, subjects are unaware of their misreporting.

Study 3 examined this possibility. Subjects reported their SAT scores on two occasions separated by 2 months. During the second (but not the first) occasion, subjects were offered an incentive for reporting accurately, one that rewarded subjects for recalling correctly and alerted them that any discrepancy between their reported and actual SAT score would be known. If subjects misreport for impression management reasons and are aware of their misreporting, then they should recall their score correctly when an incentive is offered for an accurate report. Alternatively, if subjects are truly unaware of their misreporting, then subjects should misreport their scores regardless of whether an incentive is offered for recalling accurately.

Method

Subjects   Subjects were 92 undergraduates enrolled in a personality psychology course at a large Southwestern university. Data from one subject were excluded because the SAT score she reported at Time 2 (2300) exceeded the highest attainable score on the test (1600).

Procedure   At the beginning of the semester (Time 1), subjects completed several questionnaires (most of which were irrelevant to this research) as part of a class project. One of the questionnaires included the three items used in Studies 1 and 2 asking subjects to report their SAT score,[3] whether they believed their score was accurate, and, if not, what score they believed would be accurate. two months later (Time 2) during a class exam, subjects were again asked to report their SAT scores. This time, however, an incentive was offered for reporting accurately. Subjects learned that they would receive extra credit on the exam if they accurately recalled their SAT score. In truth, all subjects received the extra credit regardless of whether they did or did not recall correctly. Finally, SAT score and current GPA were recorded from each subject's academic files.

Results and Discussion

Self-reported SAT scores   Once again, the findings from Study 1 were replicated. Subjects ($n = 34$) who believe their SAT score was inaccurate reported having a lower score ($M = 962.1$) than did subjects ($n = 58$) who believed their SAT score was accurate ($M = 1055.0$), $t(90) = 3.63$, $p < .001$. In addition, Table 1 reveals that subjects who regarded their SAT score as accurate reported a score that was markedly higher than that of subjects who believed that a higher score would be more accurate. Finally, examination of the 27 subjects who believed that a higher SAT score would be more accurate revealed that subjects with low scores boosted their score more than subjects with high scores, $r = -.49$, $p < .01$. Consistent with Studies 1 and 2, the mean estimated SAT score of the 27 subjects in Study 3 who regarded their score as inaccurate was 1080.6, 139.7 points higher than their mean reported SAT score,

$t(26) = 8.27, p < .0001$. Once again, these subjects not only viewed their SAT score as inaccurate but viewed it as substantially inaccurate.

In sum, these findings replicate Studies 1 and 2. Students with low SAT scores were more likely than students with high SAT scores to perceive their score as inaccurate. In addition, when asked to estimate a more accurate SAT score, students with lower SAT scores boosted their score more than students with higher SAT scores. The replication is noteworthy because the sample in Study 3 (students from a large, Southwestern, public university) was in many ways distinct from the samples in Studies 1 and 2 (students from a small, Eastern, selective private college). In addition, the average reported SAT score in Study 3 ($M = 1020.7$) was markedly lower than the average reported SAT score in Studies 1 ($M = 1205.6$) and 2 ($M = 1183.7$). The replication in Study 3 illustrates the robustness of the earlier findings regarding perceptions of the SAT.

Causes of misreports   The remaining analyses address why students misreport their SAT scores. Examining the highest combined SAT score reported in subjects' academic files revealed that at Time 1, 33% of subjects reported a score higher, 60% reported a score equal to, and 7% reported a score lower than the highest SAT score found in subjects' academic file. A comparison of the SAT score subjects reported receiving ($M = 1020.7$) and the highest SAT score recorded in subjects' academic files ($M = 1003.0$) revealed that the 17.6-point average inflation in SAT scores was significant, $t(91) = 2.92, p < .005$, one-tailed. Of interest, both the proportion of students misreporting their SAT scores and the magnitude of these misreports were lower in Study 3 than in Study 2. This difference may be attributable to a change in the way SAT scores were requested in Study 3 (see Note 3). Alternatively, it may indicate that other factors, such as investment in intellectual identity, may influence the magnitude to which subjects inflate their SAT reports.

Two months later when offered an incentive in the form of extra credit on an exam for reporting accurately, 36% of the subjects continued to misreport their SAT scores ($M = 1011.7$). However, the magnitude of inflation was significantly less than when no incentive was offered for reporting accurately, $t(91) = 3.04, p < .001$, one-tailed. Indeed, the magnitude of inflation dropped to an average of 9.0 points, resulting in a reported SAT score only marginally higher than the highest combined SAT score reported in subjects' academic files, $t(91) = 1.59, p < .07$, one-tailed. Also of interest, the proportion of students inflating their SAT scores dropped. At Time 2, 21% of sub-

jects reported a score higher, 64% reported a score equal to, and 15% reported a score lower than the highest SAT score found in subjects' academic file.

The finding that subjects inflated their SAT scores less when offered an incentive for reporting accurately suggests that subjects were more or less conscious of their misreporting at Time 1. This finding is consistent with an impression management explanation for misreporting. Importantly, impression management was not the only factor influencing subjects' misreporting. At Time 2, the mean reported SAT score was still higher than the highest SAT score recorded in subjects' files, albeit only marginally significantly so. Moreover, providing an incentive for reporting accurately did not increase the tendency to report SAT scores accurately. That is, roughly the same number of students misreported their scores at Time 1 and Time 2. When viewed collectively, these findings suggest that subjects were more modest in their reporting at time 2. It also suggests that the tendency to inflate SAT scores is attributable partly to impression management (subjects inflated their scores less at Time 2) and partly to self-deception (subjects nevertheless continued to inflate their scores at Time 2).

GENERAL DISCUSSION

Are students biased in the perception and presentation of their SAT scores? The findings from this research suggest that they are and provide some evidence why this is so. Regarding perceptions, a majority of students (particularly those with lower scores) perceived their test scores to be inaccurate, with most estimating that a higher score would be more accurate. In addition, low scorers were more likely to report that the test in general was invalid. Yet these students did not appear to regard the SAT scores of others to be inaccurate and seemed willing to use others' scores to make important decisions about them. Specifically, Study 2 revealed that regardless of their beliefs about the SAT, students were more likely to recommend for admission to a selective college applicants with higher SAT scores. This paradoxical finding is intriguing and suggests that some individuals may hold contradictory beliefs about the SAT.

Why do subjects perceive their test scores as inaccurate? Study 2 revealed that this perception is not attributable to the score being inconsistent with college GPA, the criterion the test was designed to predict. Subjects' average and highest recorded SAT score correlated significantly with current GPA, whereas subjects' estimated SAT score did not. Moreover, subjects' actual SAT score predicted college GPA more accurately (i.e., with less error) than did subjects' estimated SAT score.

The perception of inaccuracy may reflect a motivated bias designed to protect self-esteem. Accordingly, subjects receiving low scores perceive their scores as inaccurate to sustain an important self-image of competency and intelligence. Alternatively, the perception of inaccuracy may be cognitively based. Subjects may have used high-school GPA rather than college GPA as the standard in evaluating the veracity of their SAT score. Most subjects in Studies 1 and 2 graduated in the top 20% of their high-school class and had impressive high-school GPAs. In addition, Study 2 revealed that subjects used high-school rank, a correlate of high-school GPA, in making admission decisions about others. If high-school GPA was used as the standard, then students receiving a low test score may reasonably have concluded that their SAT score, based on a single 3-hr exam, was inaccurate, whereas their high-school GPA, forged over 3½ to 4 years, was not.

Regardless of whether one favors a motivational or cognitive explanation for subjects' perceptions, it is intriguing that subjects continued to regard their scores as inaccurate even though the scores were consistent with college GPA. This finding illustrates how persistent beliefs can be even in the face of disconforming evidence. Indeed, although we have no data bearing on the question, we suspect that subjects who viewed their test score as inaccurate, if asked, would report that their college GPA was inaccurate as well.

Regarding student presentations, Studies 2 and 3 revealed that many students misreported their SAT score, claiming a higher score than they actually received. In addition, consistent with previous research (Pryor et al., 1977), low scorers were more likely than high scorers to inflate their SAT score. The results of Study 3 suggest that the inflated scores partly reflect self-presentation. Specifically, subjects inflated their SAT scores less at Time 2 when their misreporting would be evident, than at Time 1, when their misreporting would presumably go unnoticed. Nevertheless, not all misreporting can be explained in terms of self-presentation. SAT reports at Time 2 were still inflated, although only marginally significantly so. Moreover, roughly the same number of subjects misreported their scores at Time 2 as did at Time 1. These findings indicate that subjects who inflate their scores are aware that they are misreporting but are unaware of the magnitude of their misreporting.

In sum, the purpose of this article was to investigate responses to unfavorable feedback outside the psychology laboratory by examining how students who receive relatively low SAT scores perceive and present this "failure" feedback. The findings were consistent with laboratory research, revealing biases in both perceptions and presentations of test scores among students with lower scores. Students with lower scores characterized their test scores as inaccurate and, when asked to report their scores, claimed scores higher than those they actually received. These findings indicate that even outside the confines of the psychology laboratory, individuals will go to great lengths to dismiss and distort unfavorable and inconsistent feedback.

ACKNOWLEDGMENTS

This investigation was supported in part by a Batchelor (Ford) Faculty Research Grant from Holy Cross College. Portions of this article were presented at the meeting of the Midwestern Psychological Association, May 1991, Chicago.

I thank Jeff Simpson, Royce Singleton, and Sabrina Zirkel for helpful comments on an earlier draft of this article.

REFERENCES

Bradley, G. W. (1978). Self-serving biases in the attribution processes: A reexamination of the fact or fiction question. *Journal of Personality and Social Psychology, 36,* 56–71.

Festinger, L., & Carlsmith, J. M. (1959). Cognitive consequences of forced compliance. *Journal of Abnormal and Social Psychology, 58,* 203–210.

Goleman, D. (1985). *Vital lies, simple truths: The psychology of self-deception.* New York: Simon & Schuster.

Grandy, J. (1989). *Trends in SAT scores and other characteristics of examinees planning to major in mathematics, science, or engineering* (Research Rep. No. 89–24). Princeton, NJ: Educational Testing Service.

Greenwald, A. G. (1980). The totalitarian ego: Fabrication and revision of personal history. *American Psychologist, 35,* 603–618.

Lockard, J. S., & Paulhus, D. L. (1988). *Self-deception: An adaptive mechanism?* Englewood Cliffs, NJ: Prentice-Hall.

Martin, M. W. (1985). *Self-deception and self-understanding: New essays in philosophy and psychology.* Lawrence: University Press of Kansas.

Morgan, R. (1989). *Analyses of the predictive validity of the SAT and high school grades from 1976 to 1985* (College Board Rep. No. 89–7). New York: College Entrance Examination Board.

Morganthau, T. (1990, Fall/Winter). A consumer's guide to testing. *Newsweek* [Special issue], pp. 62–68.

Pryor. J. B., Gibbons, F. X., Wicklund, R. A., Fazio, R. H., & Hood, R. (1977). Self-focused attention and self-report validity. *Journal of Personality, 45,* 513–527.

Schlenker, B. R. (1980). *Impression management: The self-concept, social identity, and interpersonal relations.* Monterey, CA: Brooks/Cole.

Shepperd, J. A., Arkin, R. M., & Slaughter, J. (1993). *Social anxiety and excuse making.* Unpublished manuscript, University of Florida, Department of Psychology, Gainesville.

Snyder, C. R., & Higgins, R. L. (1988). Excuses: Their effective role in the negotiation of reality. *Psychological Bulletin, 104,* 23–35.

Snyder, C. R., Higgins, R. L., & Stucky, R. J. (1983). *Excuses: Masquerades in search of grace.* New York: Wiley/Interscience.

Tesser, A. (1988). Toward a self-evaluation maintenance model of social behavior. In L. Berkowitz (Ed.), *Advances in experimental social psychology* (Vol. 21, pp. 181–227). San Diego: Academic.

Tesser, A., & Campbell, J. (1983). Self-definition and self-evaluation maintenance. In J. Suls & A. G. Greenwald (Eds.), *Psychological perspectives on the self* (Vol. 2, pp. 1–31). Hillsdale, NJ: Lawrence Erlbaum Associates, Inc.

Weiner, B. (1985). An attributional theory of achievement motivation and emotion. *Psychological Review, 92,* 548–573.

Whitehead, G. I, III, & Smith, S. H. (1990). The use of consensus-raising excuses as a function of the manipulation of publicness: The role of expectations of future interaction. *Journal of Personality and Social Psychology, 16,* 562–572.

NOTES

1. Some institutions, to appear more selective, compute and report SAT scores based on the sum of the highest math and highest verbal score achieved across administrations. A comparison of scores derived using this method with the SAT score subjects reported receiving revealed that the majority of subjects in this sample did not use this method themselves. Consequently, this method is not discussed further.

2. I am indebted to an anonymous reviewer for suggesting these analyses.

3. Prior to analyzing the results of Study 2, I was unaware that many students take the SAT multiple times. Realizing that this might contribute to some of the misreporting, subjects in Study 3 who took the test multiple times were instructed to report the highest combined SAT score received within a single administration of the test.

CRITICAL THINKING QUESTIONS

1. Shepperd writes that people's tendency to inflate their performance on the SAT is partly attributable to impression management. What does it mean for an effect to be partly attributable to a given theory? What other factors may be influencing people's inflation of their SAT scores?

2. The SAT has a big effect on college admission, and therefore it can have a big impact on people's lives. Do people inflate their performance on other, less important tests? What attributes of the test might lead people to inflate their performance? What attributes might deter them from inflating their performance?

3. What would have happened in this study if the subjects had known that the experimenter was going to access their real SAT scores from the college's admissions office? Would they still have inflated their estimates of their performance? Why or why not? How is this question related to impression management theory?

4. In Study 3, subjects reported their score after taking an in-class exam. How might this have affected their reports of the SAT performance? What implications does this have for the interpretation of the results of this study?

5. Chapter 2 in the textbook describes how autobiographical memories, or memories about one's own actions and behaviors, are different from other memories. What might this research on autobiographical memories predict about how people would report their SAT score? How might this research be integrated with the research in the current article?

6. Should the researchers have considered the year in college (first, second, third, fourth, or fifth) when analyzing students' reports of their scores? What are some reasons that the year in college might have mattered in this study? What are some reasons that the year in college might not have mattered?

READING 4 _____

We selected this article because it represents some of the recent and interesting research on stereotypes. As Chapter 4 describes, in the modern form of racism there is a tension between one's desire to be egalitarian and one's persistent beliefs and stereotypes about certain groups. This means that people often hold or know about stereotypes that they don't want to use. In other words, they hold stereotypes that they are trying to suppress. The research in this article finds that trying to suppress a stereotype may make it more *likely* that one will use that stereotype in the future.

The issues in this study are clearly related to Chapter 4 and its emphasis on perceiving groups, especially to the section on automatic and controlled processing of stereotypes. The authors' point is that attempts to control the use of stereotypes may make their use more automatic. There is also a less obvious connection to the research discussed in Chapter 14. Much of the research on thought suppression has focused on whether people can inhibit or suppress stressful thoughts. In particular, inhibition confrontation theory suggests that suppressing thoughts about stressful experiences can lead to more stress because these thoughts rebound in the same way as stereotypes.

In reading the article, you will notice that the authors use three studies that all address the same issue. This repetition serves a useful purpose. If the results of a study can be repeated over again, we can be more confident that the results are meaningful, and the additional study often can rule out alternative explanations of the results. Note also that Experiment 3 uses a specialized procedure called a "lexical decision task." If people are using stereotypes in making judgments, then they should be able to make these judgments more quickly, because one of the functions of stereotypes is that they simplify the processing of information. In the lexical decision task the experimenters look at the speed with which people make decisions, and they assume that if people are making faster decisions then they are making more stereotypic judgments.

Out of Mind but Back in Sight: Stereotypes on the Rebound

C. Neil Macrae, Galen V. Bodenhausen, Alan B. Milne, and Jolanda Jetten

For a variety of reasons, social perceivers may often attempt to actively inhibit stereotypic thoughts before their effects impinge on judgment and behavior. However, research on the psychology of mental control raises doubts about the efficacy of this strategy. Indeed, this work suggests that when people attempt to suppress unwanted thoughts, these thoughts are likely to subsequently reappear with even greater insistence than if they had never been suppressed (i.e., a "rebound" effect). The present research comprised an investigation of the extent to which this kind of rebound effect extends to unwanted stereotypic thoughts about others. The results provided strong support for the existence of this effect. Relative to control subjects (i.e.,
stereotype users), stereotype suppressors responded more pejoratively to a stereotyped target on a range of dependent measures. We discuss our findings in the wider context of models of mind, thought suppression, and social stereotyping.

"Thinking is easier to create than to control."

Dennett (1991, p. 301)

Much of mental life, perhaps rather paradoxically, is spent thinking the unthinkable. The desire to consume another chocolate bar, assault an obnoxious neighbor, or date a best friend's partner are the sort of unpalatable thoughts

SOURCE: C. Neil Macrae, Galen V. Bodenhausen, Alan B. Milne, and Jolanda Jetten, "Out of Mind but Back in Sight: Stereotypes on the Rebound," *Journal of Personality and Social Psychology*, 1994, Vol. 67, No. 5, 808–817. Copyright © 1994 by the American Psychological Association. Reprinted with permission.

that regularly capture our attention and imagination. While relief can be obtained by exorcising these dark impulses from consciousness (e.g., Freud, 1915/1957), daily experience attests that the resulting calm is relatively short-lived. All too often, with neither consent nor warning, these unwelcome mental specters return to haunt us. The message emerging from contemporary research on thought control confirms this observation. Suppressing unwanted thoughts, beliefs, and desires can be a trying and infuriating business. Banished from mind, these inadmissible cognitions can ironically reappear with a vengeance and vigor that makes them difficult to ignore (see Wegner 1992, 1994; Wegner & Pennebaker, 1993; Wegner & Schneider, 1989). As Wegner (1989, p. 300) soberingly summarizes, "the effects of thought suppression . . . are not usually what we want them to be."

SUPPRESSING STEREOTYPIC THOUGHTS

Perceivers' preoccupation with formerly unwanted thoughts has been documented in several studies. Once suppressed, thoughts of white bears, sex, depressing or cheerful events, and former romantic liaisons have all been shown to return, or rebound, and dominate mental life (Chandler & Wegner, 1987; Gold & Wegner, 1991; Wegner, Schneider, Carter, & White, 1987; Wegner, Schneider, Knutson, & McMahon, 1991; Wegner, Shortt, Blake, & Page, 1990; Wenzlaff, Wegner, & Klein, 1991). Insofar as the judgmental or behavioral consequences of these intrusive thoughts are relatively benign, the phenomenon of rebound effects may give little cause for concern. After all, what damage can be done if one has a peculiar mental preoccupation with white bears? Of greater worry, however, is the recognition that an obsession with a legion of other formerly unwanted thoughts (e.g., eating, smoking, trauma-induced emotion, and phobias) can have distinctly deleterious consequences (see Marlatt & Parks, 1982; Pennebaker, 1990; Polivy & Herman, 1985; Wegner, 1992, 1994; Wegner & Pennebaker, 1993; Wegner & Schneider, 1989). In particular, the reappearance of these once banished thoughts may signal the onset of depression, fear, and anxiety (Roemer & Borkovec, 1993; Wenzlaff, 1993). It may also promote the execution of a multitude of maladaptive behaviors, such as binge eating and alcohol abuse (Herman & Polivy, 1993). In the present article, we consider another domain where rebound effects may have untoward judgmental and behavioral repercussions for social perceivers, namely, the stereotype domain.

Daily life is replete with situations where, for the purpose of interactional harmony, perceivers must suppress undesirable thoughts, including stereotypic beliefs about others. Of particular irritation is the fact that these thoughts seemingly spring to mind quite unintentionally (Devine, 1989; Fiske, 1989). Once encountered, for example, a hapless Scot may elicit thoughts of insobriety in even the most egalitarian of individuals (cf. Brewer, 1988; Devine, 1989; Devine, Monteith, Zuwerink, & Elliot, 1991; Fiske & Neuberg, 1990). Stereotypic beliefs such as these are unacceptable on several counts. Not only do they violate societal (i.e., legal) norms of equality and justice (Gaertner & Dovidio, 1986), but they also transgress personal standards of fairness and open-mindedness, leading to feelings of guilt and compunction (Devine et al., 1991; Monteith, 1993; Monteith, Devine, & Zuwerink, 1993). Unsurprisingly, therefore, rather than risk the social and personal costs of expressing unacceptable stereotypic thoughts, perceivers may choose instead to banish them from consciousness, anticipating that they will be kept at bay.

Unfortunately, the lesson to be inferred from available research on mental control is that these stereotypic thoughts are indeed very likely to return (see Wegner & Pennebaker, 1993). Moreover, on their reappearance they will likely preoccupy social perceivers to an intolerable degree. Assuming that the cognitive processes involved in removing a stereotypic belief from mind are structurally comparable with those encountered when any other unwanted item is banished from consciousness, then unwanted stereotypic preconceptions about others may return to preoccupy social perceivers, just as do thoughts of white bears and chocolate cheesecake. The intentional inhibition of stereotypical thinking, therefore, may not be as effective an antidote for our inferential shortcomings as many have supposed. Although conscious attempts to suppress stereotypes may indeed produce their intended effect (i.e., nonprejudiced responses), this escape from stereotypic thinking may be short-lived at best, because the stereotypic beliefs may rebound once inhibitory mechanisms have been relaxed. Rather ironically, therefore, by actively banishing stereotypic beliefs from mind, perceivers may unwittingly hasten their return. In the present article, one of our objectives is to investigate this intriguing possibility. In two studies, we consider the extent to which formerly unwanted stereotypic thoughts reappear (i.e., rebound) and impact upon perceivers' evaluation of, and behavior toward, a stereotyped target.

THE ACT OF SUPPRESSION

How are unwanted thoughts banished from mind, and exactly why do they return to preoccupy and haunt perceivers? In a recent article, Wegner and Erber (1992) proposed a model of thought suppression that attempts to address these questions. According to the model, thought suppression relies on the simultaneous operation of two cognitive processes, one controlled and the other automatic, for its successful execution (Bargh, 1984, 1989, 1990; Hasher & Zacks, 1979; Logan, 1988; Posner & Synder, 1975; Shiffrin & Schneider, 1977). Following perceivers, intention to suppress a thought, a controlled operating process is initiated that attempts to replace the unwanted item with an available distracter. This process serves the function of providing perceivers with something other than the unwanted item to think about. As a controlled cognitive process, this search for distracters is intentional, flexible, and constrained by the availability of attentional resources (see Bargh, 1989; Logan, 1988; Shallice, 1972). Simultaneously, following the onset of the intention to suppress, an ironic monitoring process is initiated that scans the contents of consciousness for any trace of the unwanted thought (i.e., failures in mental control). If it is detected, then the controlled operating process (i.e., distracter search) is reinstated to replace the item with another distracter (see Wegner, 1992, 1994; Wegner & Erber, 1992). This automatic target search process, while intentional, occurs outside of perceivers' awareness and is unconstrained by attentional capacity (see Bargh, 1989; Wegner & Erber, 1992). As Wegner and Erber reported, the simultaneous operation of these two cognitive subprocesses is essential if thought suppression is to be successful. Perceivers, after all, must not only be capable of inhibiting a thought; they must also be able to recognize or recollect the item that is to be inhibited.

One prominent implication of Wegner and Erber's model is that, at any point in time, unwanted thoughts ought to be quite cognitively accessible, even if distracters are momentarily more salient. This is because the automatic target search process ensures that perceivers are continually sensitized to any appearance of the unwanted item. If it is detected, controlled processes then take over and replace the thought with a convenient distracter. This cognitive cycle of suppression (i.e., detection then inhibition) has several intriguing empirical implications. In particular, if one precludes perceivers' ability to execute the search for distracters (e.g., through an attenuation in their cognitive capacity), then unwanted thoughts ought to become unusually accessible to consciousness. This prediction follows directly from the model because although the effortless target search process should continue uninterrupted in the face of resource depletion (i.e., perceivers will continually locate the unwanted item), the effortful task of replacing

the unwanted thought with an appropriate distracter should be impeded under similar circumstances. In two ingenious experiments, Wegner and Erber have demonstrated this effect. Under conditions of cognitive load (i.e., resource depletion), formerly unwanted thoughts become what is termed *hyperaccessible* for perceivers.

Here, then, is a potential explanation for why perceivers display a peculiar preoccupation with once forbidden thoughts. Failures in the actual cognitive process of suppression can render unwanted items highly accessible to consciousness (see Wegner & Erber, 1992). Although Wegner and Erber's model possesses considerable explanatory power, it must be acknowledged that early demonstrations of the rebound effect do not sit comfortably within this particular interpretation (e.g., Wegner et al., 1987). In this research, after all, the cycle of suppression was neither interrupted nor inhibited in any way. Subjects were simply instructed to try not to think about a particular topic (e.g., a white bear). It seems unlikely, therefore, that their subsequent preoccupation with the formerly unwanted thought can be attributed to any inability on their part to execute the controlled distracter search process (see Wegner & Erber, 1992). At present, the favored explanation is that perceivers create cognitive associations between the unwanted thought and the selected distracters. If the distracters are therefore reencountered on a future occasion, they serve as cues to remind perceivers of the unwanted item (see Wegner et al., 1987, 1991). Although we do not dispute the veracity of this context-based explanation for the rebound effect, we suspect that unwanted thoughts can also reach consciousness through a quite different route. In the present article, accordingly, we investigate the paradoxical possibility that the actual cycle of suppression itself may create conditions that ultimately promote the reappearance of unwanted thoughts (Wegner & Erber, 1992). Our argument and experimental predictions are based on an application of Wegner and Erber's model of mental control (see also Wegner, 1994) together with well-established research on priming and construct accessibility (e.g., Bargh, Bond, Lombardi, & Tota, 1986; Bargh & Pietromonaco, 1982; Higgins, 1989; Higgins, Bargh, & Lombardi, 1985; Higgins & King, 1981).

A fundamental property of Wegner and Erber's model is that, as a consequence of the ironic monitoring process, unwanted thoughts are detected (or primed) on numerous occasions. A potential clue to the subsequent rebounds of these thoughts, therefore, may reside in an awareness of the cognitive consequences of repetitive priming. Elsewhere in the literature, after all frequency of activation has reliably been shown to be an important determinant of construct accessibility and use (e.g., Higgins et al., 1985; Srull & Wyer, 1979, 1980). The more frequently a construct is activated, the more likely it is to impinge on perceivers' judgments and evaluations. One way to conceptualize this effect is within the synapse model of construct accessibility proposed by Higgins and his associates (see Higgins, 1989; Higgins & King, 1981); Higgins et al., 1985). As Higgins (1989, p. 86) noted, "as for synapses, the decay over time of the excitation level of a construct following its last activation is slower when the construct has been frequently activated when it has been activated only once."

This quotation, we suspect, may encapsulate a potential explanation for why perceivers demonstrate a preoccupation with formerly unwanted thoughts. Relative to non-suppressors (i.e., people who can think about a topic) who activate or prime a construct relatively infrequently, suppressors, as a consequence of the ironic monitoring process, activate the unwanted construct repeatedly, even if at low levels. Within the logic of the synapse model, therefore, the action potential of the construct should dissipate or decay more slowly for suppressors (i.e., frequent activation of the construct) than for nonsuppressors (i.e., infrequent activation of the construct). Correspondingly, the former group, rather than the latter, should be more likely to display construct-related effects in their subsequent cognitions and behavior. The rebound effect, then, may be a straightforward consequence of residual construct activation following repetitive priming (see Higgins, 1989; Higgins & King, 1981; Higgins et al., 1985). In the third of our reported experiments, we investigated the effects of thought suppression on the accessibility of stereotype contents.

The present research then had two main objectives. First, we considered whether stereotypic beliefs, once suppressed, return (i.e., rebound) and impact on perceivers' evaluation of, and behavior toward, a stereotyped target (Experiments 1 and 2). Second, we considered the extent to which these rebound effects may be explicable in terms of established priming mechanisms (Experiment 3).

EXPERIMENT 1

Method

Subjects and design   Twenty-four male and female undergraduates at the University of Wales College of Cardiff were paid £1 for their participation in the experiment.

The study had a 2 (task instruction: stereotype-suppression or control) × 2 (construction: Passage 1 or Passage 2) mixed design with repeated measures on the second factor.

Procedure and stimulus materials   On each subject's arrival in the laboratory, he or she was greeted by a female experimenter and randomly assigned to one of the experimental conditions.

The experimenter then explained that the study comprised an investigation of people's ability to construct life event details from visual information. All subjects were shown a color photograph of a male skinhead. It was explained that, on the paper provided, subjects would be given 5 min to compose a brief passage describing a typical day in the life of the target. Before performing this task, half of the subjects were informed that previous psychological research has established that our impressions and evaluations of others are consistently biased by stereotypic preconceptions. In the present task, however, it was stressed that subjects should actively try to avoid thinking about the target in such a manner. We anticipated that this instruction would encourage subjects to suppress their stereotypical thoughts during the experimental task. The control subjects, in contrast, were given no such instruction before constructing the passage. We assumed therefore that these subjects would use stereotypic preconceptions to guide their construction of the target's life events.

After they completed the passage, subjects were shown a color photograph of a different male skinhead. They were then all requested to spend another 5 min constructing a story describing a day in the life of this person. Importantly, in this case, none of the subjects received any admonishment about the avoidance of stereotyping. Thus, across the two parts of the experiment, some subjects were at liberty to think stereotypically from the outset (i.e., use-use); others only after an initial period of stereotype suppressions (i.e., suppress-use). On completion of the second passage, subjects were debriefed, paid, and dismissed.

Dependent measure   The dependent variable in this experiment was the level of stereotypicality of the constructed passages.

To compute this measure, two independent raters read each passage and, using a 9-point rating scale (1 = *not at all stereotypic* and 9 = *very stereotypic*), gave an estimate of the stereotypicality of its contents. These raters were blind to experimental condition and the purpose of the study. Given the high level of agreement in their estimates, $r(46) = .812$, scores were collapsed and a single measure of the stereotypicality of each passage was calculated.

Results and Discussion

If, like other unwanted thoughts, stereotypic beliefs rebound after suppression, then a particular pattern of results

TABLE 1   Ratings of Passage Stereotypicality as a Function of Task Instruction

	Instruction	
Passage	Suppress stereotype	Control
1	5.54	6.95
2	7.83	7.08

should emerge. Specifically, when subjects are allowed to think about stereotypic beliefs that were previously suppressed, they may display a higher level of stereotypical thinking than if they had never tried to suppress the thoughts in the first place. To evaluate this possibility, we submitted the ratings of passage stereotypicality to a 2 (task instruction: stereotype suppression or control) × 2 (construction: Passage 1 or Passage 2) mixed-model analysis of variance (ANOVA) with repeated measures on the second factor. This analysis revealed a main effect of construction, $F(1, 22) = 17.81$, $p < .0004$, but as anticipated, this effect was qualified by a significant Task Instruction × Construction interaction, $F(1, 22) = 14.31$, $p < .001$ (see Table 1). Simple effects analysis conformed an effect of task instruction on the stereotypicality of each passage: Passage 1, $F(1, 41) = 15.33$, $p < .0001$; Passage 2, $F(1, 41) = 4.29$, $p < .05$. Importantly, however, the pattern of treatment means was reversed for each passage. Whereas the first passage was most stereotypic in content when constructed by control subjects (i.e., stereotype users); the second passage, in contrast, was most stereotypic when constructed by stereotype suppressors. The analysis also revealed an effect of construction for subjects in the suppression condition, $F(1, 22) = 32.02$, $p < .0001$. Unsurprisingly, these subjects constructed a more stereotypic passage (i.e., Passage 2 rather than Passage 1) when the instruction to suppress the stereotype was relaxed.

These results provide initial evidence for the rebound of stereotypic thoughts after an earlier period of suppression (cf. Gold & Wegner, 1991); Wegner et al., 1987; Wegner et al., 1990; Wegner et al., 1991; Wenzlaff et al., 1991). When subjects were allowed to express stereotypic beliefs that were previously forbidden, these beliefs had a considerable impact on their conception of a target and his daily activities. An inspection of the relevant treatment means in Table 1 (i.e., Passage 2 means) shows that these subjects demonstrated a higher level of stereotypical thinking than their counterparts (i.e., control condition) who were able to entertain and express stereotypic beliefs from the outset. This rebound effect, moreover, was not simply a conse-

quence of the performance of the control subjects across the two passages. One competing explanation for the effect could be that control subjects simply exhaust their repertoire of stereotypical thoughts in the construction of the first passage, thereby diminishing the stereotypicality of the second passage. The present results provide no support for this interpretation. Across the two passages, the control subjects produced life event information that was equivalent in stereotypicality (see Table 1). Thus, the present effect appears to reflect the rebound of formerly unwanted material after the cessation of an active inhibitory requirement.

One potential limitation of the first study is the possibility of an implicit demand effect created by the experimental procedures. Because subjects were first explicitly instructed not to use stereotypes in the passage construction task and then were given the same task without comparable instructions, they may have believed that the experimenter wanted them to use more stereotypic constructions in the second passage. Although post-experimental interviews with subjects did not substantiate this concern, it is at least possible that this sort of demand process occurred implicitly. To address this issue, we attempted to replicate the basic finding of Experiment 1 in a context that was less demand laden. Specifically, the second experiment examined the impact of stereotype suppression in one experimental context on subsequent behavior in a different context (a waiting room). In addition to reducing concerns about demand characteristics, the second experiment also addressed the important question of the extent to which the rebound effect observed in Experiment 1 would spill over into perceivers' actual behavior toward a stereotyped target. Would, for instance, the overt expression of discriminatory practices and prejudice be amplified in a situation where the contents of consciousness comprise previously unwanted stereotypic thoughts? In the second of our reported experiments, noting this possibility, we attempted to provide a demonstration of the behavioral consequences of stereotype rebound.

EXPERIMENT 2

Method

Subjects and design   Twenty-four male and female undergraduates at the University of Wales College of Cardiff were paid £1 for their participation in the experiment.

The study had a single-factor (task instruction: stereotype suppression or control) between-subjects design.

Procedure and stimulus materials   On each subject's arrival in the laboratory, he or she was greeted by a female experimenter and randomly assigned to one of the treatment conditions.

The procedure, at this stage, was identical to that of Experiment 1. Having been presented with a color photograph of a male skinhead, subjects proceeded to spend 5 min detailing a typical day in his life. As before, half of the subjects performed this task under the instruction to try to avoid thinking about the target in a category-based manner (i.e., stereotype suppressors); the others simply completed the passage with no such instruction in place (i.e., control condition).

Following their completion of the passage, the experimenter explained that she would take the subject next door to meet the person (i.e., skinhead) who was depicted in the photograph. On entering the adjacent room, however, the subject was confronted not by the skinhead but by a row of eight empty seats. A denim jacket and bag were placed on the first seat and the experimenter explained that these items belonged to the person. She then remarked that he must have popped out of the room for a few minutes, most probably to visit the toilet. Until he reappeared, each subject was instructed to occupy one of the vacant seats (i.e., Seats 2 through 8) and wait for his return. It was anticipated that subjects' seating preference would be affected by the earlier passage completion task. That is, to the extent that stereotype inhibition promotes the resurgence of stereotypical thinking, we expected stereotype suppressors, rather than subjects in the control condition, to maintain a larger social distance from the target.

Note that the implicit demand in this experiment works against the experimental hypothesis, because subjects had been instructed not to use stereotypes in thinking about the very target they were about to meet. However, because these instructions had come in the context of the initial experimental task, we assumed that subjects' suppression motivation would be relaxed once that task was completed, setting the stage for a rebound effect. Once each subject had selected a seat, the seat number was noted and the experimenter brought the study to an end. Subjects were then debriefed, paid, and dismissed.

Dependent measures   Two dependent measures were used in this study.

First, we considered the stereotypicality of the contents of the constructed passages. As before, two independent raters read each passage and gave an estimate of its stereotypicality (9-point scale). Given the level of interrater reliability in these estimates, $r(22) = .842$, scores were again collapsed to produce a single measure reflecting the stereotypicality of each passage. Second, to assess the behavioral expression of rebounded stereotypic beliefs, we noted each subject's choice of seating position. Seven seats were potentially available to the subjects, and we coded these from 1 to 7. As Seat 1 was located next to the target's belongings, successive seat numbers reflect an increase in the social distance between the subject and the target.

Results and Discussion

Passage completion   As a manipulation check, we carried out a single-factor (task instruction: stereotype suppression or control) between-subjects ANOVA on the ratings of passage stereotypicality.

As expected, this revealed a main effect of task instruction on these data, $F(1, 22) = 7.09, p < .02$. The constructed passage was more stereotypic in nature when completed by the control subjects rather than the stereotype suppressors (respective $Ms = 6.83$ vs. 5.58).

Seating position   If rebounded thoughts manifest themselves in subjects' overt behavior toward a stereotyped target, one might expect to observe the operation of this effect in subjects' choice of seating position.

That is, if stereotype suppressors, relative to control subjects, are preoccupied with previously unwanted thoughts, perhaps they will strive to maintain a larger social distance from the stereotyped target. To investigate this possibility, we submitted subjects' seating choices to a single-factor (task instruction: stereotype suppression or control) between-subjects ANOVA. As predicted, this analysis revealed an effect of task instruction on subjects' seating position, $F(1, 22) = 4.78, p < .04$. That is, stereotype suppressors chose to occupy a seat that was farther from the target than did control subjects (respective $Ms = 5.25$ vs. 4.41). Thus, it would seem that rebounded thoughts can shape social perceivers' behavior toward a stereotyped target. Whereas we acknowledge that the present behavioral correlate of stereotype rebound (i.e., seating position) may have relatively innocuous consequences for the stereotyped target, it is easy to imagine circumstances where the repercussions of this effect could be considerably more worrisome. In particular, it is conceivable, at least in principle, that stereotype rebound could precipitate overt hostility or discriminatory practices toward the members of stereotyped groups.

EXPERIMENT 3

In Experiments 1 and 2, we have revealed how formerly unwanted stereotypic thoughts can reappear and impact on perceivers' evaluation of, and behavior toward, a stereotyped target. Notwithstanding this demonstration and its obvious practical implications for our understanding of social stereotyping, an important theoretical question emerges from our findings. Exactly why is it that once-banished thoughts return and exert such a marked influence on people's behavior? At present, as was previously noted, two competing explanations strive to answer this puzzle. The first approach asserts that a disruption in the cycle of suppression, most notably the search for appropriate distracters, moderates the effect. Preclude perceivers' capacity to think about something other than the unwanted item, and the unwanted item will return to haunt them (see Wegner, 1992, 1994; Wegner & Erber, 1992). The second approach, in contrast, posits a quite different origin for the rebound effect. During suppression, perceivers are assumed to form associations in long-term memory between the unwanted item (e.g., another bottle of beer) and each of the selected distracters (e.g., the curtains or one's smelly feet). When these distracters are encountered on a subsequent occasion, they simply serve to cue or trigger the unwanted thought (Wegner et al., 1987, 1991). Although they are plausible, and indeed supported by an impressive literature, it seems improbable that either of these approaches can account for the rebound effects observed in the present research. In neither of the reported studies, after all, did we disrupt the cognitive cycle of suppression (cf. Wegner & Erber, 1992). Also, in Experiment 2, we demonstrated a potentially context-independent manifestation of the rebound effect. Despite moving subjects between rooms, thereby minimizing the cueing impact of previously selected situational distracters, we still observed a rebound effect in their behavior toward a stereotyped target (cf. Wegner et al., 1991; Wenzlaff et al., 1991).

Given these aspects of the reported research, we speculate that unwanted thoughts can reappear, or apparently reappear, in consciousness by way of a quite distinct cognitive process. Indeed, we favor the somewhat paradoxical position that the actual cycle of suppression itself may encourage the reappearance of formerly unwanted thoughts, based on insights derived from Higgins et al.'s (1985) synapse model of construct accessibility (see also Bargh, 1989; Higgins, 1989). This excitation transmission model asserts that constructs function much like the synapses of vertebrates (Kandel, 1976). Following construct activation, the decay of excitation is assumed to vary as a function of the length of priming. The more frequently a construct has been activated, the slower the subsequent dissipation of its action potential. Thus, as Higgins et al. (1985, p. 61) remark, "the more frequently a construct is primed, the more likely its action potential will remain sufficiently high to give it an advantage in subsequent processing." This priming mechanism, we suspect, may account for a range of rebound effects, including those observed in the present research. As a consequence of the ironic monitoring process that occurs during suppression, unwanted constructs are continually stimulated or primed by perceivers (see Wegner & Erber, 1992). As a result, the action potential of the unwanted construct, whether it be a stereotype or thoughts about a white bear, should dissipate slowly, thereby amplifying its impact on perceivers' subsequent information processing. In the third of our reported experiments, we evaluated this possibility. Using a lexical decision task to assess construct excitation, we investigated the accessibility of stereotype contents after a period of suppression. We anticipated that, as a direct consequence of repetitive priming (hence slower dissipation of action potential), a prior period of thought suppression would enhance the accessibility of a stereotype and its associated concepts.

Method

Subjects and design   Twenty-four male and female undergraduates at the University of Wales College of Cardiff were paid £1 for their participation in the experiment.

The study had a 2 (task instruction: stereotype suppression or control) × 2 (word type: critical or distracter) mixed design with repeated measures on the second factor.

Procedure and stimulus materials   On each subject's arrival in the laboratory, he or she was greeted by a female experimenter and randomly assigned to one of the treatment conditions.

At this stage, the experiment was identical to Experiments 1 and 2. Having been presented with a color photograph of a male skinhead, subjects spent 5 min detailing a typical day in his life. As before, half of the subjects performed this task under the instruction to suppress stereotypical thoughts; the others completed the task with no such instruction in place (i.e., control condition).

Following the completion of the passage, each subject was seated facing the screen of an Apple Macintosh Microcomputer (Mac IIvi) and requested to perform another (ostensibly unrelated) task, specifically a lexical decision task. On the presentation of a letter string in the center of the computer screen, subjects had to judge, by means of a key press, whether it was a "word" or "nonword." The list of to-be-identified letter strings comprised 14 words that were stereotypic of skinheads, 14 matched distracters, and 28 nonwords. The stereotypic words were all evaluatively unfavorable in implication and were selected on the basis of earlier pilot testing. The distracters, also derived from the earlier pilot research, were matched with the target words in terms of valence and word length, but they were irrelevant with respect to the category of skinhead. Presentation of the letter strings was randomized, for each subject, by the computer. Lexical decision times (ms) were recorded by the computer and measured using the Macintosh's Extended Time Manager. It was anticipated that residual action potential, when present, would facilitate subjects' responses to the skinhead-related words. That is, if the stereotype remained accessible, lexical decisions would be faster for the critical than for the distracter words. Moreover, the greater the action potential that was available, the greater the anticipated facilitatory priming effect. To provide supplementary baseline data, an additional 12 subjects performed the lexical decision task without previously completing a life event passage. As no stereotype was activated in this condition, facilitatory priming effects were not expected in the lexical decision task. On completion of this task, subjects were debriefed, paid, and dismissed.

Dependent measures   As before, we considered the stereotypicality of the contents of the constructed passages.

Two independent raters read each passage and gave an estimate of its stereotypicality on the 9-point scale used previously. Given the level of interrater reliability in these estimates, $r(24) = .911$, the data were collapsed to produce a single measure reflecting the stereotypicality of each passage. Lexical decision latencies were taken as an indicator of stereotype accessibility.

Results and Discussion

Passage completion   To evaluate the success of our experimental manipulation, we carried out a single-factor (task instruction: stereotype suppression or control) between-subjects ANOVA on the ratings of passage stereotypicality.

This analysis confirmed an effect of task instruction on these data, $F(1, 22) = 11.27$, $p < .003$. The constructed life event passage was more stereotypic in content when completed by the control subjects rather than the stereotype suppressors (respective $Ms = 6.83$ vs. 4.83).

Lexical decision latencies   The principal dependent measures were the mean time (ms) taken by subjects to characterize each letter string as either a "word" or a "nonword."

Incorrect classifications of the letter strings were infrequent (3.17% error rate across all the trials). Where they did occur, however, these were excluded from the statistical analysis. To measure the accessibility of stereotype contents, we submitted subjects' lexical decision latencies to a 3 (task instruction: stereotype suppression or control or baseline) × 2 (word type: critical or distracter) mixed-model ANOVA with repeated measures on the second factor. As anticipated, this revealed a Task Instruction × Word Type interaction on subjects' response times, $F(2, 33) = 4.51$, $p < .02$ (see Table 2). Simple effects analysis confirmed that both stereotype suppressors, $F(1, 33) = 20.06$, $p < .001$, and control subjects, $F(1, 33) = 4.06$, $p < .05$, responded more quickly to the critical words than the matched distracters. This then supports the intuition that the applicable stereotype is accessible for these subjects. As Table 2 reveals, however, the facilitatory effect of stereotype activation was clearly stronger for the stereotype suppressors. This conclusion gains additional empirical support from the simple effect of task instruction on the response latencies associated with the critical words, $F(2, 33) = 3.10$, $p < .05$. Post-hoc Tukey tests showed that stereotype suppressors responded more quickly to the critical words than did subjects in either of the other experimental conditions ($p < .05$).

These results, then, support the prediction that following stereotype suppression, action potential dissipates slowly from the activated construct (see Higgins et al., 1985). Relative to control subjects who were at liberty to think stereotypically during the passage-completion task, stereotype suppressors displayed a greater facilitatory priming effect on the subsequent lexical decision task. This effect, then, may help to explain why perceivers frequently display a peculiar mental preoccupation with formerly unwanted thoughts and why these thoughts can sometimes affect information processing and behavior (cf. Wegner et al., 1987; Wegner et al., 1990; Wegner et al., 1991).

TABLE 2   **Ratings of Passage Stereotypicality and Lexical Decision Latencies as a Function of Task Instruction**

	Instruction		
Dependent variable	Suppress stereotype	Control	Baseline
Passage	4.83	6.83	—
Lexical decision time (ms)			
Stereotypic traits	571ab	690a	778b
Distracters	773	782	790

Note: Means sharing a common subscript differ significantly at $p < .05$ (Tukey's honestly significant difference).

GENERAL DISCUSSION

Stereotypes on the Rebound

Social conventions and personal convictions often dictate that social perceivers should "just say no" to stereotypic thought processes, before they can impinge on judgmental outcomes and behavior directed at members of stereotyped groups (e.g., Devine, 1989; Fiske, 1989). As Devine (1989, p. 16), argued, for example, "in situations involving consciously controlled stereotype-related processes, those who score low in prejudice on an attitude scale are attempting to inhibit stereotypic responses." Although benefits are clearly to be accrued through the instigation of these inhibitory mechanisms, most notably in the form of a reduction in stereotyping and prejudice, the picture may not be as clear-cut as it first appears. In particular, as identified in the present research, there may be a range of ironic side effects associated with the seemingly functional and adaptive process of stereotype inhibition (see also Macrae, Bodenhausen, Milne, & Jetten, 1993). By means of the well-established phenomenon of postsuppression rebound (e.g., Wegner et al., 1987; Wegner et al., 1990; Wegner et al., 1991), for instance, formerly unwanted stereotypic thoughts may reappear in mind and impact on perceivers' treatment of a stereotyped target (Experiments 1 and 2). In this respect, stereotypic beliefs about others appear to behave much like any other forbidden thought. Whether the exiled item is a desire to eat junk food forever, to reveal one's undying love for a close friend, or simply to inform an Englishman that he's a touch pompous, the consequences of postsuppression rebound are equivalent in each case. Once inhibitory mechanisms are relaxed, perceivers demonstrate a pervasive preoccupation with the formerly unwanted thought, with all the pernicious implications that this entails for their ensuing cognitions and behavior (see Wegner, 1992, 1994; Wegner & Pennebaker, 1993; Wegner & Schneider, 1989). Out of sight, then, does not necessarily mean out of mind, at least where unwanted thoughts are concerned.

Extending Wegner and Erber's (1992) model of mental control, we made the seemingly paradoxical theoretical prediction that the actual process of suppression itself may promote the rebound of formerly unwanted thoughts. Our arguments were derived from an application of the synapse model of construct accessibility to thinking in this domain (Bargh et al., 1986; Bargh, Lombardi, & Higgins, 1988; Higgins, 1989; Higgins & King, 1981; Higgins et al., 1985). We suggested that postsuppression rebound may be explicable, at least in part, in terms of mechanisms that are well established in the literature on priming and construct accessibility. Our results provided strong support for this intuition (Experiment 3). Relative to subjects who were previously able to express stereotypic beliefs about a target, stereotype suppressors demonstrated greater evidence of construct activation on a subsequent lexical decision task. Moreover, the pattern of results confirmed that stereotype contents were more accessible for the suppressors than for the control subjects (i.e., stereotype users). We attributed this increased accessibility to the repetitive priming the stereotype experienced during suppression (Wegner & Erber, 1992) and the resulting diminished rate of decay of action potential from the frequently stimulated construct (Higgins et al., 1985).

Although our results are generally consistent with other contemporary research documenting ironic effects of attempts to exert mental control, most notably the work of Wegner and his colleagues (see Wegner, 1994), some potentially interesting differences can also be identified. A study conducted by Wenzlaff, Wegner, and Klein (1991, Experiment 1), for example, suggested that postsuppression rebound effects are more sizable when the context at the time of suppression is similar to the subsequent postsuppression context. In our second experiment, however, we found a rebound effect despite a change of social context (i.e., a different room in an apparently different phase of the experiment). Of course Wenzlaff et al. studied the effects of an internal, psychological context (mood), whereas in our experiment, the change of context primarily involved the external, physical environment, making direct comparisons between the studies difficult. In any event, Wenzlaff et al. did find rebound effects across contexts, but they were of a smaller magnitude than ones occurring in the same context. If anything, this suggests that the rebound effects we observed in our second experiment might have been even larger if the suppression activity had occurred in the same context as the postsuppression activity. Future research should address the issue of whether our priming explanation for rebound effects can also explain the moderating role of context similarity on the magnitude of these effects. If the psychological or physical context becomes associated with the primed but to-be-disregarded stereotype, then it may very well contribute to the (additional) activation of the stereotype when the context is maintained or reinstated.

Another interesting difference between our results and those of Wegner and his colleagues concerns the role played by mental load in the hyperaccessibility phenomenon. Elsewhere, the hyperaccessibility of once-suppressed thoughts has typically been found under conditions of resource depletion (Wegner, 1994; Wegner & Erber, 1992). In a recent study, for example, Wegner, Erber, and Bowman (cited in

Wegner, 1994) instructed subjects to complete sentence stems under conditions of either high or low time pressure. The sentences were selected so that it was possible to complete them in either relatively sexist or nonsexist ways. Some subjects were instructed to try not to be sexist in completing the sentence stems, while others were given no special instructions before the task. It was anticipated that the time-pressure manipulation would short-circuit the successful operation of the effortful operating process, setting the stage for greater sexism among those who were actively trying not to be sexist. This is precisely what happened. In contrast, our results indicate that the intention to suppress stereotypes can backfire even in the absence of any appreciable cognitive load. Because we did not manipulate resource availability during suppression, we cannot determine whether the effects we observed might have been even more pronounced under conditions of resource depletion. However, there seems to be no compelling theoretical or empirical reason to assume that hyperaccessibility can only occur under conditions of mental load. Wegner, Erber, and Bowman's no-load subjects may also have had highly accessible stereotypes when they were attempting to suppress them, but they had ample time to edit their sentence completions before speaking them. Our experimental procedures were different in that they created an experimental context in which the suppression motivation was first created, then relaxed. Once the suppression motivation is diminished, the likelihood of output editing also declines, setting the stage for our observed rebound effects, even in the absence of any cognitive load. Thus, stereotype suppression may elevate the accessibility of the stereotype regardless of load, but whether this heightened accessibility affects overt behavior depends on a number of factors that affect the person's motivation or ability to engage in output editing, of which cognitive load is only one.

The existence of a mental process that produces counterintentional results would seem to be a considerable impediment to successful adaptation and adjustment. After all, what functional utility can we attach to a process that apparently exacerbates the very tendency it is attempting to remedy? An inspection of the relevant literature on construct accessibility, however, may provide insight to this puzzle. In estimating the ultimate behavioral consequences of construct accessibility, it is essential to consider the applicability of the primed construct in relation to the available stimulus input (Bargh, 1989; Higgins, 1989; Higgins & Bargh, 1987; Higgins & Chaires, 1980; Higgins, Rholes, & Jones, 1977; Srull & Wyer, 1979). As Higgins (1989, pp. 87–88) noted, "it is the combination of a construct's prior level of excitation and its applicability to the

input that determines the likelihood that the construct will be used in judging the input." In other words, if an accessible construct, such as a social stereotype, is unrelated to the available stimulus input, it is unlikely to exert any influence on information processing. Although a stereotype may remain accessible in memory after suppression, more often than not it will be inapplicable to the stimulus information that is subsequently encountered. Hence it will have no effect on information processing. Only when some critical match is established between the activated construct and available information would one expect postsuppression rebound effects to be realized in perceivers' cognitions and behavior (for a detailed description of these effects, see Bargh, 1989; Higgins, 1989). Whereas this critical precondition may not often be satisfied in daily interaction, it must be acknowledged that, at least in principle, rebound effects may be experienced some time after the stereotype has been suppressed. Priming effects of one sort or another, after all, have been documented in the literature up to 16 months after the occurrence of the initial priming episode (see Jacoby, 1983; Sloman, Hayman, Ohta, Law, & Tulving, 1988; Smith, Stewart, & Buttram, 1992; Srull & Wyer, 1979; Tulving, Schacter, & Stark, 1982). Rather soberingly, therefore, long after their exorcism, unwanted stereotypic thoughts may return to haunt perceivers.

Is There Anybody Home?

Any consideration of exactly how perceivers inhibit unwanted stereotypic thoughts inevitably gives rise to an intractable philosophical conundrum. As Uleman (1989, p. 432) summarized, "if control is being exercised, who is ultimately in control? Doesn't there have to be a homunculus, or little person, inside the system somewhere to monitor what is going on?" Like Uleman, however, we conclude that the answer to this puzzle appears to be no (see Bargh, 1984; Dennett, 1978, 1991; Gilbert, 1989; Miller, Galanter, & Pribram, 1960; Neisser, 1967; Uleman, 1989). Although appealing, it is unlikely that some cerebral executive or general controller pulls our strings, ensuring that inappropriate stereotypic beliefs never appear in our utterances and behavior. As Dennett (1991, p. 29) remarked, "the trouble with brains . . . is that when you look in them, you discover that there's nobody home." If nobody's home, of course, then how exactly are inhibitory mechanisms selected, prioritized and instigated by perceivers? What, for instance, stops perceivers from routinely announcing that every politician encountered is an obsequious jerk? Several solutions have been offered for this problem. Dennett (1978) argued that the homunculus is simply an emergent property of the entire information-processing system (see Uleman, 1989). In reality, the function of the homunculus (e.g., mental control) can be accomplished by a large number of smaller more stupid homunculi who, importantly, remain ignorant of both their prescribed role and the overall workings of the system (see also Dennett, 1984, 1991). As Dennett (1978, p. 124) put it, "one discharges fancy homunculi from one's scheme by organizing armies of such idiots to do the work."

An influential application of this approach to issues in social cognition is Gilbert's (1989) model of dispositional inference. Within this model, an army of dullards (i.e., stupid homunculi) furnish consciousness with dispositional inferences upon which more reflective (i.e., corrective) processes may ultimately operate. The crux of the model, as Gilbert (1989) noted, is that these dullards deliver their products (i.e., dispositional inferences) to mind in a blind, unconscious, and mechanical fashion. Consciousness, in reality, has no awareness of either the existence of these basic processes or how their outputs arrive in mind (see Bargh, 1984; Dennett, 1991). Moreover, the assumption that the inferences were somehow computed directly in consciousness in the first place is little more than a seductive (but dangerous) Cartesian illusion (see Dennett, 1991).

Stereotype inhibition, then, may be regulated by processes of which we have little direct knowledge. Indeed, the intention to suppress may occur outside our conscious awareness (e.g., Fiske, 1989; Lewin, 1951; Miller et al., 1960) and in some cases beyond our direct volitional control (see Bargh, 1984). In an insightful article, Bargh (1990) has argued that many of our goal-related mental activities may not be under executive control at all. Instead, they may be initiated by features of the situational environment. Once triggered or activated by the appropriate environmental cue, these goals shape information processing without perceivers' awareness or conscious consent. Stereotype inhibition, we suspect, may be one class of mental event that benefits from this theoretical analysis. Situational features may automatically activate stereotype inhibition by way of several routes. If, for example, an inhibitory goal is frequently activated in a particular setting (e.g., do not stereotype when strangers are present), generic aspects of that setting (e.g., another person) may be sufficient to activate the goal (see Bargh, 1990; Schank & Abelson, 1977). Such a process may help to explain why public displays of individuation frequently degenerate into stereotyped responses when social perceivers are in the privacy of their own homes. Remove a critical situational cue, and inhibitory mechanisms may fail to be initiated. Also, as Bargh (1990, p. 101) reported, "societal or cultural norms

for appropriate behavior in that type of situation may be directly activated by situational features, and these norms in turn may directly activate goals and intentions to behave in normative ways." Stereotype inhibition, then, may be set in motion by factors over which we have little control and accomplished through cognitive processes of which we are largely unaware (see also Dennett, 1978, 1984, 1991; Fiske, 1989; Gilbert, 1989; Uleman, 1989; Wegner & Erber, 1992). This, however, is not as surprising as it may seem. If stereotype activation can become routinized, automated, and triggered by external stimulus cues, then there is no compelling reason why stereotype inhibition should not take a similar course (cf. Brewer, 1988; Devine, 1989; Fiske & Neuberg, 1990).

Conclusions

Many have assumed that the key to prejudice reduction lies in the controlled inhibition of stereotypical thought (Devine, 1989; Fiske, 1989). Although this may indeed be true, we have identified some surprising costs that may be associated with this process—costs that apparently derive from the act of suppression itself. As a consequence of postsuppression rebound effects, formerly unwanted stereotypic thoughts were shown to return and impact on perceivers' treatment of a stereotyped target. In Wegner and Erber's (1992) model of thought control, we have a precise cognitive specification of how perceivers banish unwanted stereotypic thoughts from mind, once an intention to suppress has been initiated. What we currently lack, however, is a detailed knowledge of the factors that precede and power the model, namely, the origins of these inhibitory intentions. In the present article, following Bargh (1990), we have suggested that these intentions may be triggered, not by executive processes, but rather by environmental cues that have become associated with stereotype inhibition. One task for future research on this topic will be to investigate this speculation.

In recent years, a substantial literature has accumulated documenting what happens when perceivers think stereotypically about others (for a comprehensive review, see Hamilton & Sherman, in press). Shifting the emphasis somewhat, we have demonstrated some intriguing effects when perceivers attempt the opposite; that is, to actively try not to think about others in a stereotypic fashion. Ultimately, the implications of these effects may prove as significant for our understanding of mental life as the insights already gleaned from work on stereotype activation. What is certain is that our investigations of stereotype inhibition have only just begun.

REFERENCES

Bargh, J. A. (1984). Automatic and conscious processing of social information. In R. S. Wyer, Jr., & T. K. Srull (Eds.), *Handbook of social cognition* (Vol. 3, pp. 1–44). Hillsdale, NJ: Erlbaum.

Bargh, J. A. (1989). Conditional automaticity: Varieties of automatic influence in social perception and cognition. In J. S. Uleman & J. A. Bargh (Eds.), *Unintended thought* (pp. 3–51). New York: Guilford Press.

Bargh, J. A. (1990). Auto-motives: Preconscious determinants of social interaction. In E. T. Higgins & R. M. Sorrentino (Eds.), *Handbook of motivation and cognition* (Vol. 2, pp. 93–130). New York: Guilford Press.

Bargh, J. A., Bond, R. N., Lombardi, W. J., & Tota, M. E. (1986). The additive nature of chronic and temporary sources of construct accessibility. *Journal of Personality and Social Psychology, 50,* 869–878.

Bargh, J. A., Lombardi, W. J., & Higgins, E. T. (1988). Automaticity of chronically accessible constructs in Person × Situation effects on person perception: It's just a matter of time. *Journal of Personality and Social Psychology, 55,* 599–605.

Bargh, J. A., & Pietromonaco, P. (1982). Automatic information processing and social perception: The influence of trait information presented outside of conscious awareness on impression formation. *Journal of Personality and Social Psychology, 43,* 437–449.

Brewer, M. B. (1988). A dual process model of impression formation. In R. S. Wyer, Jr., & T. K. Srull (Eds.), *Advances in social cognition* (Vol. 1, pp. 1–36). Hillsdale, NJ: Erlbaum.

Chandler, G., & Wegner, D. M. (1987). *The effect of thought suppression on preoccupation with associated thoughts.* Unpublished manuscript, Trinity University, San Antonio, TX.

Dennett, D. C. (1978). *Brainstorms: Philosophical essays on mind and psychology.* Cambridge, MA: MIT Press.

Dennett, D. C. (1984). *Elbow room: The varieties of free will worth having.* Cambridge, MA: MIT Press.

Dennett, D. C. (1991). *Consciousness explained.* London: Penguin.

Devine, P. G. (1989). Stereotypes and prejudice: their automatic and controlled components. *Journal of Personality and Social Psychology, 56,* 5–18.

Devine, P. G., Monteith, M. J., Zuwerink, J. R., & Elliot, A. J. (1991). Prejudice with and without compunction. *Journal of Personality and Social Psychology, 60,* 817–830.

Fiske, S. T. (1989). Examining the role of intent: Toward understanding its role in stereotyping and prejudice. In J. S. Uleman & J. A. Bargh (Eds.), *Unintended thought* (pp. 253–286). New York: Guilford Press.

Fiske, S. T., & Neuberg, S. L. (1990). A continuum model of impression formation from category-based to individuating processes: Influences of information and motivation on attention and interpretation. In M. P. Zanna (Ed.), *Advances in experimental social psychology* (Vol. 3, pp. 1–74). San Diego, CA: Academic Press.

Freud, S. (1957). Repression. In J. Strachey (Ed.), *The standard edition of the complete psychological works of Sigmund Freud* (Vol. 14, pp. 146–158). London: Hogarth Press. (Original work published 1915.)

Gaertner, S. L., & Dovidio, J. F. (1986). The aversive form of racism. In J. F. Dovidio & S. L. Gaertner (Eds.,), *Prejudice, discrimination, and racism* (pp. 61–89). San Diego, CA: Academic Press.

Gilbert, D. T. (1989). Thinking lightly about others: Automatic components of the social inference process. In J. S. Uleman & J. A. Bargh (Eds.), *Unintended thought* (pp. 189–211). New York: Guilford Press.

Gold, D. B., & Wegner, D. M. (1991). *Fanning old flames: Arousing romantic obsession through thought suppression.* Paper presented at the meeting of the American Psychological Association, San Francisco.

Hamilton, D. L., & Sherman, J. W. (in press). Stereotypes. In R. S. Wyer, Jr., & T. K. Srull (Eds.), *Handbook of social cognition* (2nd ed.). Hillsdale, NJ: Erlbaum.

Hasher, L., & Zacks, R. T. (1979). Automatic and effortful processes in memory. *Journal of Experimental Psychology: General, 108,* 356–388.

Herman, C. P., & Polivy, J. (1993). Mental control of eating: Excitatory and inhibitory food thoughts. In D. M. Wegner & J. W. Pennebaker (Eds.), *Handbook of mental control* (pp. 491–505). Englewood Cliffs, NJ: Prentice-Hall.

Higgins, E. T. (1989). Knowledge accessibility and activation: subjectivity and suffering from unconscious sources. In J. S. Uleman & J. A. Bargh (Eds.), *Unintended thought* (pp. 75–123). New York: Guilford Press.

Higgins, E. T., Bargh, J. A. (1987). Social perception and social cognition. *Annual Review of Psychology, 38,* 369–425.

Higgins, E. T., Bargh, J. A., & Lombardi, W. (1985). The nature of priming effects on categorization. *Journal of Experimental Psychology: Learning, Memory, and Cognition, 11,* 59–69.

Higgins, E. T., & Chaires, W. M. (1980). Accessibility of interrelational constructs: Implications for stimulus encoding and creativity. *Journal of Experimental Social Psychology, 16,* 348–361.

Higgins, E. T., & King, G. (1981). Accessibility of social constructs: Information-processing consequences of individual and contextual variability. In N. Cantor & J. F. Kihlstrom (Eds.), *Personality, cognition, and social interaction* (pp. 69–122). Hillsdale, NJ: Erlbaum.

Higgins, E. T., Rholes, W. S., & Jones, C. R. (1977). Category accessibility and impression formation. *Journal of Experimental Social Psychology, 13,* 141–154.

Jacoby, L. L. (1983). Remembering the data: Analyzing interactive processes in reading. *Journal of Verbal Learning and Verbal Behavior, 22,* 485–508.

Kandel, E. R. (1976). *Cellular basis of behavior: An introduction to neurobiology.* San Francisco: Freeman.

Lewin, K. (1951). Intention, will, and need. In D. Rapaport (Ed. and Trans.), *Organization and pathology of thought* (pp. 95–153). New York: Columbia University Press.

Logan, G. D. (1988). Toward an instance theory of automatization. *Psychological Review, 95,* 492–527.

Macrae, C. N., Bodenhausen, G. V., Milne, A. B., & Jetten, J. (1993). *On resisting the temptation for simplification: Cognitive costs of stereotype suppression.* Manuscript submitted for publication.

Marlatt, G. P., & Parks, G. A. (1982). Self-management of addictive behaviors. In P. Karoly & F. H. Kanfer (Eds.), *Self-management and behavior change* (pp. 443–488). New York: Pergamon Press.

Miller, G. A., Galanter, E., & Pribram, K. (1960). *Plans and the structure of behavior.* New York: Holt.

Monteith, M. J. (1993). Self-regulation of prejudiced responses: Implications for progress in prejudice-reduction efforts. *Journal of Personality and Social Psychology, 65,* 469–485.

Monteith, M. J., Devine, P. G., & Zuwerink, J. R. (1993). Self-directed versus other-directed affect as a consequence of prejudice-related discrepancies. *Journal of Personality and Social Psychology, 64,* 198–210.

Neisser, U. (1967). *Cognitive psychology.* New York: Appleton-Century-Crofts.

Pennebaker, J. W. (1990). *Opening up: The healing powers of confiding in others.* New York: Morrow.

Polivy, J., & Herman, C. P. (1985). Dieting and binging: A causal analysis. *American Psychologist, 40,* 193–201.

Posner, M. I., & Snyder, C. R. R. (1975). Attention and cognitive control. In R. L. Soloso (Ed.), *Information processing and cognition* (pp. 55–85). Hillsdale, NJ: Erlbaum.

Roemer, L., & Borkovec, T. D. (1993). Worry: Unwanted cognitive activity that controls unwanted somatic experience. In D. M. Wegner & J. W. Pennebaker (Eds.), *Handbook of mental control* (pp. 220–238). Englewood Cliffs, NJ: Prentice-Hall.

Schank, R. C., & Abelson, R. P. (1977). *Scripts, plans, goals, and understanding.* Hillsdale, NJ: Erlbaum.

Shallice, T. (1972). Dual functions of consciousness. *Psychological Review, 79,* 383–393.

Shiffrin, R. M., & Schneider, W. (1977). Controlled and automatic human information processing II: Perceptual learning, automatic attending, and a general theory. *Psychological Review, 84,* 127–190.

Sloman, S. A., Hayman, C. A. G., Ohta, N., Law, J., & Tulving, E. (1988). Forgetting in primed fragment completion. *Journal of Experimental Psychology: Learning, Memory, and Cognition, 14,* 223–239.

Smith, E. R., Stewart, T. L., & Buttram, R. T. (1992). Inferring a trait from a behavior has long-term, highly specific effects. *Journal of Personality and Social Psychology, 62,* 753–759.

Srull, T. K., & Wyer, R. S., Jr. (1979). The role of category accessibility in the interpretation of information about persons: Some determinants and implications. *Journal of Personality and Social Psychology, 37,* 1660–1672.

Srull, T. K., & Wyer. R. S., Jr. (1980). Category accessibility and social perception: Some implications for the study of person memory and interpersonal judgments. *Journal of Personality and Social Psychology, 38,* 841–856.

Tulving, E., Schacter, D. L., & Stark, H. A. (1982). Priming effects in word-fragment completion are independent of recognition memory. *Journal of Experimental Psychology: Learning, Memory, and Cognition, 8,* 336–342.

Uleman, J. S. (1989). A framework for thinking intentionally about unintended thoughts. In J. S. Uleman & J. A. Bargh (Eds.), *Unintended thoughts* (pp. 425–449). New York: Guilford Press.

Wegner, D. M. (1989). *White bears and other unwanted thoughts.* New York: Viking.

Wegner, D. M. (1992). You can't always think what you want: Problems in the suppression of unwanted thoughts. In M. P. Zanna (Ed.), *Advances in experimental social psychology* (Vol. 25, pp. 193–225). San Diego, CA: Academic Press.

Wegner, D. M. (1994). Ironic processes of mental control. *Psychological Review, 101,* 34–52.

Wegner, D. M., & Erber, R. (1992). The hyperaccessibility of suppressed thoughts. *Journal of Personality and Social Psychology, 63,* 903–912.

Wegner, D. M., & Pennebaker, J. W. (Eds.) (1993). *Handbook of mental control.* Englewood Cliffs, NJ: Prentice-Hall.

Wegner, D. M., & Schneider, D. J. (1989). Mental control: The war of the ghosts in the machine. In J. S. Uleman & J. A. Bargh (Eds.), *Unintended thought* (pp. 287–305). New York: Guilford Press.

Wegner, D. M., Schneider, D. J., Carter, S., & White, L. (1987). Paradoxical effects of thought suppression. *Journal of Personality and Social Psychology, 53,* 5–13.

Wegner, D. M., Schneider, D. J., Knutson, B., & McMahon, S. (1991). Polluting the stream of consciousness: The influence of thought suppression on the mind's environment. *Cognitive Therapy and Research, 15,* 141–152.

Wegner, D. M., Shortt, J. W., Blake, A. W., & Page, M. S. (1990). The suppression of exciting thoughts. *Journal of Personality and Social Psychology, 58,* 409–418.

Wenzlaff, R. M. (1993). The mental control of depression: Psychological obstacles to emotional well-being. In D. M. Wegner & J. W. Pennebaker (Eds.), *Handbook of mental control* (pp. 239–257). Englewood Cliffs, NJ: Prentice-Hall.

Wenzlaff, R. M., Wegner, D. M., & Klein, S. B. (1991). The role of thought suppression in the bonding of mood and thought. *Journal of Personality and Social Psychology, 60,* 500–508.

Received October 18, 1993
Revision received March 29, 1994
Accepted April 4, 1994

CRITICAL THINKING QUESTIONS

1. Macrae and his colleagues suggest that if people try to suppress the use of stereotypes, then they may be more likely to use these stereotypes in the future. Does this mean that people should go ahead and use their stereotypes? Does it mean that there is nothing that can be done about stereotyping? What does other research reported in Chapter 4 of the text have to say about this problem?

2. The researchers told the subjects in these experiments to not stereotype the person with whom they were interacting. Do you think this is different from the spontaneous stereotype suppression that people engage in when they decide that they do not want to stereotype others? In what ways might it be different? In what ways is it likely to be the same?

3. The stereotype that was used in this research—the stereotype about skinheads—is a stereotype that many people would be willing to display in public. In terms of modern racism, as it was discussed in Chapter 4, this stereotype may not conflict with the dominant egalitarian norm that most people hold, because one could argue that he or she stereotypes skinheads because they do not support this egalitarian norm. Is stereotyping a skinhead the same as using other stereotypes like those based on race and gender? In what ways is it similar? In what ways might it be different?

4. What evidence did the authors offer that subjects in these experiments were suppressing the use of stereotypes?

5. How does the speed with which people decide whether a string of letters is a word or not (the lexical decision task in Experiment 3) indicate stereotyping?

6. Have you ever experienced the rebound effect of thought suppression? Do you think this is a common occurrence? Do you think we commonly use stereotypes on the rebound?

PART II
Social Interaction

READING 5 _____

When Snyder, Tanke, and Berscheid conducted this classic investigation of self-fulfilling prophecies based on stereotypes concerning physical attractiveness, little research had been conducted on the consequences of social perception. As Chapter 3 of your textbook shows, much research had been conducted by 1977 on how people form impressions of others, but Snyder and his colleagues noted that there had been little attention paid to the question "What are the cognitive and behavioral consequences of our impressions of other people?"

In Reading 1 of this book, Rosenthal and Jacobson (1968) showed the consequences of teachers' expectations about their students' intellectual potential. They found that these expectations led to self-fulfilling prophecies. Chapter 3 defines a self-fulfilling prophecy as the process by which a perceiver's expectations about a person eventually lead that person to behave in ways that confirm those expectations. The teachers' false expectations about some of their students led the students to behave in ways consistent with these expectations, thus confirming the expectations. Snyder, Tanke, and Berscheid hypothesized that stereotypes can have similar effects. A perceiver's stereotype about some group of people may lead the perceiver to act toward individual members of this group in ways that are likely to produce behaviors that are consistent with the stereotype. Thus, even inaccurate stereotypes can lead to behavioral confirmation of the stereotypes.

The stereotype Snyder and his colleagues examined concerned physical attractiveness. As Chapter 5 of the textbook shows, physical attractiveness plays an important role in people's lives. Physically attractive individuals are judged and responded to differently than physically unattractive people in various ways. Chapter 5 describes the pervasive bias for beauty, and explains that one important cause is the what-is-beautiful-is-good stereotype: the belief that physically attractive people also have desirable personalities. The experiment reported in this paper provides evidence not only for the existence of this stereotype among their male subjects, but also for the social consequences of the stereotype. It thus demonstrates the significance of this stereotype and also suggests how it can be reinforced and strengthened even if it is wrong. Suppose that a physically attractive person does *not* have certain positive traits, such as being sociable, warm, or interesting. A perceiver's expectations about this person may still cause the perceiver to bring out sociable, warm, and interesting behavior from this person. When this happens, the perceiver's stereotype about physically attractive people is confirmed and reinforced.

Social Perception and Interpersonal Behavior: On the Self-Fulfilling Nature of Social Stereotypes

Mark Snyder
University of Minnesota

Elizabeth Decker Tanke
University of Santa Clara

Ellen Berscheid
University of Minnesota

This research concerns the self-fulfilling influences of social stereotypes on dyadic social interaction. Conceptual analysis of the cognitive and behavioral consequences of stereotyping suggests that a perceiver's actions based upon stereotyped-generated attributions about a specific target individual may cause the behavior of that individual to confirm the perceiver's initially erroneous attributions. A paradigmatic investigation of the behavioral confirmation of stereotypes involving physical attractiveness (e.g., "beautiful people are good people") is presented. Male "perceivers" interacted with female "targets" whom they believed (as a result of an experimental manipulation) to be physically attractive or physically unattractive. Tape recordings of each participant's conversational behavior were analyzed by naive observer judges for evidence of behavioral confirmation. These analyses revealed that targets who were perceived (unknown to them) to be physically attractive came to behave in a friendly, likeable, and sociable manner in comparison with targets whose perceivers regarded them as unattractive. It is suggested that theories in cognitive social psychology attend to the ways in which perceivers create the information that they process in addition to the ways that they process that information.

> Thoughts are but dreams
> Till their effects be tried
>
> —William Shakespeare[1]

Cognitive social psychology is concerned with the processes by which individuals gain knowledge about behavior and events that they encounter in social interaction, and how they use this knowledge to guide their actions. From this perspective, people are "constructive thinkers" searching for the causes of behavior, drawing inferences about people and their circumstances, and acting upon this knowledge.

Most empirical work in this domain—largely stimulated and guided by the attribution theories (e.g., Heider, 1958; Jones & Davis, 1965; Kelley, 1973)—has focused on the processing of information, the "machinery" of social cognition. Some outcomes of this research have been the specification of how individuals identify the causes of an actor's behavior, how individuals make inferences about the traits and dispositions of the actor, and how individuals make predictions about the actor's future behavior (for reviews, see Harvey, Ickes, & Kidd, 1976; Jones et al., 1972; Ross, 1977).

It is noteworthy that comparatively little theoretical and empirical attention has been directed to the other fundamental question within the cognitive social psychologist's mandate: What are the cognitive and behavioral consequences of our impressions of other people? From our vantage point, current-day attribution theorists leave the individual "lost in thought," with no machinery that links thought to action. It is to this concern that we address

ourselves, both theoretically and empirically, in the context of social stereotypes.

Social stereotypes are a special case of interpersonal perception. Stereotypes are usually simple, overgeneralized, and widely accepted (e.g., Karlins, Coffman, & Walters, 1969). But stereotypes are often inaccurate. It is simply not true that all Germans are industrious or that all women are dependent and conforming. Nonetheless, many social stereotypes concern highly visible and distinctive personal characteristics; for example, sex and race. These pieces of information are usually the first to be noticed in social interaction and can gain high priority for channeling subsequent information processing and even social interaction. Social stereotypes are thus an ideal testing ground for considering the cognitive and behavioral consequences of person perception.

Numerous factors may help sustain our stereotypes and prevent disconfirmation of "erroneous" stereotype-based initial impressions of specific others. First, social stereotypes may influence information processing in ways that serve to bolster and strengthen these stereotypes.

Cognitive Bolstering of Social Stereotypes

As information processors, humans readily fall victim to the cognitive process described centuries ago by Francis Bacon (1620/1902):

> The human understanding, when any proposition has been once laid down . . . forces everything else to add fresh support and confirmation . . . it is the peculiar and perpetual error of the human understanding to be more moved and excited by affirmatives than negatives. (pp. 23–24)

Empirical research has demonstrated several such biases in information processing. We may overestimate the frequency of occurrence of confirming or paradigmatic examples of our stereotypes simply because such instances are more easily noticed, more easily brought to mind, and more easily retrieved from memory (cf. Hamilton & Gifford, 1976; Rothbart, Fulero, Jensen, Howard, & Birrell, Note 1). Evidence that confirms our stereotyped intuitions about human nature may be, in a word, more cognitively "available" (Tversky & Kahneman, 1973) than nonconfirming evidence.

Moreover, we may fill in the gaps in our evidence base with information consistent with our preconceived notions of what evidence should support our beliefs. For example, Chapman and Chapman (1967, 1969) have demonstrated that both college students and professional clinicians perceive positive associations between particular Rorschach responses and homosexuality in males, even though these associations are demonstrably absent in real life. These "signs" are simply those that comprise common cultural stereotypes of gay males.

Furthermore, once a stereotype has been adopted, a wide variety of evidence can be interpreted readily as supportive of that stereotype, including events that could support equally well an opposite interpretation. As Merton (1948) has suggested, in-group virtues ("We are thrifty") may become outgroup vices ("They are cheap") in our attempts to maintain negative stereotypes about disliked out groups. (For empirical demonstrations of this bias, see Regan, Straus, & Fazio, 1974; Rosenhan, 1973; Zadney & Gerard, 1974.)

Finally, selective recall and reinterpretation of information from an individual's past history may be exploited to support a current stereotyped-based inference (cf. Loftus & Palmer, 1974). Thus, having decided that Jim is stingy (as are all members of his group), it may be all too easy to remember a variety of behaviors and incidents that are insufficient one at a time to support an attribution of stinginess, but that taken together do warrant and support such an inference.

Behavioral Confirmation of Social Stereotypes

The cognitive bolstering processes discussed above may provide the perceiver with an "evidence base" that gives compelling cognitive reality to any traits that he or she may have erroneously attributed to a target individual initially. This reality is, of course, entirely cognitive: It is in the eye and mind of the beholder. But stereotype-based attributions may serve as grounds for predictions about the target's future behavior and may guide and influence the perceiver's interactions with the target. This process itself may generate behaviors on the part of the target that erroneously confirm the predictions and validate the attributions of the perceiver. How others treat us is, in large measure, a reflection of our treatment of them (cf. Bandura, 1977; Mischel, 1968; Raush, 1965). Thus, when we use our social perceptions as guides for regulating our interactions with others, we may constrain their behavioral options (cf. Kelley & Stahelski, 1970).

Consider this hypothetical, but illustrative, scenario: Michael tells Jim that Chris is a cool and aloof person. Jim meets Chris and notices expressions of coolness and aloofness. Jim proceeds to overestimate the extent to which Chris' self-presentation reflects a cool and aloof disposition and underestimates the extent to which this posture was engendered by his own cool and aloof behavior toward Chris, that had in turn been generated by his own prior beliefs about Chris. Little does Jim know that Tom, who had heard that Chris was warm and friendly, found that his impressions of Chris were confirmed during their interaction. In each case, the end result of the process of "interaction guided by perceptions" has been the target person's *behavioral confirmation* of the perceiver's initial impressions of him.

This scenario makes salient key aspects of the process of behavioral confirmation in social interaction. The perceiver (either Jim or Tom) is not aware that his original perception of the target individual (Chris) is inaccurate. Nor is the perceiver aware of the causal role that his own behavior (here, the enactment of a cool or warm expressive style) plays in generating the behavioral evidence that erroneously confirms his expectations. Unbeknownst to the perceiver, the reality that he confidently perceives to exist in the social world has, in fact, been actively constructed by his own transactions with and operations upon the social world.

In our empirical research, we proposed to demonstrate that stereotypes may create their own social reality by channeling social interaction in ways that cause the stereotyped individual to behaviorally confirm the perceiver's stereotype. Moreover, we sought to demonstrate behavioral confirmation in a social interaction context designed to mirror as faithfully as possible the spontaneous generation of impressions in everyday social interaction and the subsequent channeling influences of these perceptions on dyadic interaction.

One widely held stereotype in this culture involves physical attractiveness. Considerable evidence suggests that attractive persons are assumed to possess more socially desirable personality traits and are expected to lead better lives than their unattractive counterparts (Berscheid & Walster, 1974). Attractive persons are perceived to have virtually every character trait that is socially desirable to the perceiver: "Physically attractive people, for example, were perceived to be more sexually warm and responsive, sensitive, kind, interesting, strong, poised, modest, sociable, and outgoing than persons of lesser physical attractiveness" (Berscheid & Walster, 1974, p. 169). This powerful stereotype holds for male and female perceivers and for male and female stimulus persons.

What of the validity of the physical attractiveness stereotype? Are the physically attractive actually more likable, friendly, and confident than the unattractive? Physically attractive young adults are more often and more eagerly sought out for social dates (Dermer, 1973; Krebs & Adinolphi, 1975; Walster, Aronson, Abrahams, & Rottman, 1966). Even as early as nursery school age, physical attractiveness appears to channel social interaction: The physically attractive are chosen and the unattractive are rejected in sociometric choices (Dion & Berscheid, 1974; Kleck, Richardson, & Ronald, 1974).

Differential amount of interaction with the attractive and unattractive clearly helps the stereotype persevere, for it limits the chances for learning whether the two types of individuals differ in the traits associated with the stereotype. But the point we wish to focus upon here is that the stereotype may also channel interaction so that it behaviorally confirms itself. Individuals may have different styles of interaction for those whom they perceive to be physically attractive and for those whom they consider unattractive. These differences in interaction style may in turn elicit and nurture behaviors from the target person that are in accord with the stereotype. That is, the physically attractive may actually come to behave in a friendly, likable, sociable manner—not because they necessarily possess these dispositions, but because the behavior of others elicits and maintains behaviors taken to be manifestations of such traits.

Accordingly, we sought to demonstrate the behavioral confirmation of the physical attractiveness stereotype in dyadic social interaction. In order to do so, pairs of previously unacquainted individuals (designated, for our purposes, as a perceiver and a target) interacted in a getting-acquainted situation that had been constructed to allow us to control the information that one member of the dyad (the male perceiver) received about the physical attractiveness of the other individual (the female target). To measure the extent to which the actual behavior of the target matched the perceiver's stereotype, naive observer judges, who were unaware of the actual or perceived physical attractiveness of either participant, listened to and evaluated tape recordings of the interaction.

METHOD

Participants

Fifty-one male and 51 female undergraduates at the University of Minnesota participated, for extra course credit, in a study of "the processes by which people become acquainted with each other." Participants were scheduled in pairs of previously unacquainted males and females.

The Interaction Between Perceiver and Target

To insure that participants would not see each other before their interactions, they arrived at separate experimental rooms on separate corridors. The experimenter informed each participant that she was studying acquaintance processes in social relationships. Specifically, she was investigating the differences between those initial interactions that involve nonverbal communication and those, such as telephone conversations, that do not. Thus, she explained, the participant would engage in a telephone conversation with another student in introductory psychology.

Before the conversation began, each participant provided written permission for it to be tape recorded. In addition, both dyad members completed brief questionnaires concerning such information as academic major in college and high school of graduation. These questionnaires, it was explained, would provide the partners with some information about each other with which to start the conversation.

Activating the perceiver's stereotype The getting-acquainted interaction permitted control of the information that each male perceiver received about the physical attractiveness of his female target. When male perceivers learned about the biographical information questionnaires, they also learned that each person would receive a snapshot of the other member of the dyad, because "other people in the experiment have told us they feel more comfortable when they have a mental picture of the person they're talking to." The experimenter then used a Polaroid camera to photograph the male. No mention of any snapshots was made to female participants.

When each male perceiver received his partner's biographical information form, it arrived in a folder containing a Polaroid snapshot, ostensibly of his partner. Although the biographical information had indeed been provided by his partner, the photograph was not. It was one of eight photographs that had been prepared in advance.

Twenty female students from several local colleges assisted (in return for $5) in the preparation of stimulus materials by allowing us to take Polaroid snapshots of them. Each photographic subject wore casual dress, each was smiling, and each agreed (in writing) to allow us to use her photograph. Twenty college-age men then rated the attractiveness of each picture on a 10-point scale.[2] We then chose the four pictures that had received the highest attractiveness ratings ($M = 8.10$) and the four photos that had received the lowest ratings ($M = 2.56$). There was virtually no overlap in ratings of the two sets of pictures.

Male perceivers were assigned randomly to one of two conditions of perceived physical attractiveness of their targets. Males in the attractive target condition received folders containing their partners' biographical information form and one of the four attractive photographs. Males in the unattractive target condition received folders containing their partners' biographical information form and one of the four unattractive photographs. Female targets knew nothing of the photographs possessed by their male inter-action partners, nor did they receive snapshots of their partners.

The perceiver's stereotype-based attributions   Before initi-ating his getting-acquainted conversation, each male per-ceiver rated his initial impressions of his partner on an Impression Formation Questionnaire. The questionnaire was constructed by supplementing the 27 trait adjectives used by Dion, Berscheid, and Walster (1972) in their orig-inal investigation of the physical attractiveness stereotype with the following items: intelligence, physical attrac-tiveness, social adeptness, friendliness, enthusiasm, trust-worthiness, and successfulness. We were thus able to assess the extent to which perceivers' initial impressions of their partners reflected general stereotypes linking physical at-tractiveness and personality characteristics.

The getting-acquainted conversation   Each dyad then en-gaged in a 10-minute unstructured conversation by means of microphones and headphones connected through a Sony TC-570 stereophonic tape recorder that recorded each participant's voice on a separate channel of the tape.

After the conversation, male perceivers completed the Impression Formation Questionnaires to record final im-pressions of their partners. Female targets expressed self-perceptions in terms of the items of the Impression Forma-tion Questionnaire. Each female target also indicated, on 10-point scales, how much she had enjoyed the conversa-tion, how comfortable she had felt while talking to her partner, how accurate a picture of herself she felt that her partner had formed as a result of the conversation, how typical her partner's behavior had been of the way she usually was treated by men, her perception of her own physical attractiveness, and her estimate of her partner's perception of her physical attractiveness. All participants were then thoroughly and carefully debriefed and thanked for their contribution to the study.

Assessing Behavioral Confirmation

To assess the extent to which the actions of the target women provided behavioral confirmation for the stereo-types of the men perceivers, 8 male and 4 female intro-ductory psychology students rated the tape recordings of the getting-acquainted conversations. These observer judges were unaware of the experimental hypotheses and knew nothing of the actual or perceived physical attractiveness of the individuals on the tapes. They listened, in random

order, to two 4-minute segments (one each from the begin-ning and end) of each conversation. They heard *only* the track of the tapes containing the target women's voices and rated each woman on the 34 bipolar scales of the Impres-sion Formation Questionnaire as well as on 14 additional 10-point scales; for example, "How animated and enthusi-astic is this person?", "How intimate or personal is this person's conversation?", and "How much is she enjoying herself?". Another group of observer judges (3 males and 6 females) performed a similar assessment of the male per-ceivers' behavior based upon only the track of the tapes that contained the males' voices.[3]

RESULTS

To chart the process of behavioral confirmation of social stereotypes in dyadic social interaction, we examined the effects of our manipulation of the target women's apparent physical attractiveness on (a) the male perceivers' initial impressions of them and (b) the women's behavioral self-presentation during the interaction, as measured by the observer judges' ratings of the tape recordings.

The Perceivers' Stereotype

Did our male perceivers form initial impressions of their specific target women on the basis of general stereotypes that associate physical attractiveness and desirable person-alities? To answer this question, we examined the male perceivers' initial ratings on the Impression Formation Questionnaire. Recall that these impressions were recorded *after* the perceivers had seen their partners' photographs, but *before* the getting-acquainted conversation.[4] Indeed, it appears that our male perceivers did fashion their initial impressions of their female partners on the basis of stereo-typed beliefs about physical attractiveness, multivariate $F(34, 3) = 10.19$, $p < .04$. As dictated by the physical at-tractiveness stereotype, men who anticipated physically attractive partners expected to interact with comparatively sociable, poised, humorous, and socially adept women; by contrast, men faced with the prospect of getting acquainted with relatively unattractive partners fashioned images of rather unsociable, awkward, serious, and socially inept women, all $Fs (1, 36) > 5.85$, $p < .025$.

Behavioral Confirmation

Not only did our perceivers fashion their images of their discussion partners on the basis of their stereotyped intui-tions about beauty and goodness of character, but these impressions initiated a chain of events that resulted in the behavioral confirmation of these initially erroneous inferences. Our analyses of the observer judges' ratings of the women's behavior were guided by our knowledge of the structure of the men's initial impressions of their target women's personality. Specifically, we expected to find evidence of behavioral confirmation only for those traits that had defined the perceivers' stereotypes. For example, male perceivers did not attribute differential amounts of sensitivity or intelligence to partners of differing apparent physical attractiveness. Accordingly, we would not expect that our observer judges would "hear" different amounts of intelligence or sensitivity in the tapes. By contrast, male perceivers did expect attractive and unattractive targets to differ in sociability. Here we would expect that observer judges would detect differences in sociability between conditions when listening to the women's contributions to the conversations, and thus we would have evidence of behavioral confirmation.

To assess the extent to which the women's behavior, as rated by the observer judges, provided behavioral confirmation for the male perceivers' stereotypes, we identified, by means of a discriminant analysis (Tatsuoka, 1971), those 21 trait items of the Impression Formation Questionnaire for which the mean initial ratings of the men in the attractive target and unattractive target conditions differed by more than 1.4 standard deviations.[5] This set of "stereotype traits" (e.g., sociable, poised, sexually warm, outgoing) defines the differing perceptions of the personality characteristics of target women in the two experimental conditions.

We then entered these 21 stereotype traits and the 14 additional dependent measures into a multivariate analysis of variance. This analysis revealed that our observer judges did indeed view women who had been assigned to the attractive target condition quite differently than women in the unattractive target condition, $Fm(35, 2) = 40.003$, $p < .025$. What had initially been reality in the minds of the men had now become reality in the behavior of the women with whom they had interacted—a behavioral reality discernible even by naive observer judges, who had access *only* to tape recordings of the women's contributions to the conversations.

When a multivariate analysis of variance is performed on multiple correlated dependent measures, the null hypothesis states that the vector of means is equal across conditions. When the null hypothesis is rejected, the nature of the difference between groups must then be inferred from inspection of group differences on the individual dependent measures. In this case, the differences between

the behavior of the women in the attractive target and the unattractive target conditions were in the same direction as the male perceivers' initial stereotyped impressions for fully 17 of the 21 measures of behavioral confirmation. The binomial probability that at least 17 of these adjectives would be in the predicted direction by chance alone is a scant .003. By contrast, when we examined the 13 trait pairs that our discriminant analysis had indicated did *not* define the male perceivers' stereotype, a sharply different pattern emerged. Here, we would not expect any systematic relationship between the male perceivers' stereotyped initial impressions and the female targets' actual behavior in the getting-acquainted conversations. In fact, for only 8 of these 13 measures is the difference between the behavior of the women in the attractive condition in the same direction as the men's stereotyped initial impressions. This configuration is, of course, hardly different from the pattern expected by chance alone if there were no differences between the groups (exact binomial $p = .29$). Clearly, then, behavioral confirmation manifested itself only for those attributes that had defined the male perceivers' stereotype; that is, only in those domains where the men believed that there did exist links between physical attractiveness and personal attributes did the women come to behave differently as a consequence of the level of physical attractiveness that we had experimentally assigned to them.

Moreover, our understanding of the nature of the difference between the attractive target and the unattractive target conditions identified by our multivariate analysis of variance and our confidence in this demonstration of behavioral confirmation are bolstered by the consistent pattern of behavioral differences on the 14 additional related dependent measures. Our raters assigned to the female targets in the attractive target condition higher ratings on *every* question related to favorableness of self-presentation. Thus, for example, those who were thought by their perceivers to be physically attractive appeared to the observer judges to manifest greater confidence, greater animation, greater enjoyment of the conversation, and greater liking for their partners than those women who interacted with men who perceived them as physically unattractive.[6]

In Search of Mediators of Behavioral Confirmation

We next attempted to chart the process of behavioral confirmation. Specifically, we searched for evidence of the behavioral implications of the perceivers' stereotypes. Did the male perceivers present themselves differently to target women whom they assumed to be physically attractive or unattractive? Because we had 50 dependent measures[7] of the observer judges' ratings of the males—12 more than the number of observations (male perceivers)—a multivariate analysis of variance is inappropriate. However, in 21 cases, univariate analyses of variance did indicate differences between conditions (all $ps < .05$). Men who interacted with women whom they believed to be physically attractive appeared (to the observer judges) more sociable, sexually warm, interesting, independent, sexually permissive, bold, outgoing, humorous, obvious, and socially adept than their counterparts in the unattractive target condition. Moreover, these men were seen as more attractive, more confident, and more animated in their conversation than their counterparts. Further, they were considered by the observer judges to be more comfortable, to enjoy themselves more, to like their partners more to take the initiative more often, to use their voices more effectively, to see their women partners as more attractive and, finally, to be seen as more attractive by their partners than men in the unattractive target condition.

It appears, then, that differences in the level of sociability manifested and expressed by the male perceivers may have been a key factor in bringing out reciprocating patterns of expression in the target women. One reason that target women who had been labeled as attractive may have reciprocated these sociable overtures is that they regarded their partners' images of them as more accurate, $F(1, 28) = 6.75$, $p < .02$, and their interaction style to be more typical of the way men generally treated them, $F(1,28) = 4.79$, $p < .04$, than did women in the unattractive target condition.[8] These individuals, perhaps, rejected their partners' treatment of them as unrepresentative and defensively adopted more cool and aloof postures to cope with their situations.

DISCUSSION

Of what consequence are our social stereotypes? Our research suggests that stereotypes can and do channel dyadic interaction so as to create their own social reality. In our demonstration, pairs of individuals got acquainted with each other in a situation that allowed us to control the information that one member of the dyad (the perceiver) received about the physical attractiveness of the other person (the target). Our perceivers, in anticipation of interaction, fashioned erroneous images of their specific partners that reflected their general stereotypes about physical attractiveness. Moreover, our perceivers had very different patterns and styles of interaction for those whom they perceived to be physically attractive and unattractive. These differences in self-presentation and interaction style, in

turn, elicited and nurtured behaviors of the target that were consistent with the perceivers' initial stereotypes. Targets who were perceived (unbeknownst to them) to be physically attractive actually came to behave in a friendly, likable, and sociable manner. The perceivers' attributions about their targets based upon their stereotyped intuitions about the world had initiated a process that produced behavioral confirmation of those attributions. The initially erroneous attributions of the perceivers had become real: The stereotype had truly functioned as a self-fulfilling prophecy (Merton, 1948).[9]

We regard our investigation as a particularly compelling demonstration of behavioral confirmation in social interaction. For if there is any social-psychological process that ought to exist in "stronger" form in everyday interaction than in the psychological laboratory, it is behavioral confirmation. In the context of years of social interaction in which perceivers have reacted to their actual physical attractiveness, our 10-minute getting-acquainted conversations over a telephone must seem minimal indeed. Nonetheless, the impact was sufficient to permit outside observers who had access only to one person's side of a conversation to detect manifestations of behavioral confirmation.

Might not other important and widespread social stereotypes—particularly those concerning sex, race, social class, and ethnicity—also channel social interaction so as to create their own social reality? For example, will the common stereotype that women are more conforming and less independent than men (cf. Broverman, Vogel, Broverman, Clarkson, & Rosenkrantz, 1972) influence interaction so that (within a procedural paradigm similar to ours) targets believed to be female will actually conform more, be more dependent, and be more successfully manipulated than interaction partners believed to be male? At least one empirical investigation has pointed to the possible self-fulfilling nature of apparent sex differences in self-presentation (Zanna & Pack, 1975).

Any self-fulfilling influences of social stereotypes may have compelling and pervasive societal consequences. Social observers have for decades commented on the ways in which stigmatized social groups and outsiders may fall "victim" to self-fulfilling cultural stereotypes (e.g., Becker, 1963; Goffman, 1963; Merton, 1948; Myrdal, 1944; Tannenbaum, 1938). Consider Scott's (1969) observations about the blind:

> When, for example, sighted people continually insist that a blind man is helpless because he is blind, their subsequent treatment of him may preclude his even exercising the kinds of skills that would enable him to be independent. It is in this sense that stereotypic beliefs are self-actualized. (p. 9)

And all too often it is the "victims" who are blamed for their own plight (cf. Ryan, 1971) rather than the social expectations that have constrained their behavioral options.

Of what import is the behavioral confirmation process for our theoretical understanding of the nature of social perception? Although our empirical research has focused on social stereotypes that are widely accepted and broadly generalized, our notions of behavioral confirmation may apply equally well to idiosyncratic social perceptions spontaneously formed about specific individuals in the course of every day social interaction. In this sense, social psychologists have been wise to devote intense effort to understanding the processes by which impressions of others are formed. Social perceptions are important precisely because of their impact on social interaction. Yet, at the same time, research and theory in social perception (mostly displayed under the banner of attribution theory) that have focused on the manner in which individuals process information provided them to form impressions of others may underestimate the extent to which information received in actual social interaction is a product of the perceiver's own actions toward the target individual. More careful attention must clearly be paid to the ways in which perceivers *create or construct* the information that they process in addition to the ways in which they *process* that information. Events in the social world may be as much the *effects* of our perceptions of those events as they are the *causes* of those perceptions.

From this perspective, it becomes easier to appreciate the perceiver's stubborn tendency to fashion images of others largely in trait terms (e.g., Jones & Nisbett, 1972), despite the poverty of evidence for the pervasive cross-situational consistencies in social behavior that the existence of "true" traits would demand (e.g., Mischel, 1968). This tendency, dubbed by Ross (1977) as the "fundamental attribution error," may be a self-erasing error. For even though any target individual's behavior may lack, overall, the trait-defining properties of cross-situational consistency, the actions of the perceiver himself may produce consistency in the samples of behavior available to that perceiver. Our impressions of others may cause those others to behave in consistent trait-like fashion for us. In that sense, our trait-based impressions of others are veridical, even though the same individual may behave or be led to behave in a fashion perfectly consistent with opposite attributions by other perceivers with quite different impressions of that individual. Such may be the power of the behavioral confirmation process.

REFERENCE NOTE

1. Rothbart, M., Fulero, S., Jensen, C., Howard, J., & Birrell, P. *From individual to group impressions: Availability heuristics in stereotype formation.* Unpublished manuscript, University of Oregon, 1976.

REFERENCES

Bacon, F. [Novum organum] (J. Devey, Ed.). New York: P. F. Collier & Son, 1902. (Originally published, 1620.)

Bandura, A. *Social learning theory.* Englewood Cliffs, N.J.: Prentice-Hall, 1977.

Becker, H. W. *Outsiders: Studies in the sociology of deviance.* N.Y.: Free Press, 1963.

Berscheid, E., & Walster, E. Physical attractiveness. In L. Berkowitz (Ed.), *Advances in experimental social psychology* (Vol. 7). New York: Academic Press, 1974.

Broverman, I. K., Vogel, S. R., Broverman, D. M., Clarkson, F. E., & Rosenkrantz, P. S. Sex-role stereotypes: A current appraisal. *Journal of Social Issues*, 1972, 28, 59–78.

Chapman, L., & Chapman, J. The genesis of popular but erroneous psychodiagnostic observations. *Journal of Abnormal Psychology*, 1967, 72, 193–204.

Chapman, L., & Chapman, J. Illusory correlations as an obstacle to the use of valid psychodiagnostic signs. *Journal of Abnormal Psychology*, 1969, 74, 271–280.

Dermer, M. *When beauty fails.* Unpublished doctoral dissertation, University of Minnesota, 1973.

Dion, K. K., & Berscheid, E. Physical attractiveness and peer perception among children. *Sociometry*, 1974, 37(1), 1–12.

Dion, K. K., Berscheid, E., & Walster, E. What is beautiful is good. *Journal of Personality and Social Psychology*, 1972, 24, 285–290.

Ebel, R. L. Estimation of the reliability of ratings. *Psychometrika*, 1951, 16, 407–424.

Goffman, E. *Stigma: Notes on the management of spoiled identity.* Englewood Cliffs: N.J.: Prentice-Hall, 1963.

Hamilton, D. L., & Gifford, R. K. Illusory correlation in interpersonal perception: A cognitive basis of stereotypic judgments. *Journal of Experimental Social Psychology*, 1976, 12, 392–407.

Harvey, J. H., Ickes, W. J., & Kidd, R. F. *New directions in attribution research.* Hillsdale, N.J.: Erlbaum, 1976.

Heider, F. *The psychology of interpersonal relations.* New York: Wiley, 1958.

Janis, I., & Field, P. Sex differences and personality factors related to persuasibility. In C. Hovland & I. Janis (Eds.), *Personality and persuasibility.* New Haven, Conn.: Yale University Press, 1973.

Jones, E. E., & Davis, K. E. From acts to dispositions: The attribution process in person perception. In L. Berkowitz (Ed.), *Advances in experimental social psychology* (Vol. 2). New York: Academic Press, 1965.

Jones et al. *Attribution: Perceiving the causes of behavior.* Morristown, N.J.: General Learning Press, 1972.

Jones, E. E., & Nisbett, R. E. The actor and the observer: Divergent perceptions of the causes of behavior. In E. Jones, D. Kanouse, H. Kelley, S. Valins, & B. Weiner (Eds.), *Attribution: Perceiving the causes of behavior.* New York: General Learning Press, 1972.

Karlins, M., Coffman, T. L., & Walters, G. On the fading of social stereotypes: Studies in three generations of college students. *Journal of Personality and Social Psychology*, 1969, 13, 1–16.

Kelley, H. H. The process of causal attribution. *American Psychologist*, 1973, 28, 107–128.

Kelley, H. H., & Stahelski, A. J. The social interaction basis of cooperator's and competitors' beliefs about others. *Journal of Personality and Social Psychology*, 1970, 16, 66–91.

Kleck, R. E., Richardson, S. A., & Ronald, L. Physical appearance cues and interpersonal attraction in children. *Child Development*, 1974, *45*, 305–310.

Krebs, D., & Adinolphi, A. A. Physical attractiveness, social relations, and personality style. *Journal of Personality and Social Psychology*, 1975, *31*, 245–253.

Loftus, E., & Palmer, J. Reconstruction of automobile destruction. *Journal of Verbal Learning and Verbal Behavior*, 1974, *13*, 585–589.

Merton, R. K. The self-fulfilling prophecy. *Antioch Review*, 1948, *8*, 193–210.

Mischel, W. *Personality and assessment.* New York: Wiley, 1968.

Myrdal, G. *An American dilemma.* New York: Harper and Row, 1944.

Raush, H. L. Interaction sequences. *Journal of Personality and Social Psychology*, 1965, *2*, 487–499.

Regan, D. T., Straus, E., & Fazio, R. Liking and the attribution process. *Journal of Experimental Social Psychology*, 1974, *10*, 385–397.

Rosenhan, D. L. On being sane in insane places. *Science*, 1973, *179*, 250–258.

Rosenthal, R. *On the social psychology of the self-fulfilling prophecy: Further evidence for pygmalion effects and their mediating mechanisms.* New York: M.S.S. Information Corp. Modular Publications, 1974.

Ross, L. The intuitive psychologist and his shortcomings: Distortions in the attribution process. In L. Berkowitz (Ed.), *Advances in experimental social psychology* (Vol. 10). New York: Academic Press, 1977.

Ryan, W. *Blaming the victim.* New York: Vintage Books, 1971.

Scott, R. A. *The making of blind men.* New York: Russell Sage, 1969.

Tannenbaum, F. *Crime and the community.* Boston: Ginn, 1938.

Tatsuoka, M. M. *Multivariate analysis.* New York: Wiley, 1971.

Tinsley, H. E. A., & Weiss, D. J. Interrater reliability and agreement of subjective judgments. *Journal of Counseling Psychology*, 1975, *22*, 358–376.

Tversky, A., & Kahneman, D. Availability: A heuristic for judging frequency and probability. *Cognitive Psychology*, 1973, *5*, 207–232.

Walster, E., Aronson, V., Abrahams, D., & Rottman, L. Importance of physical attractiveness in dating behavior. *Journal of Personality and Social Psychology*, 1966, *4*, 508–516.

Zadny, J., & Gerard, H. B. Attributed intentions and informational selectivity. *Journal of Experimental Social Psychology*, 1974, *10*, 34–52.

Zanna, M. P., & Pack, S. J. On the self-fulfilling nature of apparent sex differences in behavior. *Journal of Experimental Social Psychology*, 1975, *11*, 583–591.

NOTES

1. From *The Rape of Lucrece*, lines 346–353.

2. The interrater correlations of these ratings of attractiveness ranged from .45 to .92, with an average interrater correlation of .74.

3. We assessed the reliability of our raters by means of intraclass correlations (Ebel, 1951), a technique that employs analysis-of-variance procedures to determine the proportion of the total variance in ratings due to variance in the persons being rated. The intraclass correlation is the measure of reliability most commonly used with interval data and ordinal scales that assume interval properties. Because the measure of interest was the mean rating of judges on each variable, the between-rater variance was not included in the error term in calculating the intraclass correlation. (For a discussion, see Tinsley & Weiss, 1975, p. 363). Reliability coefficients for the coders' ratings of the females for all dependent measures ranged from .35 to .91 with a median of .755. For each dependent variable, a single score was constructed for each participant by calculating the mean of the raters' scores on that measure. Analyses of variance, including the time of the tape segment (early vs. late in the conversation) as a factor, revealed no more main effects of time or interactions between time and perceived attractiveness than would have been expected by chance. Thus, scores for the two tape segments were summed to yield a single score for each dependent variable. The same procedure was followed for ratings of male perceivers' behavior. In this case, the reliability coefficients ranged from .18 to .83 with a median of .61.

4. These and all subsequent analyses are based upon a total of 38 observations, 19 in each of the attractive target and unattractive target conditions. Of the original 51 dyads, a total of 48 male-female pairs completed the experiment. In each of the remaining three dyads, the male participant had made reference during the conversation to the photograph. When this happened, the experimenter interrupted the conversation and immediately debriefed the participants. Of the remaining 48 dyads who completed the experimental procedures, 10 were eliminated from the analyses for the following reasons: In 4 cases the male participant expressed strong suspicion about the photograph; in 1 case, the conversation was not tape recorded because of a mechanical problem; and in 5 cases, there was a sufficiently large age difference (ranging from 6 years to 18 years) between the participants that the males in these dyads reported that they had reacted very differently to their partners than they would have reacted to an age peer. This pattern of attrition was independent of assignment to the attractive target and unattractive target experimental conditions (x^2 = 1.27, ns).

5. After the 21st trait dimension, the differences between the experimental conditions drop off sharply. For example, the next adjective pair down the line has a difference of 1.19 standard deviations, and the one after that has a difference of 1.02 standard deviations.

6. We may eliminate several alternative interpretations of the behavioral confirmation effect. Women who had been assigned randomly to the attractive target condition were not in fact more physically attractive than those who were assigned randomly to the unattractive target condition. Ratings of the actual attractiveness of the female targets by the experimenter revealed no differences whatsoever between conditions, $t(36)$ = .00. Nor, for that matter, did male perceivers differ in their own physical attractiveness as a function of experimental condition, $t(36)$ = .44. In addition, actual attractiveness of male perceivers and actual attractiveness of female targets within dyads were independent of each other, $r(36)$ = .06.

Of greater importance, there was no detectable difference in personality characteristics of females who had been assigned randomly to the attractive target and unattractive target conditions of the experiment. They did not differ in self-esteem as assessed by the Janis-Field-Eagly (Janis & Field, 1973) measure, $F(1, 36) < 1$. Moreover, there were no differences between experimental conditions in the female targets' self-perceptions as reported after the conversations on the Impression Formation Questionnaire ($Fm < 1$). We have thus no reason to suspect that any systematic, pre-existing differences between conditions in morphology or personality can pose plausible alternative explanations of our demonstration of behavioral confirmation.

7. Two dependent measures were added between the time that the ratings were made of the female participants and the time that the ratings were made of the male participants. These measures were responses to the questions, "How interested is he in his partner?" and "How attractive does he think his partner is?"

8. The degrees of freedom for these analyses are fewer than those for other analyses because they were added to the experimental procedure after four dyads had participated in each condition.

9. Our research on behavioral confirmation in social interaction is a clear "cousin" of other demonstrations that perceivers' expectations may influence other individuals' behavior. Thus, Rosenthal (1974) and his colleagues have conducted an extensive program of laboratory and field investigations of the effects of experimenters' and teachers' expectations on the behavior of subjects in psychological laboratories and students in classrooms. Experimenters and teachers led to expect particular patterns of performance from their subjects and pupils act in ways that selectively influence or shape those performances to confirm initial expectations (e.g., Rosenthal, 1974).

Received December 6, 1976

CRITICAL THINKING QUESTIONS

1. Explain how the self-fulfilling prophecy was achieved in this experiment. How were the men's behaviors influenced by the pictures, and how did their behavior influence the women's behavior?

2. What evidence do the authors have that there was *behavioral confirmation*, rather than just that the male perceivers' or the judges' stereotypes about physical attractiveness affected their *perceptions* of the female targets' behavior?

3. Why did the researchers show a picture to only one person in each pair?

4. Do you think the results would have been similar or different if the perceivers had been women and the targets had been men? Why?

5. What role did the fundamental attribution error (see Chapter 3) play in the male perceivers' perceptions of the female targets?

6. Considering the research discussed in Chapter 3 concerning self-fulfilling prophecies and in Chapter 4 concerning stereotypes, what factors do you think would make the behavioral confirmation of the perceivers' stereotypes about physical attractiveness less likely to occur in a situation similar to that faced by subjects in this study?

READING 6

In studying the effect of relationships on helping, this article by Williamson and Clark bridges Chapters 6 and 7 in the textbook. In particular, it examines how the types of relationship that two people have affects the emotional reactions that one of these people feels when he or she helps the other. The general finding is consistent with the finding presented in Chapter 7 that people seem to feel better when they help. However, this seems to be true only when the helper wants a communal relationship with the other person; when, in contrast, the helper wants an exchange relationship, people seem to feel worse when they help.

Chapter 6 in the textbook describes the differences between communal and exchange relationships, and this study clearly shows how this distinction has important implications for predicting people's actions and responses. The article also clearly relates to the section of Chapter 7 that discusses the effects of mood on helping. Finally, the authors distinguish between positive and negative affect in this study. This basic distinction and the relationship between these two constructs are discussed in Chapter 14, which describes positive and negative affectivity.

This article is a good example of how researchers seldom just write one article and end their research there, since this article is part of a long series of work done by the authors. The study also discusses what the authors claim is a statistical artifact. They found that people may try to distance themselves from negative affect (feelings). Since people don't want to think about these feelings, there may be a limit on how much negative affect they are willing to report. And if people fail to report the negative affective in this way, then the researchers aren't able to measure it.

Impact of Desired Relationship Type on Affective Reactions to Choosing and Being Required to Help

Gail M. Williamson
University of Georgia

Margaret S. Clark
Carnegie Mellon University

Donors' reactions to choosing and being required to help were examined. Among subjects led to desire a communal relationship with the recipient, both choosing and being required to help elevated positive affect and alleviated negative affect relative to not being asked to help. Changes in affect as a result of choosing to help did not differ from changes as a result of being required to help. Among subjects led to desire an exchange relationship with the recipient, choosing to help caused positive affect to deteriorate, relative to being required to help or to not helping. Changes in affect in the required condition did not differ from those in the no-help condition. Psychological processes that may underlie these effects are discussed.

Past research suggests that providing aid can improve helpers' affective states (e.g., Batson, Coke, Jasnoski, & Hanson, 1978, Study 2; Harris, 1977, Study 3; Williamson & Clark, 1989, Studies 1 and 2; Yinon & Landau, 1987, Study 1). Researchers have argued that this occurs because people possess internalized norms that dictate that those who need help should be helped and that helping others is admirable. Thus, when people help, they feel good (Aronfreed, 1970; Berkowitz, 1972; Berkowitz & Connor, 1966; Cialdini & Kenrick, 1976; Schwartz, 1975; Schwartz & Howard, 1982).

More recently, Williamson and Clark (1989, Study 3) found evidence that affective reactions to providing help

SOURCE: Gail M. Williamson and Margaret S. Clark, "Impact of Desired Relationship Type on Affective Reactions to Choosing and Being Required to Help," *Personality and Social Psychology Bulletin*, Vol. 18, No. 1, February 1992: 10–18. Reprinted by permission of Sage Publications, Inc.

are moderated by the type of relationship that helpers desire with the recipient. Specifically, helping (relative to being unable to help) improved helpers' moods when a communal, but not an exchange, relationship was desired. We suggested two reasons for these effects. First, norms in communal relationships (e.g., most friendships and romantic involvements) but not those in exchange relationships (e.g., most interactions between strangers, acquaintances, and business associates) specify that special attention should be paid to the other's needs (Clark, Mills, & Powell, 1986) and that help should be given when the other has a need (Clark, Ouellette, Powell, & Milberg, 1987). We reasoned that because helping follows general societal norms as well as norms specific to communal relationships, people desiring a communal relationship should feel good about having helped the other. Not only have they followed the appropriate norm, they may well have promoted the desired relationship by so doing. Second, in exchange but not in communal relationships, norms indicate that the recipient of a benefit should return a comparable benefit as soon as possible (Clark & Mills, 1979; Clark & Waddell, 1985). Until that benefit is repaid, people may experience a sense of inequity and distress (Walster, Walster, & Berscheid, 1978) and decreased attraction toward the other (Clark & Mills, 1979; Clark & Waddell, 1985). We reasoned that these unpleasant feelings might override or counteract any positive feelings derived from following general societal ideals about helping those in need. Thus, helping someone with whom an exchange relationship is desired may not improve affect and may even lead to less positive feelings than not helping at all.

The present study further examined reactions to helping when communal and exchange relationships are desired. A primary goal was to more clearly differentiate the effects of helping per se on the helpers' affect in communal and in exchange relationships from the effects of knowing that help was needed but not being able to give it than was done in the original work by Williamson and Clark (1989, Study 3). In that earlier study the affect of subjects who had been induced to help was contrasted with the affect of subjects who knew help was needed but were not allowed to provide it. There was no control group in which subjects were not asked for help. Consequently, the effects of helping could not be disentangled from the effects of not being allowed to help when help was needed. In the present work, we contrasted affective reactions to helping with those of not helping in a situation in which the possibility of helping was simply not raised.

A secondary goal was to begin to identify mechanisms that might underlie the effects of helping on affective states.

Do communal helpers experience improved affect because they see themselves as good people for choosing to help? Are exchange helpers' affective states not improved by helping, or might their affective states even deteriorate because they evaluate themselves less favorably for having freely created an inequity by choosing to help? These questions were addressed by creating *two* helping conditions, one in which subjects felt they had chosen to help and another in which they were required to help. If seeing oneself as a good person plays a role in elevating affect among communal helpers, then affect should be more improved when one feels one has freely chosen to help than when one believes one has helped simply because one was required to. If less favorable self-evaluations (e.g., feeling gullible) contribute to exchange helpers' less improved (or possibly deteriorated) affect, then that effect also should be greater after choosing to help than after being required to help.

We expected that because helping fits communal norms and might promote the development of a communal relationship, among subjects desiring a communal relationship with recipient, providing help (either by choice or by requirement) would improve affect relative to not being asked to help. That is, positive affect should be higher and negative affect lower following helping than following having no opportunity to help when communal relationships are desired. Moreover, these effects were expected to be diminished (and possibly even reversed) among those desiring an exchange relationship. In a more exploratory manner, we also investigated the possibility that freely choosing to help, as opposed to being required to help, would influence these reactions. Specifically, if providing help does improve affect when communal relationships are desired *and* if perception of oneself as a good person accounts for this effect, communal helpers ought to feel better after freely choosing to help than after being required to help. If not, then other mechanisms must be considered to account for the effect. Further, if affect drops when helping occurs when exchange relationships are desired *and* if perceiving oneself as a gullible person for agreeing to help accounts for this effect, then affect ought to be lower when one has chosen to help than when one has been required to help. Again, if not, other mechanisms for any effects of helping on affect in exchange relationships must be considered.

METHOD

Overview

While participating in an experiment on word recognition, male subjects were led to desire either an exchange or a communal relationship with an attractive female who needed help. One third were induced to choose to provide the aid; one third were required to provide the aid; the remaining subjects were not asked to help. Affect was measured before and immediately after the interval in which subjects chose to help, were required to help, or received no request.[1]

Measures

In consideration of work indicating that positive and negative affect may be independent (e.g., Diener & Emmons, 1985; Warr, Barter, & Brownbridge, 1983; Zevon & Tellegen, 1982), a measure of positive and negative affect, the Positive and Negative Affect scale (PANAS), recently developed by Watson, Clark, and Tellegen (1988), was used. Although there were no a priori reasons to predict that changes in positive and negative affect would not be the mirror image of each other, it seemed important to explore the possibility that helping might have different effects on positive and negative affect.

The PANAS consists of 10 positive adjectives (PANAS-PA), *interested, excited, strong, enthusiastic, proud, alert, inspired, attentive, determined,* and *active,* and 10 negative adjectives (PANAS-NA), *distressed, upset, guilty, scared, hostile, irritable, ashamed, nervous, jittery,* and *afraid.* Affect can be assessed with the PANAS over a variety of time frames by changing the wording in the instructions for completing the scale. In this study, subjects were asked to indicate to what extent each item described the way they felt "at the present moment" on a scale from 1 (*very slightly or not at all*) to 5 (*extremely*). Watson et al. (1988) reported Cronbach's alpha coefficients for internal reliability of .89 for the PANAS-PA and .85 for the PANAS-NA as momentary measures of affect. In this study, alpha coefficients for the pretest measures were .87 for the PANAS-PA and .76 for the PANAS-NA.

Subjects

Ninety male[2] undergraduate students (mean age, 18.6 years) were recruited for an experiment on word recognition. Participation partially fulfilled a psychology course requirement. Each subject was randomly assigned to one of six conditions: (a) communal—choose to help, (b) communal—required to help, (c) communal—no help, (d) exchange—choose to help, (e) exchange—required to help, (f) exchange—no help. No subject indicated suspicions about the true purpose of the study.

Procedure

Subjects were run individually or in groups of two or three. Each sat at one of three tables facing separate walls. They were told the study focused on processes involved in recognizing words. To investigate these processes, they would perform two tasks. The experimenter said that previous research had shown performance to be affected by subjects' current moods. For this reason, moods would be measured immediately before each task so that these effects could be controlled in data analyses. The experimenter emphasized that to obtain accurate measures of performance, it was very important that subjects rate their moods according to the way they really felt at the time each measure was taken.

After giving each subject an envelope containing the first affect assessment form and materials for the first task, the experimenter requested that subjects not communicate with each other during the session. Subjects then began the first task, and the experimenter left the room. Written instructions advised subjects to complete the affect assessment before beginning the task. Then, for 10 min, subjects located and circled words in a matrix of letters (this was merely a filler task).

After the 10 min had passed, the experimenter returned, collected the first task materials and affect measures, and said she had forgotten to have them do something before they started. Supposedly, the coordinator of undergraduate education for the psychology department had asked subjects in all studies taking less than an hour to complete to listen to a tape and read some information about a research project being conducted by an undergraduate student. Because this would take only a few minutes and because it was supposed to be done before the end of the experiment, the experimenter had decided to take care of the matter before starting the second task. She then told subjects that the undergraduate researcher's name was Janet and that Janet would arrive later to talk to them. Each subject was given an audiotape cassette, a small tape player with earphones, and an envelope containing a memo from the coordinator of undergraduate education along with some information about Janet's project. Memos were printed on department stationery and signed by the actual undergraduate adviser in the department. For all conditions, they began as follows:

This semester, a number of our undergraduate psychology students are conducting experiments as independent study projects. This means that the demand for subjects is higher than usual. Consequently, we want to be sure that the time allotted to experiments (one hour of subject time for each experimental credit given) is fully utilized. Some of our faculty and graduate student experiments, such as the one you're participating in now, take considerably less than an hour to complete. Our undergraduate students are being allowed to use the rest of the allotted hour to run their own research projects, as long as this does not interfere with the experiment you signed up for. Enclosed is some information about one of our undergraduate researchers as well as some information about the research he or she is conducting.

These undergraduate projects have been judged to be ethical by our review committee. Since the experiment in which you are participating right now takes less than one hour, . . .

The way the sentence was completed served as a partial manipulation of helping condition. For subjects assigned to a choose to help condition, the sentence went on to say, "we are asking each participant in this study if he/she would consider helping out an undergraduate researcher." In the required to help conditions, the sentence continued, "we are *requiring* each participant in this study to help out an undergraduate researcher" (emphasis in original). Subjects in the no help conditions read that "we are permitting our undergraduate researchers to ask each participant in this study to help them out."[3]

Instructions indicated that subjects should listen to the tape before reading Janet's research description. Tapes and research descriptions contained further experimental manipulations. Envelopes and tapes had been placed in a box before the experiment began. Materials were drawn from the box at random, allowing the experimenter to remain unaware of assignment to condition.

For those in a communal condition, the tape said:

Hi, my name is Janet Lewis, and I'd like to tell you a little about myself and the research I'll be doing this semester. First, I'm single, 19 years old, and a psychology major. I'm from Philadelphia. I just transferred from the University of Pennsylvania, so this is my first semester at Carnegie Mellon. I don't know many people on campus, so I'm really anxious to meet new people and get to know my way around.

It was assumed that most subjects, who were predominantly unmarried freshmen, would be available for and interested in having a communal relationship (e.g., a friendship or possibly a romantic relationship) with a physically attractive other who was interested in meeting people. (As will be seen, subjects discovered that Janet was attractive soon after they listened to one of the tapes.)

For subjects in an exchange condition, the tape said:

Hi, my name is Janet Lewis, and I'd like to tell you a little about myself and the research I'll be doing this semester. First, I'm married, 19 years old, and a psychology major.

Both my husband and I are from Pittsburgh. I've been at Carnegie Mellon for two years, but I don't know many people on campus, since we spend most of our free time at family gatherings and visiting with our friends.

It was assumed that most subjects would prefer an exchange relationship with someone who was married and did not indicate interest in meeting people. Studies including measures specifically designed to tap the effectiveness of very similar manipulations (Clark, 1986; Clark & Waddell, 1985) have provided evidence for the effectiveness of both the exchange and communal manipulations.[4]

After exposing subjects to either the communal or the exchange relationship manipulation, both tapes then went on to say:

Now about my research: The psychology department has allowed me to use part of your experimenter's time to get some work done on my own research project. I will stop by later—after you've finished the experiment you're working on now—so that we can discuss my research and so that I can answer any questions you may have about it. For right now, your experimenter will give you an envelope which contains some information about the research I will be doing this semester. When you've finished with these materials, please put them all back into their envelope and give them to your experimenter. He or she will see that I get them.

At the top of each research description (which subjects read after listening to the tape) was a small photocopy of an attractive female's photograph.[5] The same photograph was used in the communal and exchange conditions. Beneath it was a brief description of Janet's research project, a study investigating the relationship between college students' study habits and their favorite leisure-time activities. For subjects assigned to a no help condition, the message went on to say that Janet did not need any help that could be given within the hour but that she might be looking for volunteer subjects later on. For subjects assigned to either a choose or a required to help condition, the message went on to say that Janet needed help in collecting some preliminary data on university students' favorite activities. In the choose to help conditions, subjects were *asked* whether they would fill out an attached questionnaire; those in the required conditions were told they *should* fill it out. Subjects in the choose and required conditions also read that Janet might be looking for volunteer subjects later on.

In the four helping conditions (communal-choose, communal-required, exchange-choose, and exchange-required), subjects completed a form listing 36 activities (e.g., going to the movies, talking on the phone, listening to records/tapes, jogging, Frisbee). They were asked to place a check mark next to those activities in which they participated at least once a week. During this time, the experimenter waited in an adjacent room. After 10 min she returned and told them to put the materials from Janet aside so they could begin the second task. Subjects were then given another envelope containing a second affect measure and materials for the second word recognition task. As before, subjects were reminded to complete the affect measure immediately before beginning the task, and the experimenter left the room.

The experimenter returned 10 min later and said the experiment was over. After collecting the second task materials, she gave each subject a "Reactions to Word Recognition Study" form to fill out. It asked three filler questions about how difficult and enjoyable the tasks were. Two additional questions served as partial checks for suspicion about the real purpose of the study: "Sometimes people's own perceptions of the task/experiment affect their performance. In your own words, what was the purpose of the study?" and "Any other comments you'd like to make about the study?" While the experimenter gave subjects these forms, she mentioned that Janet was waiting to talk to them as soon as they finished.[6] Finally, subjects were further checked for suspicion and carefully debriefed.

RESULTS

The dependent measures were changes in positive and negative affect. Change scores were calculated as differences between the sum of a subject's scores on the appropriate pretest items and the analogous sum on the posttest items. Preliminary analyses revealed no significant differences in changes in either positive or negative affect for the number of subjects participating in experimental sessions. Specifically, whether subjects participated alone or with one or two other individuals did not appear to influence changes in affect, both $Fs < 2.50$, n.s. Additional preliminary analyses revealed no differences between conditions at pretesting for either positive or negative affect. On the premanipulation measure, average positive moods (overall $M = 27.0$) and average negative moods (overall $M = 15.1$) were comparable to the norms for college students reported by Watson et al. (1988), $Ms = 29.7$ for positive moods and 14.8 for negative moods. There was a small negative correlation between changes in positive affect and changes in negative affect, $r = -.19$, $p < .04$.

Because our helping task involved recalling pleasant activities, it was possible that the task itself (rather than helping per se) had an impact on affective reactions. To investigate the possibility that differential responses on the

favorite activities survey accounted for observed differences in affect between the conditions in which help was given, we conducted a series of 2 (Communal vs. Exchange) × 2 (Choose vs. Required to Help) ANOVAs, using as dependent variables responses (yes or no) to each activity as well as a total activities measure derived by counting the activities each subject checked. Because of the number of analyses conducted (37), the alpha level for determining significance was set at $p < .01$ to control for Type I error. No significant effects were revealed for any of the individual activities or for total activities. Only one analysis revealed an effect approaching significance. Subjects in the exchange conditions tended to be more likely to report that jogging was a favored leisure activity than those in the communal conditions, $F(1, 56) = 5.20$, $p < .03$. All other F values were less than 3.76, n.s. Thus, responses on the helping task itself did not differ reliably by experimental condition.

Changes in Positive Affect

Mean changes in positive affect are shown in Figure 1. As predicted, among subjects led to desire a communal relationship, positive affect was elevated in the choose and required conditions, relative to the no help condition. Also as expected, among subjects led to desire an exchange

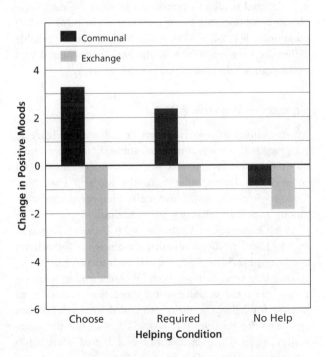

FIGURE 1 Changes in positive affect as a result of choosing or being required to help when either an exchange or a communal relationship was desired.

relationship, positive affect did not improve in the choose and required conditions. Rather, in the choose condition positive affect deteriorated, and in the required condition positive affect showed little change, relative to the no help condition.

A 2 (Communal vs. Exchange) × 3 (Choose vs. Required vs. No Help) ANOVA revealed a main effect for desired relationship type, $F(1, 84) = 18.02$, $p < .0001$, such that regardless of helping condition, the positive affect of subjects desiring a communal relationship was more elevated than that of subjects desiring an exchange relationship. The main effect for helping condition was not reliable, $F(2, 84) = 1.74$, n.s., but the interaction between helping condition and desired relationship type was significant, $F(2, 84) = 4.60$, $p < .01$.

Planned comparisons using a priori F tests revealed that positive affect improved more both in the communal-choose ($M = 3.3$) and in the communal-required ($M = 2.5$) conditions than in the communal—no help condition ($M = -0.8$), $Fs(1, 84) = 6.20$ and 4.03, respectively, both $ps < .05$. the difference between changes in the communal-choose and communal-required conditions was not reliable, $F(1, 84) = .23$, n.s. Positive affect deteriorated more in the exchange-choose condition ($M = -4.6$) than in the exchange-required condition ($M = -0.8$), $F(1, 84) = 5.25$, $p < .05$, and tended to deteriorate more in the exchange-choose condition than in the exchange-no help ($M = -1.7$) condition, $F(1, 84) = 3.00$, $p < .10$. There was no reliable difference between means in the exchange-required and exchange-no help conditions, $F(1, 84) = .31$, n.s.[7]

Changes in Negative Affect

Mean changes in negative affect are shown in Figure 2. As predicted, among communal subjects, negative affect improved (i.e., became less negative) in the choose and required conditions, relative to the no help condition. Contrary to predictions, negative affect improved somewhat among exchange subjects in all conditions.

A 2 (Communal vs. Exchange) × 3 (Choose vs. Required vs. No Help) ANOVA revealed a main effect for helping condition, $F(2,84) = 4.80$, $p < .01$, such that, regardless of relationship type, helping (both by choice and by requirement) alleviated negative affect more than receiving no request for help. The main effect of desired relationship type was not reliable, $F(1, 84) = .72$, n.s., but the interaction between helping condition and desired relationship type was significant, $F(2, 84) = 3.18$, $p < .05$.

Planned comparisons revealed that negative affect decreased (i.e., was alleviated) more in the communal-

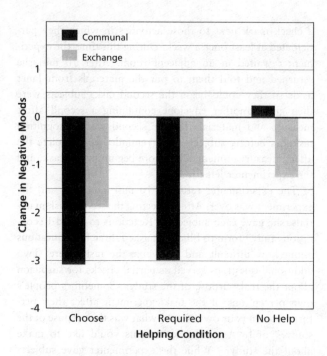

FIGURE 2 Changes in negative affect as a result of choosing or being required to help when either an exchange or a communal relationship was desired.

choose ($M = -3.1$) and communal-required ($M = -3.0$) conditions than in the communal—no help condition ($M = .02$), $Fs(1, 84) = 11.75$ and 11.25, respectively, both $ps < .01$. The difference between mean changes in the communal-choose and communal-required conditions was not reliable, $F(1, 84) = 0.01$, n.s. There were no significant differences between the exchange-choose ($M = -1.9$), exchange-required ($M = -1.3$), and exchange—no help ($M = -1.3$) conditions, all $Fs < .48$, n.s.

DISCUSSION

The present study has shown that giving help can improve one's affective state—a result consistent with prior research (e.g., Batson et al., 1978, Study 2; Harris, 1977, Study 3; Williamson & Clark, 1989, Studies 1 and 2; Yinon & Landau, 1987, Study 1). It has also shown that this effect is moderated by the type of relationship that helpers desire with the recipient. Affect improved only when a communal relationship was desired. When an exchange relationship was desired, affect did not improve. Rather, a strong tendency for choosing to help to cause positive affect to decline was observed. The moderating impact of desired relationship is consistent with prior research (Williamson &

Clark, 1989, Study 3). More important, these results move us beyond prior work, in a number of ways.

Clearly Identifying the Effects of Giving Help in Two Relationship Types

One way this research goes beyond prior work is that it allows us to separate the effects of helping in desired communal and exchange relationships from those of knowing help is needed and being unable to help. Recall that in the original study investigating the impact of desired relationship type on reactions to providing help (Williamson & Clark, 1989, Study 3), the effects of helping could not be clearly separated from those of knowing the other needed help and being unable to give it. In the present study, that problem was eliminated by contrasting the effects of helping with those of not being asked to help. Therefore, we can now state that being able to give help itself improves affect when a communal but not when an exchange relationship is desired. We can also tentatively propose that choosing to give help actually seems to cause affect to decline when an exchange relationship is desired.

Beginning to Identify Mechanisms Underlying These Effects

A second way this research moves beyond prior work is that, by including the manipulation of choice about helping, we have begun to identify mechanisms underlying reactions to providing help. In introducing this study, we suggested that perceiving oneself as a good person would seem to play a role in improving helpers' affective state if it were found that communal helpers feel better after choosing to help than after being required to help. Instead, however, subjects in the communal conditions did *not* feel better when they chose to help than when they were required to help. This finding, of course, does not provide conclusive evidence that self-perception processes are never involved in causing affect to be improved by helping. However, when combined with the fact that the same manipulation of choice did have an impact in the exchange conditions, it suggests looking elsewhere for an explanation of why helping (both by choice and by requirement) improved affect in the communal conditions in this particular study. We suspect those effects were due to (a) enjoyment derived from knowing that someone with whom a communal relationship is desired has received a benefit (Smith, Keating, & Stotland, 1989) and/or (b) perceiving that one's chances of forming the desired communal relationship have been enhanced by having personally helped the other. Future work will investigate these possibilities.

Interestingly, another argument can also be made against improved self-evaluations as a cause of the improvement in affect: If observing oneself providing aid leads to positive evaluations of the self and consequent improved affect, we might expect the improvement to be especially pronounced in the exchange conditions. After all, subjects might feel they are particularly good people for having helped even when they did not desire a close relationship with the other. The fact that this did not occur in our study suggests that self-perception processes may not account for the improvements in affect that follow helping.

Does this mean that self-perception processes had no impact in this study? No. In fact, in contrast to the communal conditions, choice did influence affect in the exchange conditions. Although being required to help did not cause affective states to deteriorate significantly when an exchange relationship was desired, choosing to help caused positive affect to deteriorate relative to being required to help. Moreover, a strong tendency for choosing to help to cause positive affect to deteriorate relative to not being asked to help was also observed. This suggests that self-perception processes may have played a role in *declines* in positive affect in the exchange conditions. In particular, seeing oneself as gullible or stupid for helping when help is not required by social norms may cause positive affect to decrease. Another possibility is that subjects may have worried that if the recipient realized they had freely chosen to help, she might erroneously perceive their behavior as indicating a desire for a communal rather than an exchange relationship. However, because she sought help with the psychology department's endorsement and because subjects did not specifically seek an opportunity to help her, we believe the latter explanation is less likely than the former.

Investigating the Impact of Helping on Positive and Negative Affect Separately

Finally, this study goes beyond prior research by demonstrating that among exchange helpers, helping may not influence negative affect in the same way it influences positive affect. In the present study, choosing to help resulted in declines in exchange helpers' positive affect without analogous increases in negative affect. This was not a predicted effect.

However, a reasonable explanation is that there may be a ceiling on the level of negative affect people are willing to report or will allow themselves to experience under less than extraordinary circumstances. The data provide some support for this idea in that subjects never reported increased negative affect. In addition, premanipulation mean positive affect was considerably higher than premanipulation mean negative affect. Scores on each scale could vary from 10 to 50. Pretest scores on the positive affect scale averaged 27.0. In contrast, average pretest scores on the negative affect scale were 15.1. In other words, prior to the experimental manipulation, mean positive affect was around the midpoint of the scale, but mean negative affect was close to the bottom. Watson et al. (1988) report similar average scores for college students on these scales.

It may be that a score of 15 represents about the highest amount of negative affect that subjects are willing to admit experiencing. Other research (e.g., Sommers, 1984) shows that people in negative moods are not liked as much as people in positive moods. Subjects may implicitly know this and be hesitant to report increases in negative emotions (e.g., guilt, hostility, upset). Alternatively, it may be that when people experience increased negative affect, they actively try to control those feelings (Clark & Isen, 1982). Thus, a score of 15 may represent the most negative affect that subjects actually experience under ordinary circumstances. Either or both of these possibilities can explain why negative affect did not increase in the present study.

Finally, note that the *only* significant effects on negative affect occurred in the communal conditions, where both being required and choosing to help significantly decreased negative affect. These results are also consistent with the "ceiling" explanation. People may be reluctant to report experiencing more than minimal negative affect, but they should not hesitate to report declines in whatever negative feelings they have acknowledged earlier. It could even be argued that this result is especially impressive because there was so little room for negative affect to decline (from a pretest average of only 15 to an absolute minimum of 10).

If the lack of effects on negative feelings indeed resulted from reluctance to admit experiencing much negative affect on a self-report measure, then a less obtrusive measure might reveal effects not found in the present work. However, if the lack of effects was due to subjects' active efforts to counter negative feelings, then our results may reflect reality.

Concluding Comments

In sum, the present study provides additional evidence that helping is beneficial to helpers. However, like prior work (Williamson & Clark, 1989, Study 3), it suggests that when one helps a stranger, this benefit may be limited to situations in which a communal relationship is desired with the recipient. Indeed, the findings show that choosing to help can even make one feel worse under certain conditions.

They also suggest that seeing the other benefit and/or promoting a desired relationship may underlie improvements in affect when communal relationships are desired. In contrast, feeling gullible or stupid about having helped when one would rather not may underlie the observed tendency for affect to deteriorate after choosing to help when exchange relationships are desired.

Do we believe that people never feel good about helping someone with whom they prefer to have an exchange relationship? No. For instance, when they help in an emergency, people may feel good regardless of desired relationship type, because overriding societal norms about helping in dire circumstances are stronger than those about helping in mundane situations (as in the present study). Further work is needed to precisely identify underlying mechanisms and boundary conditions of affective reactions to providing help. Finally, we would note that although we see no theoretical reason that our present results should not generalize to females, to be absolutely confident that they would, future work should include female as well as male subjects.

REFERENCES

Aronfreed, J. (1970). The socialization of altruistic and sympathetic behavior: Some theoretical and experimental analyses. In J. Macaulay & L. Berkowitz (Eds.), *Altruism and helping behavior* (pp. 103–126). Orlando, FL: Academic Press.

Batson, C. D., Coke, J. S., Jasnoski, M. L., & Hanson, M. (1978). Buying kindness: Effect of an extrinsic incentive for helping on perceived altruism. *Personality and Social Psychology Bulletin, 4,* 86–91.

Berkowitz, L. (1972). Social norms, feelings, and other factors affecting helping and altruism. In L. Berkowitz (Ed.), *Advances in experimental social psychology* (Vol. 6). Orlando, FL: Academic Press.

Berkowitz, L., & Connor, W. H. (1966). Success, failure, and social responsibility. *Journal of Personality and Social Psychology, 4,* 664–669.

Cialdini, R. B., & Kenrick, D. T. (1976) Altruism as hedonism: A social development perspective on the relationship of negative mood state and helping. *Journal of Personality and Social Psychology, 34,* 907–914.

Clark, M. S. (1986). Evidence for the effectiveness of manipulations of desire for communal versus exchange relationships. *Personality and Social Psychology Bulletin, 12,* 414–425.

Clark, M. S., & Isen, A. M. (1982). Toward understanding the relationship between feeling states and social behavior. In A. Hastorf & A. M. Isen (Eds.), *Cognitive social psychology* (pp. 73–108). New York: Elsevier North-Holland.

Clark, M. S., & Mills, J. (1979). Interpersonal attraction in exchange and communal relationships. *Journal of Personality and Social Psychology, 37,* 12–24.

Clark, M. S., Mills, J., & Powell, M. C. (1986). Keeping track of needs in communal and exchange relationships. *Journal of Personality and Social Psychology, 51,* 333–338.

Clark, M. S., Ouellette, R., Powell, M. C., & Milberg, S. (1987). Recipient's mood, relationship type, and helping. *Journal of Personality and Social Psychology, 53,* 94–103.

Clark, M. S., & Waddell, B. (1985). Perception of exploitation in communal and exchange relationships. *Journal of Social and Personal Relationships, 2,* 403–413.

Diener, E., & Emmons, R. A. (1985). The independence of positive and negative affect. *Journal of Personality and Social Psychology, 47,* 1105–1117.

Harris, M. B. (1977). Effects of altruism on mood. *Journal of Social Psychology, 102,* 197–208.

Schwartz, S. H. (1975). The justice of need and the activation of humanitarian norms. *Journal of Social Issues, 31,* 111–136.

Schwartz, S. H., & Howard, J. A. (1982). Helping and cooperation: A self-based motivational model. In V. J. Derlega & J. Grzelak (Eds.), *Cooperation and helping behavior: Theories and research* (pp. 327–353). Orlando, FL: Academic Press.

Sommers, S. (1984). Reported emotions and conventions of emotionality among college students. *Journal of Personality and Social Psychology, 46,* 207–215.

Smith, K. D., Keating, J. P., & Stotland, E. (1989). Altruism reconsidered: The effect of denying feedback on a victim's status to empathic witnesses. *Journal of Personality and Social Psychology, 57,* 641–650.

Walster, E., Walster, B., & Berscheid, E. (1978). *Equity theory and research.* Newton, MA: Allyn & Bacon.

Warr, P., Barter, J., & Brownbridge, G. (1983). On the independence of positive and negative affect. *Journal of Personality and Social Psychology, 44,* 644–651.

Watson, D., Clark, L. A., & Tellegen, A. (1988). Development and validation of brief measures of positive and negative affect. *Journal of Personality and Social Psychology, 54,* 1063–1070.

Williamson, G. M., & Clark, M. S. (1989). Providing help and desired relationship type as determinants of changes in moods and self-evaluations. *Journal of Personality and Social Psychology, 56,* 722–734.

Yinon, Y., & Landau, M. O. (1987). On the reinforcing value of helping behavior in a positive mood. *Motivation and Emotion, 11,* 83–93.

Zevon, M. A., & Tellegen, A. (1982). The structure of mood change: An idiographic/nomothetic analysis. *Journal of Personality and Social Psychology, 43,* 111–123.

NOTES

1. As an exploratory measure, all subjects also received a later request for help from the same female. However, no significant differences were observed on this measure, and consequently the results are not reported in this article.

2. Subjects of just one sex were run as part of our effort to keep as many variables aside from those in which we had an immediate theoretical interest constant and because we had no theoretical reason to suspect males and females would show different patterns of reactions to helping when exchange versus communal relationships were desired. Males in particular were selected simply because the available subject population included many more males than females.

3. As will be seen, subjects in the no help conditions were subsequently advised that Janet did not need any help that could be given within the remainder of the hour.

4. For example, in the Clark (1986) study, subjects were first exposed to the communal or to the exchange manipulation. Then, under the guise of a study on impression formation, they rated the degree to which they would follow communal norms (as expressed in seven statements) and exchange norms (as expressed in seven statements) in a relationship with the target. They also selected the type of relationship they would most like to have with the target from a list of two typically exchange and two typically communal relationships. Results revealed that subjects exposed to the communal manipulation were significantly more likely to say they would conform to communal norms when with the other (e.g., they would enjoy responding to the other's need; would like the other to respond to their needs) relative to conforming to exchange norms (e.g., if they received something of value from the other, they would immediately return something comparable; if they gave something of value to the other, they would expect repayment soon afterward) than subjects exposed to the exchange manipulation. Moreover, a significantly greater proportion of subjects exposed to the communal manipulation than of those exposed to the exchange manipulation said they would choose to have a type of relationship believed to be typically communal in nature (i.e., a friendship) with the other, as opposed to choosing a type of relationship believed to be typically exchange in nature (i.e., an acquaintanceship or a businesslike relationship).

5. Before the experiment, this photo had been selected from a group of nine photos of college-age women. Twenty undergraduate students (6 males and 14 females) independently rated each photo on a scale of 1 (*extremely unattractive*) to 5 (*extremely attractive*). The one used in the present studies received a mean rating of 4 (somewhat attractive).

6. It was at this point that the second request occurred. After passing out the "Reactions to Word Recognition Study" forms, the experimenter said that Janet had asked her to give each subject another envelope and wanted subjects to respond to its contents before she came in to talk to them. This envelope contained a second request for help. As mentioned previously, this measure yielded no results and consequently will not be discussed further.

7. Although not all comparisons were orthogonal to one another, they were all theoretically meaningful and clearly called for by our a priori hypotheses and questions.

CRITICAL THINKING QUESTIONS

1. What are some of the reasons, suggested by the authors, that people may feel bad when they help others in an exchange relationship? Are there other reasons that people may feel bad in this situation?

2. In this study positive and negative affect do not seem to be related. Why do you think this is?

3. In this experiment subjects helped by acting as a subject for another student in a psychology experiment. Do you think this is the same as helping someone why may have a more significant problem? In what ways is it likely to be similar? In what ways is it likely to be different?

4. The authors suggest several reasons why people may feel good when helping other people. Can you think of other reasons?

5. When subjects chose to help and when they were required to help they often had the same reaction. What was the exception to this statement? Why might choosing versus being required to help someone not make a difference to people? Why might it make a difference?

6. What implications does this study have for the mood-maintenance explanation of helping described in Chapter 7 of the textbook?

READING 7

Understanding the causes of human aggression is an important mission for social psychology in this increasingly violent world. One of the first and most influential social psychological theories concerning aggression was the frustration-aggression hypothesis. This hypothesis, described in the book *Frustration and Aggression* by John Dollard and his colleagues in 1939, is the dual proposition that frustration always elicits the motive to aggress, and aggression is always caused by frustration. This hypothesis sparked a great amount of research, including research illustrating the important concept of displaced aggression. As is discussed in Chapter 8 of your textbook, the frustration-aggression hypothesis has been revised and modified in various ways since it was first introduced in 1939. Inspired by this research but also recognizing its limitations, Leonard Berkowitz offered an important contribution to our understanding of the situational determinants of aggression by emphasizing the roles of anger and thought on aggression.

Berkowitz argued that when people are angry, they are in a state of readiness to aggress. Frustration is only one cause of anger. Whether or not an angered person will behave aggressively depends, in part, on whether aggression-enhancing cues are present in the situation. As is summarized in Chapter 8, any object or external characteristic that is associated with successful aggression or with the negative affect of pain or unpleasantness can serve as an aggression-enhancing situational cue. Berkowitz proposed that the presence of such a cue in a situation can automatically increase the likelihood of aggression.

The aggression-enhancing cue examined in the study reported in this reading was the presence of weapons. Berkowitz and LePage addressed the question of "whether weapons can serve as aggression-eliciting stimuli, causing an angered individual to display stronger violence than he would have shown in the absence of such weapons." Note that Berkowitz and LePage did not investigate whether the presence of weapons would prompt people to use the weapons to aggress; rather, they examined the more subtle, and potentially pervasive, point of whether the presence of weapons would increase the underlying *likelihood* of responding aggressively— that is, even if the weapons are not used in the actual aggression. As you read this article, consider the implications of this research for understanding aggression in general, but also for the ongoing debates about gun control and the prevalence of violence depicted in the media.

Weapons as Aggression-Eliciting Stimuli

Leonard Berkowitz and Anthony LePage
University of Wisconsin

An experiment was conducted to test the hypothesis that stimuli commonly associated with aggression can elicit aggressive responses from people ready to act aggressively. One hundred male university students received either 1 or 7 shocks, supposedly from a peer, and were then given an opportunity to shock this person. In some cases a rifle and revolver were on the table near the shock key. These weapons were said to belong, or not to belong, to the available target person. In other instances there was nothing on the table near the shock key, while for a control group 2 badminton racquets were on the table near the key. The greatest number of shocks was given by the strongly aroused Ss (who had received 7 shocks) when they were in the presence of the weapons. The guns had evidently elicited strong aggressive responses from the aroused men.

Human behavior is often goal directed, guided by strategies and influenced by ego defenses and strivings for cognitive consistency. There clearly are situations, however, in which these purposive considerations are relatively unimportant

SOURCE: Leonard Berkowitz and Anthony LePage, "Weapons as Aggression-Eliciting Stimuli," *Journal of Personality and Social Psychology*, 1967, Vol. 7, No. 2, 202–207. Copyright © 1967 by the American Psychological Association. Reprinted with permission.

regulators of action. Habitual behavior patterns become dominant on these occasions, and the person responds relatively automatically to the stimuli impinging upon him. Any really complete psychological system must deal with these stimulus-elicited, impulsive reactions as well as with more complex behavior patterns. More than this, we should also be able to specify the conditions under which the various behavior determinants increase or decrease in importance.

The senior author has long contended that many aggressive actions are controlled by the stimulus properties of the available targets rather than by anticipations of ends that might be served (Berkowitz, 1962, 1964, 1965). Perhaps because strong emotion results in an increased utilization of only the central cues in the immediate situation (Easterbrook, 1959; Walters & Parke, 1964), anger arousal can lead to impulsive aggressive responses which, for a short time at least, may be relatively free of cognitively mediated inhibitions against aggression or, for that matter, purposes and strategic considerations.[1] This impulsive action is not necessarily pushed out by the anger, however. Berkowitz has suggested that appropriate cues must be present in the situation if aggressive responses are actually to occur. While there is still considerable uncertainty as to just what characteristics define aggressive cue properties, the association of a stimulus with aggression evidently can enhance the aggressive cue value of this stimulus. But whatever its exact genesis, the cue (which may be either in the external environment or represented internally) presumably elicits the aggressive response. Anger (or any other conjectured aggressive "drive") increases the person's reactivity to the cue, possibly energizes the response, and may lower the likelihood of competing reactions, but is not necessary for the production of aggressive behavior.[2]

A variety of observations can be cited in support of this reasoning (cf. Berkowitz, 1965). Thus, the senior author has proposed that some of the effects of observed violence can readily be understood in terms of stimulus-elicited aggression. According to several Wisconsin experiments, observed aggression is particularly likely to produce strong attacks against anger instigators who are associated with the victim of the witnessed violence (Berkowitz & Geen, 1966, 1967; Geen & Berkowitz, 1966). The frustrater's association with the observed victim presumably enhances his cue value for aggression, causing him to evoke stronger attacks from the person who is ready to act aggressively.

More direct evidence for the present formulation can be found in a study conducted by Loew (1965). His subjects, in being required to learn a concept, either aggressive or nature words, spoke either 20 aggressive or 20 neutral words aloud. Following this "learning task," each subject

was to give a peer in an adjacent room an electric shock whenever this person made a mistake in his learning problem. Allowed to vary the intensity of the shocks they administered over a 10-point continuum, the subjects who had uttered the aggressive words gave shocks of significantly greater intensity than did the subjects who had spoken the neutral words. The aggressive words had evidently evoked implicit aggressive responses from the subjects, even though they had not been angered beforehand, which then led to the stronger attacks upon the target person in the next room when he supposedly made errors.

Cultural learning shared by many members of a society can also associate external objects with aggression and thus affect the objects' aggressive cue value. Weapons are a prime example. For many men (and probably women as well) in our society, these objects are closely associated with aggression. Assuming that the weapons do not produce inhibitions that are stronger than the evoked aggressive reactions (as would be the case, e.g., if the weapons were labeled as morally "bad"), the presence of the aggressive objects should generally lead to more intense attacks upon an available target than would occur in the presence of a neutral object.

The present experiment was designed to test this latter hypothesis. At one level, of course, the findings contribute to the current debate as to the desirability of restricting sales of firearms. Many arguments have been raised for such a restriction. Thus, according to recent statistics, Texas communities having virtually no prohibitions against firearms have a much higher homicide rate than other American cities possessing stringent firearm regulations, and J. Edgar Hoover has maintained in *Time* magazine that the availability of firearms is an important factor in murders (Anonymous, 1966). The experiment reported here seeks to determine how this influence may come about. The availability of weapons obviously makes it easier for a person who wants to commit murder to do so. But, in addition, we ask whether weapons can serve as aggression-eliciting stimuli, causing an angered individual to display stronger violence than he would have shown in the absence of such weapons. Social significance aside, and at a more general theoretical level, this research also attempts to demonstrate that situational stimuli can exert "automatic" control over socially relevant human actions.

METHOD

Subjects

The subjects were 100 male undergraduates enrolled in the introductory psychology course at the University of

Wisconsin who volunteered for the experiment (without knowing its nature) in order to earn points counting toward their final grade. Thirty-nine other subjects had also been run, but were discarded because they suspected the experimenter's confederate (21), reported receiving fewer electric shocks than was actually given them (7), had not attended to information given them about the procedure (9), or were run while there was equipment malfunctioning (2).

Procedure

General design Seven experimental conditions were established, six organized in a 2 × 3 factorial design, with the seventh group serving essentially as a control. Of the men in the factorial design, half were made to be angry with the confederate, while the other subjects received a friendlier treatment from him. All of the subjects were then given an opportunity to administer electric shocks to the confederate, but for two-thirds of the men there were weapons lying on the table near the shock apparatus. Half of these people were informed the weapons belonged to the confederate in order to test the hypothesis that aggressive stimuli which also were associated with the anger instigator would evoke the strongest aggressive reaction from the subjects. The other people seeing the weapons were told the weapons had been left there by a previous experimenter. There was nothing on the table except the shock key when the last third of the subjects in both the angered and nonangered conditions gave the shocks. Finally, the seventh group consisted of angered men who gave shocks with two badminton racquets and shuttlecocks lying near the shock key. This condition sought to determine whether the presence of *any* object near the shock apparatus would reduce inhibitions against aggression, even if the object were not connected with aggressive behavior.

Experimental manipulations When each subject arrived in the laboratory, he was informed that two men were required for the experiment and that they would have to wait for the second subject to appear. After a 5-minute wait, the experimenter, acting annoyed, indicated that they had to begin because of his other commitments. He said he would have to look around outside to see if he could find another person who might serve as a substitute for the missing subject. In a few minutes the experimenter returned with the confederate. Depending upon the condition, this person was introduced as either a psychology student who had been about to sign up for another experiment or as a student who had been running another study.

The subject and confederate were told the experiment was a study of physiological reactions to stress. The stress would be created by mild electric shocks, and the subjects could withdraw, the experimenter said, if they objected to these shocks. (No subjects left.) Each person would have to solve a problem knowing that his performance would be evaluated by his partner. The "evaluations" would be in the form of electric shocks, with one shock signifying a very good rating and 10 shocks meaning the performance was judged as very bad. The men were then told what their problems were. the subject's task was to list ideas a publicity agent might employ in order to better a popular singer's record sales and public image. The other person (the confederate) had to think of things a used-car dealer might do in order to increase sales. The two were given 5 minutes to write their answers, and the papers were then collected by the experimenter who supposedly would exchange them.

Following this, the two were placed in separate rooms, supposedly so that they would not influence each other's galvanic skin response (GSR) reactions. The shock electrodes were placed on the subject's right forearm, and GSR electrodes were attached to fingers on his left hand, with wires trailing from the electrodes to the next room. The subject was told he would be the first to receive electric shocks as the evaluation of his problem solution. The experimenter left the subject's room saying he was going to turn on the GSR apparatus, went to the room containing the shock machine and the waiting confederate, and only then looked at the schedule indicating whether the subject was to be angered or not. He informed the confederate how many shocks the subject was to receive, and 30 seconds later the subject was given seven shocks (angered condition) or one shock (nonangered group). The experimenter then went back to the subject, while the confederate quickly arranged the table holding the shock key in the manner appropriate for the subject's condition. Upon entering the subject's room, the experimenter asked him how many shocks he had received and provided the subject with a brief questionnaire on which he was to rate his mood. As soon as this was completed, the subject was taken to the room holding the shock machine. Here the experimenter told the subject it was his turn to evaluate his partner's work. For one group in both the angered and nonangered conditions the shock key was alone on the table (no-object groups). For two other groups in each of these angered and nonangered conditions, however, a 12-gauge shotgun and a .38-caliber revolver were lying on the table near the key (aggressive-weapon conditions). One group in both the angered and nonangered conditions was informed the weapons belonged to the subject's partner. The subjects given this treatment had been told earlier that their partner was a student who had been conducting an experiment.[3] They now were reminded of this, and the experimenter said the weapons were being used in some way by this person in his research (associated-weapons condition); the guns were to be disregarded. The other men were told simply the weapons "belong to someone else" who "must have been doing an experiment in here" (un-associated-weapons group), and they too were asked to disregard the guns. For the last treatment, one group of angered men found two badminton racquets and shuttle-cocks lying on the table near the shock key, and these people were also told the equipment belonged to someone else (badminton-racquets group).

Immediately after this information was provided, the experimenter showed the subject what was supposedly his partner's answer to his assigned problem. The subject was reminded that he was to give the partner shocks as his evaluation and was informed that this was the last time shocks would be administered in the study. A second copy of the mood questionnaire was then completed by the subject after he had delivered the shocks. Following this, the subject was asked a number of oral questions about the experiment, including what, if any, suspicions he had. (No doubts were voiced about the presence of the weapons.) At the conclusion of this interview the experiment was explained, and the subject was asked not to talk about the study.

Dependent Variables

As in nearly all the experiments conducted in the senior author's program, the number of shocks given by the subjects serves as the primary aggression measure. However, we also report here findings obtained with the total duration of each subject's shocks, recorded in thousandths of a minute. Attention is also given to each subject's rating of his mood, first immediately after receiving the partner's evaluation, and again immediately after administering shocks to the partner. These ratings were made on a series of 10 13-point bipolar scales with an adjective at each end, such as "calm-tense" and "angry-not angry."

RESULTS

Effectiveness of Arousal Treatment

Analyses of variance of the responses to each of the mood scales following the receipt of the partner's evaluation indicate the prior-shock treatment succeeded in creating differences in anger arousal. The subjects getting seven shocks

rated themselves as being significantly angrier than the subjects receiving only one shock ($F = 20.65$, $p < .01$). There were no reliable differences among the groups within any one arousal level. Interestingly enough, the only other mood scale to yield a significant effect was the scale "sad-happy." The aroused–seven-shocks men reported a significantly stronger felt sadness than the men getting one shock ($F = 4.63$, $p > .05$).

Aggression Toward Partner

A preliminary analysis of variance of the shock data for the six groups in the 3×2 factorial design yielded the findings shown in Table 1. As is indicated by the significant inter-action, the presence of the weapons significantly affected the number of shocks given by the subject when the subject had received seven shocks. A Duncan multiple-range test was then made of the differences among the seven conditions means, using the error variance from a seven-group one-way analysis of variance in the error term. The mean number of shocks administered in each experimental condition and the Duncan test results are given in Table 2. The hypothesis guiding the present study receives good support. The strongly provoked men delivered more frequent electrical attacks upon their tormentor in the presence of a weapon than when nonaggressive objects (the badminton racquet and shuttlecocks) were present or when only the shock key was on the table. The angered subjects gave the greatest number of shocks in the presence of the weapons associated with the anger instigator, as predicted, but this group was not reliably different from the angered–unassociated-weapons conditions. Both of these groups expressing aggression in the presence of weapons were significantly more aggressive than the angered–neutral-object condition, but only the associated-weapons condition differed significantly from the angered–no-object group.

Some support for the present reasoning is also provided by the shock-duration data summarized in Table 3. (We

TABLE 1   Analysis of Variance Results for Number of Shocks Given by Subjects in Factorial Design

Source	df	MS	F
No. shocks received (A)	1	182.04	104.62*
Weapons association (B)	2	1.90	1.09
A × B	2	8.73	5.02*
Error	84	1.74	

*p < .01

TABLE 2   Mean Number of Shocks Given in Each Condition

Condition	Shocks received	
	1	7
Associated weapons	2.60$_a$	6.07$_d$
Unassociated weapons	2.20$_a$	5.67$_{cd}$
No object	3.07$_a$	4.67$_{bc}$
Badminton racquets	—	4.60$_b$

Note: Cells having a common subscript are not significantly different at the .05 level by Duncan multiple-range test. There were 10 subjects in the seven-shocks-received–badminton-racquets group and 15 subjects in each of the other conditions.

might note here, before beginning, that the results with duration scores—and this has been a consistent finding in the present research program—are less clear-cut than the findings with number of shocks given.) The results indicate that the presence of weapons resulted in a decreased number of attacks upon the partner, although not significantly so, when the subjects had received only one shock beforehand. The condition differences are in the opposite direction, however, for the men given the stronger provocation. Consequently, even though there are no reliable differences among the groups in this angered condition, the angered men administering shocks in the presence of weapons gave significantly longer shocks than the nonangered men also giving shocks with guns lying on the table. The angered–neutral-object and angered–no-object groups, on the other hand, did not differ from the nonangered–no-object condition.

Mood Changes

Analyses of covariance were conducted on each of the mood scales, with the mood ratings made immediately after the subjects received their partners' evaluation held constant in order to determine if there were condition differences in mood changes following the giving of shocks to the partner. Duncan range tests of the adjusted condition means yielded negative results, suggesting that the attacks on the partner did not produce any systematic condition differences. In the case of the felt anger ratings, there were very high correlations between the ratings given before and after the shock administration, with the Pearson *rs* ranging from .89 in the angered–unassociated-weapons group to .99 in each of the three unangered conditions. The subjects could have felt constrained to repeat their initial responses.

DISCUSSION

Common sense, as well as a good deal of personality theorizing both influenced to some extent by an egocentric view of human behavior as being caused almost exclusively by motives within the individual, generally neglect the type of weapons effect demonstrated in the present study. If a person holding a gun fires it, we are told either that he wanted to do so (consciously or unconsciously) or that he pulled the trigger "accidentally." The findings summarized here suggest yet another possibility: The presence of the weapon might have elicited an intense aggressive reaction from the person with the gun, assuming his inhibitions against aggression were relatively weak at the moment. Indeed, it is altogether conceivable that many hostile acts which supposedly stem from unconscious motivation really arise because of the operation of aggressive cues. Not realizing how these situational stimuli might elicit aggressive behavior, and not detecting the presence of these cues, the observer tends to locate the source of the action in some conjectured underlying, perhaps repressed, motive. Similarly, if he is a Skinnerian rather than a dynamically oriented clinician, he might also neglect the operation of aggression-eliciting stimuli by invoking the concept of operant behavior, and thus sidestep the issue altogether. The sources of the hostile action, for him, too, rest within the individual, with the behavior only steered or permitted by discriminative stimuli.

Alternative explanations must be ruled out, however, before the present thesis can be regarded as confirmed. One obvious possibility is that the subjects in the weapons condition reacted to the demand characteristics of the situation as they saw them and exhibited the kind of behavior they thought was required of them. ("These guns on the table mean I'm supposed to be aggressive, so I'll give many shocks.") Several considerations appear to negate this

TABLE 3   Mean Total Duration of Shocks Given in Each Condition

Condition	Shocks received	
	1	7
Associated weapons	17.93$_c$	46.93$_a$
Unassociated weapons	17.33$_c$	39.47$_{ab}$
No object	24.47$_{bc}$	34.80$_{ab}$
Badminton racquets	—	34.90$_{ab}$

Note: The duration scores are in thousandths of a minute. Cells having a common subscript are not significantly different at the .05 level by Duncan multiple-range test. There were 10 subjects in the seven-shocks-received–badminton-racquet group and 15 subjects in each of the other conditions.

explanation. First, there are the subjects' own verbal reports. None of the subjects voiced any suspicions of the weapons and, furthermore, when they were queried generally denied that the weapons had any effect on them. But even those subjects who did express any doubts about the experiment typically acted like the other subjects. Thus, the eight nonangered-weapons subjects who had been rejected gave only 2.50 shocks on the average, while the 18 angered–no-object or neutral-object men who had been discarded had a mean of 4.50 shocks. The 12 angered-weapon subjects who had been rejected, by contrast, delivered an average of 5.83 shocks to their partner. These latter people were evidently also influenced by the presence of weapons.

Setting all this aside, moreover, it is not altogether certain from the notion of demand characteristics that only the angered subjects would be inclined to act in conformity with the experimenter's supposed demands. The nonangered men in the weapons group did not display a heightened number of attacks on their partner. Would this have been predicted beforehand by researchers interested in demand characteristics? The last finding raises one final observation. Recent unpublished research by Allen and Bragg indicates that awareness of the experimenter's purpose does not necessarily result in an increased display of the behavior the experimenter supposedly desires. Dealing with one kind of socially disapproved action (conformity), Allen and Bragg demonstrated that high levels of experimentally induced awareness of the experimenter's interests generally produced a decreased level of the relevant behavior. Thus, if the subjects in our study had known the experimenter was interested in observing their *aggressive* behavior, they might well have given less, rather than more, shocks, since giving shocks is also socially disapproved. This type of phenomenon was also not observed in the weapons conditions.

Nevertheless, any one experiment cannot possibly definitely exclude all of the alternative explanations. Scientific hypotheses are only probability statements, and further research is needed to heighten the likelihood that the present reasoning is correct.

REFERENCES

Anonymous. A gun-toting nation. *Time*, August 12, 1966.

Berkowitz, L. *Aggression: A social psychological analysis.* New York: McGraw-Hill, 1962.

Berkowitz, L. Aggressive cues in aggressive behavior and hostility catharsis. *Psychological Review*, 1964, 71, 104–122.

Berkowitz, L. The concept of aggressive drive: Some additional considerations. In L. Berkowitz (Ed.), *Advances in experimental social psychology.* Vol. 2. New York: Academic Press, 1965. Pp. 301–329.

Berkowitz, L., & Geen, R. G. Film violence and the cue properties of available targets. *Journal of Personality and Social Psychology*, 1966, 3, 525–530.

Berkowitz, L., & Geen, R. G. Stimulus qualities of the target of aggression: A further study. *Journal of Personality and Social Psychology*, 1967, 5, 364–368.

Buss, A. *The psychology of aggression.* New York: Wiley, 1961.

Easterbrook, J. A. The effect of emotion on cue utilization and the organization of behavior. *Psychological Review*, 1959, 66, 183–201.

Geen, R. G., & Berkowitz, L. Name-mediated aggressive cue properties. *Journal of Personality*, 1966, 34, 456–465.

Loew, C. A. Acquisition of a hostile attitude and its relationship to aggressive behavior. Unpublished doctoral dissertation, State University of Iowa, 1965.

Walters, R. H., & Parke, R. D. Social motivation, dependency, and susceptibility to social influence. In L. Berkowitz (Ed.), *Advances in experimental social psychology.* Vol. 1. New York: Academic Press, 1964. Pp. 231–276.

NOTES

1. Cognitive processes can play a part even in impulsive behavior, most notably by influencing the stimulus qualities (or meaning) of the objects in the situation. As only one illustration, in several experiments by the senior author (cf. Berkowitz, 1965) the name applied to the available target person affected the magnitude of the attacks directed against this individual by angered subjects.

2. Buss (1961) has advanced a somewhat similar conception of the functioning of anger.

3. This information evidently was the major source of suspicion; some of the subjects doubted that a student running an experiment would be used as a subject in another study, even if he were only an undergraduate. This information was provided only in the associated-weapons conditions, in order to connect the guns with the partner, and, consequently, this ground for suspicion was not present in the unassociated-weapons groups.

(Received October 5, 1966)

CRITICAL THINKING QUESTIONS

1. What were the separate roles played by anger and by the presence of weapons in eliciting aggressive responses? How did the combination of anger and the presence of weapons affect subjects' responses?

2. Do you think the results would have been different if the confederates had been women rather than men? If the subjects had been women rather than men? If the subjects and confederates had been of different races? Why do you think these variations would, or

would not, have made a difference? Could these differences, or lack of differences, be explained by the theoretical and empirical discussions presented in this reading?

3. What implications does this research have for the debates about gun control? That is, does the research suggest that the prevalence of weapons should increase the likelihood of aggressive behavior? Why or why not?

4. What implications, if any, does this research have for the issue of media depictions of violence?

5. Other than the presence of availability of weapons, what aggression-eliciting cues are there in your environment? Should policies be adopted to reduce the prevalence of such cues?

6. In what ways is this research consistent with the social learning theory discussed in Chapter 8? In what ways is this research consistent and inconsistent with the original formulation of the frustration-aggression hypothesis?

READING 8

We chose this article because it clearly describes an important program of research that relates alcohol use to several aspects of social psychology. Since alcohol use and abuse are a prevalent part of our lives, it seemed appropriate to examine its effects on social psychological phenomena. The article notes that although many people enjoy drinking alcohol and its effects are not all bad, its effects on our perceptions and thinking can be a two-headed monster. The myopia that alcohol creates can lead to destructive behavior as well as addiction.

This article is particularly relevant to Chapters 7 and 8 because it describes how alcohol can lead to increased helping and how it can lead to destructive aggression. The effects of alcohol on self-awareness and self-enhancement, concepts discussed in Chapter 2, are also discussed in this article. Those students with interests in clinical psychology should note the relevance that social psychology can have for clinical issues.

This article describes a program of research rather than one or a few studies in detail, and so it is slightly different than most of the articles in this reader. That is, it covers more studies than most of the articles, but it covers them at a more general level of detail. If you are interested in learning more about the specifics of any of the studies described, we encourage you to find the citations in the reference section and read the relevant articles.

Alcohol Myopia: Its Prized and Dangerous Effects

Claude M. Steele and Robert A. Josephs
University of Michigan

This article explains how alcohol makes social responses more extreme, enhances important self-evaluations, and relieves anxiety and depression, effects that underlie both the social destructiveness of alcohol and the reinforcing effects that make it an addictive substance. The theories are based on alcohol's impairment of perception and thought— the myopia it causes—rather than on the ability of alcohol's pharmacology to directly cause specific reactions or on expectations associated with alcohol's use. Three conclusions are offered (a) Alcohol makes social behaviors more extreme by blocking a form of response conflict. (b) The same process can inflate self-evaluations. (c) Alcohol myopia, in combination with distracting activity, can reliably reduce anxiety and depression in all drinkers by making it difficult to allocate attention to the thoughts that provoke these states. These theories are discussed in terms of their significance for the prevention and treatment of alcohol abuse.

Alcohol abuse has become the nation's most costly health problem. This has happened largely because, as a threat to public health, alcohol is a two-headed beast; it causes behaviors that are destructive of others and society, on one hand, and holds millions in the grip of addiction, on the other. As a source of antisocial behavior, alcohol is implicated in nearly 70% of fatal automobile accidents, 65% of murders, 88% of knifings, 65% of spouse battering, 55% of violent child abuse, 60% of burglaries, and so on, causing the National Commission on the Causes and Prevention of Violence (1970) to conclude that "no other psychoactive substance is associated with violent crimes, suicide, and automobile accidents more than alcohol" (p. 641). For some individuals, of course, drinking alcohol becomes something they cannot control—the other head of the beast. In 1985, nearly 10.5 million people in the United States were addicted to alcohol (Williams, Stinson, Parker, Harford, & Noble, 1987). We hasten to point out, however, that alcohol is not all bad. Most drinkers know that it can be a social lubricant, and as we show later, even a spur to altruism. Still, the price we pay for these benefits, as individuals and as a society, is frequently disastrous. When the cost of lost production, crime, and accidents due to alcohol are totaled and added to the cost of treating alcohol addiction—both heads of the beast—the bill comes to over $117 billion a year (U.S. Department of Health and Human Services, 1987).

SOURCE: Claude M. Steele and Robert A. Josephs, "Alcohol Myopia: Its Prized and Dangerous Effects," *American Psychologist*, August 1990, Vol. 45, No. 8, 921–933. Copyright © 1990 by the American Psychological Association. Reprinted with permission.

In explaining how alcohol has these socially significant effects, a straightforward idea has dominated the thinking of laymen and scientists alike: Such effects stem directly from the pharmacological properties of alcohol, much the way relaxation stems from the pharmacological properties of valium. We know, for example, that people often drink alcohol to get the effects they assume it will directly cause: relaxation, a better mood, courage, social ease, and so on (e.g., Goldman, Brown, & Christiansen, 1987; Leigh, 1989; Maisto, Connors, & Sachs, 1981). This idea explains both heads of the beast; some of these direct effects, such as aggression and hostility, can be socially destructive, and others, such as relaxation and tension reduction, are reinforcing enough to make alcohol a potentially addictive substance. In recent years we have learned that drinking can have effects that are mediated not by alcohol but by the self-fulfillment of expectations about alcohol's effects or by the use of drinking to excuse reprehensible behavior (cf. Critchlow, 1986; Marlatt & Rohsenow, 1980). Still, we know that alcohol has profound social psychological effects that are independent of expectancy effects—a fact demonstrated throughout the literature (cf. Hull & Bond, 1986; Steele & Southwick, 1985) and in the self-destructiveness of many real-life alcohol effects. In explanation of such true alcohol effects, the idea persists that they stem *directly* from the pharmacological properties of the drug.

As research has accumulated, however, this idea has had to face a frustrating fact: Alcohol's effects on human social behaviors and emotions vary widely and are highly irregular. Studies show that alcohol intoxication can make us frighteningly aggressive (e.g., Zeichner & Phil, 1979, 1980) yet more altruistic (e.g., Steele, Critchlow, & Liu, 1985); it can relieve stressful anxiety and tension (e.g., Levenson, Sher, Grossman, Newman, & Newlin, 1980; Polivy, Schueneman, & Carlson, 1976) yet also increase anxiety and tension (e.g., Abrams & Wilson, 1979; Keane & Lisman, 1980); it can inflate our egos (e.g., Banaji & Steele, 1989) yet lead to "crying-in-one's beer" depression (e.g., Josephs & Steele, 1990; Steele & Josephs, 1988); and so on. Some of this variability could stem from alcohol having different effects on different people, that is, from individual differences in reactivity to alcohol. Distinctive physiological (cf. Schuckit, 1987) and personality-based (e.g., Hull, Young, & Jouriles, 1986) reactions to alcohol have been documented. But because alcohol can affect the social behaviors and emotions of all drinkers, not just those with special reactivities, such differences cannot explain the variability of these effects in the vast majority of drinkers. Nor can such differences explain the variability in these effects within drinkers (i.e., that alcohol has these effects on any one person only irregularly). In their influential book, *Drunken Comportment*, MacAndrew and Edgerton (1969) put it this way:

> The same man, in the same bar, drinking approximately the same amount of alcohol, may, on three nights running, be, say, surly and belligerent on the first evening, the spirit of amiability on the second, and morose and withdrawn on the third. (p. 15)

Thus, a basic puzzle remains: How can this single drug, aside from the effects of drinking expectancies and individual differences in reactivity to alcohol, have such varied and irregular social psychological effects?

In addressing this puzzle, Steele and his colleagues (e.g., Steele & Josephs, 1988; Steele & Southwick, 1985) have been led consistently to a particular kind of explanation. They see these effects as stemming from alcohol's general impairment of perception and thought—an effect of alcohol that occurs in every person every time alcohol is consumed. In the theories that follow, alcohol intoxication is viewed as affecting social behavior and emotion largely through an interaction of the *myopia* it causes—the short-sighted information processing that is part of alcohol intoxication—and the nature of the cues impinging on the person during intoxication. These are mixed models in the sense that alcohol's social and emotional effects are attributed to both pharmacological and environmental influences. In the present article, we describe the evolution of this idea in the field and in our work and offer what we hope is a broadened view of how alcohol has the effects it has.

The work of the Steele group has focused on three classes of socially significant alcohol effects: (a) *drunken excess,* alcohol's tendency to make social actions more extreme or excessive—the transformation, for example, of socially hesitant persons into friendly backslappers, or a person well informed about the health risks of promiscuity into a sexual risk taker; (b) *drunken self-inflation,* its ability to inflate our egos and enable us sometimes to view ourselves through rosier glasses; and (c) *drunken relief,* its ability, under some conditions, to relieve psychological stresses such as depression and anxiety. These effects of the drug underlie both heads of the alcohol beast; that drunken excess is the source of much of the social destructiveness caused by alcohol and that the other two effects, drunken self-inflation and relief, are powerful reinforcers that may underlie, to a significant degree, alcohol's addictiveness. We turn first to alcohol's effect on social behavior.

PSYCHOLOGY OF DRUNKEN EXCESS: ROLE OF INHIBITION CONFLICT

Alcohol intoxication frequently makes people aggress more, self-disclose more, gamble more, be more amorously or socially assertive, and so on, than they would if they were sober. That alcohol can cause these effects is reliable fact (cf. Hull & Bond, 1986; Pernanen, 1976; Steele & Southwick, 1985). These are the prized and dangerous effects of the drug. And as we noted earlier, it is possible to rule out or rule as incomplete, several explanations for this drunken excess. Alcohol cannot be a direct cause of such effects because if it were, they would occur every time anyone takes a drink. Also, having a special reactivity to alcohol could not be the sole cause of such excess inasmuch as alcohol has these effects in all drinkers, not just the small subpopulation of drinkers with special reactivities. Finally, all drunken excess could not be mediated by drinking expectancies (i.e., the self-fulfillment of how one believes alcohol will make one behave or the use of drinking to excuse excessive behaviors). Research shows that alcohol has these effects even when expectancies are controlled for (cf. Hull & Bond, 1986; Steele & Southwick, 1985); also, it just does not make sense that such real-life drunken excesses as gambling away one's fortune, engaging in risky sex, or assaulting and even killing people one loves, could occur from drinking expectancies alone. As these possibilities are ruled out, however, the basic question reemerges: Through what process or processes does alcohol itself cause such excess?

In answer to this question, a line of reasoning began to emerge: Perhaps alcohol can cause excessive social behaviors indirectly, by somehow preventing the drinker from responding normally to impinging cues. In this view, the kind of behavior that occurs during intoxication reflects, in largest part, the nature of the external and internal cues impinging on the person, rather than on a specific pharmacological capacity of the drug or on some special reactivity of the drinker. Thus, whether the same drunk is surly and belligerent one night, and the spirit of amiability the next depends significantly on the cues that influence behavior and emotion during intoxication, cues that vary from person to person, occasion to occasion, and culture to culture. But what exactly is the nature of the alcohol impairment that essentially lets circumstantial cues have freer reign over behavior?

The answer seems to be an impairment of perception and thought. That alcohol intoxication impairs these functions is documented in the experience of even casual drinkers and in research showing that alcohol intoxication impairs nearly every aspect of information processing: the ability to abstract and conceptualize (e.g., Kastl, 1969; Tarter, Jones, Simpson, & Vega, 1971), the ability to encode large numbers of situational cues (e.g., Washburne, 1956), the ability to use several cues at the same time (Medina, 1970; Moskowitz & Depry, 1968), the use of active and systematic encoding strategies (Rosen & Lee, 1976), the cognitive elaboration needed to encode meaning from incoming information (e.g., Birnbaum, Johnson, Hartley & Taylor, 1980), and so on. But two general impairments are most critical in this line of thinking.

1. Alcohol intoxication consistently restricts the range of cues that we can perceive in a situation. When we are drunk we simply attend to and encode fewer available cues, internal as well as external.

2. Alcohol intoxication reduces our ability to process and extract meaning from the cues and information we do perceive. When we are drunk we are less able to elaborate incoming information, to relate it to existing knowledge, and thereby to extract meaning from it. (See Huntley, 1973, and Schneider, Dumais, & Shiffrin, 1984, for particularly good illustrations of these two alcohol impairment effects.) Like the bar mitzvah food in an old Woody Allen joke, the information we receive when we are drunk is bad and there isn't enough of it. Alcohol makes us the captive of an impoverished version of reality in which the breadth, depth, and time line of our understanding is constrained. It causes what we have called an *alcohol myopia,* a state of shortsightedness in which superficially understood, immediate aspects of experience have a disproportionate influence on behavior and emotion, a state in which we can see the tree, albeit more dimly, but miss the forest altogether.

The first researchers to explain a social effect of alcohol in these terms were interested in the relation of alcohol to human aggression (cf. Pernanen, 1976; Taylor & Leonard, 1983; Zeichner & Phil, 1979). Their argument was as follows: Alcohol limits one's perceiving and thinking so as to leave one still able to respond to salient, immediate cues, but less able (than if one were sober) to respond to more peripheral cues and embedded meanings. Therefore, when the salient cues elicit violence and the peripheral ones inhibit it, alcohol intoxication releases violence.

Here is a laboratory example: Zeichner and Phil (1979) recruited male subjects, for a pain-perception/reaction-time experiment and after allowing them to ingest either alcohol or placebo drinks, they gave each subject a noxious tone (through earphones) that subjects believed was delivered by another "partner" subject. The actual subject was to stop the tone by giving the partner an electric shock as fast as possible. The intensity and duration of this retaliation measured subjects' aggression. The partner, of course, was not a real person but a computer that in the critical condition, matched the subjects' shock with a second noxious tone of equal intensity and duration—an "eye-for-an-eye." Clearly, the smart thing to do in this condition would be to give one's partner only a mild shock, and then one would get only a mild tone in return. But to be smart, one has to be mindful of the tone contingency. In a nutshell, the sober subjects played it smart, giving very little shock in this eye-for-an-eye condition, whereas the intoxicated subjects plunged ahead, giving nearly three times as much shock. Presumably, the myopia experienced by the intoxicated subjects allowed them access to the provoking stimuli, because of their immediacy and salience, but blurred their appreciation of the delayed inhibiting contingencies, allowing them to be more aggressive than their sober cohorts by a factor of 7 standard deviations.

If this reasoning could explain the relation of alcohol to human aggression, Steele and his colleagues (cf. Steele et al., 1985; Steele & Southwick, 1985) reasoned that it might explain alcohol's effect on other social behaviors as well. Alcohol might foster helping, for example, not through any special capacity to make people helpful and warm toward their fellow man, but simply because it places people under the control of immediate cues capable of eliciting helpfulness. Through the myopia it causes, alcohol may tie us to a roller-coaster ride of immediate impulses arising from whatever cues are salient.

But something is missing from this picture. It explains how alcohol can have varied social effects, but it doesn't explain when they will occur. What is missing is the identity of some factor, or set of factors, that determines the occurrence of drunken excess. To address this problem, Steele and his colleagues (Steele et al., 1985; Steele & Southwick, 1985) tried to identify the kind of situation in which alcohol myopia would lead to excess. This led to the hypothesis that it would do this in situations that, if the person were sober, would involve a certain response conflict, *inhibition conflict,* in which a response provoked by salient, strong cues is also inhibited by other strong cues that require further processing to grasp. The aforementioned aggression procedure illustrates this conflict. The provoking tone, at the moment it occurred, was more salient to the subject than the idea that his aggression would be retaliated against, an idea that at that moment required further processing to access. Our reasoning is this: If one is sober in this kind of situation, the salient, provoking cues can move one to respond, yet one can also search out, become aware of, and understand other now-relevant cues that might inhibit the response (i.e., possible

negative consequences, relevant inhibiting standards of conduct, inhibiting cues in the situation, other more appropriate responses, etc.). As a result, one can hold back the response. If one is intoxicated in this situation, however, the resulting myopia allows the influence of salient provoking cues but reduces the influence of inhibiting cues and meanings, many of which require further processing to access. In this sense, the inhibition conflict is preempted, or blocked. As a result, alcohol leads to excess. What we can't see or appreciate, we can't use, and when alcohol intoxication prevents us from using cues that might otherwise inhibit a response, we respond more extremely.

The other equally important part of this idea is the implication that alcohol intoxication does not generally lead to excess in situations that do not involve this kind of conflict. In situations without these conflicting response pressures—in which cues provoking the response are weak, or cues inhibiting the response are weak, or both sets of cues are weak—the myopia that alcohol causes will not change the balance of pressures bearing on the response. (It would only block inhibiting cues that are already weak or weaken inhibition against a response tendency that was weak to begin with.) In these situations, drunk people should behave no more extremely than sober people. The point here is that whether alcohol intoxication results in drunken excess can depend in large part on the situational strength of a simple condition—inhibition conflict.

Consider this real-life example. You have just had an angering argument with your landlord, the kind of argument that makes you want to take his head off on sight. As you are milling around at a neighborhood cocktail party that evening, you turn from the eggplant dip to the wine table and encounter him face to face. If you are sober in this situation, you should experience the kind of response conflict we are describing. The salient cue of his presence will provoke in you an impulse to tell him off on the spot, yet with just an instance's further consideration you realize that if you do this you will cause a terrible scene, embarrass yourself, and maybe even get evicted the next day. Thus, you grit your teeth and hold in your tirade. Our point is that this kind of situation—characterized by such conflicting response pressures—can trigger drunken excess. Thus, if you should encounter your landlord after being three or four drinks into the evening, his presence, as a salient cue, should still provoke your anger, but the myopia that alcohol causes should reduce your access to the negative consequences of telling him off. As a result, a legendary scene erupts and the next day you are homeless.

Let us say now that you are not angry at your landlord or that you are vacating your apartment anyway and nobody is left at the party when you encounter him. Neither of these situations would involve inhibition conflict. Either there is no salient cue provoking your anger or there are no consequences to be accessed that would inhibit your anger if you wanted to express it. In situations like these, the myopia that alcohol causes will not change the balance of pressures bearing on the response and you should behave pretty much the same way drunk or sober. If you are not angry at him, the mere myopia of alcohol intoxication would not make you tell him off for no reason; of if you are angry at him but have nothing to lose from a tirade, you would probably tell him off even without the aid of alcohol.

To summarize, the central assumption of this reasoning is that alcohol myopia restricts attention and thought to the most salient cues in a setting, whatever they may be, and that this is a general process through which alcohol influences social behavior. In this process, the primary determinants of social behavior during intoxication, as during sobriety, are the internal and external cues that become salient to the actor (rather than specific pharmacological effects of alcohol or special alcohol reactivities of some drinkers). Sometimes these will be cues that provoke only a weak response, and not much will happen; sometimes these will even be cues capable of inhibiting a response;[1] and sometimes, of course, these will be strong response-provoking cues. Even then, alcohol intoxication may add little to the extremeness of the response. If there are few inhibiting pressures that further processing would access, then alcohol's impairment of this processing will do little to make the response more extreme. But when further processing would access inhibiting pressures, the myopia of alcohol intoxication should occlude these pressures, disinhibiting the response. It is this latter kind of situation that we call *inhibition conflict.*

One more consideration: The amount one drinks should also make a difference; 12 drinks would probably have greater effect on one's behavior at the cocktail party than would 3. This is because alcohol's impairment of perceptual and cognitive functioning—that is, alcohol myopia—increases with dosage (e.g., Jones & Vega, 1972). The greater the myopia, the more thoroughly peripheral cues and embedded meanings will be occluded from awareness and the greater should be alcohol's disinhibiting effect in conflict situations.

If this reasoning is correct, it should be possible to find support among existing studies of alcohol's effect on social behavior. To this end, Steele and Southwick (1985) identified every study, published or unpublished, that had ever tested the effect of alcohol on some human social

behavior. They came up with 34 studies in all, and from these they compiled a set of 121 comparisons of treatment conditions in which all factors were equal, except that one group in the comparison got alcohol and the other one did not. Their expectation, of course, was that in comparisons for which the social response was under strong inhibition conflict, alcohol would have a large effect, in the sense that intoxicated subjects would respond more extremely than the sober subjects in the comparison, but that under weak conflict conditions, alcohol would have little or no effect—and also, that this tendency would increase with the level of alcohol in subjects' blood.

We believe that anyone who is familiar with the conflict idea could glance at the method sections of these studies and tell that inhibition conflict varied considerably from one experimental condition to the next. In the aggression studies, for example, many conditions established intense inhibition conflict of the sort we have described, but others established clearly weak conflict, as when subjects were neither provoked to aggress nor inhibited from doing so. In gambling studies, betting was sometimes under the strong conflict of large possible gains and large possible losses, yet in other conditions it was under the weak conflict of large possible gains and only small possible losses (e.g., a cheap raffle ticket). Still, not anticipating our theory, none of these studies had explicitly manipulated conflict. Thus, the classification of alcohol effects, whether the response involved was under strong or weak inhibition conflict, had to be one of judgment. It turned out, however, that these judgments could be made with great reliability. Steele and Southwick (1985) agreed in their ratings of conflict for 96% of the comparisons. And for a subsample of 60 comparisons, their judgments agreed with 83% of those made by independent judges who, blind to the hypothesis and the results of the studies, used their own coding rules. One more technical point: The dependent variable for each comparison was how much more extreme the behavior of alcohol subjects was compared with that of the no-alcohol subjects. To use a scale common to all comparisons, these differences were expressed in standard deviation units—in essence, how many standard deviations more extreme were the intoxicated subjects than were their sober control subjects.

It will probably surprise no one to learn that intoxicated subjects were generally more extreme than their sober control subjects, 0.69 standard deviation over the entire set of comparisons. They gambled more, looked longer at sexual slides, gave more shock to their opponents, self-disclosed more, and so on. In strong support of our theory, however, these effects varied dramatically with the level of inhibition conflict of the response. Intoxicated subjects were a full standard deviation more extreme than their sober counterparts ($M = 1.06$) under strong conflict and only nonsignificant 0.10 standard deviation more extreme ($M = 0.14$) under weak conflict. Figure 1 presents mean alcohol effects broken down by conflict and degree of intoxication. Here the powerful mediating effect of conflict is even clearer. When conflict was strong and intoxicated subjects had blood alcohol levels (BALs) above .06, they were a full 1.4 standard deviations more extreme than their sober control subjects. In percentage terms they were, on average, more extreme than 95% of the control subjects. Even at low levels of intoxication, strong conflict led to significant alcohol effects ($M = 0.38$). Clearly though, it is the combination of strong inhibition conflict and higher BAL that caused whatever extreme drunken excess was evidenced in these studies.

Table 1 breaks down alcohol effect sizes by level of conflict and type of social behavior and shows that the pattern of bigger alcohol effects under strong conflict holds for all but two of the social behaviors studied.[2] Also, an analysis of expectancy effects in this literature—the difference between subjects who believed they had consumed alcohol and those who believed they had not, all other factors held constant—showed that unlike real alcohol effects, expectancy effects did not vary with rated conflict. This result, presented in Figure 2, makes an important point: Even though expectancy effects are substantial—people

TABLE 1   Effect Size Means by Level of Conflict and Type of Social Behavior

Type of social behavior	Conflict level			
	High		**Low**	
	M	**n**	**M**	**n**
Aggression	1.32	32	0.17	30
Assertiveness	—	—	0.54	1
Human conflict	0.89	1	0.01	3
Drinking	0.88	2	−0.38	8
Eating	0.02	3	0.58	3
Gambling	0.38	2	0.05	6
Mirth	—	—	0.10	6
Moral judgment	—	—	−0.17	2
Risk taking	0.48	2	0.66	3
Self-disclosure	1.34	3	0.07	4
Sexual interest	0.42	4	−0.06	4
Yielding	—	—	0.29	2

Note: Ms are not given for cells of the table for which there is only one effect size.

who believed they had consumed alcohol behaved almost 0.50 standard deviation more extreme than did people who believed they had not—they cannot explain the pattern of alcohol effects. That is, because expectancy effects do not vary with conflict, they could not have mediated, in any way, the observed relation between alcohol effects and conflict.

There is a gratifying thoroughness about meta-analysis; but in the end, largely because conflict had to be judged post hoc, this one could not stand as a test of the conflict idea, although it was encouraging. Also, aggression studies dominate this analysis, as they do the literature in general, raising some question about how well these findings represent alcohol's effect on the full range of social behaviors.

Thus, to test the idea experimentally and to examine its generalizability, Steele et al. (1985) tested the effect of alcohol on helping, a frequently conflictual prosocial behavior. They created a situation in the laboratory that was a little like being asked by a friend to stay and help paint after you'd already helped him move in all day. Subjects crossed out *a*s and *e*s in a paragraph of legal jargon for as many repetitions as they could do in 17 min. Then, just as they expected to relax for the remaining 25 min of the experiment, the experimenter appealed to each of them to help by doing more repetitions. This merciless procedure, it was assumed, would establish a strong conflict between the impulse to help (aroused by the immediate, urgent, face-to-face appeal) and a strong desire not to do any more of this

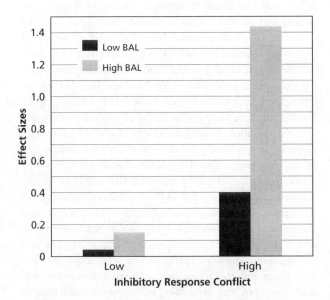

FIGURE 1   Alcohol Effect Sizes by Level of Inhibition Conflict and Blood Alcohol Level (BAL)

boring task. A weak conflict condition was established by only weakly pressuring subjects to help (through a written appeal at the bottom of a questionnaire). One half of the subjects had consumed enough alcohol before the proof-reading task to bring their BALs to .04 at the time of the request, whereas the other half had consumed only a pla-cebo drink. It was expected, of course, that alcohol would increase helping in the strong conflict condition but not in the weak conflict condition, and that is exactly what happened. Over two experiments, this basic procedure was varied to test whether merely believing that one had con-sumed alcohol would increase helping—it didn't—and whether the effect of conflict was robust over slightly different BALs and operational definitions—it was.

Illustrating the real-world generality of the drinking–helping relationship, Lynn (1988) found that as patrons in a Columbus, Ohio restaurant drank more alcohol, they gave bigger tips—clearly an otherwise conflicted act of helping—even when the size of the check was held constant. As far as conflicted helping is concerned, alcohol is apparently a milk of human kindness.

We believe this evidence clarifies several things about social drunkenness. First, it identifies an important process through which alcohol contributes to these effects. *As far as drunken comportment is concerned, alcohol need not be a direct cause, a releaser of special alcohol reactivities (the devil's potion), or an inconsequential concomitant of drinking expectancy effects, but can affect social behavior by blocking inhibition conflict, that is, by freeing motivated responses from inhibiting cues.* And second, it identifies a

pervasive condition under which alcohol causes drunken excess: in simplest terms, whenever salient cues provoke a person to do something that if he were sober, remoter cues and thoughts would pressure him to inhibit. This evidence makes drunken excess a more predictable phenomenon. If one can specify, even roughly, the degree of inhibition conflict a response is under in a setting, one can predict the extent to which alcohol intoxication is likely to make it excessive. The research we have described shows that, for the most part, this is a rather straightforward speci-fication, both with regard to judging existing situations (the meta-analysis) and with regard to constructing situa-tions that manipulate the level of this conflict (the helping experiments).[3, 4]

With respect to the generalizability of these conclusions, an interesting fact about alcohol's effect on rat learning is worth noting: Alcohol seems to impair this learning only in paradigms that involve response conflict (cf. Brown, Mans-field, & Skurdal, 1980; Cappell & Herman, 1972; Gray, 1978). In the passive-avoidance paradigm, for example, in which the rat must learn to inhibit a tendency to approach a punishing goal area, or in the extinction paradigm in which the animal must learn to inhibit dominant responses so that new ones can be learned, alcohol consistently re-tards learning by impairing inhibition. Drunk rats in these paradigms plunge ahead, following their immediate im-pulses, regardless of the consequences. Sober rats play it safe. Yet in nonconflictual, instrumental learning paradigms in which the animal simply has to initiate a response to gain reward or avoid or terminate punishment, it is sur-prising that alcohol has no consistent effect. Thus, just like its effect on human social behavior, alcohol seems to impair rat learning through the particular effect of impair-ing the animal's ability to hold back motivated responses in light of conflicting pressures. We have no idea whether this impairment happens in rats the same way it does in people. For the rat data, Gray preferred the physiological explana-tion that alcohol changes the electrical activity in an area of the brain specifically linked to inhibitory control. Brown et al., however, offered evidence that alcohol has this conflict-reducing effect by reducing the influence of the weakest response tendency in these conflicts, regardless of whether it is excitatory or inhibitory. They show that alcohol can actually increase inhibition in circumstances in which inhibition cues are stronger than excitatory cues, and among several possible explanations, suggest that alcohol "interferes with the organism's ability to attend simultane-ously to sets of cues demanding incompatible behaviors, so that only the more salient ones are effectively processed" (p. 430)—a view indistinguishable from our notion of

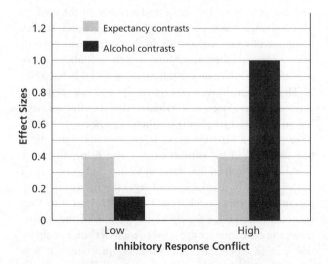

FIGURE 2   Alcohol and Drinking Expectancy Effect Sizes by Level of Inhibition Conflict

myopia. Thus, the important suggestion of these data, which supports the generalizability of our findings and theory, is that alcohol affects rat conflict behavior in much the same way it affects human conflict behavior. It frees responses initiated by the most salient cues from the conflicting pressures of less salient cues, and it may do this in both species through the myopic processing it causes.

Another point worth stressing is the demonstration in the present work of alcohol's own influence on human social behaviors. This may seem painfully obvious. Nonetheless, in recent years, estimates of alcohol's role in causing drunken excess have trended downward. When tests of these effects are aggregated without regard to conflict, the overall social impact of alcohol appears surprisingly modest. This could be seen in our own meta-analysis. And the same result in several recent reviewers of the balanced-placebo literature (Critchlow, 1986; Hull & Bond, 1986; Marlatt & Rohsenow, 1980; Reinarman & Leigh, 1987) led reviews to conclude that alcohol has consistent effects on nonsocial behaviors (cognitive and motor performance) but that drinking affects social behavior more through the effects of drinking expectancies. As we hope we have shown here, a vastly different picture emerges when alcohol's social effects are broken down by the level of inhibition conflict the response is under. Under conditions of strong conflict, even doses of alcohol that typify just moderate social drinking (i.e., BALs between .06 and .14) have massive effects on social behavior, making intoxicated subjects more extreme than 95% of their sober controls (all of this with drinking expectancies held constant). Under the right conditions, then, very common conditions, alcohol has quite profound influences on these behaviors, influences that explain perhaps more plausibly than do expectancies alcohol's relation to extreme, self-threatening behaviors such as violent crime and risky sex.

DRUNKEN SELF-INFLATION: ALCOHOL AS THE EGO'S ELIXIR

It is possible to make another generalization of alcohol's conflict-blocking effect, one that connects this work more closely to the other head of the alcohol beast, alcohol addiction. Not long ago, Banaji and Steele (1989, 1990) considered whether this effect of alcohol would generalize from the case of simple response conflict to the higher realm of intrapsychic conflicts—in particular, to conflicts over how well to evaluate oneself. Their reasoning began with the long-known fact that people have a powerful need to think positively of themselves, especially along dimensions that are important to them (e.g., Greenwald, 1980;

James, 1915; Steele, 1988; Tesser, 1988). Yet, even when one is in full possession of one's faculties, it can be disappointingly easy to call to mind information that contradicts these desired self-images—establishing, in a real sense, a self-evaluative conflict. Consider the aspiring classical pianist, for example, who wants deeply to view himself as having a great talent but, whenever he begins to think this way, readily accesses deficiencies in his playing and comparisons to others that inhibit this evaluation. This kind of conflict, in some form or another, at one time or another, haunts us all. Banaji and Steele (1989) proposed that through the myopia it causes, alcohol may disinhibit these self-evaluative conflicts. That is, when immediate cues (such as topic of conversation) arouse a strong impulse for a favorable evaluation along some important dimension of the self-concept, alcohol myopia should allow us to experience the impulse and at the same time impair access to more remote, inhibiting information. In this way, alcohol intoxication may inflate our self-evaluations, especially along important dimensions. Thus, when the question of talent arises during intoxication, our aspiring pianist, having less access to his deficiencies, ranks himself as worthy of a recording contract.

To test this idea, Banaji and Steele (1989) had subjects rate the personal importance of 35 trait dimensions and their "real" and "ideal" standing on each dimension, both before and after they were made intoxicated or had consumed a placebo drink—and that was all there was to the study. They found that getting drunk significantly inflated the self, *but only on traits that were both important to subjects and for which, before drinking, they had acknowledged that their "real" self was considerably worse than their "ideal" self.* On these strong-conflict traits (i.e., those five with the largest and most important ideal–real discrepancies on the pretest) intoxicated subjects significantly bettered their ratings of their real selves after drinking, but for weak-conflict traits (i.e., the five smallest and least important ideal–real discrepancies) alcohol had no such effect. Placebo drinks caused no change on any traits (see Figure 3). Also, additional experiments replicated these results and showed that they did not occur because of alcohol's elevation of mood.

On the basis of these data, alcohol causes conceit in much the same way it causes a tirade at a neighborhood cocktail party. It impairs the processing capacity needed to inhibit strong impulses toward these things, impulses aroused by immediate, salient cues, external or internal. The importance of these data to our discussion is their demonstration of the generalizability of alcohol as a conflict disinhibitor and the fact that this capacity of alcohol extends to intrapsychic, self-evaluative conflicts as well as response conflicts.

Herein too is a suggestion of how people can come to have reliable drinking reactions of the sort we know in real life, as for example, a "mean drunk" or a "sentimental drunk," seemingly distinctive individual reactions to alcohol. The reliable experience of certain inhibition conflicts, even intrapsychic ones, in situations in which a person consumes alcohol can cause, through alcohol's disinhibition of these conflicts, reliable drinking reactions. For example, the reliable experience of strong ego needs at gatherings of his colleagues, disinhibited by alcohol, could make our aspiring pianist a reliably egotistical drunk in these settings. This would not occur because of alcohol's pharmacological capacity to cause egotism in general or in people with special alcohol reactivities, but because of alcohol's general ability, through the myopia it causes, to disinhibit otherwise inhibited impulses.

Also, the fact that alcohol can be an elixir for such conflicts suggests that when conflicts become chronic, they may entice alcohol use and, in this way, provide a groundwork for addiction. Alcohol may bring our aspiring pianist so close to his ideal state, for example, as to make the drug powerfully reinforcing psychologically, and if he continues to seek this reinforcement, even physiologically addictive. We now turn to the problem of alcohol addiction.

DRUNKEN RELIEF: ALCOHOL AND THE ALLOCATION OF ATTENTION TO ONE'S WORRIES

As we began to focus on the problem of how alcohol affects psychological stress, we encountered a familiar pattern of highly varied and irregular effects. Alcohol affects a variety of psychological stresses (e.g., anxiety, depression, and fear), and as with social behavior, it does so only intermittently. Sometimes it even increases these stresses (cf. Cappell & Greely, 1987; Steele & Josephs, 1988; Wilson, 1988). But before tackling this puzzle, we offer a word about why it is important.

It should be kept in mind that alcoholism has several causes. Recently, evidence has suggested that some forms of alcoholism have a significant genetic basis (Cloninger, Bohman, & Sigvardsson, 1981; Goodwin 1976, 1979; Petrakis, 1985). The evidence is strongest for early onset alcohol addiction that is associated with a general disposition toward impulsive and antisocial behavior; however, it is important to stress that genes are not the only cause of alcoholism. Estimates of variation in the incidence of alcoholism due to genes—that is, the heritability of alcoholism—range from near 0 to 60%, and recent estimates are closer to 30% (see Searles, 1988, for a thorough review). The important implication, then, is that environmentally induced processes (even allowing for some incidence of alcoholism stemming from Gene × Environment interactions) have the most powerful influence on the development of alcoholism.

And this is where behavioral psychology enters the picture. It proposes that learning is an important source of alcoholism: Alcohol does something that is reinforcing to the individual; this effect increases the frequency of drinking; the drinking response then generalizes to other situations and conditions; tolerance of alcohol eventually develops so that more alcohol is needed to produce the same reinforcing effect; and as the addiction is fully developed,

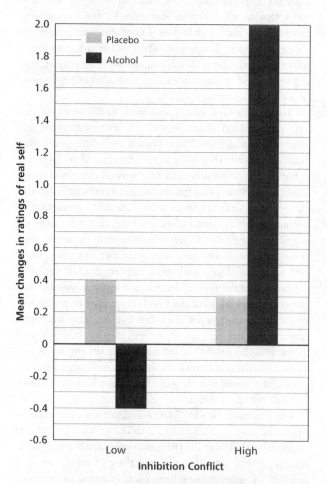

FIGURE 3   Changes in Rating of the Real Self by Conflict Level of the Trait Level of the Trait Dimension and Alcohol

one experiences uncomfortable withdrawal symptoms if drinking is stopped (cf. Bandura, 1969; Marlatt, 1976). The principal reinforcing effect of alcohol is presumed to be relief from psychological stress, stated more generally as *tension* in Conger's (1956) classic tension-reduction hypothesis.

It is this effect that the behavioral etiology of alcohol addiction is presumed to begin, and it is here that the evidence is disturbingly inconsistent. Relevant studies are about equally divided between those reporting a tension-reducing effect of alcohol, those reporting the opposite effect, and those reporting no effect on such varied psychological stresses as social anxiety, depression, and fear (cf. Cappell & Greely, 1987; Marlatt, 1976; Steele & Josephs, 1988; Wilson, 1988).

Thus, a familiar question presented itself: How can the same drug have such varied and irregular effects on psychological stress? Drinking expectancies (cf. Hull & Bond, 1986; Marlatt, 1976) and distinctive individual reactivities to alcohol (cf. Hull et al., 1986; Levenson, Oyama, & Meek, in press; Sher, 1987) again play some role in this variability, but alcohol can have powerful effects on these states even when expectancies are held constant and even among the vast majority of drinkers who have no special reactivity to the drug.

If alcohol myopia could help explain the variability of alcohol's effects on social behavior, might it do the same for alcohol's effects on psychological stress? We came to the idea that as far as the stresses that come from worry are concerned (e.g., anxiety, depression, fear), whether alcohol reduces them in human beings may depend to a significant degree on the single factor of whether the drinker is doing something while he is intoxicated. The reasoning here begins with the central things we know about alcohol myopia: that it restricts attention to the salient, immediate aspects of experience and that it reduces processing capacity so that a greater proportion of this capacity has to be devoted to the demands of immediate, ongoing activity. Thus, when the drinker is doing something that requires attention and thought, alcohol myopia pressures him to attend to and think about that activity over less salient worries. That is, during intoxication, one may simply not have the processing resources to engage in a salient, ongoing activity like watching TV and to brood over one's worries at the same time.

The same idea suggests one condition under which alcohol should increase worry. This should be the case whenever in the absence of distracting activity, troubling thoughts are highly salient and easily understood. Then alcohol's narrowing of perception should focus attention onto these salient worries, and its impairment of thought should make it more difficult to rationalize or in some other way cognitively defend against them, resulting in a crying-in-one's-beer effect.

Let us pursue an example. You get home from work one day worried about the poor raise you received and the continuing atmosphere of underappreciation you suffer. Because it is hot outside you fix yourself a tall gin and tonic to drink while you watch the nightly news. As the alcohol takes hold and as your processing resources become more occupied with the news broadcast, you will probably experience a fading away of your worries, but if you should decide to turn off the news and sit quietly, that same tonic might cause you to cry into it.

Here, then, we have an account of alcohol's effects on psychological stress that suggests how these effects can be so varied and irregular. In this view, alcohol can affect a variety of psychological stresses through its ability to screen out of awareness, in conjunction with activity, a common source of these states, that is, the thoughts that cause them. The variation in these effects, to an important degree, depends on what the drinker is doing while he or she is intoxicated. We have called this reasoning the *attention-allocation model* because it views alcohol and activity as affecting psychological stress by affecting how much attention one can pay to one's worries. It is not, of course, an explanation of alcohol's effect on all stresses, but rather of its effect on psychological stresses that arise from our thinking (e.g., those forms of anxiety, depression, and fear) that are rooted in disturbing thoughts and thought processes. Still, if this reasoning held up to test, it would identify a pervasive reinforcing effect of alcohol, one on which a learning model of addiction could rest quite comfortably. To find out, we tested the effect of alcohol and activity on both anxiety and depression. Because both sets of studies produced similar results and have been published elsewhere (Josephs & Steele, 1990; Steele & Josephs, 1988; Steele, Southwick & Pagano, 1986), we summarize only the anxiety studies to illustrate the general pattern of findings.

In the first of these experiments, intoxicated and sober subjects learned that immediately after a period of 15 minutes they would give a speech on "What I dislike most about my body and physical appearance" to be evaluated by psychology graduate students—a piece of news that, as one might imagine, raised anxiety in sober and intoxicated subjects alike. One half of the intoxicated and sober subjects then engaged in a distracting activity for the next 7 minutes (they rated the aesthetic features of art slides), while the other half did nothing for this period of time (hooked up to a false recording electrode, they sat quietly, ostensibly providing baseline physiological measures). Subjects' anxiety was measured again 7 minutes into this rating/waiting period, and then, after extensive debriefing, the experiment was over. The only subjects who experienced a reduction of anxiety during this period were those who were intoxicated and rated art slides. By the end of this brief period, these subjects had recovered entirely from the anxiety caused by news of the speech (some even had to be reminded of the upcoming speech). It worsened among intoxicated subjects who did nothing during this period. For subjects in the other conditions, anxiety either did not improve or worsened.

This effect was replicated in a second experiment as well, further supporting the view that when the drinker is not distracted and stressful cognitions are salient, alcohol actually increases psychological stress—in this case, anxiety.

The argument here is that alcohol and activity reduce psychological stress through the one–two punch of pharmacologically weakening attentional capacities and then occupying them with immediate activity rather than worry. How much worry is reduced should depend on how much attentional capacity has been reduced by alcohol and on how much attention the distracting activity requires. Josephs

and Steele (1990) tested this reasoning—and thus the hypothesized mediational processes—by varying the amount of attention required by the distracting activity. Over two experiments, using the anticipatory anxiety paradigm described earlier, subjects were exposed to a no-activity condition and to four conditions that involved increasingly demanding versions of the slide-rating task (i.e., these versions varied from the undemanding task of answering easy questions about the color and contents of the slides to the extremely demanding task of answering more difficult questions while the slides were continuously presented for only three-second exposures). Figure 4 presents the average changes in anxiety over the rating/waiting period for these conditions. Again, alcohol without distraction significantly increased anxiety, illustrating the danger of drinking with nothing else to do. In the other conditions, the more demanding the distracting task, the more alcohol reduced anxiety, until in the condition with the most demanding task, the activity itself, without the aid of alcohol, was sufficient to reduce anxiety.

These data, we believe, support an important conclusion: *Even modest accompanying distraction transforms alcohol intoxication from a sometime reducer of psycho-*

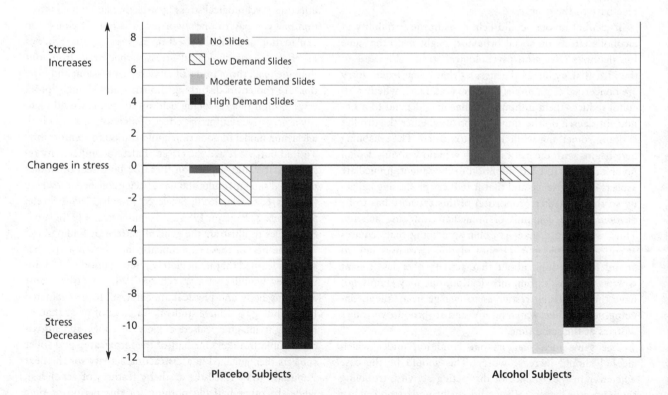

FIGURE 4   Changes in Anxiety Over an Upcoming Stressful Speech by Level of Distraction and Alcohol

logical stress into a strong, reliable one that consistently reduces this stress at even moderate doses for all drinkers. This explains in a simple way how such common drinking experiences as a beer and TV sports or cocktails and conversation can have strong relieving effects that can underlie a behavioral etiology of alcoholism in all drinkers, even when the alcohol involved, taken without these activities, would not.[5] This is not to say that accompanying distraction is always needed for alcohol to reduce psychological stress. Clearly, extreme, near-ataxic doses of alcohol can prevent worry without distraction by preventing thought of any sort. Also, alcohol has been shown to reduce anxiety (most consistently on measures of cardiovascular activity) among some subtypes of subjects—for example, the children of alcoholics (Levenson et al., in press; Sher, 1987) and those individuals who are high in self-consciousness (e.g., Hull et al., 1986)—apparently without accompanying distraction (although variation in experimental procedures makes the role of distraction in these effects difficult to assess; see Wilson, 1988, for a more thorough discussion of these effects). Still, our findings show that even slight distraction greatly increases the magnitude and reliability of alcohol's stress-reducing effect for all drinkers.

The Steele and Josephs (1988) and Joseph and Steele (1990) studies have shown also that alcohol can increase psychological stress in the absence of distraction. This is not to say that this will happen every time one drinks without distraction. As we just noted, alcohol may reduce some forms of stress more or less directly for some people. Also, whether alcohol has an anxiogenic effect depends a great deal on how available and strong the stressful cognitions are during intoxication. We failed to get this effect in the Steele et al. (1986) studies when the stressor was a past event and was less believed by the subjects, but we got it reliably in the Josephs and Steele and Steele and Josephs studies when the stressor was strong, upcoming, and salient. Similarly Wilson (1988) reported a clear anxiogenic effect of alcohol among a group of interacting alcoholics, but only when a strong social stressor was made the focus of their attention. Thus, without accompanying distraction a beer can make one cry into it, but only if one's troubles are obvious like the nose on one's face.

Such data, we would like to believe, suggest a new understanding of how alcohol can affect psychological stress. To an important degree, these effects are mediated indirectly through the conjunctive effects of alcohol myopia and the demands of ongoing activity. This view has several advantages: (a) It identifies an important and pervasive condition—a distracting activity—under which alcohol has the reliable tension-relieving effect that behavioral scientists have for so long seen as a central root of alcoholism. (b) It shows how alcohol intoxication can be reinforcing even though many of its physiological effects (i.e., nausea, confused thinking, impaired motor control, slurred speech, fatigue, and hangovers), especially during the descending limb of the BAL curve, are so stressful. The protection against psychological distress that one gets from alcohol and distraction may easily outweigh these discomforts. (c) It suggests that chronic psychological stress, whether it stems from the circumstances of one's life or from dispositional factors, is an important susceptibility to alcohol addiction. It creates the conditions under which drinking alcohol (and distraction) can be chronically reinforcing, suggesting that effective treatment of alcoholism would entail treatment of one's troubles as much as one's drinking.

A few comments in closing: Two facts about the effect of alcohol on social behavior and psychological stress have been particularly difficult to explain: (a) the variety of these effects, the fact that alcohol affects so many social behaviors and stresses, and (b) the irregularity of these effects, the fact that they occur only intermittently. In addressing these puzzlements, we have used a strategy focused on alcohol's impairment of perception and thought (the myopia it causes) rather than on other pharmacological properties of the drug, individual reactivities to the drug, or expectancies associated with its use. We offer three conclusions:

1. First, aside from the effects of drinking expectancies, alcohol itself can make human social behavior more extreme. It does this primarily by blocking a form of response conflict. When salient cues strongly motivate a response that, if one were sober, would be inhibited by further access to other cues and meanings (i.e., under inhibition conflict), alcohol myopia makes the response more extreme by reducing access to the inhibiting cues. Aside from such response conflict, alcohol does not appear to have much effect on social behaviors.

2. Alcohol can have profound effects on the depression and anxiety that arise from worries. This can depend on whether alcohol intoxication is accompanied by distracting activity and on the processing demands of the activity. Together with distraction, alcohol can forge a highly reinforcing and reliable diversion tactic for all drinkers, a means of effectively keeping one's mind off one's worries. Without accompanying distraction, however, alcohol myopia can backfire as a palliative, restricting attention to salient troubles and worsening affect.

3. Alcohol is a reliable means of self-inflation; during intoxication one gets closer to the self of one's dreams. Whether alcohol has this effect depends on whether an

important self-evaluative conflict has been made salient. When this happens, alcohol intoxication apparently leaves enough capacity to experience the need for self-regard but not enough to access the reasons for humility.

We offer with some confidence conclusions that describe the effects of alcohol and the conditions that mediate them; we offer more cautiously the conclusions that describe the mediational processes. We still lack a certain kind of direct evidence (a) that alcohol's disinhibition of response conflict is associated with less use of inhibiting cues, (b) that in conjunction with distraction, alcohol's effect on depression and anxiety is associated with variation in attention to one's worries, or (c) that alcohol self-inflation is associated with less processing of self-deflating information. Some of our findings get quite close to this type of evidence, for example, the finding that the effect of alcohol and activity on anxiety varies with the processing demands of the activity. Also, of course, we have been able to rule out alternative explanations we have come up with over the years. Nonetheless, whatever the fruits of these theories, they must still be taken as essentially working theories.

The most certain and practical fruit of this research so far is the identification of general conditions that mediate alcohol's prized and dangerous effects. We can now say that it is largely the nature and level of inhibition conflict that determines whether alcohol intoxication fosters behavioral excesses from altruism to aggression; also, it is whether a distracting activity accompanies alcohol intoxication that determines whether it will uniformly reduce tension or deepen despair. We hope this research underscores the importance of alcohol's social psychological effects in effort to understand, prevent, and treat the ill effects of this drug.

REFERENCES

Abrams, D. B., & Wilson, G. T. (1979). Effects of alcohol on social anxiety in women: Cognitive versus physiological processes. *Journal of Abnormal Psychology, 88,* 161–173.

Banaji, M. R., & Steele, C. M. (1989). The social cognition of alcohol use. *Social Cognition, 7,* 137–151.

Banaji, M. R., & Steele, C. M. (in press). *Alcohol and self-inflation.* Unpublished manuscript, Yale University.

Bandura, (1969). *Principles of behavior modification.* New York: Holt, Rinehart, & Winston.

Birnbaum, I. M., Johnson, M. K., Hartley, J. T., & Taylor, T. H. (1980). Alcohol and elaborative schemas for sentences. *Journal of Experimental Psychology: Human Learning and Memory, 6,* 293–300.

Brown, J. S., Mansfield, J. G., & Skurdal, A. J. (1980). An interference-reduction theory of the effects of ethanol on conflict behavior. *Physiological Psychology, 8,* 423–432.

Cappell, D., & Greely, S. (1987). Alcohol and tension reduction: An update on research and theory. In H. T. Blane & K. E. Leonard (Eds.), *Psychological theories of drinking and alcoholism* (pp. 1–44). New York: Guilford Press.

Cappell, H., & Herman, C. P. (1972). Alcohol and tension reduction. *Quarterly Journal of Studies on Alcohol, 33,* 33–64.

Cloninger, C. R., Bohman, M., & Sigvardsson, S. (1981). Inheritance of alcohol abuse: Cross-fostering analysis of adopted men. *Archives of General Psychiatry, 38,* 861–868.

Conger, J. J. (1956). Alcoholism: Theory, problem, and challenge: II. Reinforcement theory and the dynamics of alcoholism. *Quarterly Journal of Studies on Alcohol, 17,* 296–305.

Critchlow, B. (1986). The powers of John Barleycorn: Beliefs about the effects of alcohol on social behavior, *American Psychologist, 41,* 751–764.

Goldman, M. S., Brown, S. A., & Christiansen, B. A. (1987). Expectancy theory: Thinking about drinking. In H. T. Blane & K. E. Leonard (Eds.), *Psychological theories of drinking and alcoholism* (pp. 181–226). New York: Guilford Press.

Goodwin, D. W. (1976). Adoption studies of alcoholism. *Journal of Operational Psychiatry, 7,* 54–63.

Goodwin, D. W. (1979). Alcoholism and heredity: A review and hypothesis. *Archives of General Psychiatry, 36,* 57–61.

Gray, J. A. (1978). The neuropsychology of anxiety. *British Journal of Psychology, 69,* 417–434.

Greenwald, A. G. (1980). The totalitarian ego: Fabrication and revision of personal history. *American Psychologist, 35,* 603–618.

Hasin, D. S., & Martin, J. L. (1989). *Alcohol use, alcoholism, and sexual behavior in New York City gay men.* Unpublished manuscript, Columbia University College of Physicians and Surgeons.

Hull, J. G., & Bond, Jr., C. F. (1986). Social and behavioral consequences of alcohol consumption and expectancy: A meta-analysis. *Psychological Bulletin, 99,* 347–360.

Hull, J. G., & Young, R. D. (1983) Self-consciousness, self-esteem, and success-failure as determinants of alcohol consumption in male social drinkers. *Journal of Personality and Social Psychology, 44,* 1097–1109.

Hull, J. G., Young, R. D., & Jouriles, E. (1986). Applications of the self-awareness model of alcohol consumption: Predicting patterns of use and abuse. *Journal of Personality and Social Psychology, 51,* 790–796.

Huntley, M. S., Jr. (1973). Effects of alcohol and fixation-task difficulty on choice reaction time to extrafoveal stimulation. *Quarterly Journal of Studies on Alcohol, 34,* 89–103.

James, W. (1915). *Psychology, briefer course.* New York: Holt.

Jones, B. M., & Vega, A. (1972). Cognitive performance measured on the ascending and descending limb of the blood alcohol curve. *Psychopharmacologia, 23,* 99–114.

Josephs, R. A., & Steele, C. M. (1990). The two faces of alcohol myopia: Attentional mediation of psychological stress. *Journal of Abnormal Psychology, 99,* 115–126.

Kastl, A. J. (1969). Changes in ego functioning under alcohol. *Quarterly Journal of Studies on Alcohol, 30,* 371–380.

Keane, T. M., & Lisman, S. A. (1980). Alcohol and social anxiety in males: Behavioral, cognitive, and physiological effects. *Journal of Abnormal Psychology, 89,* 213–223.

Leigh, B. (1989). In search of the seven dwarfs: Issues of measurement and meaning in alcohol expectancy research. *Psychological Bulletin, 105,* 361–373.

Levenson, R. W., Oyama, O. N., & Meek, P. S. (in press). Greater
reinforcement from alcohol for those at risk: Parental risk,
personality risk, and gender. *Journal of Abnormal Psychology.*

Levenson, R. W., Sher, K. J., Grossman, L. M., Newman, J., &
Newlin, D. B. (1980). Alcohol and stress response dampening:
Pharmacological effects, expectancy, and tension reduction.
Journal of Abnormal Psychology, 89, 528–538.

Lynn, M. (1988). The effects of alcohol consumption on restaurant
tipping. *Personality and Social Psychology Bulletin, 14,* 87–91.

MacAndrew, C., & Edgerton, R. B. (1969). *Drunken comportment: A social explanation.* Chicago: Aldine.

Maisto, S. A., Connors, G. J., & Sachs, P. R. (1981). Expectation
as a mediator in alcohol intoxication: A reference level model.
Cognitive Therapy and Research, 5, 1–18.

Marlatt, G. A. (1976). Alcohol, stress, and cognitive control. In
I. G. Sarason & C. D. Spielberger (Eds.), *Stress and Anxiety*
(Vol. 3, pp. 271–296). Washington, DC: Hemisphere.

Marlatt, G. A., & Rohsenow, D. (1980). Cognitive processes in
alcohol use: Expectancy and the balanced placebo design. In
N. K. Mello (Ed.), *Advances in substance abuse: Behavioral and
biological research* (pp. 159–199). Greenwich, CT: JAI Press.

Medina, E. L. (1970). The role of the alcoholic in accidents and
violence. In R. E. Popham (Ed.), *Alcohol and alcoholism* (pp.
350–355). Toronto, Canada: University of Toronto Press.

Moskowitz, H., & DePry, D. (1968). Differential effect of alcohol
on auditory vigilance and divided attention. *Quarterly Journal
of Studies on Alcohol, 29,* 54–67.

National Commission on the Causes and Prevention of Violence.
(1970). *Crimes of violence.* Washington, DC: U.S. Government
Printing Office.

Pernanen, K. (1976). Alcohol and crimes of violence. In B. Kissin
& H. Begleiter (Eds.), *The biology of alcoholism: Vol. 4. Social
aspects of alcoholism* (pp. 351–444). New York: Plenum Press.

Petrakis, E. (1985). Sex differences and specificity of anticipation
of coincidence. *Perceptual and Motor Skills, 61,* 1135–1138.

Polivy, J., Schueneman, A. L., & Carlson, K. (1976). Alcohol and
tension reduction: Cognitive and physiological effects. *Journal
of Abnormal Psychology, 85,* 595–600.

Reinarman, C., & Leigh, B. C. (1987). Culture, cognition, and
disinhibition: Notes on sexuality and alcohol in the age of
AIDS. *Contemporary Drug Problems, Fall,* 435–460.

Rosen, L. J., & Lee, C. L. (1976). Acute and chronic effects of
alcohol use on organizational processes in memory. *Journal of
Abnormal Psychology, 85,* 309–317.

Schneider, W., Dumais, S. T., & Shiffrin, R. M. (1984). Automatic
and control processing and attention. In R. Parasuraman &
D. R. Davies (Eds.), *Varieties of attention* (pp. 1–27). New
York: Academic Press.

Schuckit, M. A. (1987). Biological vulnerability to alcoholism.
Journal of Consulting and Clinical Psychology, 55, 301–309.

Searles, J. S. (1988). The role of genetics in the pathogenesis of
alcoholism. *Journal of Abnormal Psychology, 97,* 153–167.

Sher, K. J. (1987). Stress response dampening. In H. T. Blane &
K. E. Leonard (Eds.), *Psychological theories of drinking and
alcoholism* (pp. 227–271). New York: Guilford Press.

Stall, R., McKusick, L., Wiley, J., & Coates, T. J. (1986). Alcohol
and drug use during sexual activity and compliance with safe
sex guidelines for AIDS: The AIDS behavioral research project.
Health Education Quarterly, 13, 359–371.

Steele, C. M. (1988). The psychology of self-affirmation: Sustaining
the integrity of the self. In L. Berkowitz (Ed.), *Advances in

experimental social psychology* (Vol. 21, pp. 261–302). New
York: Academic Press.

Steele, C. M., Critchlow, E., & Liu, T. J. (1985). Alcohol and
social behavior: 2. The helpful drunkard. *Journal of Personality
and Social Psychology, 48,* 35–46.

Steele, C. M., & Josephs, R. A. (1988). Drinking your troubles
away: 2. An attention-allocation model of alcohol's effect on
psychological stress. *Journal of Abnormal Psychology, 97,*
196–205.

Steele, C. M., & Southwick, L. (1985). Alcohol and social behavior: 1. The psychology of drunken excess. *Journal of Personality
and Social Psychology, 48,* 18–34.

Steele, C. M., Southwick, L., & Pagano, R. (1986). Drinking your
troubles away: The role of activity in mediating alcohol's
reduction of psychological stress. *Journal of Abnormal Psychology, 95,* 173–180.

Tarter, R. E., Jones, B. M., Simpson, C. D., & Vega, A. (1971).
Effects of task complexity and practice on performance during
acute alcohol intoxication. *Perceptual and Motor Skills, 37,*
307–313.

Taylor, S. P., & Leonard, K. E. (1983). Alcohol and human aggression. In R. G. Goreen & E. I. Donnerstein (Eds.), *Aggression: Theoretical and empirical reviews* (pp. 77–102). New
York: Academic Press.

Tesser, A. (1988). Toward a self-evaluation maintenance model of
social behavior. In L. Berkowitz (Ed.), *Advances in experimental
social psychology* (Vol. 21, pp. 181–222). New York: Academic
Press.

U.S. Department of Health and Human Services. (1987). *Report to
Congress: Toward a national plan to combat alcohol abuse and
alcoholism.* Washington, DC: U.S. Government Printing Office.

Washburne, C. (1956). Alcohol, self, and the group. *Quarterly
Journal of Studies on Alcohol, 17,* 108–123.

Williams, G. D., Stinson, F. S., Parker, D. A., Harford, T. C., &
Noble, J. (1987). Demographic trends, alcohol abuse, and
alcoholism. *Alcohol and Health and Research World, 15,*
80–83.

Wilson, G. T. (1988). Alcohol and anxiety. *Behavior Research and
Therapy, 26,* 369–381.

Zeichner, A., & Phil, R. O. (1979). Effects of alcohol and behavior
contingencies on human aggression. *Journal of Abnormal Psychology, 88,* 153–160.

Zeichner, A., & Phil, R. O. (1980). Effects of alcohol and instigator intent on human aggression. *Journal of Studies on Alcohol, 41,* 265–276.

NOTES

1. We do not assume that cues provoking a response will always
be more salient than cues inhibiting it, or that alcohol myopia
somehow makes this so. Consider the example in which cues inhibiting aggression (e.g., the presence of several policemen standing
in front of an individual at the bar) are more salient than cues
provoking it (e.g., a hissed insult from an antagonist at the back of
the barroom). Here, alcohol myopia may actually reduce aggression by narrowing the drinker's attention to the more salient
inhibiting policemen, causing him or her to miss the more remote,
provoking insult (a possibility brought to our attention by friends
and colleagues, Jay Hull, David Kuykendall, Barbara Leigh,
Kipling Williams, Ron Van Treuren, and Mark Zanna). Although

in this way the logic of alcohol myopia suggests the possibility of drunken inhibition (see Brown, Mansfield, & Skurdal, 1980, for evidence of this effect in animal conflict learning paradigms) as well as drunken excess, it is the latter effect that occupies researchers in this field, as it is through this effect that alcohol has its most important social effects, both prized and dangerous.

One might also ask whether there are strong inhibition conflicts in which both motivating and inhibiting meanings are so salient that alcohol myopia would not impair the influence of inhibiting cues and thus would not disinhibit the response. Although this is ultimately an empirical question, we doubt that such situations arise very often. Once a strong response tendency is aroused, inhibition of that tendency requires further processing even when inhibiting cues are highly salient. One's attention and thought must get past the immediate cues arousing the tendency, past the tendency itself and the orientation it forces on perception and thought, and access other cues and standards relevant to the response and grasp their inhibitory significance. All of this takes processing beyond that required for the response to be aroused in the first place, even when cues and meanings of potential inhibitory significance are highly salient. It is this processing that we argue is impaired by alcohol. Thus, even when cues that would inhibit a response are highly salient—policeman-at-the-elbow situations, as they are known in British jurisprudence—we would expect alcohol myopia to weaken their influence, allowing a motivated response to be more extreme.

2. The studies measuring alcohol's effect on eating behavior used very low doses of alcohol and allowed almost no time for absorption. This may have contributed to the weak alcohol effects in these studies.

3. We do caution, however, that inhibition conflict may be difficult to judge in situations in which it is difficult to judge the relative salience and strength of response-relevant cues. This was not a significant problem in the research we have reported (both the experiments and the studies in the meta-analysis) because these investigations were designed explicitly to test alcohol's effect on particular responses. Thus, the salience and strength of response-relevant cues was fairly straightforward to judge, and to the extent that any of this research generalizes to real-life (as we believe it does), we expect that much of the time these judgments will be reliable there as well. Nonetheless, there are settings in which these judgments are not straightforward. An example comes from research on alcohol's role in risky sex (i.e., sex in which the risk of contracting AIDS is high; e.g., Hasin & Martin, 1989; Stall, McKusick, Wiley, & Coates, 1986). Without specific information

about the dispositions of the actors and the circumstances of their encounter, it may be difficult to judge whether cues leading to sexual arousal or to the fear of AIDS are more salient or stronger in a given situation. In such situations, although we believe that alcohol's effect is mediated by the level of inhibition conflict the relevant response is under, independent evidence of the relative cue salience and strength may be necessary before sound predictions from the theory can be made.

4. We assume that alcohol's blocking of inhibition conflict is a general mediator of drunken excess in the sense that it can cause excess in all drinkers who have consumed alcohol to the point of intoxication. This assumption, plus the finding that alcohol intoxication caused no excess in the absence of inhibition conflict in any of the research reviewed, might suggest that disinhibition of conflict is the only process through which alcohol causes excess. Here we offer a caution. Most of this research used normal and heavy social drinkers as subjects, mostly college students. It is thus conceivable that it undersampled subcategories of problem drinkers who because of special reactivities to alcohol (cf. Schuckit, 1987) might show drunken excess even in the absence of inhibition conflict. We know of no evidence linking such reactivities to drunken excess. But because of this sampling limitation, we fall short of concluding that alcohol's disinhibition of conflict is the only route to drunken excess. We do conclude, however, that it is a general route that can cause drunken excess in all drinkers, even if in addition to its effect, other processes can cause this effect in some drinkers.

5. Anyone familiar with Hull and Young's, 1983, self-awareness model of alcohol use might wonder how much our results stem from alcohol's reduction of self-awareness. Hull and Young have proposed that alcohol can reduce stress by reducing self-awareness, the higher order processing related to the encoding of information in relation to the self. Thus, alcohol may have reduced stress in these studies by reducing subjects' sensitivity to the self-relevant threat inherent in the stressors. This model does not seem to fit our findings; in particular, the fact that alcohol actually increased stress in reaction to the speech when subjects were not distracted does not fit. Whatever self-awareness-reducing effects alcohol had in this condition were overridden by its effect of focusing subjects' attention onto the stressful speech. The alcohol and activity condition may well have reduced self-awareness in the process of occupying subjects' attention with the task. But this is essentially the same argument as our own: The combination of alcohol myopia and occupying activity made it difficult for subjects to process stressful cognitions about the stressor or its relevance to the self.

CRITICAL THINKING QUESTIONS

1. Steele and Josephs make the strong claim that the results of their research cannot be explained by the pharmacological effects of alcohol. How are the effects of alcohol myopia different from the pharmacological effects of alcohol?

2. The authors emphasize that the social effects of alcohol only occur when there is inhibition conflict. What do they mean by inhibition conflict?

3. The studies discussed in this paper all examine the effects of alcohol in a laboratory. Are the effects of alcohol different at a bar? At a fraternity party?

4. The authors argue that alcohol usually reduces anxiety and depression, but that under some conditions it can increase these emotional reactions. When is alcohol likely to reduce anxiety and depression and when is it likely to increase these reactions?

5. Chapter 8 of the textbook argues that situational cues can lead to aggressive responses. How might alcohol myopia affect the relationship between these situational cues and aggression?
6. Besides aggression, helping, and self-evaluation, what other social behaviors might alcohol myopia affect?

PART III
Social Influence

READING 9

Milgram's research on destructive obedience is perhaps the most famous, memorable, and dramatic research in the history of social psychology. It taught a surprising lesson about people's vulnerability to the commands of authority. We, along with the authors of your textbook, felt that this book of readings should include Milgram's firsthand account of his research procedure and of the results of the first complete demonstration of this procedure.

As the theoretical and empirical perspectives discussed in Chapter 9 of your textbook indicate, social influence plays an important role in our lives. To a large extent, conformity and obedience bind civilization together. These same ties, however, can prevent individuals from expressing their true beliefs, from behaving in ways dictated by their conscience. This sometimes terrifying battle between one's own inner voice and the voice of authority is the drama of Milgram's research.

Milgram's research is made clear in the first two paragraphs of the reading. After reading this article, refer to Chapter 9's summary of Milgram's and others' research on obedience that was inspired by this classic and controversial publication.

Behavioral Study of Obedience

Stanley Milgram
Yale University

This article describes a procedure for the study of destructive obedience in the laboratory. It consists of ordering a naive S to administer increasingly more severe punishment to a victim in the context of a learning experiment. Punishment is administered by means of a shock generator with 30 graded switches ranging from Slight Shock to Danger: Severe Shock. The victim is a confederate of the E. The primary dependent variable is the maximum shock the S is willing to administer before he refuses to continue further. 26 Ss obeyed the experimental commands fully, and administered the highest shock on the generator. 14 Ss broke off the experiment at some point after the victim protested and refused to provide further answers. The procedure created extreme levels of nervous tension in some Ss. Profuse sweating, trembling, and stuttering were typical expressions of this emotional disturbance. One unexpected sign of tension—yet to be explained—was the regular occurrence of nervous laughter, which in some Ss developed into uncontrollable seizures. The variety of interesting behavioral dynamics observed in the experiment, the reality of the situation for the S, and the possibility of parametric variation within the framework of the procedure, point to the fruitfulness of further study.

Obedience is as basic an element in the structure of social life as one can point to. Some system of authority is a requirement of all communal living, and it is only the man dwelling in isolation who is not forced to respond, through defiance or submission, to the commands of others. Obedience, as a determinant of behavior, is of particular relevance to our time. It has been reliably established that from 1933–45 millions of innocent persons were systematically slaughtered on command. Gas chambers were built, death camps were guarded, daily quotas of corpses were produced with the same efficiency as the manufacture of appliances. These inhumane policies may have originated in the mind of a single person, but they could only be carried out on a massive scale if a very large number of persons obeyed orders.

Obedience is the psychological mechanism that links individual action to political purpose. It is the dispositional cement that binds men to systems of authority. Facts of recent history and observation in daily life suggest that for many persons obedience may be a deeply ingrained behavior tendency, indeed, a prepotent impulse overriding training in ethics, sympathy, and moral conduct. C. P. Snow (1961) points to its importance when he writes:

When you think of the long and gloomy history of man, you will find more hideous crimes have been committed in the name of obedience than have ever been committed in the name of rebellion. If you doubt that, read William Shirer's "Rise and Fall of the Third Reich." The German

SOURCE: Milgram, Stanley, "Behavioral Study of Obedience," *Journal of Abnormal and Social Psychology*, 1963, Vol. 67, No. 4, 371–378. Copyright © renewed 1991 by Alexandra Milgram. Permission granted by Alexandra Milgram.

Officer Corps were brought up in the most rigorous code of obedience . . . in the name of obedience they were party to, and assisted in, the most wicked large scale actions in the history of the world [p. 24].

While the particular form of obedience dealt with in the present study has its antecedents in these episodes, it must not be thought all obedience entails acts of aggression against others. Obedience serves numerous productive functions. Indeed, the very life of society is predicated on its existence. Obedience may be ennobling and educative and refer to acts of charity and kindness, as well as to destruction.

General Procedure

A procedure was devised which seems useful as a tool for studying obedience (Milgram, 1961). It consists of ordering a naive subject to administer electric shock to a victim. A simulated shock generator used, with 30 clearly marked voltage levels that range from 15 to 450 volts. The instrument bears verbal designations that range from Slight Shock to Danger: Severe Shock. The responses of the victim, who is a trained confederate of the experimenter, are standardized. The orders to administer shocks are given to the naive subject in the context of a "learning experiment" ostensibly set up to study the effects of punishment on memory. As the experiment proceeds the naive subject is commanded to administer increasingly more intense shocks to the victim, even to the point of reaching the level marked Danger: Severe Shock. Internal resistances become stronger, and at a certain point the subject refuses to go on with the experiment. Behavior prior to this rupture is considered "obedience," in that the subject complies with the commands of the experimenter. The point of rupture is the act of disobedience. A quantitative value is assigned to the subject's performance based on the maximum intensity shock he is willing to administer before he refuses to participate further. Thus for any particular subject and for any particular experimental condition the degree of obedience may be specified with a numerical value. The crux of the study is to systematically vary the factors believed to alter the degree of obedience to the experimental commands.

The technique allows important variables to be manipulated at several points in the experiment. One may vary aspects of the source of command, content and form of command, instrumentalities for its execution, target object, general social setting, etc. The problem, therefore, is not one of designing increasingly more numerous experimental conditions, but of selecting those that best illumi-

nate the *process* of obedience from the sociopsychological standpoint.

Related Studies

The inquiry bears an important relation to philosophic analyses of obedience and authority (Arendt, 1958; Friedrich, 1958; Weber, 1947), an early experimental study of obedience by Frank (1944), studies in "authoritarianism" (Adorno, Frenkel-Brunswik, Levinson, & Stanford, 1950; Rokeach, 1961), and a recent series of analytic and empirical studies in social power (Cartwright, 1959). It owes much to the long concern with *suggestion* in social psychology, both in its normal forms (e.g., Binet, 1900) and in its clinical manifestations (Charcot, 1881). But it derives, in the first instance, from direct observation of a social fact; the individual who is commanded by a legitimate authority ordinarily obeys. Obedience comes easily and often. It is a ubiquitous and indispensable feature of social life.

METHOD

Subjects

The subjects were 40 males between the ages of 20 and 50, drawn from New Haven and the surrounding communities. Subjects were obtained by a newspaper advertisement and direct mail solicitation. Those who responded to the appeal believed they were to participate in a study of memory and learning at Yale University. A wide range of occupations is represented in the sample. Typical subjects were postal clerks, high school teachers, salesmen, engineers, and laborers. Subjects ranged in educational level from one who had not finished elementary school, to those who had doctorate and other professional degrees. They were paid $4.50 for their participation in the experiment. However, subjects were told that payment was simply for coming to the laboratory, and that the money was theirs no matter what happened after they arrived. Table 1 shows the proportion of age and occupational types assigned to the experimental condition.

Personnel and Locale

The experiment was conducted on the grounds of Yale University in the elegant interaction laboratory. (This detail is relevant to the perceived legitimacy of the experiment. In further variations, the experiment was dissociated from the university with consequences for performance.) The role of experimenter was played by a 31-year-old high school teacher of biology. His manner was impassive, and his

TABLE 1   Distribution of Age and Occupational Types in the Experiment

Occupations	20–29 years *n*	30–39 years *n*	40–50 years *n*	Percentage of total (occupations)
Workers, skilled and unskilled	4	5	6	37.5
Sales, business, and white-collar	3	6	7	40.0
Professional	1	5	3	22.5
Percentage of total (Age)	20	40	40	

Note: Total *N* = 40.

appearance somewhat stern throughout the experiment. He was dressed in a gray technician's coat. The victim was played by a 47-year-old accountant, trained for the role; he was of Irish-American stock, whom most observers found mild-mannered and likable.

Procedure

One naive subject and one victim (an accomplice) performed in each experiment. A pretext had to be devised that would justify the administration of electric shock by the naive subject. This was effectively accomplished by the cover story. After a general introduction on the presumed relation between punishment and learning, subjects were told:

> But actually, we know *very little* about the effect of punishment on learning, because almost no truly scientific studies have been made of it in human beings.
>
> For instance, we don't know how *much* punishment is best for learning—and we don't know how much difference it makes as to who is giving the punishment, whether an adult learns best from a younger or an older person than himself—or many things of that sort.
>
> So in this study we are bringing together a number of adults of different occupations and ages. And we're asking some of them to be teachers and some of them to be learners.
>
> We want to find out just what effect different people have on each other as teachers and learners, and also what effect *punishment* will have on learning in this situation.
>
> Therefore, I'm going to ask one of you to be the teacher here tonight and the other one to be the learner.
>
> Does either of you have a preference?

Subjects then drew slips of paper from a hat to determine who would be the teacher and who would be the

learner in the experiment. The drawing was rigged so that the naive subject was always the teacher and the accomplice always the learner. (Both slips contained the word "Teacher.") Immediately after the drawing, the teacher and learner were taken to an adjacent room and the learner was strapped into an "electric chair" apparatus.

The experimenter explained that the straps were to prevent excessive movement while the learner was being shocked. The effect was to make it impossible for him to escape from the situation. An electrode was attached to the learner's wrist, and electrode paste was applied "to avoid blisters and burns." Subjects were told that the electrode was attached to the shock generator in the adjoining room.

In order to improve credibility the experimenter declared, in response to a question by the learner: "Although the shocks can be extremely painful, they cause no permanent tissue damage."

Learning task   The lesson administered by the subject was a paired-associate learning task. The subject read a series of word pairs to the learner, and then read the first word of the pair along with four terms. The learner was to indicate which of the four terms had originally been paired with the first word. He communicated his answer by pressing one of four switches in front of him, which in turn lit up one of four numbered quadrants in an answerbox located atop the shock generator.

Shock generator   The instrument panel consists of 30 lever switches set in a horizontal line. Each switch is clearly labeled with a voltage designation that ranges from 15 to 450 volts. There is a 15-volt increment from one switch to the next going from left to right. In addition, the following verbal designations are clearly indicated for groups of four switches going from left to right: Slight Shock, Moderate Shock, Strong Shock, Very Strong Shock, Intense Shock, Extreme Intensity Shock, Danger: Severe Shock. (Two switches after this last designation are simply marked XXX.)

Upon depressing a switch: a pilot light corresponding to each switch is illuminated in bright red; an electric buzzing is heard; an electric blue light, labeled "voltage energizer," flashes; the dial on the voltage meter swings to the right; various relay clicks are sounded.

The upper left-hand corner of the generator is labeled Shock Generator, Type ZLB, Dyson Instrument Company, Waltham, Mass. Output 15 Volts–450 Volts.

Details of the instrument were carefully handled to insure an appearance of authenticity. The panel was engraved by precision industrial engravers, and all components were of high quality. No subject in the experiment suspected that the instrument was merely a simulated shock generator.[1]

Sample shock   Each naive subject is given a sample shock on the shock generator, prior to beginning his run as teacher. This shock is always 45 volts, and is applied by pressing the third switch of the generator. The shock is applied to the wrist of the naive subject, and has its source in a 45-volt battery wired into the generator. This further convinces the subject of the authenticity of the generator.

Shock instructions   The subject is told to administer a shock to the learner each time he gives a wrong response. Moreover—and this is the key command—the subject is instructed to "move one level higher on the shock generator each time the learner flashes a wrong answer." He is also instructed to announce the voltage level before administering a shock. This serves to continually remind subjects of the increasing intensity of shocks administered to the learner.

Preliminary and regular run   Pretests revealed that the procedure of reading words and administering shocks requires some practice before it can be handled smoothly. Therefore, immediately preceding the regular run, the teacher is given a preliminary series of 10 words to read to the learner. There are 3 neutral words in the practice series (i.e., words that the learner answers correctly), so that shocks are administered for 7 of the words, with the maximum shock at 105 volts (moderate shock). Almost all subjects master the procedure by the time the preliminary run is over.

Subjects are then presented with a second list, and are told that the procedure is the same as for the first list; the experimenter adds, however:

> When you get to the bottom of the list, repeat it over again, and continue giving shocks, until the learner has learned all the pairs correctly.

The experimenter instructs the subject to,

> start from 15 volts and increase the shock level one step each time the learner gives a wrong answer.

Feedback from the victim   In all conditions the learner gives a predetermined set of responses to the word pair test, based on a schedule of approximately three wrong answers to one correct answer. In the present experimental condition no vocal response or other sign of protest is heard from the learner until Shock Level 300 is reached. When the 300-volt shock is administered, the learner pounds on the wall of the room in which he is bound to the electric chair. The pounding can be heard by the subject. From this

point on, the learner's answers no longer appear on the four-way panel.

At this juncture, subjects ordinarily turn to the experimenter for guidance. The experimenter instructs the subject to treat the absence of a response as a wrong answer, and to shock the subject according to the usual schedule. He advises the subjects to allow 5–10 seconds before considering no response as a wrong answer, and to increase the shock level one step each time the learner fails to respond correctly. The learner's pounding is repeated after the 315-volt shock is administered; afterwards he is not heard from, nor do his answers reappear on the four-way signal box.

Experimenter feedback   At various points in the experiment the subject may turn to the experimenter for advice on whether he should continue to administer shocks. Or he may indicate that he does not wish to go on. It was important to standardize the experimenter's responses to these inquiries and reactions.

If the subject indicated his unwillingness to go on, the experimenter responded with a sequence of "prods," using as many as necessary to bring the subject into line.

> Prod 1: Please continue. *or* Please go on.
> Prod 2: The experiment requires that you continue.
> Prod 3: It is absolutely essential that you continue.
> Prod 4: You have no other choice, you *must* go on.

The prods were always made in sequence: Only if Prod 1 had been unsuccessful, could Prod 2 be used. If the subject refused to obey the experimenter after Prod 4, the experiment was terminated. The experimenter's tone of voice was at all times firm, but not impolite. The sequence was begun anew on each occasion that the subject balked or showed reluctance to follow orders.

Special prods. If the subject asked if the learner was liable to suffer permanent physical injury, the experimenter said:

> Although the shocks may be painful, there is no permanent tissue damage, so please go on. [Followed by Prods 2, 3, and 4 if necessary.]

If the subject said that the learner did not want to go on, the experimenter replied:

> Whether the learner likes it or not, you must go on until he has learned all the word pairs correctly. So please go on. [Followed by Prods 2, 3, and 4 if necessary.]

Dependent Measures

The primary dependent measure for any subject is the maximum shock he administers before he refuses to go any further. In principle this may vary from 0 (for a subject who refuses to administer even the first shock) to 30 (for a subject who administers the highest shock on the generator). A subject who breaks off the experiment at any point prior to administering the thirtieth shock level is termed a *defiant* subject. One who complies with experimental commands fully, and proceeds to administer all shock levels commanded, is termed an *obedient* subject.

Further records With few exceptions, experimental sessions were recorded on magnetic tape. Occasional photographs were taken through one-way mirrors. Notes were kept on any unusual behavior occurring during the course of the experiments. On occasion, additional observers were directed to write objective descriptions of the subjects' behavior. The latency and duration of shocks were measured by accurate timing devices.

Interview and dehoax Following the experiment, subjects were interviewed; open-ended questions, projective measures, and attitude scales were employed. After the interview, procedures were undertaken to assure that the subject would leave the laboratory in a state of well being. A friendly reconciliation was arranged between the subject and the victim, and an effort was made to reduce any tensions that arose as a result of the experiment.

RESULTS

Preliminary Notions

Before giving an account of the experimental results, it is instructive to consider how persons predict others will perform when commanded to administer powerful shocks to another person. Fourteen Yale seniors, all psychology majors, were provided with a detailed description of the experimental situation. They were asked to reflect carefully on it, and to predict the behavior of 100 hypothetical subjects. More specifically, they were instructed to plot the distribution of obedience of "100 Americans of diverse occupations, and ranging in age from 20 to 50 years," who were placed in the experimental situation.

There was considerable agreement among the respondents on the expected behavior of hypothetical subjects. All respondents predicted that only an insignificant minority would go through to the end of the shock series. (The estimates ranged from 0 to 3%; i.e., the most "pessimistic" member of the class predicted that of 100 persons, 3 would continue through to the most potent shock available on the shock generator—450 volts.) The class mean was 1.2%. The question was also posed informally to colleagues of the author, and the most general feeling was that few if any subjects would go beyond the designation Very Strong Shock.

Results of Experiment I

Subjects accept situation With few exceptions subjects were convinced of the reality of the experimental situation, that they were administering shocks to another person, and the most potent shocks were extremely painful. In the postexperimental interview subjects were asked: "How painful to the learner were the last few shocks that you administered to him?" Subjects were instructed to indicate their answers on a printed 14-point scale ranging from "Not at all painful" to "Extremely painful." The modal response was 14 (Extremely painful) with the mean at 13.42.

Signs of extreme tension Many subjects showed signs of nervousness in the experimental situation, and especially upon administering the more powerful shocks. In a large number of cases the degree of tension reached extremes that are rarely seen in sociopsychological laboratory studies. Subjects were observed to sweat, tremble, stutter, bite their lips, groan, and dig their fingernails into their flesh. These were characteristic rather than exceptional responses to the experiment.

One sign of tension was the regular occurrence of nervous laughing fits. Fourteen of the 40 subjects showed definite signs of nervous laughter and smiling. The laughter seemed entirely out of place, even bizarre. Full-blown, uncontrollable seizures were observed for 3 subjects. On one occasion we observed a seizure so violently convulsive that it was necessary to call a halt to the experiment. The subject, a 46-year-old encyclopedia salesman, was seriously embarrassed by his untoward and uncontrollable behavior. In the post-experimental interviews subjects took pains to point out that they were not sadistic types, and that the laughter did not mean they enjoyed shocking the victim.

Distribution of scores It had been conjectured that persons would not, in general, agree to administer shocks beyond the level designated as Very Strong Shock. The distribution of maximum shocks for this experiment is shown in Table 2. The obtained distribution of scores deviates radically from the prediction.

Upon command of the experimenter, each of the 40 subjects went beyond the expected breakoff point. No subject stopped prior to administering Shock Level 20. (At this level—300 volts—the victim kicks on the wall and no longer provides answers to the teacher's multiple-choice questions.)

TABLE 2   Distribution of Breakoff Points

Verbal designation and voltage indication	Number of subjects for whom this was maximum shock
Slight Shock	
15	0
30	0
45	0
60	0
Moderate Shock	
75	0
90	0
105	0
120	0
Strong Shock	
135	0
150	0
165	0
180	0
Very Strong Shock	
195	0
210	0
225	0
240	0
Intense Shock	
255	0
270	0
285	0
300	5
Extreme Intensity Shock	
315	4
330	2
345	1
360	1
Danger: Severe Shock	
375	1
390	0
405	0
420	0
XXX	
435	0
450	26

Of the 40 subjects, 5 refused to obey the experimental commands beyond the 300-volt level. Four more subjects administered one further shock, and then refused to go on. Two broke off at the 330-volt level, and 1 each at 345, 360, and 375 volts. Thus a total of 14 subjects defied the experimenter. It is instructive to reprint their remarks at the point of defiance, as transcribed from the tape recordings:

[0124] I think he's trying to communicate, he's knocking. . . . Well it's not fair to shock the guy . . . these are terrific volts. I don't think this is very humane. . . . Oh, I can't go on with this; no, this isn't right. It's a hell of an experiment. The guy is suffering in there. No, I don't want to go on. This is crazy. [Subject refused to administer more shocks.]

[0123] He's banging in there. I'm gonna chicken out. I'd like to continue, but I can't do that to a man. . . . I'm sorry I can't do that to a man. I'll hurt his heart. You take your check. . . . No really, I couldn't do it.

These subjects were frequently in a highly agitated and even angered state. Sometimes, verbal protest was at a minimum, and the subject simply got up from his chair in front of the shock generator, and indicated that he wished to leave the laboratory.

Of the 40 subjects, 26 obeyed the orders of the experimenter to the end, proceeding to punish the victim until they reached the most potent shock available on the shock generator. At that point, the experimenter called a halt to the session. (The maximum shock is labeled 450 volts, and is two steps beyond the designation: Danger: Severe Shock.) Although obedient subjects continued to administer shocks, they often did so under extreme stress. Some expressed reluctance to administer shocks beyond the 300-volt level, and displayed fears similar to those who defied the experimenter; yet they obeyed.

After the maximum shocks had been delivered, and the experimenter called a halt to the proceedings, many obedient subjects heaved sighs of relief, mopped their brows, rubbed their fingers over their eyes, or nervously fumbled cigarettes. Some shook their heads, apparently in regret. Some subjects had remained calm throughout the experiment, and displayed only minimal signs of tension from beginning to end.

DISCUSSION

The experiment yielded two findings that were surprising. The first finding concerns the sheer strength of obedient tendencies manifested in this situation. Subjects have learned from childhood that it is a fundamental breach of moral conduct to hurt another person against his will. Yet, 26 subjects abandon this tenet in following the instructions of an authority who has no special powers to enforce his commands. To disobey would bring no material loss to the subject; no punishment would ensue. It is clear from the remarks and outward behavior of many participants that in punishing the victim they are often acting against their own values. Subjects often expressed deep disapproval of shocking a man in the face of his objections, and others denounced it as stupid and senseless. Yet the majority complied with the experimental commands. This outcome was surprising from two perspectives: first, from the standpoint of predictions made in the questionnaire described earlier. (Here, however, it is possible that the remoteness of the respondents from the actual situation, and the difficulty of conveying to them the concrete details of the experiment, could account for the serious underestimation of obedience.)

But the results were also unexpected to persons who observed the experiment in progress, through one-way mirrors. Observers often uttered expressions of disbelief upon seeing a subject administer more powerful shocks to the victim. These persons had a full acquaintance with the details of the situation, and yet systematically underestimated the amount of obedience that subjects would display.

The second unanticipated effect was the extraordinary tension generated by the procedures. One might suppose that a subject would simply break off or continue as his conscience dictated. Yet, this is very far from what happened. There were striking reactions of tension and emotional strain. One observer related:

I observed a mature and initially poised businessman enter the laboratory smiling and confident. Within 20 minutes he was reduced to a twitching, stuttering wreck, who was rapidly approaching a point of nervous collapse. He constantly pulled on his earlobe, and twisted his hands. At one point he pushed his fist into his forehead and muttered: "Oh God, let's stop it." And yet he continued to respond to every word of the experimenter, and obeyed to the end.

Any understanding of the phenomenon of obedience must rest on an analysis of the particular conditions in which it occurs. The following features of the experiment go some distance in explaining the high amount of obedience observed in the situation.

1. The experiment is sponsored by and takes place on the grounds of an institution of unimpeachable reputation, Yale University. It may be reasonably presumed that the personnel are competent and reputable. The importance of this background authority is now being studied by conducting a series of experiments outside of New Haven, and without any visible ties to the university.

2. The experiment is, on the face of it, designed to attain a worthy purpose—advancement of knowledge about learning and memory. Obedience occurs not as an end in itself, but as an instrumental element in a situation that the subject construes as significant, and meaningful. He may not be able to see its full significance, but he may properly assume that the experimenter does.

3. The subject perceives that the victim has voluntarily submitted to the authority system of the experimenter. He is not (at first) an unwilling captive impressed for involuntary service. He has taken the trouble to come to the laboratory presumably to aid the experimental research. That he later becomes an involuntary subject does not alter the fact that, initially, he consented to participate without qualification. Thus he has in some degree incurred an obligation toward the experimenter.

4. The subject, too, has entered the experiment voluntarily, and perceives himself under obligation to aid the experimenter. He has made a commitment, and to disrupt the experiment is a repudiation of this initial promise of aid.

5. Certain features of the procedure strengthen the subject's sense of obligation to the experimenter. For one, he has been paid for coming to the laboratory. In part this is canceled out by the experimenter's statement that:

Of course, as in all experiments, the money is yours simply for coming to the laboratory. From this point on, no matter what happens, the money is yours.[2]

6. From the subject's standpoint, the fact that he is the teacher and the other man the learner is purely a chance consequence (it is determined by drawing lots) and he, the subject, ran the same risk as the other man in being assigned the role of learner. Since the assignment of positions in the experiment was achieved by fair means, the learner is deprived of any basis of complaint on this count. (A similar situation obtains in Army units, in which—in the absence of volunteers—a particularly dangerous mission may be assigned by drawing lots, and the unlucky soldier is expected to bear his misfortune with sportsmanship.)

7. There is, at best, ambiguity with regard to the prerogatives of a psychologist and the corresponding rights of his subject. There is a vagueness of expectation concerning what a psychologist may require of his subject, and when he is overstepping acceptable limits. Moreover, the experiment occurs in a closed setting, and thus provides no opportunity for the subject to remove these ambiguities by discussion with others. There are few standards that seem directly applicable to the situation, which is a novel one for most subjects.

8. The subjects are assured that the shocks administered to the subject are "painful but not dangerous." Thus they assume that the discomfort caused the victim is momentary, while the scientific gains resulting from the experiment are enduring.

9. Through Shock Level 20 the victim continues to provide answers on the signal box. The subject may construe this as a sign that the victim is still willing to "play the

game." It is only after Shock Level 20 that the victim repudiates the rules completely, refusing to answer further.

These features help to explain the high amount of obedience obtained in this experiment. Many of the arguments raised need not remain matters of speculation, but can be reduced to testable propositions to be confirmed or disproved by further experiments.[3]

The following features of the experiment concern the nature of the conflict which the subject faces.

10. The subject is placed in a position in which he must respond to the competing demands of two persons: the experimenter and the victim. The conflict must be resolved by meeting the demands of one or the other; satisfaction of the victim and the experimenter are mutually exclusive. Moreover, the resolution must take the form of a highly visible action, that of continuing to shock the victim or breaking off the experiment. Thus the subject is forced into a public conflict that does not permit any completely satisfactory solution.

11. While the demands of the experimenter carry the weight of scientific authority, the demands of the victim spring from his personal experience of pain and suffering. The two claims need not be regarded as equally pressing and legitimate. The experimenter seeks an abstract scientific datum; the victim cries out for relief from physical suffering caused by the subject's actions.

12. The experiment gives the subject little time for reflection. The conflict comes on rapidly. It is only minutes after the subject has been seated before the shock generator that the victim begins his protests. Moreover, the subject perceives that he has gone through but two-thirds of the shock levels at the time the subject's first protests are heard. Thus he understands that the conflict will have a persistent aspect to it, and may well become more intense as increasingly more powerful shocks are required. The rapidity with which the conflict descends on the subject, and his realization that it is predictably recurrent may well be sources of tension to him.

13. At a more general level, the conflict stems from the opposition of two deeply ingrained behavior dispositions: first, the disposition not to harm other people, and second, the tendency to obey those whom we perceived to be legitimate authorities.

REFERENCES

Adorno, T., Frenkel-Brunswik, Else, Levinson, D. J., & Sanford, R. N. *The authoritarian personality.* New York: Harper, 1950.

Arendt, H. What was authority? In C. J. Friedrich (Ed.), *Authority.* Cambridge: Harvard Univer. Press, 1958. Pp. 81–112.

Binet, A. *La suggestibilité.* Paris: Schleicher, 1900.

Buss, A. H. *The psychology of aggression.* New York: Wiley, 1961.

Cartwright, S. (Ed.) *Studies in social power.* Ann Arbor: University of Michigan Institute for Social Research, 1959.

Charcot, J. M. *Oeuvres complètes.* Paris: Bureaux du Progrès Médical, 1881.

Frank, J. D. Experimental studies of personal pressure and resistance. *J. Gen. Psychol.,* 1944, 30, 23–64.

Friedrich, C. J. (Ed.). *Authority.* Cambridge: Harvard Univer. Press, 1958.

Milgram, S. Dynamics of obedience. Washington: National Science Foundation, 25 January 1961. (Mimeo)

Milgram, S. Some conditions of obedience and disobedience to authority. *Hum. Relat.,* 1964, in press.

Rokeach, M. Authority, authoritarianism, and conformity. In I. A. Berg & B. M. Bass (Eds.), *Conformity and deviation.* New York: Harper, 1961. Pp. 230–257.

Snow, C. P. Either-or. *Progressive,* 1961 (Feb.), 24.

Weber, M. *The theory of social and economic organization.* Oxford: Oxford Univer. Press, 1947.

NOTES

1. A related technique, making use of a shock generator, was reported by Buss (1961) for the study of aggression in the laboratory. Despite the considerable similarity of technical detail in the experimental procedures, both investigators proceeded in ignorance of the other's work. Milgram provided plans and photographs of his shock generator, experimental procedure, and first results in a report to the National Science Foundation in January 1961. This report received only limited circulation. Buss reported his procedure 6 months later, but to a wider audience. Subsequently, technical information and reports were exchanged. The present article was first received in the Editor's office on December 27, 1961; it was resubmitted with deletions on July 27, 1962.

2. Forty-three subjects, undergraduates at Yale University, were run in the experiment without payment. The results are very similar to those obtained with paid subjects.

3. A series of recently completed experiments employing the obedience paradigm is reported in Milgram (1964).

(Received July 27, 1962)

CRITICAL THINKING QUESTIONS

1. What aspects of the situation faced by the subjects in this study do you think were most influential in causing the subjects to obey? Would you have been vulnerable to these factors? Do you think that most people today would show similar levels of obedience? Do

you think that most people today would show a great deal of obedience in a situation in which their team coach, or their employer, was the authority? Why or why not?

2. When Milgram asked people to predict how many subjects in his study would obey completely and give shocks through the end of the shock series (450 volts), none of the respondents predicted that more than 3 percent of the subjects would show this level of obedience, and most thought that fewer than 2 percent would. Similarly, when students today learn about this study, almost none believes that he or she would come close to the maximum level of obedience. Yet in the study reported in this paper, 65 percent of the subjects obeyed all the way through the shock series. How can you explain this disparity? What role does the fundamental attribution error (see Chapter 3) play in this?

3. Why do you think Milgram designed the situation so that the shock levels started from only 15 volts and increased in steps of only 15 volts each? How do you think the results would have been affected if this procedure had been shortened by starting at a higher voltage or having increments much larger than 15 volts.

4. In this paper Milgram wrote that the technique he designed to study obedience "allows important variables to be manipulated at several points in the experiment." What manipulations of variables do you think would increase the levels of obedience observed? What manipulations would decrease obedience?

5. Chapter 1 of your textbook discusses the question of ethics in social psychological research and what steps have been taken in recent years to help protect the welfare research participants. Milgram's research has generated many debates about the ethics of the research. What are the pros and cons of doing research such as Milgram's? If you were an experimenter in Milgram's research, how would you have wanted to conduct the debriefing of the subjects at the conclusion of the study so that they would feel better about themselves? If you were on a review board that was deciding whether to let Milgram conduct his study, how would you vote? Why?

6. One of the factors Milgram emphasizes in explaining the destructive obedience observed in his study was the perceived legitimate authority of the experimenter. Compare the power of the experimenter in this situation with the power that each of the following has on individuals' likelihood to obey destructive commands: high-status peers, role models, coaches, groups of people, employers, the police, the military, and the government. Do these comparisons suggest that the results of Milgram's research have any implications for real-world tendencies to obey authority? Explain.

READING 10

This article is one of the first and most famous studies of cognitive dissonance theory, a theory discussed in detail in Chapter 10. In this study, Festinger and Carlsmith put their subjects through a dull task. Some subjects were then induced to lie to another person (actually a confederate) by telling the person that they found the task enjoyable. They received either $1 or $20 for telling this lie. Festinger and Carlsmith found that subjects who received $1 for telling the lie later reported that they enjoyed the task more than did the subjects who received $20. Festinger and Carlsmith interpreted these results as consistent with cognitive dissonance theory. They argued that there is an inconsistency between saying a task is fun when one knows that it is boring. The subjects who were paid $20 for saying the task was fun, however, knew why they said it was fun—they did it for the money. This resolves the inconsistency and they had little reason to experience cognitive dissonance. On the other hand, $1 is hardly a justification for lying, so the subjects who were paid only a dollar were likely to experience cognitive dissonance. To resolve the dissonance, they changed their attitude about the task. By coming to think that the task was indeed somewhat enjoyable, these subjects would no longer have reason to feel badly about telling someone else that the task was enjoyable.

Chapter 10 in the textbook describes cognitive dissonance theory and the role that this study played in the development of the theory. It also notes the importance of this study for the alternative models that they try to explain why people change their attitudes to justify their behaviors.

In reading this article, you can appreciate the inventiveness that Festinger and Carlsmith used in creating the experimental situation. It has been a model in this respect for almost all social psychologists. The description of dissonance theory in the introduction is somewhat technical, but note how the authors apply the results to the theory in the discussion section.

Cognitive Consequences of Forced Compliance

Leon Festinger and James M. Carlsmith
Stanford University

What happens to a person's private opinion if he is forced to do or say something contrary to that opinion? Only recently has there been any experimental work related to this question. Two studies reported by Janis and King (1954; 1956) clearly showed that, at least under some conditions, the private opinion changes so as to bring it into closer correspondence with the overt behavior the person was forced to perform. Specifically, they showed that if a person is forced to improvise a speech supporting a point of view with which he disagrees, his private opinion moves toward the position advocated in the speech. The observed opinion change is greater than for persons who only hear the speech or for persons who read a prepared speech with emphasis solely on elocution and manner of delivery. The authors of these two studies explain their results mainly in terms of mental rehearsal and thinking up new arguments. In this way, they propose, the person who is forced to improvise a speech convinces himself. They present some evidence, which is not altogether conclusive, in support of this explanation. We will have more to say concerning this explanation in discussing the results of our experiment.

Kelman (1953) tried to pursue the matter further. He reasoned that if the person is induced to make an overt statement contrary to his private opinion by the offer of some reward, then the greater the reward offered, the greater should be the subsequent opinion change. His data, however, did not support this idea. He found, rather, that a large reward produced less subsequent opinion change that did a smaller reward. Actually, this finding by Kelman is consistent with the theory we will outline below but, for a number of reasons, is not conclusive. One of the major

SOURCE: Leon Festinger and James M. Carlsmith (1959). *Journal of Abnormal and Social Psychology, 58,* 203–210.

weaknesses of the data is that not all subjects in the experiment made an overt statement contrary to their private opinion in order to obtain the offered reward. What is more, as one might expect, the percentage of subjects who complied increased as the size of the offered reward increased. Thus, with self-selection of who did and who did not make the required overt statement and with varying percentages of subjects in the different conditions who did make the required statement, no interpretation of the data can be unequivocal.

Recently, Festinger (1957) proposed a theory concerning cognitive dissonance from which come a number of derivations about opinion change following forced compliance. Since these derivations are stated in detail by Festinger (1957, Ch. 4), we will here give only a brief outline of the reasoning.

Let us consider a person who privately holds opinion "X" but has, as a result of pressure brought to bear on him, publicly stated that he believes "not X."

1. This person has two cognitions which, psychologically, do not fit together: one of these is the knowledge that he believes "X," the other the knowledge that he has publicly stated that he believes "not X." If no factors other than his private opinion are considered, it would follow, at least in our culture, that if he believes "X" he would publicly state "X." Hence, his cognition of his private belief is dissonant with his cognition concerning his actual public statement.

2. Similarly, the knowledge that he has said "not X" is consonant with (does fit together with) those cognitive elements corresponding to the reasons, pressures, promises of rewards and/or threats of punishment which induced him to say "not X."

3. In evaluating the total magnitude of dissonance, one must take account of both dissonances and consonances. Let us think of the sum of all the dissonances involving some particular cognition as "D" and the sum of all the consonances as "C." Then we might think of the total magnitude of dissonance as being a function of "D" divided by "D" plus "C."

Let us then see what can be said about the total magnitude of dissonance in a person created by the knowledge that he said "not X" and really believes "X." With everything else held constant, this total magnitude of dissonance would decrease as the number and importance of the pressures which induced him to say "not X" increased.

Thus, if the overt behavior was brought about by, say, offers of reward or threats of punishment, the magnitude of dissonance is maximal if these promised rewards or threatened punishments were just barely sufficient to induce the person to say "not X." From this point on, as the promised rewards or threatened punishment become larger, the magnitude of dissonance becomes smaller.

4. One way in which the dissonance can be reduced is for the person to change his private opinion so as to bring it into correspondence with what he has said. One would consequently expect to observe such opinion change after a person has been forced or induced to say something contrary to his private opinion. Furthermore, since the pressure to reduce dissonance will be a function of the magnitude of the dissonance, the observed opinion change should be greatest when the pressure used to elicit the overt behavior is just sufficient to do it.

The present experiment was designed to test this derivation under controlled, laboratory conditions. In the experiment we varied the amount of reward used to force persons to make a statement contrary to their private views. The prediction [from 3 and 4 above] is that the larger the reward given to the subject, the smaller will be the subsequent opinion change.

PROCEDURE

Seventy-one male students in the introductory psychology course at Stanford University were used in the experiment. In this course, students are required to spend a certain number of hours as subjects (Ss) in experiments. They choose among the available experiments by signing their names on a sheet posted on the bulletin board which states the nature of the experiment. The present experiment was listed as a two-hour experiment dealing with "Measures of Performance."

During the first week of the course, when the requirement of serving in experiments was announced and explained to the students, the instructor also told them about a study that the psychology department was conducting. He explained that, since they were required to serve in experiments, the department was conducting a study to evaluate these experiments in order to be able to improve them in the future. They were told that a sample of students would be interviewed after having served as Ss. They were urged to cooperate in these interviews by being completely frank and honest. The importance of this announcement will become clear shortly. It enabled us to measure the opinions of our Ss in a context not directly connected with our experiment and in which we could reasonably expect frank and honest expressions of opinion.

When the S arrived for the experiment on "Measures of Performance" he had to wait for a few minutes in the secretary's office. The experimenter (E) then came in, introduced himself to the *S* and, together, they walked into the laboratory room where the *E* said:

> This experiment usually takes a little over an hour but, of course, we had to schedule it for two hours. Since we have that extra time, the introductory psychology people asked if they could interview some of our subjects. [Offhand and conversationally.] Did they announce that in class? I gather that they're interviewing some people who have been in experiments. I don't know much about it. Anyhow, they may want to interview you when you're through here.

With no further introduction or explanation the *S* was shown the first task, which involved putting 12 spools onto a tray, emptying the tray, refilling it with spools, and so on. He was told to use one hand and to work at his own speed. He did this for one-half hour. The *E* then removed the tray and spools and placed in front of the *S* a board containing 48 square pegs. His task was to turn each peg a quarter turn clockwise, then another quarter turn, and so on. He was told again to use one hand and to work at his own speed. The *S* worked at this task for another half hour.

While the *S* was working on these tasks, the *E* sat, with a stop watch in his hand, busily making notations on a sheet of paper. He did so in order to make it convincing that this was what the *E* was interested in and that these tasks, and how the *S* worked on them, was the total experiment. From our point of view the experiment had hardly started. The hour which the *S* spent working on the repetitive, monotonous tasks was intended to provide, for each *S* uniformly, an experience about which he would have a somewhat negative opinion.

After the half hour on the second task was over, the *E* conspicuously set the stop watch back to zero, put it away, pushed his chair back, lit a cigarette, and said:

> O.K. Well, that's all we have in the experiment itself. I'd like to explain what this has been all about so you'll have some idea of why you were doing this. [*E* pauses.] Well, the way the experiment is set up is this. There are actually two groups in the experiment. In one, the group you were in, we bring the subject in and give him essentially no introduction to the experiment. That is, all we tell him is what he needs to know in order to do the tasks, and he has no idea of what the experiment is all about, or what it's going to be like, or anything like that. But in the other group, we have a student that we've hired that works for us regularly, and what I do is take him into the next room where the subject is waiting—the same room you were waiting in before—and I introduce him as if he had just finished being a subject in the experiment. That is, I say: "This is so-and-so, who's just finished the experiment, and

I've asked him to tell you a little of what it's about before you start." The fellow who works for us then, in conversation with the next subject, makes these points [The *E* then produced a sheet headed "For Group B" which had written on it: It was very enjoyable, I had a lot of fun, I enjoyed myself, it was very interesting, it was intriguing, it was exciting. The *E* showed this to the *S* and then proceeded with his false explanation of the purpose of the experiment.] Now, of course, we have this student do this, because if the experimenter does it, it doesn't look as realistic, and what we're interested in doing is comparing how these two groups do on the experiment—the one with this previous expectation about the experiment, and the other, like yourself, with essentially none.

Up to this point the procedure was identical for *S*s in all conditions. From this point on they diverged somewhat. Three conditions were run, Control, One Dollar, and Twenty Dollars, as follows:

Control Condition

The *E* continued:

> Is that fairly clear? [Pause.] Look, that fellow [looks at watch] I was telling you about from the introductory psychology class said he would get here a couple of minutes from now. Would you mind waiting to see if he wants to talk to you? Fine. Why don't we go into the other room to wait? [The *E* left the *S* in the secretary's office for four minutes. He then returned and said:] O.K. Let's check and see if he does want to talk to you.

One and Twenty Dollar Conditions

The *E* continued:

> Is that fairly clear how it is set up and what we're trying to do? [Pause.] Now, I also have a sort of strange thing to ask you. The thing is this. [Long pause, some confusion and uncertainty in the following, with a degree of embarrassment on the part of the *E*. The manner of the *E* contrasted strongly with the preceding unhesitant and assured false explanation of the experiment. The point was to make it seem to the *S* that this was the first time the *E* had done this and that he felt unsure of himself.] The fellow who normally does this for us couldn't do it today—he just phoned in, and something or other came up for him—so we've been looking around for someone that we could hire to do it for us. You see, we've got another subject waiting [looks at watch] who is supposed to be in that other condition. Now Professor _____, who is in charge of this experiment, suggested that perhaps we could take a chance on your doing it for us. I'll tell you what we had in mind: the thing is, if you could do it for us now, then of course you would know how to do it, and if something like this

should ever come up again, that is, the regular fellow couldn't make it, and we had a subject scheduled, it would be very reassuring to us to know that we had somebody else we could call on who knew how to do it. So, if you would be willing to do this for us, we'd like to hire you to do it now and then be on call in the future, if something like this should ever happen again. We can pay you a dollar (twenty dollars) for doing this for us, that is, for doing it now and then being on call. Do you think you could do that for us?

If the *S* hesitated, the *E* said things like, "It will only take a few minutes," "The regular person is pretty reliable; this is the first time he has missed," or "If we needed you we could phone you a day or two in advance; if you couldn't make it, of course, we wouldn't expect you to come." After the *S* agreed to do it, the *E* gave him the previously mentioned sheet of paper headed "For Group B" and asked him to read it through again. The *E* then paid the *S* one dollar (twenty dollars), made out a hand-written receipt form, and asked the *S* to sign it. He then said:

> O.K., the way we'll do it is this. As I said, the next subject should be here by now. I think the next one is a girl. I'll take you into the next room and introduce you to her, saying that you've just finished the experiment and that we've asked you to tell her a little about it. And what we want you to do is just sit down and get into a conversation with her and try to get across the points on that sheet of paper. I'll leave you alone and come back after a couple of minutes. O.K.?

The *E* then took the *S* into the secretary's office where he had previously waited and where the next *S* was waiting. (The secretary had left the office.) He introduced the girl and the *S* to one another saying that the *S* had just finished the experiment and would tell her something about it. He then left saying he would return in a couple of minutes. the girl, an undergraduate hired for this role, said little until the *S* made some positive remarks about the experiment and then said that she was surprised because a friend of hers had taken the experiment the week before and had told her that it was boring and that she ought to try to get out of it. Most *Ss* responded by saying something like "Oh, no, it's really very interesting. I'm sure you'll enjoy it." The girl, after this listened quietly, accepting and agreeing to everything the *S* told her. The discussion between the *S* and the girl was recorded on a hidden tape recorder.

After two minutes the *E* returned, asked the girl to go into the experimental room, thanked the *S* for talking to the girl, wrote down his phone number to continue the fiction that we might call on him again in the future and

then said: "Look, could we check and see if that fellow from introductory psychology wants to talk to you?"

From this point on, the procedure for all three conditions was once more identical. As the *E* and the *S* started to walk to the office where the interviewer was, the *E* said: "Thanks very much for working on those tasks for us. I hope you did enjoy it. Most of our subjects tell us afterward that they found it quite interesting. You get a chance to see how you react to the tasks and so forth." This short persuasive communication was made in all conditions in exactly the same way. The reason for doing it, theoretically, was to make it easier for anyone who wanted to persuade himself that the tasks had been, indeed, enjoyable.

When they arrived at the interviewer's office, the *E* asked the interviewer whether or not he wanted to talk to the *S*. The interviewer said yes, the *E* shook hands with the *S*, said good-bye, and left. The interviewer, of course, was always kept in complete ignorance of which condition the *S* was in. The interview consisted of four questions, on each of which the *S* was first encouraged to talk about the matter and was then asked to rate his opinion or reaction on an 11-point scale. The questions are as follows:

1. Were the tasks interesting and enjoyable? In what way? In what way were they not? Would you rate how you feel about them on a scale from −5 to +5 where −5 means they were extremely dull and boring, +5 means they were extremely interesting and enjoyable, and zero means they were neutral, neither interesting nor uninteresting.

2. Did the experiment give you an opportunity to learn about your own ability to perform these tasks? In what way? In what way not? Would you rate how you feel about this on a scale from 0 to 10 where 0 means you learned nothing and 10 means you learned a great deal.

3. From what you know about the experiment and the tasks involved in it, would you say the experiment was measuring anything important? That is, do you think the results may have scientific value? In what way? In what way not? Would you rate your opinion on this matter on a scale from 0 to 10 where 0 means the results have no scientific value or importance and 10 means they have a great deal of value and importance.

4. Would you have any desire to participate in another similar experiment? Why? Why not? Would you rate your desire to participate in a similar experiment again on a scale from −5 to +5, where −5 means you would definitely dislike to participate, +5 means you would definitely like to participate, and 0 means you have no particular feeling about it one way or the other.

As may be seen, the questions varied in how directly relevant they were to what the *S* had told the girl. This point will be discussed further in connection with the results.

At the close of the interview the S was asked what he thought the experiment was about and, following this, was asked directly whether or not he was suspicious of anything and, if so, what he was suspicious of. When the interview was over, the interviewer brought the S back to the experimental room where the E was waiting together with the girl who had posed as the waiting S. (In the control condition, of course, the girl was not there.) The true purpose of the experiment was then explained to the S in detail, and the reasons for each of the various steps in the experiment were explained carefully in relation to the true purpose. All experimental Ss in both One Dollar and Twenty Dollar conditions were asked, after this explanation, to return the money they had been given. All Ss, without exception, were quite willing to return the money.

The data from 11 of the 71 Ss in the experiment had to be discarded for the following reasons:

1. Five Ss (three in the One Dollar and two in the Twenty Dollar condition) indicated in the interview that they were suspicious about having been paid to tell the girl the experiment was fun and suspected that that was the real purpose of the experiment.
2. Two Ss (both in the One Dollar condition) told the girl that they had been hired, that the experiment was really boring but they were supposed to say it was fun.
3. Three Ss (one in the One Dollar and two in the Twenty Dollar condition) refused to take the money and refused to be hired.
4. One S (in the One Dollar condition), immediately after having talked to the girl, demanded her phone number saying he would call her and explain things, and also told the E he wanted to wait until she was finished so he could tell her about it.

These 11 Ss were, of course, run through the total experiment anyhow and the experiment was explained to them afterwards. Their data, however, are not included in the analysis.

Summary of Design

There remain, for analysis, 20 Ss in each of the three conditions. Let us review these briefly: 1. *Control condition.* These Ss were treated identically in all respects to the Ss in the experimental conditions, except that they were never asked to, and never did, tell the waiting girl that the experimental tasks were enjoyable and lots of fun. 2. *One Dollar condition.* These Ss were hired for one dollar to tell a waiting S that tasks, which were really rather dull and boring,

were interesting, enjoyable, and lots of fun. 3. *Twenty Dollar condition.* These Ss were hired for twenty dollars to do the same thing.

RESULTS

The major results of the experiment are summarized in Table 1 which lists, separately for each of the three experimental conditions, the average rating which the Ss gave at the end of each question on the interview. We will discuss each of the questions on the interview separately, because they were intended to measure different things. One other point before we proceed to examine the data. In all the comparisons, the Control condition should be regarded as a baseline from which to evaluate the results in the other two conditions. The Control condition gives us, essentially, the reactions of Ss to the tasks and their opinions about the experiment as falsely explained to them, without the experimental introduction of dissonance. The data from the other conditions may be viewed, in a sense, as changes from this baseline.

How Enjoyable the Tasks Were

The average ratings on this question, presented in the first row of figures in Table 1, are the results most important to the experiment. These results are the ones most directly relevant to the specific dissonance which was experimentally created. It will be recalled that the tasks were purposely arranged to be rather boring and monotonous. And, indeed, in the Control condition the average rating was −.45, somewhat on the negative side of the neutral point.

TABLE 1   Average Ratings on Interview Questions For Each Condition

	Experimental Condition		
Question on Interview	Control (N = 20)	One Dollar (N = 20)	Twenty Dollars (N = 20)
How enjoyable tasks were (rated from −5 to +5)	−.45	+1.35	−.05
How much they learned (rated from 0 to 10)	3.08	2.80	3.15
Scientific importance (rated from 0 to 10)	5.60	6.45	5.18
Participate in similar exp. (rated from −5 to +5)	−.62	+1.20	−.25

In the other two conditions, however, the Ss told someone that these tasks were interesting and enjoyable. The resulting dissonance could, of course, most directly be reduced by persuading themselves that the tasks were, indeed, interesting and enjoyable. In the One Dollar condition, since the magnitude of dissonance was high, the pressure to reduce this dissonance would also be high. In this condition, the average rating was +1.35, considerably on the positive side and significantly different from the Control condition at the .02 level[1] ($t = 2.48$).

In the Twenty Dollar condition, where less dissonance was created experimentally because of the greater importance of the consonant relations, there is correspondingly less evidence of dissonance reduction. The average rating in this condition is only –.05, slightly and not significantly higher than the Control condition. The difference between the One Dollar and Twenty Dollar conditions is significant at the .03 level ($t = 2.22$). In short, when an S was induced, by offer of reward, to say something contrary to his private opinion, this private opinion tended to change so as to correspond more closely with what he had said. The greater the reward offered (beyond what was necessary to elicit the behavior) the smaller was the effect.

Desire to Participate in a Similar Experiment

The results from this question are shown in the last row of Table 1. This question is less directly related to the dissonance that was experimentally created for the Ss. Certainly, the more interesting and enjoyable they felt the tasks were, the greater would be their desire to participate in a similar experiment. But other factors would enter also. Hence, one would expect the results on this question to be very similar to the results on "how enjoyable the tasks were" but weaker. Actually, the result, as may be seen in the table, are in exactly the same direction, and the magnitude of the mean differences is fully as large as on the first question. The variability is greater, however, and the differences do not yield high levels of statistical significance. The difference between the One Dollar condition (+1.20) and the Control condition (–.62) is significant at the .08 level ($t = 1.78$). The difference between the One Dollar condition and the Twenty Dollar condition (–.25) reaches only the .15 level of significance ($t = 1.46$).

The Scientific Importance of the Experiment

This question was included because there was a chance that differences might emerge. There are, after all, other ways in which the experimentally created dissonance could be reduced. For example, one way would be for the S to magnify for himself the value of the reward he obtained. This, however, was unlikely in this experiment because money was used for the reward and it is undoubtedly difficult to convince oneself that one dollar is more than it really is. There is another possible way, however. The Ss were given a very good reason, in addition to being paid, for saying what they did to the waiting girl. The Ss were told it was necessary for the experiment. The dissonance could, consequently, be reduced by magnifying the importance of this cognition. The more scientifically important they considered the experiment to be, the less was the total magnitude of dissonance. It is possible, then, that the results on this question, shown in the third row of figures in Table 1, might reflect dissonance reduction.

The results are weakly in line with what one would expect if the dissonance were somewhat reduced in this manner. The One Dollar condition is higher than the other two. The difference between the One and Twenty Dollar conditions reaches the .08 level of significance on a two-tailed test ($t = 1.79$). The difference between the One Dollar and Control conditions is not impressive at all ($t = 1.21$). The result that the Twenty Dollar condition is actually lower than the Control condition is undoubtedly a matter of chance ($t = 0.58$).

How Much They Learned From the Experiment

The results on this question are shown in the second row for figures in Table 1. The question was included because, as far as we could see, it had nothing to do with the dissonance that was experimentally created and could not be used for dissonance reduction. One would then expect no differences at all among the three conditions. We felt it was important to show that the effect was not a completely general one but was specific to the content of the dissonance which was created. As can be readily seen in Table 1, there are only negligible differences among conditions. The highest t value for any of these differences is only 0.48.

DISCUSSION OF A POSSIBLE ALTERNATIVE EXPLANATION

We mentioned in the introduction that Janis and King (1954; 1956) in explaining their findings, proposed an explanation in terms of the self-convincing effect of mental rehearsal and thinking up new arguments by the person who had to improvise a speech. Kelman (1953), in the previously mentioned study, in attempting to explain the unexpected finding that the persons who complied in the moderate reward condition changed their opinion more than in the high reward condition, also proposed the same kind of explanation. If the results of our experiment are to be taken as strong corroboration of the theory of cognitive dissonance, this possible alternative explanation must be dealt with.

Specifically, as applied to our results, this alternative explanation would maintain that perhaps, for some reason, the *S*s in the One Dollar condition worked harder at telling the waiting girl that the tasks were fun and enjoyable. That is, in the One Dollar condition they may have rehearsed it more mentally, thought up more ways of saying it, may have said it more convincingly, and so on. Why this might have been the case is, of course, not immediately apparent. One might expect that, in the Twenty Dollar condition, having been paid more, they would try to do a better job of it than in the One Dollar condition. But nevertheless, the possibility exists that the *S*s in the One Dollar condition may have improvised more.

Because of the desirability of investigating this possible alternative explanation, we recorded on a tape recorder the conversation between each *S* and the girl. These recordings were transcribed and then rated, by two independent raters, on five dimensions. The ratings were, of course, done in ignorance of which condition each *S* was in. The reliabilities of these ratings, that is, the correlations between the two independent raters, ranged from .61 to .88, with an average reliability of .71. The five ratings were:

1. The content of what the *S* said *before* the girl made the remark that her friend told her it was boring. The stronger the *S*'s positive statements about the tasks, and the more ways in which he said they were interesting and enjoyable, the higher the rating.

2. The content of what the *S* said *after* the girl made the above-mentioned remark. This was rated in the same way as for the content before the remark.

3. A similar rating of the over-all content of what the *S* said.

4. A rating of how persuasive and convincing the *S* was in what he said and the way in which he said it.

5. A rating of the amount of time in the discussion that the *S* spent discussing the tasks as opposed to going off into irrelevant things.

The mean ratings for the One Dollar and Twenty Dollar conditions, averaging the ratings of the two independent raters, are presented in Table 2. It is clear from examining the table that, in all cases, the Twenty Dollar condition is slightly higher. The differences are small, however, and only on the rating of "amount of time" does the difference between the two conditions even approach significance. We are certainly justified in concluding that the *S*s in the One

TABLE 2   Average Ratings of Discussion Between Subject and Girl

Dimension Rated	Condition		
	One Dollar	Twenty Dollars	Value of *t*
Content before remark by girl (rated from 0 to 5)	2.26	2.62	1.08
Content after remark by girl (rated from 0 to 5)	1.63	1.75	0.11
Over-all content (rated from 0 to 5)	1.89	2.19	1.08
Persuasiveness and conviction (rated from 0 to 10)	4.79	5.50	0.99
Time spent on topic (rated from 0 to 10)	6.74	8.19	1.80

Dollar condition did not improvise more nor act more convincingly. Hence, the alternative explanation discussed above cannot account for the findings.

SUMMARY

Recently, Festinger (1957) has proposed a theory concerning cognitive dissonance. Two derivations from this theory are tested here. These are:

1. If a person is induced to do or say something which is contrary to his private opinion, there will be a tendency for him to change his opinion so as to bring it into correspondence with what he has done or said.

2. The larger the pressure used to elicit the overt behavior (beyond the minimum needed to elicit it) the weaker will be the above-mentioned tendency.

A laboratory experiment was designed to test these derivations. Subjects were subjected to a boring experience and then paid to tell someone that the experience had been interesting and enjoyable. The amount of money paid the subject was varied. The private opinions of the subjects concerning the experiences were then determined.

The results strongly corroborate the theory that was tested.

REFERENCES

Festinger, L. A. *Theory of cognitive dissonance.* Evanston, Ill: Row Peterson, 1957.

Janis, I. L., & King, B. T. The influence of role-playing on opinion change. *J. Abnorm. Soc. Psychol.*, 1954, 49, 211–218.

Kelman, H. Attitude change as a function of response restriction. *Hum. Relat.*, 1953, 6, 185–214.

King, B. T., & Janis, I. L. Comparison of the effectiveness of improvised versus non-improvised role-playing in producing opinion changes. *Hum. Relat.*, 1956, 9, 177–186.

NOTES

1. All statistical tests referred to in this paper are two-tailed.

Received November 18, 1957.

CRITICAL THINKING QUESTIONS

1. According to Festinger and Carlsmith, why did the offer of $20 reduce cognitive dissonance?
2. According to Festinger and Carlsmith, subjects who were paid $1 to lie felt cognitive dissonance between their actual experience and the lie they told, and they resolved this dissonance by changing their perception of their experience. Why did they resolve dissonance in this way? Are there other ways they could have reduced the dissonance?
3. What is the importance of the fact that the results from 11 subjects were excluded from the analyses? Does this make the results of this experiment suspect?
4. How would self-perception theory described in Chapter 2 and Chapter 10 explain the results of this experiment? How would self-affirmation theory described in Chapter 10 explain the results of this experiment.
5. How is this study related to the study described in Reading #2, in which children's intrinsic motivation was undermined by a reward? How would cognitive dissonance theory explain the results of that study?
6. Do people often experience cognitive dissonance in their everyday lives? How do they tend to resolve cognitive dissonance?

READING 11 _____

This article demonstrates both the impact of culture and some of the basic processes of persuasion. Han and Shavitt found that in Korea, a collectivistic culture, people were more easily persuaded by appeals to ingroup benefit, harmony, and family integrity. In contrast, in the United States, an individualistic culture, people are more easily persuaded by appeals to individual benefits, preferences, personal success, and independence. Han and Shavitt also found that the frequency of certain kinds of advertisements in these two countries reflected these differences in effectiveness.

Chapter 10 describes the basic processes involved in persuasion, and this study suggests that those basic processes can be affected by one's culture of origin. The discussion of the effects of culture on the self-concept in Chapter 2 parallels the findings in this study. Also note the parallels between this research and the research on culture that is discussed in the contexts of fundamental attribution error (Chapter 3) and conformity (Chapter 9).

This article uses a combination of methods; it examines both the persuasiveness of advertisements in the laboratory and the actual frequency of advertisements outside the laboratory. Using both of these methods improves the quality of the research, but it does make the methodology harder to understand. As you read the studies, make sure you can identify whether it is a study examining the frequency of advertisements or an experimental study examining the impact of advertisements.

Persuasion and Culture: Advertising Appeals in Individualistic and Collectivistic Societies

Sang-pil Han
Hanyang University, Seoul, Korea

Sharon Shavitt
University of Illinois, Urbana-Champaign

Two studies examined the extent to which a core dimension of cultural variability, individualism–collectivism (Hofstede, 1980, 1983; Triandis, 1990), is reflected in the types of persuasive appeals that tend to be used and that tend to be effective in different countries. Study 1 demonstrated that magazine advertisements in the United States, an individualistic culture, employed appeals to individual benefits and preferences, personal success, and independence to a greater extent than did advertisements in Korea, a collectivistic culture. Korean advertisements employed appeals emphasizing ingroup benefits, harmony, and family integrity to a greater extent than did U.S. ads. Study 2, a controlled experiment conducted in the two countries, demonstrated that in the U.S. advertisements emphasizing individualistic benefits were more persuasive, and ads emphasizing family or ingroup benefits were less persuasive than they were in Korea. In both studies, however, product characteristics played a role in moderating these overall

differences: Cultural differences emerged strongly in Studies 1 and 2 for advertised products that tend to be purchased and used with others, but were much less evident for products that are typically purchased and used individually. © 1994 Academic Press, Inc.

Individualism–collectivism is perhaps the most basic dimension of cultural variability identified in cross-cultural research. Concepts related to this dimension have been employed in several social science domains (cf. Triandis, McCusker, & Hui, 1990), and the individualism–collectivism dimension has come to be regarded as "central to an understanding of cultural values, of work values, of social systems, as well as in the studies of morality, the structure of constitutions, and cultural patterns" (Triandis, Brislin, & Hui, 1988). Several recent studies have suggested that individualism and collectivism are contrasting cultural syndromes that are associated with a broad pattern of

SOURCE: "Persuasion and Culture: Advertising Appeals in Individualistic and Collectivistic Societies" by Sang-pil Han and Sharon Shavitt, *Journal of Experimental Social Psychology 30*, 326–350. Copyright © 1991 by Academic Press, Inc. Reprinted by permission.

differences in individual's social perceptions and social behavior, including differences in the definition of self and its perceived relation to ingroups and outgroups (Markus & Kitayama, 1991), in the endorsement of values relevant to individual vs group goals (Triandis et al., 1990), and in the pattern and style of social interactions (cf. Triandis, 1990).

However, little is known about the implications of these cultural differences for another social process that is fundamental to every culture: persuasion. Persuasive communications transmit and reflect the values of a culture. Persuasive messages are used to obtain the compliance that achieves the personal, political, and economic ends valued in the culture. Although social influence has always been a central arena of research in social psychology, little is understood about what differences exist in the types of persuasive appeals used in different cultures (see Burgoon, Dillard, Doran, & Miller, 1982; Glenn, Witmeyer, & Stevenson, 1977). Even less is known about the effectiveness of different appeal types in different cultures.

What types of persuasive appeals are prevalent in individualistic versus collectivistic cultures? And how do members of these different cultures differ in the extent to which they are persuaded by these appeals? This paper presents an exploration of these questions.

Our studies focused on cross-cultural differences in advertising, a form of persuasive communication that is highly prevalent in many societies, both individualist and collectivist. The studies examined how this core dimension of cultural variability is reflected in the types of advertising appeals employed in two countries (the United States and Korea) that have been shown to differ greatly on the individualism–collectivism dimension (Hofstede, 1980, 1983). The research also investigated the relative *effectiveness* of individualistic and collectivistic advertising appeals in the United States and Korea. Moreover, the research looks beyond overall cultural differences in advertising content and persuasiveness to identify factors that may moderate these differences.

Individualism and Collectivism

Individualism–collectivism is perhaps the broadest and most widely used dimension of cultural variability for cultural comparison (Gudykunst and Ting-Toomey, 1988). Hofstede (1980) described individualism–collectivism as the relationship between the individual and the collectivity that prevails in a given society. In individualistic cultures, individuals tend to prefer independent relationships to others and to subordinate ingroup goals to their personal

goals. In collectivistic cultures, on the other hand, individuals are more likely to have interdependent relationships to their ingroups and to subordinate their personal goals to their ingroup goals. Individualistic cultures are associated with emphases on independence, achievement, freedom, high levels of competition, and pleasure. Collectivistic cultures are associated with emphases on interdependence, harmony, family security, social hierarchies, cooperation, and low levels of competition (see Triandis, 1989, 1990; Triandis et al., 1990, for supporting evidence and discussions of the antecedents and consequences of individualism and collectivism).

Individualistic and collectivistic cultures are characterized by important differences in members' social perceptions and social behavior. Members of these cultures have very different construals of the self, of others, and of the interdependence of the two (Markus & Kitayama, 1991). The self is defined in terms of ingroup memberships (e.g., family and ethnic identity) to a greater extent in collectivistic cultures than individualistic cultures. Moreover, there is evidence suggesting that members of collectivistic cultures perceive their ingroups to be more homogeneous than their outgroups, whereas the reverse is true among persons in individualistic societies (Triandis et al., 1990). These cultural differences in the perceived relation of the self to others have been shown to have many other cognitive, emotional, and behavioral consequences (see Markus & Kitayama, 1991).

The individualistic cultural pattern is found in most northern and western regions of Europe and in North America, whereas the collectivistic cultural pattern is common in Asia, Africa, Latin America, and the Pacific (Hofstede, 1980, 1983). In the present studies, the United States and Korea were selected to represent individualistic and collectivistic cultures, respectively. These countries were selected based on Hofstede's (1980, 1983) studies of individualism–collectivism in over 50 countries, which indicated that the United States is highly individualistic with a score of 91 on a 100-point individualism scale, whereas Korea is clearly on the collectivistic side with a score of 18.

Persuasion and Culture

We expected that advertisements in the United States and Korea would reflect their indigenous individualistic or collectivistic cultural orientation. We also expected that the persuasiveness of certain types of ad appeals would differ in these two cultures. There are several reasons to hypothesize a link between these cultural patterns and persuasion processes.

First, previous content analyses of advertising have demonstrated differences between countries in the prevalence of various types of ad content, including emotional content, informative content, comparative content, and the use of humor (e.g, Hong, Muderrisoglu, & Zinkhan, 1987; Madden, Caballero, & Matsukubo, 1986; Martenson, 1987; Miracle, 1987; Renforth & Raveed, 1983; Tansey, Hyman, & Zinkhan, 1990; Weinberger & Spotts, 1989; Zandpour, Chang, & Catalano, 1992), although ads have not always been found to reflect their indigenous cultures (e.g., Marquez, 1975; Mueller, 1987). The roles of individualism and collectivism have not been investigated in these content analyses, although the findings have suggested that cultural factors often influence the types of ads employed in different countries.

Furthermore, researchers in the field of communication have argued that the persuasive styles employed by speakers may vary from culture to culture (Burgoon et al., 1982), and that the effectiveness of those strategies may vary, as well (Bronfenbrenner, 1964; Wedge, 1968). For example, research by Glenn et al. (1977) suggested that Americans prefer a persuasive style based on inductive reasoning. Soviets tend to rely on deductive logic and axiomatic principles, and members of the Arab culture tend to use an affective or intuitive style of persuasive communication. As Glenn et al. (1977) argued, it is reasonable to assume that those who are attempting to persuade others will "select approaches consistent with their own past experiences within the cultures to which they belong, and that they are selected, in part, on the basis of their ability to handle a style congruent with the culture" (p. 53).

Research on individualism and collectivism has also suggested a link between culture and attitudinal processes. When asked to endorse attitude statements or to rate the personal importance of values linked to family integrity, welfare of the ingroup, and the importance of personal goals, subjects' ratings tend to correspond with the orientation of their particular culture. In collectivistic cultures, members are less likely to emphasize hedonism and more likely to emphasize ingroup obligations than in individualistic societies (Triandis, Bontempo, Betancourt, Bond, Leung, Brenes, Georgas, Hui, Marin, Setiadi, Sinha, Verma, Spangenberg, Touzard, & de Montmollin, 1986; Triandis, Bontempo, Villareal, Asai, & Lucca, 1988; Triandis et al., 1990). Such differences in culturally endorsed attitudes and values may be reflected in the tendency to use, and to accept, persuasive appeals that emphasize these different values.

Finally, research has shown that perceived social norms, roles, and values are major determinants of behavioral intentions in collectivist cultures, whereas individual likes and dislikes as well as perceived costs and benefits are weighted more heavily by individualists (Davidson, Jaccard, Triandis, Morales, & Diaz-Guerrero, 1976). This suggests that persuasive appeals that emphasize social norms and roles versus individual preferences and benefits may be more effective in changing behavioral intentions in collectivistic versus individualistic cultures.

Based on these findings, we expected that different types of advertising appeals would tend to be employed and to be effective in the U.S. and Korea. Specifically, appeals emphasizing family expectations, relations with ingroups, and group benefits—i.e., collectivistic appeals—would be more prevalent in Korean advertising, whereas messages emphasizing a concern with individual benefits, personal success, and independence—i.e., individualistic appeals—would be more prevalent in American advertising. We also expected that ads emphasizing these culturally relevant values would be more persuasive than ads emphasizing other values.

Moderating Factors

Although cultural orientation may be reflected in the prevalence and effectiveness of different types of appeals overall, these cultural differences may be moderated by other factors.

Product characteristics   Products differ in the goals that are associated with them and, therefore, in the types of benefits that are sought from them. As a result, appeals addressing different types of benefits are effective for different types of products (Shavitt, 1990).

Shared versus personal product categories appeared to be potentially important in moderating differences between individualistic and collectivistic cultures. *Shared products* were defined as ones for which the decision making process involved in purchase and the pattern of product usage are likely to include family members or friends (e.g., home appliances, groceries, and furniture). *Personal products,* conversely, were defined as ones for which the purchase decision and product usage are usually done by an individual (e.g., fashion apparel, cosmetics, personal care products).

How would these product characteristics moderate cultural differences in the content and persuasiveness of appeals? Shared products, which offer benefits both for the individual and for the group, could plausibly be advertised both in terms of individualistic and collectivistic appeals. For such products, cultural differences in the value placed on individual versus collective benefits could be manifested in the types of appeals that are typically employed and that are persuasive. In contrast, personal products, which offer primarily personal benefits and are typically used individually, are not likely to be convincingly promoted in terms of group-oriented or collectivistic appeals. Instead, they are likely to be promoted in terms of individual benefits, even in cultures where group benefits are highly valued. Thus, the nature of the product may constrain the degree to which cultural differences in individualism–collectivism are likely to be manifested in advertising (see Shavitt, Lowrey, & Han, 1992, for a similar point about how products constrain individual differences in advertising effectiveness).

Involvement   The concept of involvement has played a central role in theory and research on advertising and persuasion. Involvement has been defined and operationalized in a variety of ways (see Greenwald & Leavitt, 1984; Johnson & Eagly, 1989). The present research focused on involvement as the extent to which the information in a message is potentially important or personally relevant to outcomes desired by the message recipient (e.g., Petty & Cacioppo, 1986). Persuasion processes under conditions of high involvement differ from those under low involvement. Many studies have shown that involvement can moderate the effects of other message factors, including message content, on attitude change (e.g., Kahle & Homer, 1985; Petty & Cacioppo, 1979; Petty, Cacioppo, & Schumann, 1983).

Involvement could also moderate cultural differences in persuasion. Under high involvement conditions, when an ad presents information that is relevant to an anticipated decision (Petty et al., 1983), there may be a greater tendency to evaluate the product in terms of criteria that one considers particularly important, including cultural value standards. Under low involvement, however, one may be responsive to a wider variety of benefits. The possible role of involvement in moderating cultural differences in ad persuasiveness was investigated in Study 2.

STUDY 1

The first study assessed the extent to which advertising content in the U.S. and Korea reflects its indigenous individualistic or collectivistic cultural pattern. By examining the role of product characteristics, the study also attempted to identify conditions under which these cultural differences are most likely to emerge.

Method

Sample of advertisements   One popular news magazine and one woman's magazine in each country were chosen for the study. The periodicals selected as being representative of American news and women's magazines were *Newsweek* and *Redbook,* respectively. The comparable magazines for Korea were *Wolgan Chosun* and *Yosong Donga.* In order to achieve sample comparability, the two magazines were selected from each country based on their similarity in format and target audience (Mueller, 1987). The time span studied was January 1987 through December 1988. Every third month's issues was included in the sample. Two hundred product ads from each country were randomly selected from the sample.

Coding of advertisements   A manual for coding the ads was developed from theory-based factors identified by previous research on individualism–collectivism (Hofstede, 1980; Hui, 1984; Triandis et al. 1986, 1988). The individualistic classification included, (1) appeals about individuality or independence, (2) reflections of self-reliance with hedonism or competition, (3) emphasis on self-improvement or self-realization, and (4) emphasis on the benefits of the product to the consumer (you). The collectivistic classification included, (1) appeals about family integrity, (2) focus on group integrity or group well-being, (3) concerns about others or support of society, (4) focus on interdependent relationships with others, and (5) focus on group goals. A fuller description of the coding scheme is presented in Appendix A.[1]

The advertisements of each country were evaluated by four judges. For each country's ads, coding was performed by two native speakers from that country (Americans for U.S. ads and Koreans for Korean ads). In addition, two bilingual coders coded both the U.S. and Korean ads. These bilingual coders were native Koreans, who lived in the United States for several years and were fluent in English. Coders were ignorant of the purposes of the study, and independently rated the degree of individualistic or collectivistic content for each of the ads on two 3-point scales [1 = not at all individualist (collectivistic), 2 = somewhat, 3 = very].[2] Discrepancies in coding were settled by a fifth judge for the U.S. data, and by discussion among coders for the Korean data. The average correlation between the Korean coders' ratings was $r = .80$, and the average correlation of the American coders' ratings was $r = .84$, which are within acceptable ranges suggested by Kassarjian (1977). Moreover, the bilinguals' coding was highly correlated both with Koreans' coding of Korean ads (mean $r = .85$) and with Americans' coding of U.S. ads (mean $r = .82$), suggesting that possible cross-cultural differences in interpreting the meaning of ad content did not pose a serious threat to the reliability of the coding.

Selection of personal vs shared products Personal vs shared product categories were determined on the basis of a survey in which 24 American students and 24 Korean students rated 44 consumer products and services in terms of, (1) the decision making process involved in purchase (1 = never discuss with their family or friends whether to purchase, 5 = always discuss), and (2) usage pattern (1 = used mostly individually, 5 = used mostly with other members of family or friends). The correlations between the two mean scores across all products were high (American data, $r = .81$; Korean data, $r = .74$), and no differences were obtained between countries in the mean rating of the personal products or in the mean rating of the shared products. Thus, an average of the two items across all 48 respondents was used to classify products as personal or shared. Although many products could perhaps be classified as personal in some situations and shared in others, we believe that our classification adequately captured basic differences in the way the products tend to be purchased and used. See Appendix B for a complete listing of these products.

Results

U.S. ads were expected to be rated as more individualistic and less collectivistic than Korean ads. However, product category was expected to moderate these effects such that the differences between countries would be greater for shared than for personal products.

Table 1 shows the mean ratings of individualism and collectivism as a function of country and product category. An analysis of variance with country (United States vs Korea) and product type (personal vs shared) as between-subject factors and rating type (individualism vs collectivism ratings) as a within-subject factor yielded a significant main effect of rating type ($F(1, 396) = 72.21$; $p < .0001$) indicating that, overall, ads tended to be rated higher in individualism than in collectivism. More importantly, a significant interaction of country × rating type emerged ($F(1, 396) = 44.69$; $p < .0001$) indicating as expected that the relative ratings of ads on individualism and collectivism differed for U.S. vs Korean ads. Simple main effects tests demonstrated that U.S. ads were rated significantly higher in individualism than Korean ads ($F(1, 398) = 14.98$; $p < .001$), whereas Korean ads were rated significantly higher in collectivism than U.S. ads ($F(1, 398) = 42.86$; $p < .001$).

The interaction of product category × rating type was also significant ($F(1, 396) = 39.10$; $p < .0001$), indicating that the relative ratings of ads for individualism and

TABLE 1   Individualism and Collectivism Ratings in U.S. and Korean Advertisements

	U.S. ads[a,b]	Korean ads[a,b]	Overall[c,d]
Individualism ratings			
Personal products*	2.07	1.91	1.99
Shared products*	1.88	1.50	1.69
Overall*	1.98	1.70	
Collectivism ratings			
Personal products*	1.11	1.32	1.22
Shared products*	1.25	1.89	1.57
Overall*	1.19	1.61	

Note: Ratings were made on two 3-point scales, where 1 indicated "not at all individualistic (or collectivistic)" and "very."
* Mean ratings for U.S. and Korean ads differed significantly at $p < .005$.
[a] For personal products, individualism and collectivism ratings differed significantly at $p < .005$.
[b] For shared products, individualism and collectivism ratings differed signficantly at $p < .005$.
[c] Individualism ratings for personal and shared products differed significantly at $p < .005$.
[d] Collectivism ratings for personal and shared products differed signficantly at $p < .005$.

collectivism differed for personal vs shared products. Simple effects tests indicated that ads for personal products were rated significantly higher in individualism than ads for shared products ($F(1, 398) = 17.78$; $p < .0001$), whereas ads for shared products were rated significantly higher in collectivism than ads for personal products ($F(1, 398) = 27.95$; $p < .0001$).

However, as expected, the two-way interactions were qualified by a country × product category × rating type interaction ($F(1, 392) = 11.42$; $p < .001$), indicating as expected that product category moderated the differences in the ratings of Korean vs U.S. ads. That is, the differences were greater for shared than for personal products. Further analysis revealed that the interaction of country × rating type was significant within each product category, indicating that ratings of U.S. versus Korean ads differed reliably for both product types (personal products: $F(1, 194) = 7.35$; $p < .01$; shared products: $F(1, 202) = 42.76$; $p < .0001$). But within-group comparisons suggested as expected that cultural differences in advertising were much more evident for shared products than for personal products. For personal products, individualism ratings were higher than collectivism ratings for *both* U.S. and Korean ads (U.S. ads: $t(96) = 11.58$; $p < .001$; Korean ads: $t(98) = 5.36$; $p < .001$). In contrast, for shared products, individualism ratings were higher than collectivism ratings for U.S. ads ($t(102) = 7.73$; $p < .001$), whereas collectivism ratings were higher than individualism ratings for Korean ads ($t(100) =$ 2.93; $p < .005$).

Discussion

The data supported the hypothesis that individualism–collectivism, a basic dimension of cultural variability, is reflected in the content of advertising in different cultures. As expected, U.S. ads were rated as more individualistic and less collectivistic than Korean ads. That is, U.S. ads were more likely than Korean ads to emphasize self-reliance, self-improvement, and personal rewards, and less likely to emphasize family well-being, ingroup goals, and interdependence.

Importantly, this overall difference was not uniform across products. Cross-cultural differences emerged for both product categories, but were greater for shared than for personal products. The ratings of U.S. and Korean ads suggested that personal products tended to be promoted more in terms of individualistic than collectivistic appeals in both countries. This was as expected, since personal products offer predominantly personal or individually experienced benefits, and thus are unlikely to be promoted with group-oriented appeals. However, shared products tended to be promoted differently in the two countries—more in terms of individualistic appeals in the United States and more in terms of collectivistic appeals in Korea. This may be because shared products, which offer both individual and collective benefits, can be convincingly promoted in terms of either type of benefit, allowing cultural differences in the value placed on these benefits to influence the types of appeals that are employed.

STUDY 2

Study 2 was conducted to investigate cultural differences in the relative *effectiveness* of individualistic and collectivistic appeals. In this experiment, subjects in the United States and in Korea read advertisements that employed individualistic or collectivistic appeals, and completed measures assessing the persuasiveness of those ads. Overall, we expected individualistic appeals to be more persuasive in the United States and collectivistic appeals to be more persuasive in Korea. Additionally, as in Study 1, we examined the role of personal vs shared products in moderating the hypothesized cultural differences. Cultural differences in the persuasiveness of appeals were expected to be greater for shared than for personal products, for the reasons described earlier.

The possible moderating role of ad recipients' level of involvement was also investigated. Based on previous research we reasoned that, under high involvement, when ad information is relevant to an anticipated decision (e.g., Petty et al., 1983), one may be more likely to evaluate products in terms of criteria that are considered highly important, including cultural value standards. Under low involvement, however, one may be responsive to a wider variety of appeals, and thus cultural values may play a more limited role.

Personal and Shared Products

These were chosen from the list of products identified in the Study 1 survey. *Chewing gum* and *running shoes* were chosen as the personal products. *Detergents* and *clothes irons* were selected as the shared products. These products were chosen because (1) they were expected to be equally familiar to subjects in both countries, and (2) appeal types for these products could be readily manipulated.

Involvement

The perceived personal relevance of the ads that subjects read was manipulated. Subjects in the high involvement condition were led to anticipate purchase decisions regarding the advertised products, whereas low involvement subjects were not (see Method).

Method

Subjects American participants were 64 persons between the ages of 18 and 27 recruited through notices placed in University of Illinois campus buildings, promising $4 for participation. Korean participants were 64 persons between the ages of 18 and 27 enrolled in introductory communication and advertising classes at a major university in Seoul.

Involvement manipulation Involvement was manipulated in two ways. On subjects' initial instructions sheet, Americans in the high involvement condition were informed that the advertised products were scheduled to be advertised in medium-sized cities throughout the Midwest, including their own city (Champaign–Urbana), whereas subjects in the low involvement condition were informed that the products were scheduled to be advertised only in foreign countries. For Koreans, involvement was manipulated with comparable statements (i.e., products to be advertised in Seoul vs foreign countries). To strengthen the involvement manipulation, all subjects in the high involvement condition were also told that they would be asked to make a purchase decision regarding the advertised products in the study. Subjects in the low involvement condition were not led to anticipate a purchase decision.

These procedures were designed to enhance or reduce the personal relevance of the advertisements. Previous research has consistently found this sort of method to be effective in manipulating outcome-relevant involvement (e.g., Kahle & Homer, 1985; Petty et al., 1983; Sanbonmatsu, Shavitt, & Sherman, 1991).

Materials All of the advertisements were written first in English. Then, a series of double-translations with decentering (Brislin, 1980) was employed to translate the ads into the Korean versions.[3] Many of the headlines and illustrations for both the individualistic and collectivistic ads were taken from actual magazine ads, enhancing the realism of the stimulus ads. One pair of advertisements (one individualistic and one collectivistic ad) was created for each of the four products. Each ad consisted of only a headline and illustrations. Individualistic ads featured such headlines as "Treat yourself to a breath of freshening experience," and "Easy walking. Easy exercise. Easy weight loss. It's easy when you have the right shoes." Collectivistic ads featured such headlines as, "Share the Freedent breath freshening experience." and "Easy walking. Easy exercise. The shoes for your family." Individualistic ads generally featured pictures of individuals, whereas collectivistic ads generally featured pictures of groups of people. The product was also pictured in each ad.[4]

Presentation of ads Each subject read and responded to all four pairs of ads. The order of the four products subjects read about was counterbalanced in a pairwise balanced Latin-square design. The order of appeals within each pair of ads was also counterbalanced such that an individualistic ad was read first for one personal and one shared product (either for chewing gum and detergent, or for running shoes and iron), and a collectivistic appeal was read first for the other products.

Dependent measures Subjects rated their purchase intention for the advertised brand on a 4-point scale, anchored by "I definitely would/would not buy it." They also responded to two attitude measures, each consisting of three semantic differential scales anchored at −4 and +4. The first measure assessed their attitude toward the ad (scale anchors: bad–good, negative–positive, and disliked–liked). The second assessed their overall impression of the brand (scale anchors: undesirable–desirable, unsatisfactory–satisfactory, and bad–good). Subjects also compared the persuasiveness of the two ads in the pair by responding to a six-item questionnaire, including such items as "Overall, which ad do you think is better?" "Which one appeals to you more?" and "Which ad do you think would be more successful?"

Such a measure has been used successfully in previous studies to assess the relative persuasiveness of ads (Snyder & DeBono, 1985, 1987).

As a check on the classification of products as personal vs shared, subjects rated each product in terms of (1) their purchase decision process (1 = never discuss with family or friends prior to purchase, 5 = always), and (2) usage (1 = used mostly individually, 5 = used mostly with family or friends). As a check on the involvement manipulation, subjects completed three 9-point scales (1 = not at all, 9 = very much), on which they rated (1) how much they paid attention to the study, (2) how interesting the study was, and (3) how much attention they paid to the ads.

Procedure Subjects participated in groups of 12 to 20. They were told that they would evaluate a series of print advertisements currently being studied by researchers at a major advertising firm. Subjects were asked to react to the ads as naturally and spontaneously as possible, the way they would as ordinary consumers. After reading the first ad for the first product, they rated their purchase intention and their attitude toward the ad and the brand. Next, subjects read the second ad for the first product and then completed the questionnaire on which they compared the persuasiveness of the two ads in the pair. In this way, they read and responded to the four pairs of ads in turn. Finally, subjects completed the manipulation checks, and were then debriefed, paid (U.S. subjects), and dismissed.

Results

Manipulation checks As a check on the personal–shared classification of products, subjects had rated each product in terms of the involvement of others in their (1) purchase decision and (2) product usage. An average of the two 5-point items was used, with 5 being a highly shared product. Subjects' responses yielded a pattern consistent with *a priori* classifications of the products (and with the results of the same survey conducted for Study 1). Higher ratings were given to products that were classified as shared (United States, $M = 3.17$; Korea, $M = 3.39$) than those classified as personal (United States, $M = 1.89$; Korea, $M = 1.96$). An analysis of variance with product type as a within-subject variable and country as a between-subjects variable indicated that this main effect for product type was significant ($F(1, 124) = 346.56$; $p < .0001$). In addition, when ratings were examined for each product individually, the findings were supportive for all products.

Subjects' levels of attention, interest, and involvement were assessed as a check on the involvement manipulation. Because the three 9-point scales were internally consistent

(Cronbach's alpha = .79), an involvement index was created by averaging the items. Subjects' mean ratings in both countries were higher in the high involvement conditions (United States, $M = 7.58$; Korea, $M = 7.33$) than the low involvement conditions (United States, $M = 6.44$; Korea, $M = 6.38$), a significant main effect ($F(1, 95) = 19.17$; $p < .001$). No other effects were significant.

Persuasiveness of Appeals

Attitude index Subjects had rated their purchase intention and attitudes toward the ad and the brand in response to the first ad they read in each pair of ads for a product. Thus, half of the subjects provided these ratings to one ad for each product, and the other half responded to the other ad. These three ratings were substantially intercorrelated (mean $r = .66$) and were combined to yield a single attitude index. Because they were made on different scales, the ratings were transformed to z-scores before being averaged. The means of this standardized attitude index showed, as expected, that U.S. subjects were more persuaded overall when the ads presented individualistic ($M = 0.22$) rather than collectivistic ($M = -0.20$) appeals, whereas Koreans were more persuaded overall when the ads presented collectivistic ($M = 0.19$) rather than individualistic ($M = -0.23$) appeals.

Mean attitude index scores are shown in Table 2. These data were submitted to an analysis of variance with appeal type (individualistic vs collectivistic) and product type (personal vs shared) as within-subject variables and country (United States vs Korea), involvement (high vs low), and counterbalance order of products and of ads as between-subjects variables. This yielded a significant country × appeal type interaction ($F(1, 93) = 26.24$; $p < .0001$), indicating as predicted that the relative effectiveness of the two appeal types differed in the United States versus Korea. Moreover, pairwise comparisons of the effectiveness of the two appeal types within each country, as well as comparisons of the effectiveness of each appeal type in the United States vs Korea, were all significant (p's < .05).

However, as expected, this effect was moderated by product type. For shared products, U.S. subjects responded more favorably to individualistic appeals than collectivistic appeals, whereas the opposite was the case for Korean subjects (see Table 2). This pattern also emerged for personal products, but less strongly. Although the country × appeal type interaction was significant within each product category (personal products: $F(1, 124) = 4.99$; $p < .05$; shared products: $F(1, 125) = 39.49$; $p < .0001$), there was a significant country × product category × appeal type

TABLE 2 Persuasiveness of Individualistic and Collectivistic Appeals in the United States and Korea

	U.S. Subjects	Korean Subjects
Low involvement[a]		
Indidivualistic appeals		
Personal products	.11	−.03
Shared products	.41	−.59
Overall[b]	.26	−.29
Collectivistic appeals		
Personal products	−.11	.09
Shared products	−.24	−.12
Overall	−.17	.01
High involvement[a]		
Indidivualistic appeals		
Personal products	.09	−.21
Shared products	.32	−.12
Overall[b]	.19	−.17
Collectivistic appeals		
Personal products	−.18	.19
Shared products	−.26	.53
Overall	−.22	.36
Overall[c]		
Individualistic appeals		
Personal products	.10	−.12
Shared products[d]	.34	−.34
Collectivistic appeals		
Personal products	−.13	.14
Shared products[d]	−.25	.25

Note: Tabled values are the standardized scores on the attitude index (the average of standardized scores across three evaluative measures).
[a] Over all products, mean attitude index ratings differed significantly between individualistic and collectivistic appeals for U.S. subjects and for Korean subjects (p's < .05, 2-tailed. (Comparisons within and between product types were not conducted within level of involvement.)
[b] Over all products, mean attitude index ratings differed significantly between countries at $p < .05$, 2-tailed.
[c] For personal products, differences in attitude ratings between individualistic and collectivistic appeals were nonsignificant for U.S. subjects and for Korean subjects. For shared products, these differences were significant for U.S. subjects and for Korean subjects (p's < .0001, 2-tailed).
[d] U.S. and Korean ratings differed significantly at $p < .001$ (2-tailed).

interaction ($F(1, 93) = 6.42$; $p < .05$), indicating that the magnitude of the overall cultural differences in the persuasiveness of these appeals depended on what type of product was being advertised. Moreover, for personal products, pairwise comparisons of the effectiveness of the two appeal types within each country, as well as comparisons of the effectiveness of each appeal type in the United States vs

Korea, were all nonsignificant. In contrast, for shared products, these comparisons were all significant (p's < .05).

Level of involvement did not moderate how strongly subjects in the United States and Korea differed in their responses to these appeals (see Table 2). The country × involvement × appeal type interaction was nonsignificant ($F(1, 93)$ = .55; n.s.). Moreover, the tendency for product category to moderate cultural differences in the persuasiveness of appeals was not itself moderated by subjects' level of involvement. There was no country × product type × involvement × appeal type interaction ($F(1, 93)$ = 0.31; n.s.).[5]

Comparative ratings   After reading a pair of ads for a product, subjects had completed a questionnaire on which they compared the persuasiveness of the two ads. Because responses on this six-item questionnaire were internally consistent (Cronbach's alpha coefficients calculated for each product ranged from .71 to .90), an index was created in which a score of 1 was assigned each time subjects favored the collectivistic ad and a 0 each time they favored the individualistic ad. Thus, for each product, a 0–6 ad comparison index was created in which higher scores indicated greater favorability toward collectivistic appeals (see Snyder & DeBono, 1985).

The means on this index suggested that U.S. subjects favored individualistic appeals (M = 2.30) more than did Koreans (M = 3.15). An analysis of variance with country, involvement, counterbalance order of products and of ads as between-subjects variables and product type as a within-subject variable indicated that this difference between countries was significant ($F(1, 95)$ = 13.20; p < .0001). Also, comparisons of these ratings to the midpoint (3.0), to determine whether the ratings reflected a significant preference for one type of appeal, indicated that U.S. subjects significantly preferred individualistic ads ($t(63)$ = 4.43; p < .0001), whereas Korean subjects did not show a significant preference ($t(63)$ = 1.01; n.s.).

These differences, however, depended on the type of product being advertised. For personal products, both U.S. subjects (M = 2.12) and Korean subjects (M = 2.36) favored individualistic ads. For shared products, U.S. subjects favored individualistic ads (M = 2.45) whereas Koreans favored collectivistic ads (M = 3.95). The main effect of product type was significant ($F(1, 95)$ = 21.40; p < .0001), reflecting the fact that, across countries, comparative ratings of ads were significantly influenced by product category. More importantly, the country × product type interaction was significant ($F(1, 95)$ = 9.70; p < .005), demonstrating that product category moderated the cultural

differences observed in responses to these appeals. In addition, tests comparing these ratings to the midpoint (3.0) indicated that for personal products, the preference for individualistic ads was significant in both countries (United States, $t(62)$ = 4.25; p < .001; Korea, $t(63)$ = 2.92; p < .01). For shared products, U.S. subjects significantly preferred individualistic ads ($t(63)$ = 2.52; p < .02) and Korean subjects significantly favored collectivistic ads ($t(63)$ = 4.72; p < .001).

Level of involvement did not appear to moderate substantially the cultural differences in the persuasiveness of individualistic versus collectivistic appeals, as evidenced by a nonsignificant country × involvement interaction ($F(1, 95)$ = 1.15; n.s.). Under high involvement, U.S. subjects favored individualistic appeals (M = 2.34; $t(31)$ = 2.66; p < .05), whereas Koreans favored collectivistic appeals (M = 3.56; $t(31)$ = 2.28; p < .05). Under low involvement, U.S. subjects still favored individualistic appeals (M = 2.26; $t(30)$ = 3.66; p < .01), whereas Koreans evidenced no significant preference (M = 2.83; $t(31)$ = .84; n.s.). Moreover, the country × involvement × product type interaction was nonsignificant ($F(1, 95)$ = 1.81; n.s.). The only other significant effect was a country × involvement × product type × counterbalance order of products interaction ($F(3, 95)$ = 3.57; p < .05), which was not theoretically interpretable.

Discussion

Members of individualistic and collectivistic societies responded differently to ads emphasizing individualistic versus collectivistic appeals. Subjects in the United States were more persuaded overall by ads emphasizing individualistic benefits; whereas subjects in Korea tended to be more persuaded by ads emphasizing collectivistic benefits. This was reflected in more favorable attitude ratings for those products advertised with culturally consistent appeals, and in a preference (significant in the United States) for culturally consistent ads when comparing them with culturally inconsistent appeals.

As expected, however, this cultural difference did not emerge uniformly across products. It emerged strongly for shared products on both the attitude index and the comparative measure. It also emerged, but was diminished, on the attitude index for personal products. However, when making direct comparisons of the persuasiveness of the ads for personal products, both U.S. and Korean subjects favored individualistic appeals as expected (i.e., cultural differences did not emerge). Thus, the type of product advertised moderated cultural differences in the persuasiveness of the ads. It is not clear why comparative evaluations of the ads suggested a stronger moderating role of product category than did the absolute attitude ratings that were taken after the first ad in each pair. One possibility is that when comparing two ads for a product directly, the goals or standards that subjects typically associated with the product became more salient through the contrast between the appeals. That is, for personal products, which offer predominantly personal or individually experienced benefits, standards associated with those benefits became more salient. For shared products, which offer both personal and group benefits, standards or goals valued by the culture became more salient. Previous research has suggested that the goals associated with products are more salient when ad appeals are presented in pairs (rather than separately) prior to evaluating them, heightening the persuasiveness of appeals relevant to those goals (Shavitt, 1990).

We had reasoned that the influence of cultural value standards on product evaluations may be greater under high than low involvement. However, subjects' level of involvement did not significantly moderate cultural differences in the persuasiveness of these appeals. This suggests that cultural value standards may play a role in evaluating certain products regardless of the degree to which the advertisement is personally relevant. That is, such standards may be employed somewhat automatically in product evaluation.

Alternatively, it is possible that other standards would have been used under low involvement if the stimulus ads would have provided some alternative bases for forming evaluations. Recall that the ads in this study consisted of only a headline and illustrations, which focused largely on the individualistic or collectivist benefit being touted. Had other types of reasons for purchasing the product also been presented in the ads, low involvement subjects may have been more responsive than high involvement subjects to these other benefits, and involvement may have played a greater role in moderating the cultural differences observed in the persuasiveness of appeals. More research is needed to explore this possibility.

GENERAL DISCUSSION

The present research examined how individualism–collectivism, a core dimension of cultural variability, is reflected in the advertising appeals employed in the United States and Korea, countries that have been shown to differ on this dimension (Hofstede, 1980, 1983). It also investigated the relative effectiveness of ad appeals emphasizing culturally relevant values versus appeals targeting other values. On the basis of the converging pattern of results

from a content analysis and an experimental investigation conducted in two countries, it is evident that cultural differences in individualism–collectivism play an important role in persuasion processes both at the societal and the individual level, influencing the prevalence and the effectiveness of different types of advertising appeals.

Study 1, a content analysis of existing magazine advertisements, demonstrated that ads in the U.S. use individualistic appeals to a greater extent, and collectivistic appeals to a lesser extent, than do Korean advertisements. Study 2, an experiment conducted in the United States and Korea, demonstrated that the effectiveness of these types of appeals differed in the two countries. In the United States, advertisements that emphasized individualistic benefits were more persuasive, overall, than ads that emphasized family or ingroup benefits. The reverse was true in Korea.

Although cultural orientation was reflected in the prevalence and effectiveness of different types of appeals overall, the extent to which the advertised products were likely to be purchased and used individually (personal products) or with others (shared products) moderated the cultural differences observed in both studies. For shared products, there were strong differences between the United States and Korea in the prevalence and effectiveness of appeals. For personal products, however, individualistic appeals were generally favored in both countries.

This suggests that product characteristics can constrain the role of cultural differences in the prevalence and persuasiveness of advertising appeals. Personal products, which offer predominantly individually-experienced benefits, are unlikely to be convincingly promoted in terms of collectivistic benefits. Thus, such products provide little opportunity for cultural differences in individualism–collectivism to be reflected in advertising use and persuasion. Shared products, however, can be convincingly promoted both in terms of benefits to the individual and to the group, and thus provide an opportunity for these cultural differences to be manifested (for similar findings on the role of product characteristics in constraining individual differences in persuasion, see Shavitt et al. 1992).

Limitations in the Generalizability of the Results

Some limitations must be kept in mind in interpreting these results. First, our research involved only one country from each culture. Although the United States and Korea differ greatly in terms of individualism and collectivism, they do not necessarily represent all aspects of this dimension. Collectivism or individualism can take different forms in different countries (see Triandis et al., 1990). Thus, the present findings should be viewed as preliminary. Further research is needed including other individualistic and collectivistic countries in order to establish further the role of this dimension in persuasion processes.

In Study 1, advertisements from only two magazines in each country were studied. Although these magazines cannot be considered representative of all advertising media in each country, it is important to keep in mind that advertisers as a rule do not produce different ads for different media vehicles. They produce campaigns, in which the same ads highlighting the same product benefits are run in several vehicles (e.g., *Newsweek, Harper's, The New Yorker*) and even in different media (e.g., magazines, billboards). Thus, if one samples across a number of media and vehicles, one will find overlap in the ads that are run (consider the ubiquitous "Joe Camel" or Absolut Vodka campaigns). It should also be noted that the titles we employed represent mainstream, mass-circulation magazines in two major categories of consumer publications—news magazines and women's magazines. Their advertisers include most consumer product categories, from automobiles and appliances to groceries and clothing. Thus, although our sample of magazines was small, the ads that appeared in them are broadly representative of the types of claims made for a wide range of products promoted in mass market campaigns.

In Study 2, only two products were used in each product category. However, the products we selected represent a range of items in each category. For instance, whereas detergents and irons are similar in terms of being shared products, they differ greatly in terms of cost and the length of their purchase cycle. Thus, marketers would classify them into two fundamentally different product categories (packaged goods versus durable goods). Chewing gum and athletic shoes also differ on many dimensions, although they are both personal products. Therefore, although the sample of products employed was small, we believe the products within each category are varied enough to represent a broader range of items in the marketplace.

Our studies examined only print advertisements. As such, they do not provide evidence about the generalizability of the findings to broadcast advertising in individualistic versus collectivistic cultures. Unlike print ads, television ads might be especially likely to feature collectivistic appeals because exposure to TV ads often takes place in family or group contexts. If that is the case, then our research on print ads may have overestimated the differences between American and Korean ads. Still, it should be noted that examinations of television commercials in the United States, Korea, and Japan and have pointed to a number of differences, some of which (e.g., the types of peer groups shown

as models) appear consistent with our findings (Bu & Condry, 1991; and see Miracle, 1987, for a relevant non-empirical analysis).

Data collection in our studies focused exclusively on contemporary advertising. Clearly, analyzing advertising usage and effectiveness over a longer period would provide more reliable comparisons between cultures. Another advantage of a longitudinal design would be the information it provides about whether advertising appeals within a culture have changed and whether appeals across cultures have converged (e.g., Tansey et al., 1990). For example, as American "baby boomers" move through their child-bearing years, one might expect U.S. advertising strategies (and their persuasiveness) to reflect the resulting changes in consumers' collectivistic, family-oriented concerns. Research is needed to examine the effects of such demographic changes on cultural differences in the values reflected in advertising.

Further research is also needed to establish the generalizability of our findings to other, noncommercial forms of persuasive appeals. For example, previous studies of cultural differences in persuasive communication (e.g., Bronfenbrenner, 1964; Glenn et al., 1977; Wedge, 1968) often focused on interpersonal communication about political issues. Perhaps individualistic and collectivistic cultures also differ in the persuasive strategies that they favor in political and diplomatic arenas, as well as in commercial communications.

It should be noted that individualistic self-interest tends to be poorly correlated with Americans' social policy attitudes. Instead, there is evidence that Americans often justify their policy attitudes (e.g., attitudes toward racial policies) with symbolic arguments about shared social values (Sears & Kinder, 1971; Sears & McConahay, 1973). Among these social values, however, a strong belief in the ethic of individualism and self-reliance has been found to underlie many Americans' attitudes toward racial policies (Sniderman & Hagen, 1985). It is possible, then, that our cross-cultural findings would generalize to the public policy domain in terms of the types of values that are invoked in the policy advocacies of individualistic and collectivistic societies.

Some strengths of these studies should also be noted. First, the procedures minimized potential translation difficulties, which have posed serious problems in cross-cultural research (Brislin, 1980; Miracle, 1990). In Study 1, ads were not translated from one language to another. Instead, both native speakers and bilinguals evaluated all ads. The high correlations between the codings of bilinguals and native speakers (both Americans and Koreans) indicated that possible linguistic or cultural differences in interpretation of the ad content did not pose a serious problem in the coding. In Study 2, where translation of stimulus ads was necessary, a series of double-translations with decentering (Brislin, 1980) was employed to achieve equivalence in meaning and smooth, natural-sounding phrasing in the English and Korean versions of the ads. Thus, the studies minimized language difficulties that can be associated with cross-cultural research.

Moreover, the present research employed multiple methods (content analysis and experimental design) to investigate cultural differences in persuasion processes. Multimethod approaches are deemed highly desirable in cross-cultural research (Hui & Triandis, 1985; Triandis et al., 1990) because each method has inherent limitations. Content analysis monitors social phenomena ubobtrusively as they occur (maximizing external validity), but often does not allow causal relations between variables to be inferred (low internal validity). In contrast, experimental research limits variation to the manipulated factors so that causal relations can be established, maximizing internal validity. But such manipulations may not resemble social phenomena in their natural settings, and thus may be low in external validity (Neuman, 1989). Employing these two complementary methodologies, the present studies converged on the same individualistic and collectivistic categories of advertising appeals, and demonstrated cultural differences in both the prevalence and effectiveness of these types of appeals.

It should also be noted that previous work investigating differences in social behavior and social perceptions in individualistic and collectivistic cultures, reviewed earlier, has yielded results that parallel the present studies (see Markus & Kitayama, 1991; Triandis, 1989, 1990, Triandis et al., 1990). The consistency of our analysis of advertising with several prior studies of self-definitions, ingroup relations, values, and behavioral intentions increases confidence in the validity of the present findings.

APPENDIX A

Scoring Criteria for Cultural Variation

1. *Criteria for Classifications as Individualistic Appeals*

   Appeals about individuality or independence
     "The art of being unique"
     "She's got a style all her own"
   Reflections of self-reliance with hedonism or competition (mostly expressed in pictures, not in headlines)
     "Alive with pleasure!"
     "Self-esteem"
   Emphasis on self-improvement or self-realization

   "My own natural color's come back. Only better, much better"
     "You, only better"
   Emphasis on the benefits of the product to the consumer (you)
     "How to protect the most personal part of the environment. Your skin."
     "A quick return for your investment"
   Focus on ambition
     "A leader among leaders"
     "Local hero"
   Focus on personal goals
     "With this new look I'm ready for my new role"
     "Make your way through the crowd"

2. *Criteria for Classification as Collectivistic Appeals*

   Appeals about family integrity
     "A more exhilarating way to provide for your family"
   Focus on group integrity or group well-being
     "We have a way of bringing people closer together"
     "Ringing out the news of business friendships that really work"
   Concerns about others or support of society
     "We share our love with seven wonderful children"
     "We devote ourselves to contractors"
   Focus on interdependent relationships to others
     "Successful partnerships"
     "Celebrating a half-century of partnership"
   Focus on group goals
     "The dream of prosperity for all of us"
     "Sharing is beautiful"
   References to harmony with others
     "Your business success: Harmonization with Sunkyong"
   Focus on others' happiness
     "Mom's love-Baby's happiness"
   Paying attention to the views of others
     "Our family agrees with the selection of home-furnishings"

APPENDIX B

Selection of Product Categories

Personal	Shared
Women's sanitary pads	Soft drinks
Cosmetics	Groceries
Haircare (shampoo, mousse)	Baby products (e.g.,
Lingerie	diapers, cereal)

Personal	Shared
Suntan lotion	Coffee/tea
Greeting cards	Toothpaste
Gift wrap	Laundry products/soap
Kitchen utensils	Over-the-counter medicines
Perfume	Baby clothing
Watches	Batteries
Electric shaver	Corporate advertising
Personal copiers/typewriters	Insurance
Jewelry	Washer/dryer/iron
Fashion apparel	Air conditioners
Credit cards	Camera/telephone
Sunglasses	Television/VCR
Jeans	Computer
Wine	Airline tickets
	Automobiles
	Hotel/resort
	accommodations
	Home furnishings

REFERENCES

Brislin, R. W. (1980). Translation and content analysis of oral and written material. In H. Triandis & J. W. Berry (Eds.), *Handbook of cross-cultural psychology* (v. 2, pp. 389–444). Boston: Allyn and Bacon.

Bronfenbrenner, U. (1964). Allowing for Soviet perceptions. In R. Fisher (Ed.), *International conflict and behavioral science*. New York: Basic Books.

Bu, K. H., & Condry, J. C. (1991). *Children's commercials in the U.S. and Korea.* Paper presented at the Biennial Convention of the Society for Research in Child Development, Seattle, April.

Burgoon, M., Dillard, J., Doran, N., & Miller, M. (1982). Cultural and situational influences on the process of persuasive strategy selection. *International Journal of Intercultural Relations, 6,* 85–100.

Davidson, A. R., Jaccard, J. J., Triandis, H. C., Morales, M. L., & Diaz-Guerrero, R. (1976). Cross-cultural model testing: Toward a solution of the emic–etic dilemma. *International Journal of Psychology, 11,* 1–13.

Glenn, E. S., Witmeyer, D., & Stevenson, K. A. (1977). Cultural styles of persuasion. *International Journal of Intercultural Relations, 3,* 52–65.

Greenwald, A. G., & Leavitt, C. (1984). Audience involvement in advertising: Four levels. *Journal of Consumer Research, 11,* 581–592.

Gudykunst, W. B., & Ting-Toomey, S. (1988). *Culture and interpersonal communication.* Newbury Park, CA: Sage.

Hofstede, G. (1980). *Culture's consequences: International differences in work-related values.* Beverly Hills, CA: Sage.

Hofstede, G. (1983). Dimensions of national cultures in fifty countries and three regions. In J. Deregowski et al. (Eds.) *Explications in cross-cultural psychology.* Lisse, The Netherlands: Swets and Zeitlinger.

Hong, J., Muderrisoglu, A., & Zinkhan, G. (1987). Cultural differences and advertising expression: A comparative content analysis of Japanese and U.S. magazine advertising. *Journal of Advertising, 16*(1), 55–62.

Hui, C. H. (1984). *Individualism–collectivism: Theory, measurement and its relation to reward allocation.* Unpublished doctoral dissertation, University of Illinois at Urbana–Champaign.

Hui, C. H., & Triandis, H. C. (1985). Measurement in cross-cultural psychology: A review and comparison of strategies. *Journal of Cross-Cultural Psychology, 16,* 131–152.

Johnson, B. T., & Eagly, A. H. (1989). Effects of involvement on persuasion: A meta-analysis. *Psychological Bulletin, 106,* 290–314.

Kahle, L. R., & Homer, P. M. (1985). Physical attractiveness of the celebrity endorser: A social adaptation perspective. *Journal of Consumer Research, 11,* 954–961.

Kassarjian, H. H. (1977). Content analysis in consumer research. *Journal of Consumer Research, 4,* 8–18.

Madden, C., Caballero, M., & Matsukubo, S. (1986). Analysis of information content in U.S. and Japanese magazine advertising. *Journal of Advertising, 15*(3), 38–45.

Markus, H. R., & Kitayama, S. (1991). Culture and the self: Implications for cognition, emotion, and motivation. *Psychological Review, 98,* 224–253.

Marquez, F. T. (1975). The relationship of advertising and culture in the Philippines. *Journalism Quarterly, 52*(3), 436–442.

Martenson, R. (1987). Advertising strategies and information content in American and Swedish advertising. *International Journal of Advertising, 6,* 133–144.

Miracle, G. (1987). Feel–do–learn: An alternative sequence underlying Japanese response to television commercials. In F. Feasley (Ed.), *Proceedings of the 1987 conference of the American Academy of Advertising* (pp. 73–78).

Miracle, G. (1990). Research methodology to resolve problems of equivalency in cross-cultural advertising research. In P. Stout (Ed.), *Proceedings of the 1990 conference of the American Academy of Advertising* (pp. 197–198).

Mueller, B. (1987). Reflections of culture: An analysis of Japanese and American advertising appeals. *Journal of Advertising Research, 27,* 51–59.

Neuman, W. R. (1989). Parallel content analysis: Old paradigms and new proposals. In G. Comstock (Ed.), *Public communication and behavior.* San Diego: Academic Press.

Petty, R. E., & Cacioppo, J. T. (1979). Issue involvement can increase or decrease persuasion by enhancing message-relevant cognitive responses. *Journal of Personality and Social Psychology, 37,* 1915–1926.

Petty, R. E., & Cacioppo, J. T. (1986). *Communication and persuasion: Central and peripheral routes to attitude change.* New York: Springer-Verlag.

Petty, R. E., Cacioppo, J. T., & Schumann, D. (1983). Central and peripheral routes to advertising effectiveness: The moderating role of involvement. *Journal of Consumer Research, 10,* 134–148.

Renforth, W., & Raveed, S. (1983). Consumer information cues in television advertising: A cross country analysis. *Journal of the Academy of Marketing Science, 11*(3), 216–225.

Sanbonmatsu, D. M., Shavitt, S., & Sherman, S. J. (1991). The role of personal relevance in the formation of distinctiveness-based illusory correlations. *Personality and Social Psychology Bulletin, 17,* 124–132.

Sears, D. O., & Kinder, D. R. (1971). Racial tensions and voting in Los Angeles. In W. Z. Hirsch (Ed.), *Los Angeles: Viability and prospects for metropolitan leadership*. New York: Praeger.

Sears, D. O., & McConahay, J. (1973). *The new urban Blacks and the Watts riot*. Boston: Houghton Mifflin.

Shavitt, S. (1990). The role of attitude objects in attitude functions. *Journal of Experimental Social Psychology, 26*, 124–148.

Shavitt, S., Lowrey, T. M., & Han, S. (1992). Attitude functions in advertising: The interactive role of products and self-monitoring. *Journal of Consumer Psychology, 1*(4), 337–364.

Sniderman, P. M., & Hagen, M. G. (1985). *Race and inequality: A study in American values*. Chatham, NJ: Chatham House.

Snyder, M., & DeBono, K. (1985). Appeals to image and claims about quality: Understanding the psychology of advertising. *Journal of Personality and Social Psychology, 49*, 586–597.

Snyder, M., & DeBono, K. (1987). A functional approach to attitudes and persuasion. In M. P. Zanna, J. M. Olson, & C. P. Herman (Eds.). *Social influence: The Ontario symposium, Volume 5* (pp. 107–125). Hillsdale: NJ: Erlbaum.

Tansey, R., Hyman, M. R., & Zinkhan, G. M. (1990). Cultural themes in Brazilian and U.S. auto ads: A cross-cultural comparison. *Journal of Advertising, 19*(2), 30–39.

Triandis, H. C. (1989). The self and social behavior in differing cultural contexts. *Psychological Review, 96*(3), 506–520.

Triandis, H. C. (1990). Cross-cultural studies of individualism and collectivism. In J. Berman (Ed.), *Nebraska symposium on motivation*. Lincoln: University of Nebraska Press.

Triandis, H. C., Bontempo, R., Betancourt, H., Bond, M., Leung, K., Brenes, A., Georgas, J., Hui, C. H., Marin, G., Setiadi, B., Sinha, J. B. P., Verma, J., Spangenberg, J., Touzard, H., & de Montmollin, G. (1986). The measurement of etic aspects of individualism and collectivism across cultures. *Australian Journal of Psychology, 38*(3), 257–267.

Triandis, H. C., Bontempo, R., Villareal, M. J., Asai, M., & Lucca, N. (1988). Individualism and collectivism: Cross-cultural perspectives on self-ingroup relationships. *Journal of Personality and Social Psychology, 54*, 323–338.

Triandis, H. C., Brislin, R., & Hui, C. H. (1988). Cross-cultural training across the individualism-collectivism divide. *International Journal of Intercultural Relations, 12*, 269–289.

Triandis, H. C., McCusker, C., & Hui, C. H. (1990). Multimethod probes of individualism and collectivism. *Journal of Personality and Social Psychology, 59*, 1006–1020.

Wedge, B. (1968). Communication analysis and comprehensive diplomacy. In A. S. Hoffman (Ed.), *International communication and the new diplomacy*. Bloomington: Indiana Univ. Press.

Weinberger, M. B., & Spotts, H. E. (1989). Humor in U.S. versus U.K. TV commercials: A comparison. *Journal of Advertising, 18*(2), 39–44.

Zandpour, F., Chang, C., & Catalano, J. (1992). Stories, symbols, and straight talk: A comparative analysis of French, Taiwanese, and U.S. TV Commercials. *Journal of Advertising Research, 32*(1), 25–38.

NOTES

1. It should be noted that the individualistic and collectivistic classifications were generally appropriate to both U.S. and Korean ads. However, direct references to harmony with others did not appear in U.S. ads, only in a small number (<10) of Korean ads.

2. In addition to these quantitative ratings, coders also classified the primary emphasis of each advertisement into one of three categories ("individualistic," "collectivistic," or "neither"). 74% of the ads were classified as either individualistic or collectivistic. Thus, the primary emphasis of most of the ads appeared to be captured by the coding categories.

However, one difficulty with these categories is that the use of the labels "individualistic" and "collectivistic" in the coding scheme may have triggered coders' own stereotypes about Korean vs. U.S. culture. Thus, even though coders were unaware of the hypotheses of the study, it is possible that their coding reflected cultural stereotypes that were consistent with those hypotheses. Future use of this coding scheme should ideally avoid use of the terms "individualistic" and "collectivistic" and substitute culture-irrelevant terms or labels.

3. This type of translation refers to "a process by which one set of materials is not translated with as little change as possible into another language. Rather material in one language is changed so that there will be a smooth, natural-sounding version in the second language . . . decentering means that the research project is not centered around any one culture or language" (Brislin, 1980, p. 433). Double-translation with decentering, in part, enables equivalency of message stimuli (meaning and familiarity) to be achieved between the two cultures.

4. A pilot study verified that these pairs of ads differed in terms of their individualism–collectivism. Ten native speakers from each country, who were blind to the hypotheses, rated the ads in their native language. They were shown pairs of ads and were asked which one they thought emphasized individualistic and which emphasized collectivistic appeals. All judges in both countries correctly classified all ads into the categories they had been designed to represent.

It was also important to determine whether individualistic and collectivistic ads differed on important dimensions other than their individualism–collectivism, such as their comprehensibility, familiarity of arguments, or readability. To assess the comparability of the ads on these dimensions, the same ten judges from each country evaluated a randomly ordered set of the ads. For each ad, they rated (1) how technically well-written this ad was, (2) how easy it was to understand the ad, and (3) how often they had seen such a set of arguments for purchasing any product (cf. Shavitt, 1990). Their ratings were nearly identical for the individualistic and collectivistic appeals for every product in each country.

5. Although other effects were also significant in this analysis, none of them were associated with a theoretically meaningful pattern of means. The effects of involvement × product type, country × involvement × product type, counterbalance order of products, product order × involvement, product order × involvement × country, product order × involvement × ad order, and product order × involvement × product type were statistically significant. None of these interactions involve the appeal type factor, and thus none of them have implications for our conclusions regarding the persuasiveness of individualistic versus collectivistic appeals.

Received: June 3, 1993;
revised: January 10, 1994;
accepted: January 10, 1994

CRITICAL THINKING QUESTIONS

1. Han and Shavitt studied students from Korea and the United States to examine individualistic and collectivistic cultures. Are countries the same as cultures? Are there cultural differences within the United States, for example, that would lead to differences in persuasiveness similar to those found between Korea and the United States in the research?

2. Han and Shavitt found that culture seemed to matter for some products more than for others. Why might this be? What implications does this have for the interpretation of their results?

3. How did Han and Shavitt select the ads that they catalogued in Study 1? Is this procedure appropriate? How did they code the ads in Study 1? Does this procedure adequately categorize the ads?

4. In Study 2, Han and Shavitt measured persuasion by asking subjects their intention to buy products. Does this procedure make sense? How are intentions to buy products related to the actual buying of products? What would the theory of planned behavior say about the intention to buy products?

5. In Study 2, subjects were supposed to react to ads as naturally as they could. Can subjects in the laboratory react to ads in a natural way, the same way they would to ads on television or in magazines? Are there steps that research can take in the lab to increase the experimental realism of the procedure—that is, the degree to which the procedure involves the subjects and leads them to behave naturally and spontaneously (see Chapter 1)?

6. How is the research discussed in Chapter 2 of the textbook concerning the effects of culture on the self-concept related to the findings in this article? How is the research discussed in Chapter 3 concerning the effects of culture on the fundamental attribution error related to the findings in this article?

READING 12 _____

This article represents some of the most innovative contemporary research on persuasion. It examines how trying to persuade others, and their response to this attempt, affects one's own receptiveness to persuasion. The research is especially interesting because it begins to examine the dialogue that often accompanies persuasive appeals. The studies generally find that people are more persuaded by people whom they have influenced in the past than by people whom they were unable to influence. This effect is especially strong when the person making the arguments has good arguments. The study clearly shows that these effects are not due to other causes.

The article touches on almost all of the basic processes of persuasion discussed in Chapter 10. The impact of the communicator and the message are discussed thoroughly. In addition, the article is related to the discussions of the norm of reciprocity in the contexts of helping (Chapter 7) and compliance (Chapter 9). The article provides an interesting integration of these different areas of research. In reading this study, you will see how carefully the authors establish that their results are not due to alternative explanations. You might ask yourself how their studies were designed to rule out these alternative explanations.

When Tactical Pronouncements of Change Become Real Change: The Case of Reciprocal Persuasion

Robert B. Cialdini, Beth L. Green, and Anthony J. Rusch
Arizona State University

In 3 experiments, Ss' public statements of attitude change conformed to the norm of reciprocity, in that the most change on a topic was accorded to a persuader who had yielded to the S's earlier persuasive attempt on a prior topic, and the least such change was accorded to a persuader who had resisted the S's persuasive attempt. This tendency was unaffected by perceptions of the persuader's likability and intelligence, personal relevance of the topic, and strength of the arguments. Private change matched the pattern of public change only when the arguments Ss received were strong, and Ss could (mistakenly) attribute much of their reciprocation-induced change to the cogency of the arguments. Implications are discussed for the internalization of socially desirable conduct.

There is good evidence that a rule for reciprocity governs much of human experience: We report liking those who report liking us (Byrne & Rhamey, 1965; Condon & Crano, 1988); we cooperate with cooperators and compete with competitors (Braver, 1975; Rosenbaum, 1980); we self-disclose to those who have disclosed themselves to us (Cunningham, Strassberg, & Haan, 1986); we try to harm

those who have tried to harm us (Dengerink, Schnedler, & Covey, 1978); in negotiations, we make concessions to those who have made concessions to us (Axelrod, 1984; Cialdini et al., 1975); and we provide gifts, favors, services, and aid to those who have provided us with these things (see Cialdini, 1988, for review).

Of course, as with any form of action, there are variations in the way that the rule for reciprocity manifests itself. For instance, in certain long-term relationships, such as families and close friendships, the pure, tit-for-tat version of reciprocation may not occur. In these "communal" relationships, what is exchanged reciprocally is not a precise set of actions but, rather, the willingness to provide what the other needs, when it is needed (Clark, Mills, & Powell, 1986; Mills & Clark, 1982). It is noteworthy that even in these types of exchanges, then, there remains a fundamental commitment to reciprocity.

Impressed with its generality across behavioral domains and societal groups, some social scientists (e.g., Berkowitz, 1972; Cialdini, 1988; Gouldner, 1960) have accorded the rule for reciprocity the status of a social norm (one that obligates individuals to return the form of behavior they

SOURCE: Robert B. Cialdini, Beth L. Green, and Anthony J. Rusch, "When Tactical Pronouncements of Change Become Real Change: The Case of Reciprocal Persuasion," *Journal of Personality and Social Psychology*, 1992, Vol. 63, No. 1, 30–40. Copyright © 1992 by the American Psychological Association. Reprinted with permission.

have received) that is said to maximize the outcomes of the individual who abides by it and of the societal group that enculturates it (Axelrod, 1984). Indeed, certain anthropologists have called the obligation to give back what we have gotten a central (Tiger & Fox, 1971) or *the* central (Leakey & Lewin, 1978) characteristic of being human.

It is odd, then, that there is no evidence showing that the obligation to reciprocate applies to one major and heavily researched form of human behavior—reported persuasion. There are no data to our knowledge indicating that, if someone reports being persuaded by us on Topic A, we will act on an obligation to accede to that person's persuasion attempt on Topic B. One reason for the dearth of evidence in this regard may be the difficulty in documenting that such a reciprocal reaction on our part was due to a desire to reciprocate, rather than to other factors. For example, using average college students as subjects, Cialdini and his associates (Cialdini, Braver, & Lewis, 1974; Cialdini & Mirels, 1976) have demonstrated that persuaders come to view a target who has yielded to their persuasive arguments as more intelligent and likable as a consequence. Thus, if we found ourselves yielding to the arguments of someone who had yielded to ours on a prior topic, our acquiescence could be attributed not to the desire to reciprocate the act but to the increased favorability of the communicator in our eyes.

There is a crucial difference between the two explanations. If our shift is based on the perceived credibility of the communicator, then the change we exhibit should be genuine, manifesting itself not just on our public report of persuasion to the communicator but on more private measures as well. If, on the other hand, our shift is based on the more tactical and self-presentational desire to conform to the dictates of the reciprocity rule in our culture, then the effect should appear principally in our public report of attitude change to the communicator who had previously yielded to us.

The possibility that statements of opinion would be structured to meet tactical goals of a social nature is consistent with a long-standing (though never prominent) recognition within the discipline that attitude expressions serve multiple functions, only one of which may be to accurately represent genuine feelings (Cialdini, Levy, Herman, & Evenbeck, 1973; Cooper & Jones, 1969; Jones, 1964; Kelman, 1961; McGuire & Millman, 1965; Tedeschi, Schlenker, & Bonoma, 1971). In addition, more recently, theorists have begun to insist that reports of attitude change can only be fully understood through formulations that consider the reporter's interpersonal motives (Chaiken,

Liberman, & Eagly, 1989; Johnson & Eagly, 1989; Lippe & Elkin, 1987).

The purpose of the present research was twofold. First, we wished to test whether reports of attitude change appear in a reciprocal pattern, such that individuals admit to greater change in response to the persuasive arguments of a communicator who has yielded to the individuals' persuasive attempts on an earlier topic. To this end, we arranged for subjects to deliver a persuasive message on an initial topic to a fellow subject (actually an experimental confederate) who either publicly yielded to or resisted the persuasive attempt or who (in a control condition) did not respond to it. Then, on a second topic, all subjects received a (rather weak) persuasive communication from the confederate and were asked to report to the confederate the extent to which they changed their own opinions in response to it. These statements of change constituted the major dependent measure of the research and were expected to show a reciprocal pattern such that the greatest admitted change would be reported to communicators who had previously yielded to the subjects' arguments, whereas the least such change would be reported to communicators who had previously resisted them.

The second purpose of this research was to determine whether the predicted pattern of reported change (if obtained) could have been uniquely caused by the tendency to abide by the reciprocity norm. That is, we wondered whether this pattern would appear when other possible causes—such as genuine persuasion resulting from differing perceptions of communicator positivity—were eliminated. To attempt to answer this causal question we took three steps. First, we provided all subjects with prior, equivalent information about the intelligence and likability of the confederate. It was hoped that this procedure would hold constant subjects' perceptions of the communicator's positivity. Second, we added to the design an independent variable—topic relevance—that would not be expected to affect subjects' statements of change if these statements were merely public claims of a tactical sort but that would be expected to influence those statements if they reflected genuine opinion shifts flowing from perceptions of the communicator's positivity. That is, Petty and Cacioppo (1986) and Petty, Cacioppo, and Goldman (1981) have shown that perceptions of a communicator's positivity shifted subjects' opinions only on topics of low personal relevance to the subjects. By manipulating topic relevance in the present research, we could observe whether subjects' tendency toward reciprocal persuasion appeared only on a low-relevance topic (in keeping with a communicator positivity mediator of the effect) or appeared on both high- and low-relevance topics (in keeping with the rule for reciprocation). Third, in addition to recording subjects' attitude change statements made in the presence of the communicator, we included a measure taken in private. In this fashion, it was possible to compare the amount of persuasion reported with the communicator present and absent.

On the basis of the earlier reviewed literature indicating that the obligation to reciprocate is a powerful motivator of human social conduct and on the basis of considerable research indicating that individuals frequently make attitude statements to achieve social goals, tactical goals, or both (Braver, Linder, Corwin, & Cialdini, 1977; Cialdini et al., 1973; Cooper & Jones, 1969; Davis & Florquist, 1965; Johnson & Eagly, 1989; Jones, 1964; McGuire & Millman, 1965), we made the following predictions: First, subjects would report the greatest amount of change to a communicator who had yielded to their arguments on a prior topic and would report the least such change to a communicator who had resisted their arguments. Second, this basic pattern would be similar for topics on which the subjects felt either high or low personal involvement. Third, the pattern of attitude statements made by subjects in private would not conform to the pattern of public statements.

EXPERIMENT 1

Method

Subjects Forty-two introductory psychology students at Arizona State University (ASU) participated in partial fulfillment of course requirements. Data from 5 of the subjects were omitted from the analysis because of accurate suspicions regarding the experimental ruses or hypotheses.[1] These 5 subjects were spread about evenly across the levels of the major independent variable of the study, such that 2 were in the *yield* condition, 2 were in the *control* condition, and 1 was in the *resist* condition.

Design and procedure After appearing at a laboratory room to participate in an "interpersonal interaction" experiment, the subject and a same-sex experimental confederate (posing as a fellow subject) were seated in desks separated by a partition that prevented visual contact but allowed verbal exchange.

Initial attitude assessment and manipulation of topic relevance. The subject and confederate first filled out a questionnaire assessing their attitudes on eight topics that they were told were "currently under consideration by various national, state and local legislative bodies." One of the topics concerned a proposal to require comprehensive senior examinations at their university, either in the next year

(high relevance) or in 10 years (low relevance). This manipulation was patterned after the procedures used repeatedly and successfully by Petty and Cacioppo (1986) to vary the degree of personal relevance of the senior comprehensive exams issue. A second topic in the initial questionnaire concerned a proposal to lower the drinking age in Arizona to 18 years. Subjects indicated on 9-point scales how favorable or unfavorable they felt about each of the eight proposals.

After collecting the questionnaires, the experimenter informed the participants that they would be assigned one topic apiece and would be asked to write three arguments supporting their opinions on that topic. Allegedly at random, the subject was always assigned to the drinking age issue and the confederate to the senior comprehensive issue. The experimenter explained that the participants would be reading each other's arguments, but because one purpose of the study was to explore how having different amounts of information might influence interpersonal interaction, one of them would be receiving some biographical information about the other. A rigged drawing was staged, which invariably determined that the subject would receive the biographical sketch. The sketch consisted of bogus feedback from a number of previously administered tests,[2] showing the confederate to have scored in the average range for intelligence, likability, and anxiety. This information was provided in an attempt to equate across conditions the subjects' perceptions of the confederate's positivity. While the experimenter went to "obtain the biographical information off the computer," the subject and confederate were each to write three arguments supporting their positions on their assigned topic.

First interaction and manipulation of prior persuasion. The experimenter returned and gave the biographical sketch to the subject, who read it and returned it to the experimenter. The experimenter then gave the subject's arguments on the drinking age issue to the confederate and instructed him or her to read them carefully before summarizing his or her opinion on the topic for the subject. Before leaving the room to allow the participants to interact on the topic, the experimenter (except in the control condition) pointed to a large 100-point scale affixed to the wall, the end points of which were labeled (1) *disagree totally with proposal* and (100) *agree totally with proposal,* saying that because some people are more visually than verbally oriented, the participants might want to use the scale on the wall to help them convey their opinions to one another. When the experimenter left, the confederate read the subject's statements and responded in one of three ways designed to manipulate the subject's success in persuasion.

In the yield condition, the confederate stated that, despite initially holding an opinion opposed to that of the subject, the subject's arguments made sense, and he or she now agreed more with the subject. Using the scale on the wall, the confederate indicated that his or her initial attitude had been about 10 scale points from midscale in the direction opposite to the subject's position, but now it was about 20 points from midscale in the same direction as the subject's position. For example, if the subject's statements were in favor of lowering the drinking age, the confederate would say, "Well, I read your arguments, and they make sense. In fact, I would say that before I read your arguments, I was about a 40 on the scale, but after reading your arguments, now I'm about a 70," thereby showing that the subject's arguments successfully changed the confederate's view.

In the resist condition, the confederate indicated that his or her opinion on the scale had not moved from being 10 scale points from midscale in the direction opposite to the subject's. For example, if the subject favored lowering the drinking age, the confederate would say, "Well, I read your arguments, and they make sense; but I really don't think I've changed my mind any. I'd say that before I read your arguments I was about a 40, and I still am."

In the control condition, the experimenter did not instruct the participants to interact in any way. Therefore, no verbal exchange took place on the drinking issue.

Ratings of the confederate's positivity.   The experimenter returned and handed out a Personal Assessment Questionnaire, consisting of ten 7-point scales, five of which assessed likability (*likable, good, friendly, warm,* and *enjoyable*) and five of which assessed intelligence (*worthy of respect, intelligent, wise, perceptive,* and *knowledgeable of current events*). The participants were instructed to use the scales to rate their perceptions of the other.

Second interaction and public report of persuasion.   In the second interaction, the subject was given the confederate's argument's supporting the proposal to require senior comprehensive exams at ASU, either in 10 years (low relevance) or in the next year (high relevance). These arguments, designed to be weak in order to reduce argument-based attitude change, were (a) By the time you're a senior, what difference does one more test make? (b) They have senior comprehensives at other schools, I don't see why we shouldn't have them at ASU; and (c) They couldn't make a senior comprehensive at ASU too hard, so I don't think it would be a big deal to have one.

On leaving the room, the experimenter instructed all subjects to summarize their opinions on this issue to one another by using the scale on the wall. After allowing the

subject time to read the arguments, the confederate asked the subject to indicate where "you would have put yourself on the scale before reading my arguments, and where you would put yourself now." The number of units of change the subject indicated was secretly recorded by the confederate and constituted the measure of publicly reported attitude change.

Measure of persuasion taken in private.   On returning, the experimenter began to hand out "a final questionnaire" and discovered that there was only one left, which was given to the confederate to complete while the experimenter left the room to retrieve another questionnaire. The confederate had finished the questionnaire by the time the experimenter returned and, consequently, was dismissed, allowing the subject to complete the questionnaire in private. This sequence of events was staged to ensure the subject that the confederate would not have access to the subject's answers, thus facilitating honest responding to the attitude-related items on the questionnaire. The final questionnaire contained 12 opinion statements concerning the topics that subjects had responded to on the initial attitude questionnaire. Three of the statements involved the topic of senior comprehensive examinations: "Senior comprehensives should be used because they ensure that the students have retained what they have learned"; "Students who have passed their previous classes do not need to take comprehensive exams"; and "No students should have to undergo the added stress of comprehensive exams in order to graduate from college." Subjects indicated their agreement or disagreement with each statement by responding to a 9-point Likert-type scale, ranging from *totally agree* to *totally disagree.* The average of subjects' responses to the three senior-exam-related statements constituted our index of privately measured persuasion. Averaging subjects' responses over these three statements was deemed warranted by high interitem correlations among them ($\alpha = .87$). On the basis of pilot work, we felt comfortable that this three-item index was comparable in sensitivity to our single-item measure of publicly reported attitude; the correlation between control subjects' comprehensive exam attitude scores on the two measures was $r(12) = .90$, $p < .001$.

Results

Analyses to determine the impact of subject sex on responding within our paradigm produced no significant effects. Consequently, all subsequent analyses did not include that variable.

Public change   Table 1 shows the average number of units of public change reported in the various cells of the design.

TABLE 1   Mean Units of Publicly Reported Change: Experiment 1

Topic relevance	Prior persuasion		
	Yield	Control	Resist
Low			
M	27.50	10.00	7.50
n	6	7	6
High			
M	26.43	24.80	5.00
n	7	5	6
M	26.92	16.17	6.25

An analysis of variance (ANOVA) was performed on subjects' reports of attitude change to the communicator on the senior exams topic. In keeping with our first prediction, subjects declared the greatest amount of change to a communicator who had yielded to their arguments on the drinking age topic (26.92) and declared the least amount of change to a communicator who had resisted their arguments on the drinking age topic (6.25), with control subjects reporting an intermediate amount of change (16.17), $F(2, 31) = 5.44$, $p < .009$. Simple effects tests within the significant main effect showed that it was composed of two marginally significant components: yield versus control, $t(34) = -1.74$, $p < .09$; and resist versus control, $t(34) = 1.57$, $p < .12$.

There was no significant main effect of the topic relevance manipulation ($F < 1$). More important, consistent with our second prediction, there was no significant interaction between the prior persuasion and topic relevance factors, $F(2, 31) = 1.13$. Within the low-relevance conditions, the prior persuasion effect was marginally significant, $F(2, 31) = 3.04$, $p < .062$; whereas, in the high-relevance conditions, it was conventionally significant, $F(2, 31) = 3.60$, $p < .04$. Tukey tests performed on the set of six means found no two means to be significantly different from one another.

Private change   To compute a measure of private change on the senior exams topic, we subtracted each subject's score on the final attitude measure (taken in private) from that subject's score on the initial attitude measure (taken at the outset of the experiment). An ANOVA on those change scores produced no significant main or interaction effects (all $Fs < 1.08$).[3] However, the means for the prior persuasion conditions did approximate the shape of the pattern found on the public measure of change: yield = 1.87; con-

trol = 1.11; and resist = 1.03.[4] To ensure that the significant reciprocal pattern obtained on the public measure of change was truly different from the nonsignificant reciprocal pattern found on the private measure we performed an analysis in which the public and private measures of change were treated as repeated measures. In other words, we performed a $2 \times 3 \times 2$ mixed ANOVA, with a within-subjects factor labeled *type-of-change measure* (public or private). If that analysis generated a significant interaction between the prior persuasion factor and the type-of-change measure factor, we would have evidence that the effects of prior persuasion on the two kinds of change were truly different, as predicted. That analysis did produce a significant Prior Persuasion × Type-of-Change Measure interaction, $F(2, 31) = 5.37$, $p < .01$; in short, the significant reciprocal pattern found on the public-change scores was significantly different from the nonsignificant reciprocal pattern found on the private-change scores. No other interactions approached significance; however, because of a metric difference between the two types of change scores, there was a significant type-of-change measure main effect, $F(1, 31) = 38.45$, $p < .01$.

Additional Measures   We also submitted subjects' perceptions of the confederate's likability and intelligence to ANOVAs to determine if we had succeeded in equating these perceptions across conditions of the experiments. Evidence that we did succeed in this regard comes from the fact that no main or interaction effects proved significant for either analysis. Furthermore, an examination of the means relative to the crucial prior persuasion factor indicated that for both sets of perceptions a pattern emerged that was distinct from that of the public attitude-change measure: For likability, yield = 5.75, control = 5.17, and resist = 5.50; for intelligence, yield = 5.50, control = 4.97, and resist = 5.32.

Discussion

The results of our first study were quite congruent with our predictions. First, in keeping with the expectation that admissions of persuasion would be tactically generated to conform to the rule for reciprocity, subject's statements of attitude change appeared in a reciprocal pattern, such that the greatest change was reported to a persuader who had yielded to the subjects' arguments on a prior topic, and the least such change was reported to a persuader who had resisted the subjects' arguments. Moreover, this basic reciprocal pattern (a) was not different for topics of high or low personal relevance, (b) was not significant on the measure of private change, and (c) did not match the pattern of subjects' perceptions of the persuader's intelligence or likability. This last result, especially, seemed to reduce the likelihood that the reciprocal change effect was mediated by perceptions of the communicator's positivity. To provide further evidence in this regard, we conducted an analysis of covariance (ANCOVA) on both the public- and private-change measures using likability and intelligence as covariates. The results were identical to those of the original ANOVAs we had conducted. That is, no effects approached significance except the prior persuasion main effect on the public-change measure, $F(2, 28) = 6.84$, $p < .001$.

Despite the overall support for our hypotheses in Experiment 1, we saw several reasons to replicate and extend our findings. First, Experiment 1 included no manipulation check on the personal relevance variable, thereby reducing the certainty with which we could make the claim that the reciprocal public change effect occurred both for issues of low and high personal relevance. Second, the cell *ns* of that initial study were quite small, further reducing confidence in the generality of that effect. That is, it is possible that the failure to obtain an interaction between the personal relevance factor and the prior persuasion factor was not due to the robustness of the reciprocal change effect but was due to inadequate cell sizes that resulted in a weak statistical test of the interaction. Finally, an alternate conceptual explanation remained conceivable for the findings of Experiment 1. Perhaps, having their persuasive arguments accepted, not commented on, or rejected put subjects in different moods, respectively, that temporarily affected the way that they viewed the persuader's arguments. If, as seems plausible, the subjects who had succeeded in convincing the confederate were feeling most happy, whereas those who had failed were feeling least happy, the results of Experiment 1 could be explained as mere mood-based effects. One research tradition has shown that, after exposure to positive mood induction procedures, people react more favorably to a variety of stimuli (Clark & Waddell, 1983; Howard & Barry, 1990; Isen, Shalker, Clark, & Karp, 1978; Manis, Cornell, & Moore, 1974), including persuasive appeals (Razran, 1938). It seemed possible, then, that the reciprocal pattern observed on the public-change measure was not mediated by a tendency for reciprocation at all. Instead, it may have reflected the current mood states of the subjects and the corresponding degree of favorability they accorded to any stimuli they processed while in those experimentally modified moods; and perhaps the reciprocal pattern appeared only on the public-change measure because, by the time subjects were administered the private-change measure, the mood state differences among the three groups of subjects had dissipated. To

compensate for these three weaknesses of Experiment 1, we undertook a second study.

EXPERIMENT 2

The alternative account of our earlier findings that we wished to test required that mood differences be present among the yield, control, and resist condition subjects at the time of the subjects' exposure to the persuader's arguments. Therefore, we reasoned that, if we could eliminate any mood differences (that may have been produced by the manipulation of prior persuasion in our experimental setting) before subjects got the chance to hear the arguments and to publicly report attitude change, and if the reciprocal pattern nonetheless appeared, we would have evidence against the mood-based interpretation of our prior results. To this end, in Experiment 2, we interpolated a mood-neutralizing activity between the manipulation of the prior persuasion factor and subjects' reports of attitude change to the confederate. We also included a mood-check measure to assess the degree to which the activity succeeded in removing any potential mood differences. In addition, to ensure that our effect was not unique to the scale that participants used to report their public changes, we substituted a 9-point scale for the 100-point scale we used in Experiment 1. Finally, in an attempt to enhance confidence in the generality of the reciprocal change effect for both low- and high-relevance issues, we added a manipulation check on personal relevance, and we greatly increased our cell sizes so as to allow for a more powerful test of the interaction between the personal relevance and the prior persuasion factors.

Method

Subjects   Participants were 102 introductory psychology students at ASU, the data from 7 of whom were removed from the analysis because of accurate suspicions regarding the experimental ruses or hypotheses—2 from the yield condition, 2 from the control condition, and 3 from the resist condition.

Procedure   The procedure was identical to that of Experiment 1, with the following exceptions. First, in the initial interaction, yield condition subjects heard the confederate admit to 2 units of change in their direction on a 9-point scale (e.g., from a 4 to a 6), rather than the 30 units of change on a 100-point scale used in Experiment 1; subjects in the resist condition heard the confederate admit to remaining unchanged (e.g., at 4). Second, to allow for the dissipation of any mood changes associated with having been yielded to or resisted during the first interaction, after subjects rated the confederate's likability and intelligence, they (along with the confederate) rated the pleasantness of a series of 26 nature photographs. This photograph-rating task was designed to equate subjects' moods by providing a uniform, mildly pleasant activity that would dissipate existing mood differences by virtue of distraction and the passage of time (Isen, Clark, & Schwartz, 1976). Immediately following the task, participants rated their current moods on a set of eight 7-point scales—labeled as *happy, anxious, sad, low spirited, feeling good, elated, agitated,* and *feeling low.* The scales were anchored by the terms *not at all* (1) and *very much* (7). The final procedural modification involved the introduction of three questions, after the private attitude measure had been administered, designed to check on the success of the experimental manipulations. Two of the questions checked whether the topic relevance manipulation had been properly implemented. One asked subjects to indicate how "personally relevant" the senior exams issue was to them (on a 9-point scale); the other asked what year the exams were proposed to begin. The third question asked subjects whether the "other subject" had changed his or her mind on the drinking age proposal during the first interaction; this constituted the check on the prior persuasion factor.

Results

Public change   An ANOVA generated only one reliable effect for subjects' public reports of change, the main effect of prior persuasion, $F(2, 89) = 7.52$, $p < .001$. As can be seen in Table 2, the pattern of the means appeared in the same form as in our prior study (yield = 1.84, control = 1.00, and resist = 0.79). As in Study 1, the main effect of prior persuasion was composed of a pair of influences— the twin tendencies to reciprocate yielding and resisting.

TABLE 2   Mean Units of Publicly Reported Change: Experiment 2

Topic relevance	Prior persuasion		
	Yield	Control	Resist
Low			
M	2.00	0.84	0.86
n	16	19	14
High			
M	1.69	1.19	0.71
n	16	16	14
M	1.84	1.00	0.79

However, in the present study, simple effects tests demonstrated that prior yielding produced a substantially greater reciprocal response than did prior resistance, which by itself was not significant: yield versus control, $t(92) = -3.1$, $p < .01$; control versus resist, $t(92) = 0.8$.

Neither the main effect for topic relevance nor its interaction with prior persuasion approached significance ($Fs < 1$). Within the low-relevance conditions, the prior persuasion effect was significant, $F(2, 89) = 5.53$, $p < .01$; whereas, in the high-relevance condition, it was marginally significant, $F(2, 89) = 2.74$, $p < .07$. Tukey tests performed on the set of six means found only one pair of means to be significantly different from one another at the .05 level— the low relevance-yield and the high relevance-resist cell means.

Private change   Consistent with the results of Experiment 1, an ANOVA produced no significant effects on the measure of private change (all $Fs < 1.20$). The means for the yield, control, and resist conditions, respectively, were 0.94, 0.68, and 1.38.[5] Although the pattern of the means for the private measure of change did not match that for public reports of change, we again performed a $2 \times 3 \times 2$ mixed ANOVA, using type-of-change measure as a within-subjects factor to ensure that the effects of the prior persuasion factor were truly different for the two types of measured change. That analysis produced only one effect that even approached significance, the expected Prior Persuasion × Type-of-Change interaction, $F(2, 89) = 4.73$, $p < .01$.

Additional measures   Three questions served as checks on the experimental manipulations. Two of the questions assessed the effectiveness of the topic relevance manipulation. The first asked subjects to indicate the extent—from *extremely* (1) to *not at all* (9)—to which the senior exams issue was relevant to them. An ANOVA found a significant effect for the topic relevance factor such that high-relevance condition subjects rated the topic as more personally relevant (4.07) than did the low-relevance condition subjects (5.71), $F(1, 89) = 12.07$, $p < .001$; no other effects approached significance ($Fs < 1.35$). A second check on the relevance manipulation asked subjects to state the number of years before the senior exams were proposed to be put into place; all but 1 of the subjects answered correctly. A third question, functioning as our check on the prior persuasion manipulation, asked subjects to recall whether the "other subject" had changed on the drinking age issue in the first interaction; once again, all but 1 subject responded correctly. We interpret these findings to indicate that our experimental manipulations did work as intended.

An ANOVA was conducted on the combined eight adjective scales designed to measure subjects' mood. There were no differences among subjects on the mood measure (all $Fs < 2.5$). The combined mood-score means on the prior persuasion factor were 5.30, 4.87, and 5.10 for the yield, control, and resist conditions, respectively.

Finally, we analyzed the likability and intelligence ratings of the confederate and, unlike in Experiment 1, found main effects for prior persuasion, such that control condition subjects rated the confederate as less likable (5.20) and less intelligent (4.98) than did the yield condition subjects (5.62 and 5.31, respectively) or the resist condition subjects (5.64 and 5.59, respectively). For likability, $F(2, 89) = 3.95$, $p < .025$; for intelligence, $F(2, 89) = 4.66$, $p < .012$. Although reliable, the pattern of means for these measures is different from that of the public-change measure; thus, perceptions of confederate likability or intelligence cannot be easily evoked as explanations of the reciprocal form of publicly reported change. Additional evidence in this regard comes once again from an ANOVA using likability and intelligence ratings as covariates. That analysis produced the identical pattern of effects generated by our original ANOVAs. That is, only one effect proved significant—the main effect for prior persuasion on the public measure of change, $F(2, 87) = 6.36$, $p < .01$. Our best guess as to the reason that control subjects rated the confederate least positively is that, at the time they made their ratings, they had had the least interaction with the confederate, who had offered polite and reasonable responses to the subjects' persuasion attempts (only) in the other two conditions.

Discussion

Our intent in Experiment 2 was to gain confidence that the reciprocal form of publicly reported persuasion found in Experiment 1 would (a) apply whether the personal relevance of the issue was low or high and (b) appear when we eliminated the explanatory relevance of possible mood differences among our subject groups. In the first regard, despite remaining in the uncomfortable position of trying to support the null hypothesis, we found no hint of a Prior Persuasion × Personal Relevance interaction, even though our personal relevance manipulation check was successful, and there was considerable power in the statistical test of the interaction. In the second regard, through the inclusion of a mood-neutralizing task activity and a mood measure, we were able to ensure and document that no differences in mood existed across our subject groups prior to their public reports of attitude change. Yet the reciprocal relationship appeared again in those public reports,

rendering a mood-based interpretation of that relationship improbable.

EXPERIMENT 3

In support of our argument that the predicted reciprocal pattern of publicly reported change observed in our subjects resulted from a tendency to conform to the rule of reciprocation, we have never found the reciprocal pattern emerging to any significant degree in subjects' private reports of change. That is, if subjects' public statements of change only reflected tactical attempts to live up to the norm of reciprocity (rather than reflecting genuine changes in attitude), we expected that the public changes would not be matched by private changes. That expectation received support in both of our reported studies, as well as in extensive pilot work conducted preparatory to those studies.

With that point safely made, however, it seemed beneficial to consider the circumstances under which public changes of the sort our subjects asserted would become internalized as private changes. For example, there is good reason to believe that if, in our experimental paradigm, subjects were exposed to strong arguments on the senior exams issue (rather than to the weak arguments we had been using), they would show the reciprocal pattern on both the public and the private measures of change. What is more, that reasoning suggests that the private changes would not spring directly from the persuasive power of the strong arguments but from attributional processes that took argument strength into account.

There is a substantial body of research to indicate that individuals see as causal those features of a setting that are salient (see Fiske & Taylor, 1991, for a review). It is our view that in Experiments 1 and 2, the manipulation of prior persuasion made salient the norm of reciprocity for our subjects, who then conformed to its dictates on the measure of publicly reported change. Furthermore, because the arguments the confederate used were quite weak, subjects had little basis for attributing anything to themselves but tactical motives for those public changes. Therefore, when the time came for subjects to record their genuine attitudes toward the senior exams topic, there was no good reason for them to suppose that they actually believed what they had reported. Accordingly, we found no effects of our experimental manipulations on the private-change measures in either of the two experiments using weak arguments.

A very different attributional sequence would apply, though, were subjects to be confronted with strong arguments. Because of the power of the reciprocity norm, it would still be our expectation that subjects would show a reciprocal pattern of change on the public measure. However, when asked to reflect on their true attitudes in private, subjects would now find another salient and plausible cause for their public changes—the presence of strong arguments. Thus, in assigning any causal weight for their public changes to the cogency of the arguments, subjects would be expected to attribute to themselves corresponding private changes. To use a somewhat different theoretical language, subjects exposed to strong arguments prior to their publicly reported changes could discount (Kelley, 1972) the exclusive role of the reciprocity rule in bringing about whatever changes occurred and could assign at least some of the causality to genuine persuasion.

We saw three benefits of testing this expectation. First, we would be able to observe whether our basic finding would appear outside of the weak-argument settings of the prior experiments. It was conceivable that when the arguments were strong, they would carry the day and would overwhelm the role of reciprocity as an influence on subjects' public reports of change. Second, in addition to examining the generality of the reciprocal effect, conducting a study that used strong arguments would provide valuable theoretical information. As discussed previously, we could identify certain conditions under which tactically reciprocated change statements would become internalized as private changes. A last benefit would be methodological. That is, a critic could argue that the lack of a significant effect on the private-change measure in either of the prior studies may be best accounted for, not by the theoretical arguments we have suggested, but by the possibility that our private-change measure was too insensitive to detect real change. Should we find the significant reciprocal change pattern predicted in Experiment 3 on the private measure, however, such an explanation would become improbable.

Method

Subjects Participants were 101 introductory psychology students at ASU, the data from 5 of whom were removed from the analysis because of accurate suspicions regarding the experimental ruses or hypotheses—1 from the yield condition, 2 from the control condition, and 2 from the resist condition.

Procedure The procedure was identical to that of Experiment 2, with two exceptions. The first was implemented because pilot testing of the strong arguments under control condition circumstances indicated that these arguments produced an average of two full units of publicly reported change—an amount of change equivalent to that declared by the confederate in our yield condition. Therefore, the

possibility existed that, when strong arguments were used, a ceiling effect would artifactually obscure genuinely reciprocated public change. That is, if we used strong arguments in our experimental paradigm, yield condition subjects could reciprocate perfectly (the two units of change the confederate had earlier ceded to them) and yet show no more change than the control condition subjects. Consequently, a true act of reciprocation among yield condition subjects could not be observed from the data. To eliminate this potential ceiling effect problem, yield condition subjects in Experiment 3 heard the confederate change four units in the subjects' direction on the drinking age topic, thereby allowing subjects to exhibit an amount of change (in return) greater than that produced by the cogency of the strong arguments alone.

The second modification was to substitute three strong arguments for the three weak arguments that had been used in all prior experiments. These strong arguments were adapted from those developed by Petty and Cacioppo (1986) to offer powerful support for the senior exams proposal.[6]

Results

Public Change As in the earlier studies, an ANOVA generated a significant main effect for prior persuasion on the public-change measure, $F(2, 90) = 9.35$, $p < .001$. The means displayed in Table 3 document that, once more, evidence for reciprocated change appeared in these public reports (yield = 3.29, control = 2.27, and resist = 1.71). Simple effects tests demonstrated that the greater part of this effect was attributable to the tendency of subjects to reciprocate yielding: yield versus control, $t(94) = -2.7$, $p < .01$; control versus resist, $t(94) = 1.51$, $p < .12$.

TABLE 3   Mean Units of Publicly Reported Change: Experiment 3

Topic relevance	Prior persuasion		
	Yield	Control	Resist
Low			
M	3.71	2.20	1.57
n	17	15	14
High			
M	2.89	2.33	1.82
n	19	15	17
M	3.29	2.27	1.71

Neither the effect for topic relevance nor its interaction with prior persuasion approached significance ($Fs < 1.35$). Within the low-relevance condition, the prior persuasion effect was significant, $F(2, 91) = 8.56$, $p < .01$; whereas, within the high-relevance condition, it was marginally significant, $F(2, 91) = 2.26$, $p < .12$. Tukey tests performed on the set of six means found two pairs of means to be significantly different from one another: low relevance–yield versus low relevance–resist; and low relevance–yield versus high–relevance resist.

Private change   An ANOVA produced only one significant effect on the private measure of change, the main effect of prior persuasion, $F(2, 90) = 3.31$, $p < .04$. As predicted, the pattern of means for that effect was similar in form (yield = 2.48, control = 1.51, and resist = 1.34) to that of publicly reported change.[7] Indeed, the parallel form of the public- and private-change measures even extended to the simple effects within the prior persuasion main effect. That is, as with the public-change measure, the greater part of the main effect for private change was due to a tendency for subjects to reciprocate yielding: yield versus control, $t(93) = -1.95$, $p < .055$; control versus resist, $t(93) = 0.43$, *ns*. The similarity of the two change patterns was further affirmed in a $2 \times 3 \times 2$ mixed ANOVA using type-of-change measure as a within-subjects factor. The crucial Prior Persuasion × Type-of-Change interaction was far from significant ($F < 1$), as were all other interactions.

Additional measures   The items that documented the success of our topic relevance manipulation in Experiment 2 showed evidence of comparable success in the present experiment. That is, high-relevance condition subjects rated the topic of senior exams as more personally relevant (3.02) than did low-relevance condition subjects (5.20), $F(1, 89) = 20.48$, $p < .001$; and 96% of the subjects remembered correctly the number of years proposed for the exams to be implemented. Similarly, our check on the prior persuasion manipulation showed that 97% of the experimental subjects remembered correctly whether the confederate had changed on the drinking age issue. On the basis of these data, we felt confident that the independent variables of Experiment 3 had been properly manipulated.

The combined measure of subject mood was also submitted to an ANOVA and, as in Experiment 2, showed no significant effects (all $Fs < 1.68$; $Ms = 5.48, 5.06$, and 5.10, for the yield, control, and resist conditions, respectively).

As in Experiment 2, separate ANOVAs on the likability and intelligence ratings each produced only one effect that approached significance, the main effect of prior persuasion: for likability, $F(2, 90) = 4.16$, $p < .02$; for intelligence,

$F(2, 90) = 3.35$, $p < .04$. However, the pattern of means for these effects (for likability, yield = 5.66, control = 4.99, and resist = 5.32; for intelligence, yield = 5.55, control = 4.94, and resist = 5.21) did not conform to those of either of the measures of attitude change. As with Studies 1 and 2, ANOVA analysis using likability and intelligence ratings as covariates produced the same pattern of effects as did our ANOVAs on the public- and private-change measures. That is, only two effects proved significant—the main effect for prior persuasion on the measure of public change, $F(2, 89) = 8.09$, $p < .001$; and the main effect for prior persuasion on the measure of private change, $F(2, 88) = 3.24$, $p < .05$.

Discussion

Aside from replicating for a third time the reciprocal pattern of reported attitude change, the results of Experiment 3 enhanced confidence in the robustness of this effect. That is, it appears that not only does this basic reciprocal relationship emerge whether the topic is of low or high personal relevance but whether the arguments received are weak or strong. It was not the case that exposing subjects to powerful arguments from a communicator overwhelmed and rendered insignificant the tendency to reciprocate announced persuasion. In fact, when comparing the size of the reciprocal effects found across our three experiments, it seems that the introduction of strong arguments produced no diminution of effect at all.

Of more theoretical interest was the emergence for the first time of corresponding patterns on the measures of public and private attitude change. It appears that subjects exposed to cogent arguments for attitude change were led to overestimate the causal role of those arguments in bringing about their (primarily reciprocation-motivated) public reports of change; consequently, they attributed to themselves amounts of genuine, private change proportional to their tactical announcements of public change. What the results of Experiment 3 may reveal, then, is a case of one classic form of misattribution, wherein individuals whose responding is due to a particular motivational factor are led to mistakenly assign causality for their responses to the action of some other salient and plausible cause (L. Ross, Rodin, & Zimbardo, 1969; Storms & Nisbett, 1970; Valins & Ray, 1967).[8]

Before making too much of this attributional interpretation of findings, it would be wise to recognize a pair of reasons for withholding strong confidence in it at this point—aside from the fact that argument strength was not manipulated directly within the three studies. First, we have provided no internal evidence that subjects actually found the strong arguments of Study 3 to be more persuasive than the weak arguments of Studies 1 and 2; we relied, instead, on the work of other investigators who validated the strength of these arguments on students at a different university at a different time (see Petty & Cacioppo, 1986). More important, to this point we have provided no evidence for the major premise of our attributional account—that subjects publicly announcing change in response to strong arguments would be more likely to attribute their shifts to the inherent cogency of the arguments, whereas subjects publicly announcing change in response to weak arguments would be more likely to attribute their shifts to social factors.

To provide evidence in each of these arenas, a separate study was conducted with 33 students at ASU who participated for class credit. Each student received a questionnaire containing a set of the three weak arguments concerning comprehensive examinations that we had used in Studies 1 and 2, as well as a set of the three strong arguments we had used in Study 3. After rating each argument in a set on 7-point scales along the dimensions strong–weak, convincing–unconvincing, and persuasive–unpersuasive, subjects were asked to imagine that the set of arguments had been presented to them by a fellow student and that they had announced to the student that they had become more favorable toward comprehensive examinations as a result.

At this point, subjects were asked to rate on a 9-point scale the extent to which their announced change was likely to have been due to argument quality or social factors; the scale was anchored by the statements *I was truly influenced by the arguments' quality* (1) and *I was responding to social factors in the situation* (9). This question was asked both after subjects had rated the strong set of arguments and after they had rated the weak set of arguments; the order of presentation of the strong and weak argument sets was counterbalanced across subjects.

The ANOVAs supported both of the previously untested assumptions of our attributional formulation. First, as expected, the strong arguments were rated as stronger, more convincing, and more persuasive than the weak arguments, all $Fs(1, 32) > 55.82$, $ps < .001$. Second, subjects attributed more of their conceived public change to the quality of the arguments (and less to social factors) after reading the strong argument set ($M = 3.8$) than after reading the weak argument set ($M = 6.0$), $F(1, 27) = 15.01$, $p < .001$. It appears, then, that the findings of this study lend additional plausibility to the attributional account of our earlier results; although by no means do these findings ultimately confirm that account, as considerable further

support is required before strong confidence can be had. Nonetheless, our preferred attributional explanation offers an array of intriguing implications for future work, as is discussed in the following section.

GENERAL DISCUSSION

Despite an absence of prior evidence, it appears from the present program of work that the rule for reciprocity does indeed govern public declarations of persuasion. In all three of our experiments, subjects publicly reported the greatest persuasion from another's arguments on a topic if that other had yielded to the subjects' persuasive attempt on an earlier topic, whereas they reported the least such persuasion if the other had resisted their earlier attempt at influence. Furthermore, this tendency for publicly reciprocated persuasion was powerful enough to occur in a basic form that was unaffected by such factors as perceptions of the persuader's likability and intelligence, personal relevance of the topic under consideration, and strength of the arguments received.

It is worthy of note that in all three experiments, the tendency to reciprocate public attitude change was stronger in the yield conditions than in the resist conditions. In keeping with our focus on the social functions of attitude expressions, we favor an impression-management interpretation of this difference. That is, prior research has indicated that individuals are aware that they will be judged as less intelligent and likable by a persuader if they resist the persuasive attempt (Braver et al., 1977). Thus, it appears that, although they invariably reported the least public change to a persuader who had previously resisted their appeals, our subjects may have tempered the degree of their own stated resistance out of a desire to manage their positivity in the persuader's eyes. Nonetheless, the tendency of resist condition subjects to admit less change than control subjects was a reliable one that proved significant when the respective effects were combined across the three studies, $Z = 2.2$, $p < .03$.

The Indirect Role of Argument Strength in Producing Private Change

The factor of argument strength is worth special consideration, as it provides insight into the circumstances under which purely tactical, public pronouncements of change may become internalized as genuine change. Only when subjects were exposed to powerful arguments on an issue did their privately recorded changes conform to the reciprocal pattern of their publicly reported changes. However, it appears that when the correspondence of public and private change did occur, it came about as a side effect rather than as a direct effect of argument strength. That is, because subjects heard equally cogent arguments from yielding and resisting persuaders, it is not possible to assign subjects' differential private changes simply to the power of the arguments they heard. A more satisfactory, though admittedly still speculative, account of the role of argument strength in our findings is one that gives it the status of a discounting cue.

Recall that in all three experiments, our subjects publicly yielded to a persuader in accord with the norm of reciprocity. However, in Experiments 1 and 2, when the persuader's arguments were inherently weak, the subjects had little basis for assuming that those public changes were anything but simple responses to normative prescriptions; therefore, as is suggested by the results of our questionnaire study, they likely inferred no genuine persuasion from their public declarations of persuasion. This finding is consistent with the results of research showing that individuals who behave in a normative fashion typically will not make internal attributions to themselves on the basis of that behavior if it occurs in public. For example, Cialdini, Eisenberg, Shell, and McCreath (1987) found that elementary school children who made a commitment to help other children came to see themselves as more altruistic if the commitment had taken place in private, but not if it had occurred in public.

In Experiment 3, subjects once again changed publicly in accord with the dictates of the reciprocity norm; but, for the first time in our research program, they had a salient and plausible cause other than reciprocity for that change—the cogency of the persuader's message. Thus, when asked to register their true attitudes in private, subjects could no longer dismiss their public assertions of change as plainly and purely tactical; instead, as our questionnaire study suggests, the situation required them to allow for the causal role of genuine, argument-based persuasion—hence, the high degree of similarity between the patterns of public and private change.

Speculative Implications for the Internalization of Desirable Conduct

Certain insights that can be derived from the present research may be applied to the problem of arranging for individuals to incorporate desirable behavioral tendencies into their self-concepts. One difficulty in getting another to adopt a particular behavior pattern is that extrinsic pressures used to instigate the desired behavior may often back-fire. That is, these pressures can undermine one's attitude toward an action as well as one's subsequent performance of it by convincing a person that he or she did not engage in the act for any intrinsic reason (e.g., Fazio, 1981; Lepper & Greene, 1978; M. Ross, 1975). A standard solution suggested for this problem is to minimize the size of the extrinsic pressures designed to instigate the behavior. However, this may not always be feasible or desirable.

For instance, in many situations the target of influence may be unwilling to perform the desired action when low levels of personal, material, or social pressure are applied, requiring an intensification of extrinsic pressure to produce any compliance. The implications of our research suggest that under these circumstances, an influence agent who felt forced to use such heightened pressures to generate compliance would be well advised to use a discounting cue as well. For example, a supervisor who felt required to "pull rank" to get a subordinate to improve job performance should do so in conjunction with a set of additional reasons for that improvement (e.g., that it is consistent with the subordinate's past behavior or personal traits or long-term interests).

Similarly, a parent who has to assert his or her authority in pressing a child toward prosocial behavior through the use of extrinsic forces should not abandon the use of intrinsic reasons in the process (e.g., "You're a good boy, Timmy, and good boys share"). The implication from our research is that, even if an intrinsic reason is not a sufficient motivator of desired conduct, it may still operate as an internalizer of that conduct by serving as a discounting cue that undermines the perceived influence of the extrinsic cause. Thus, in a reversal of the traditional overjustification effect (Lepper & Greene, 1978), it might be possible to undermine the child's extrinsic interest in an activity by presenting a superfluous but plausible intrinsic reason for it. As long as the intrinsic reason remains present and salient in the situation for the child, it retains the potential, through the process of misattribution, to affect self-view. We would expect this to be especially true if, later, the parent focused on the intrinsic reason as the functional cause (e.g., "I knew you'd share your toys because you're a generous boy").

This focusing process might also be effective in leading adults to make dispositional attributions for their socially desirable actions that have arisen through the external pressures of societal norms. That is, if as Cialdini, Reno, and Kallgren (1990) have argued, norms affect behavior powerfully only when they are strong and salient, it could be counterproductive to reduce the magnitude of these extrinsic influences in situations where normative conduct is desirable. Yet, to the extent that the external normative pressures are sizable, they are more likely to be perceived as causal, and the favored conduct is less likely to be internalized. To avoid this dilemma, an influence agent might plan to focus individuals on normative forces prior to the opportunity for desirable action (e.g., to give blood or conserve energy or preserve the environment) but to refocus the individuals on intrinsic reasons for that action after it is done and is thereby ripe for causal analysis. Research indicating that individuals assign causal weight to those factors that are focal in their attention (see Fiske & Taylor, 1991, for a review) would support the effectiveness of such an approach. Of course, additional work designed to test this speculation directly would be required to provide heightened confidence in it.

REFERENCES

Axelrod, R. (1984). *The evolution of cooperation*. New York: Basic Books.

Berkowitz, L. (1972). Social norms, feelings, and other factors affecting helping and altruism. In L. Berkowitz (Ed.), *Advances in experimental social psychology* (Vol. 6, pp. 63–108). San Diego, CA: Academic Press.

Braver, S. L. (1975). Reciprocity, cohesiveness, and cooperation in two-person games. *Psychological Reports, 36*, 371–378.

Braver, S. L., Linder, D. E., Corwin, T. T., & Cialdini, R. B. (1977). Some conditions that affect admissions of attitude change. *Journal of Experimental Social Psychology, 13*, 565–576.

Byrne, D., & Rhamey, R. (1965). Magnitude of positive and negative reinforcements as a determinant of attraction. *Journal of Personality and Social Psychology, 2*, 884–889.

Chaiken, S., Liberman, A., & Eagly, A. H. (1989). Heuristic and systematic processing within and beyond the persuasion context. In J. S. Uleman & J. A. Bargh (Eds.), *Unintended thought: Limits of awareness, attention, and control* (pp. 212–252). New York: Guilford Press.

Cialdini, R. B. (1988). *Influence: Science and practice* (2nd ed.). Glenview, IL: Scott, Foresman.

Cialdini, R. B., Braver, S. L., & Lewis, S. K. (1974). Attributional bias and the easily persuaded other. *Journal of Personality and Social Psychology, 30*, 631–637.

Cialdini, R. B., Eisenberg, N., Shell, R., & McCreath, H. (1987). *British Journal of Social Psychology, 26*, 237–245.

Cialdini, R. B., Levy, A., Herman, C. P., & Evenbeck, S. (1973). Attitudinal politics: The strategy of moderation. *Journal of Personality and Social Psychology, 25*, 100–108.

Cialdini, R. B., & Mirels, H. L. (1976). Sense of personal control and attributions about yielding and resisting persuasion targets. *Journal of Personality and Social Psychology, 33*, 395–402.

Cialdini, R. B., Reno, R. R., & Kallgren, C. A. (1990). A focus theory of normative conduct: Recycling the concept of norms to reduce littering in public places. *Journal of Personality and Social Psychology, 58*, 1015–1026.

Cialdini, R. B., Vincent, J. E., Lewis, S. K., Catalan, J., Wheeler, D., & Darby, B. L. (1975). Reciprocal concessions procedure for inducing compliance: The door-in-the-face technique. *Journal of Personality and Social Psychology, 31*, 206–215.

Clark, M. S., Mills, J., & Powell, M. (1986). Keeping track of needs in communal and exchange relationships. *Journal of Personality and Social Psychology, 51*, 333–338.

Clark, M. S., & Waddell, B. A. (1983). Effects of moods on thoughts about helping, attraction, and information acquisition. *Social Psychology Quarterly, 46*, 31–35.

Condon, J. W., & Crano, W. D. (1988). Inferred evaluation and the relation between attitude similarity and interpersonal attraction. *Journal of Personality and Social Psychology, 54*, 789–797.

Cooper, J., & Jones, E. E. (1969). Opinion divergence as a strategy to avoid being miscast. *Journal of Personality and Social Psychology, 13*, 23–30.

Cunningham, J. A., Strassberg, D. S., & Haan, B. (1986). Effects of intimacy and sex-role congruency of self-disclosure. *Journal of Social and Clinical Psychology, 4*, 393–401.

Davis, K. E., & Florquist, C. C. (1965). Perceived threat and dependence as determinants of the tactical usage of opinion conformity. *Journal of Experimental Social Psychology, 1*, 219–236.

Dengerink, H. A., Schnedler, R. W., & Covey, M. K. (1978). Role of avoidance in aggressive responses to attack and no attack. *Journal of Personality and Social Psychology, 36*, 1044–1053.

Fazio, R. H. (1981). On the self-perception explanation of the overjustification effect. *Journal of Experimental Social Psychology, 17*, 417–426.

Fiske, S. T., & Taylor, S. E. (1991). *Social cognition* (2nd ed.). New York: Random House.

Gouldner, A. W. (1960). The norm of reciprocity: A preliminary statement. *American Sociological Review, 25*, 161–178.

Howard, D. J., & Barry, T. E. (1990). The evaluative consequences of experiencing unexpected favorable events. *Journal of Marketing Research, 27*, 51–60.

Isen, A. M., Clark, M., & Schwartz, M. F. (1976). Duration of the effects of good mood on helping: "Footprints on the sands of time." *Journal of Personality and Social Psychology, 34*, 385–393.

Isen, A. M., Shalker, T., Clark, M., & Karp, L. (1978). Affect, accessibility of material in memory, and behavior: A cognitive loop? *Journal of Personality and Social Psychology, 36*, 1–12.

Johnson, B. T., & Eagly, A. H. (1989). Effects of involvement on persuasion: A meta-analysis. *Psychological Bulletin, 104*, 290–314.

Jones, E. E. (1964). *Ingratiation: A social psychological analysis*. New York: Appleton-Century-Crofts.

Kelley, H. H. (1972). Attribution in social interaction. In E. E. Jones, D. E. Kanouse, H. H. Kelley, S. Valins, & B. Weiner (Eds.), *Attribution: Perceiving the causes of behavior* (pp. 1–26). Morristown, NJ: General Learning Press.

Kelman, H. C. (1961). Processes of opinion change. *Public Opinion Quarterly, 25*, 57–78.

Leakey, R., & Lewin, R. (1978). *People of the lake*. New York: Anchor Press.

Leippe, M. R., & Elkin, R. A. (1987). When motives clash: Issue involvement and response involvement as determinants of persuasion. *Journal of Personality and Social Psychology, 52,* 269–278.

Lepper, M. R., & Greene, D. (Eds.). (1978). *The hidden costs of reward.* Hillsdale, NJ: Erlbaum.

Manis, M., Cornell, S. D., & Moore, J. C. (1974). Transmission of attitude-relevant information through a communication chain. *Journal of Personality and Social Psychology, 30,* 81–94.

McGuire, W. J., & Millman, S. (1965). Anticipatory belief lowering following forewarning of a persuasive attack. *Journal of Personality and Social Psychology, 2,* 471–479.

Mills, J., & Clark, M. S. (1982). Exchange and communal relationships. In L. Wheeler (Ed.), *Review of personality and social psychology* (Vol. 3, pp. 121–144). Beverly Hills, CA: Sage.

Petty, R. E., & Cacioppo, J. T. (1986). The elaboration likelihood model of persuasion. In L. Berkowitz (Ed.), *Advances in experimental social psychology* (Vol. 19, pp. 123–205). San Diego, CA: Academic Press.

Petty, R. E., Cacioppo, J. T., & Goldman, R. (1981). Personal involvement as a determinant of argument-based persuasion. *Journal of Personality and Social Psychology, 41,* 847–855.

Razran, G. H. S. (1938). Conditioning away social bias by the luncheon technique. *Psychological Bulletin, 35,* 693.

Rosenbaum, M. E. (1980). Cooperation and competition. In P. B. Paulus (Ed.), *The psychology of group influence* (pp. 23–41). Hillsdale, NJ: Erlbaum.

Ross, L. (1977). The intuitive psychologist and his shortcomings. In L. Berkowitz (Ed.), *Advances in experimental social psychology* (Vol. 10, pp.174–221). San Diego, CA: Academic Press.

Ross, L., Rodin, J., & Zimbardo, P. G. (1969). Toward an attribution therapy: The reduction of fear through induced cognitive–emotional misattribution. *Journal of Personality and Social Psychology, 12,* 279–288.

Ross, M. (1975). Salience of reward and intrinsic motivation. *Journal of Personality and Social Psychology, 32,* 245–254.

Storms, M. D., & Nisbett, R. E. (1970). Insomnia and the attribution process. *Journal of Personality and Social Psychology, 16,* 319–328.

Tedeschi, J. T., Schlenker, B. R., & Bonoma, T. V. (1971). Cognitive dissonance: Private ratiocination or public spectacle? *American Psychologist, 26,* 685–695.

Tiger, L., & Fox, R. (1971). *The imperial animal.* New York: Holt, Rinehart & Winston.

Valins, S., & Ray, A. A. (1967). Effects of cognitive desensitization on avoidance behavior. *Journal of Personality and Social Psychology, 7,* 345–350.

NOTES

1. The determination of whether a subject's data would be dropped from the analysis was made on the basis of his or her written responses to a pair of postexperimental questions inquiring into suspicions about the nature of the experimental hypotheses and ruses. A judge (Robert B. Cialdini) read these responses while blind to subjects' experimental conditions and eliminated data from subjects whose suspicions were sufficiently accurate to discredit their data.

2. The plausible availability of such information was made possible by a battery of tests that had been administered to all introductory psychology students in the 2nd week of the semester. It was from this mass testing session that the biographical sketch was said to have come.

3. An alternative analysis was performed in which the initial attitude measure was covaried on the final attitude measure. In this study and all subsequent studies, this analysis of covariance approach produced results that were invariably comparable to those of the change-score analysis. Consequently, we have chosen to present the more intuitively accessible change-score results.

4. Although no significant differences were found within the design on the private measure, for the sake of completeness we present the means for each of the six experimental cells herein, with the low-relevance mean appearing first within each level of the prior persuasion factor: yield = 2.22 and 1.57; control = .86 and 1.47; and resist = 1.22 and .83. Tukey tests performed on these six means found no two significantly different from one another.

5. Although no significant differences were found within the design on the private measure, for the sake of completeness we present the means for each of the six experimental cells of Study 2, with the low-relevance mean appearing first within each level of the prior persuasion factor: yield = 1.10 and .77; control = .47 and .92; and resist = 1.24 and 1.52. Tukey tests performed on these six means found no two significantly different from one another.

6. Those strong arguments were (a) I just read an article about how at Duke University when they started using senior comps the overall GPA went up about 30%, so maybe if we had them at ASU, it would make people study more and get better grades; (b) The article also said that at graduate and medical schools they give preference to students that have comprehensive exams, so I think that if we had them here, it would make ASU graduates more competitive; and (c) I know students at most Ivy League schools have to take senior comps, and I think if we had them here, then ASU would become more prestigious and lose its reputation as being such a "party school."

7. Means for each of the six cells were as follows, with the low-relevance mean presented first in each level of the prior persuasion factor: yield = 3.31 and 1.77; control = 1.51 and 1.51; and resist = 1.69 and 1.06. The Prior Persuasion × Topic Relevance interaction was nonsignificant, $F(2, 90) = 1.27$. Within the low-relevance conditions, the prior persuasion main effect was significant, $F(2, 90) = 4.15$, $p < .02$; within the high-relevance conditions, it was nonsignificant, $F(2, 90) = .56$. Tukey tests on the set of six means found only one pair that differed significantly from one another—the means for the low relevance–yield and the high relevance–resist cells.

8. One potential implication of our attributional account of the private change in Experiment 3 is that the reverse pattern should have occurred in Experiments 1 and 2. That is, resist condition subjects' relative lack of public change in the face of the combination of weak arguments and prior resistance could have led them to attribute the least private change to themselves. Such an attributional pattern seems unlikely, however, given evidence that individuals rarely make confident attributions based on the lack of action (L. Ross, 1977).

Received February 19, 1991
Revision received November 18, 1991
Accepted January 2, 1992

CRITICAL THINKING QUESTIONS

1. Cialdini, Green, and Rusch examined persuasion over time as two people tried to persuade each other. In what contexts does this type of persuasion occur in everyday life? In what ways was the procedure in these studies different from what occurs in everyday life?

2. The authors suggest that a rule for reciprocity affects many different types of interactions. What interactions do they suggest it affects? Can you think of other interactions where a rule for reciprocity does not affect people's interactions?

3. What were the procedures in the control condition of Study 1? What was the purpose of this condition?

4. What is the difference between public change and private change? What might it mean if people have public change but not private change?

5. Drawing on research described in Chapter 10, how does the strength of arguments typically affect the persuasion process? How did the strength of the arguments affect persuasion in the research reported in this article?

6. At the end of the discussion section the authors speculate about how the results of the current study could be used to get people to internalize desirable consequences. Could these same processes be used for less noble ends—like getting people to internalize undesirable conduct? How does this affect the value of the research?

PART IV
Applying Social Psychology

READING 13

In Chapter 12 of your textbook, Elizabeth Loftus's theory of reconstructive memory is discussed in the context of eyewitness testimony. Reconstructive memory is the theory that eyewitness memory can be altered by exposure to information after the event. Loftus and her colleagues have conducted a number of studies consistent on this concept. This theory has generated a great deal of research and controversy. The concept of reconstructive memory has important implications for several basic and applied issues, and it is an important integration of social influence and social perception.

In the classic article by Loftus and Palmer presented here, one can see the authors take some early steps toward creating and developing the theory of reconstructive memory. With a very simple manipulation, Loftus and Palmer show how susceptible, and therefore potentially inaccurate, people's memories for details about an event are. As you read this article, consider how much greater the impact might have been if the event witnessed had been more ambiguous, if the biasing questions had been stronger and more numerous, if the witnesses had been in a more aroused state, if the witnesses had been children, and so on.

As you read the article, you can also consider the debate mentioned in the textbook about whether postevent information such as the wording of the questions actually alters the witnesses' memory, or whether their memory for the event is the same but their responses to the questions are affected. (Thus, if they later were asked more fair questions, would their responses be more accurate?) For which side of the debate do Loftus and Palmer argue?

Reconstruction of Automobile Destruction: An Example of the Interaction Between Language and Memory

Elizabeth F. Loftus and John C. Palmer
University of Washington

Two experiments are reported in which subjects viewed films of automobile accidents and then answered questions about events occurring in the films. The question, "About how fast were the cars going when they smashed into each other?" elicited higher estimates of speed than questions which used the verbs collided, bumped, contacted, or hit in place of smashed. On a retest one week later, those subjects who received the verb smashed were more likely to say "yes" to the question, "Did you see any broken glass?", even though broken glass was not present in the film. These results are consistent with the view that the questions asked subsequent to an event can cause a reconstruction in one's memory of the event.

How accurately do we remember the details of a complex event, like a traffic accident, that has happened in our presence? More specifically, how well do we do when asked to estimate some numerical quantity such as how long the accident took, how fast the cars were traveling, or how much time elapsed between the sounding of a horn and the moment of collision?

It is well documented that most people are markedly inaccurate in reporting such numerical details as time, speed, and distance (Bird, 1927; Whipple, 1909). For example, most people have difficulty estimating the duration of an event, with some research indicating that the tendency is to overestimate the duration of events which are complex (Block, 1974; Marshall, 1969; Ornstein, 1969). The judgment of speed is especially difficult, and practically every automobile accident results in huge variations from one witness to another as to how fast a vehicle was actually traveling (Gardner, 1933). In one test administered to Air Force personnel who knew in advance that they would be questioned about the speed of a moving automobile, estimates ranged from 10 to 50 mph. The car they watched was actually going only 12 mph (Marshall, 1969, p. 23).

Given the inaccuracies in estimates of speed, it seems likely that there are variables which are potentially powerful in terms of influencing these estimates. The present research was conducted to investigate one such variable, namely, the phrasing of the question used to elicit the speed judgment. Some questions are clearly more suggestive than others. This fact of life has resulted in the legal concept of a leading question and in legal rules indicating when leading questions are allowed (*Supreme Court Reporter,* 1973). A leading question is simply one that, either by its form or content, suggests to the witness what answer is desired or leads him to the desired answer.

In the present study, subjects were shown films of traffic accidents and then they answered questions about the accident. The subjects were interrogated about the speed of the vehicles in one of several ways. For example, some subjects were asked, "About how fast were the cars going when they hit each other?" while others were asked, "About how fast were the cars going when they smashed into each other?" As Fillmore (1971) and Bransford and McCarrell (in press) have noted, *hit* and *smashed* may involve specification of differential rates of movement. Furthermore, the two verbs may also involve differential specification of the likely consequences of the events to which they are referring. The impact of the accident is apparently gentler for *hit* than for *smashed*.

EXPERIMENT 1

Method

Forty-five students participated in groups of various sizes. Seven films were shown, each depicting a traffic accident. These films were segments from longer driver's education films borrowed from the Evergreen Safety Council and the Seattle Police Department. The length of the film segments ranged from 5 to 30 sec. Following each film, the subjects received a questionnaire asking them first to, "give an account of the accident you have just seen," and then to answer a series of specific questions about the accident. The critical question was the one that interrogated the subject about the speed of the vehicles involved in the collision. Nine subjects were asked, "About how fast were the cars going when they hit each other?" Equal numbers of the remaining subjects were interrogated with the verbs *smashed, collided, bumped,* and *contacted* in place of *hit*. The entire experiment lasted about an hour and a half. A different ordering of the films was presented to each group of subjects.

Results

Table 1 presents the mean speed estimates for the various verbs. Following the procedures outlined by Clark (1973), an analysis of variance was performed with verbs as a fixed effect, and subjects and films as random effects, yielding a significant quasi F ratio $F'(5.55) = 4.65$, $p < .005$.

Some information about the accuracy of subjects' estimates can be obtained from our data. Four of the seven films were staged crashes; the original purpose of these films was to illustrate what can happen to human beings when cars collide at various speeds. One collision took place at 20 mph, one at 30, and two at 40. The means estimates of speed for these four films were: 37.7, 36.2, 39.7 and 36.1 mph, respectively. In agreement with previous work, people are not very good at judging how fast a vehicle was actually traveling.

Discussion

The results of this experiment indicate that the form of a question (in this case, changes of a single word) can markedly and systematically affect a witness's answer to that question. The actual speed of the vehicles controlled little variance in subject reporting, while the phrasing of the question controlled considerable variance.

Two interpretations of this finding are possible. First, it is possible that the differential speed estimates result merely from response-bias factors. A subject is uncertain whether to say 30 mph or 40 mph, for example and the verb *smashed* biases his response towards the higher estimate. A second interpretation is that the question form causes change in the subject's memory representation of the accident. The verb *smashed* may change a subject's memory such that he "sees" the accident as being more severe than it actually was. If this is the case, we might expect subjects to "remember" other details that did not actually occur, but are commensurate with an accident occurring at higher speeds. The second experiment was designed to provide additional insights into the origin of the differential speed estimates.

TABLE 1   Speed Estimates for the Verbs Used in Experiment 1

Verb	Mean speed estimate
Smashed	40.8
Collided	39.3
Bumped	38.1
Hit	34.0
Contacted	31.8

EXPERIMENT II

Method

One hundred and fifty students participated in this experiment, in groups of various sizes. A film depicting a multiple car accident was shown, followed by a questionnaire. The film lasted less than 1 min; the accident in the film lasted 4 sec. At the end of the film, the subjects received a questionnaire asking them first to describe the accident in their own words, and then to answer a series of questions about the accident. The critical question was the one that interrogated the subject about the speed of the vehicles. Fifty subjects were asked, "About how fast were the cars going when they smashed into each other?" Fifty subjects were asked, "About how fast were the cars going when they hit each other?" Fifty subjects were not interrogated about vehicular speed.

One week later, the subjects returned and without viewing the film again they answered a series of questions about the accident. The critical question here was, "Did you see any broken glass?" which the subjects answered by checking "yes" or "no." This question was embedded in a list totalling 10 questions, and appeared in a random position in the list. There was no broken glass in the accident but since broken glass is commensurate with accidents occurring at high speed, we expected that the subjects who had been asked the *smashed* question might more often say "yes" to this critical question.

Results

The mean estimate of speed for subjects interrogated with *smashed* was 10.46 mph; with *hit* the estimate was 8.00 mph. These means are significantly different, $t(98) = 2.00$, $p < .05$.

Table 2 presents the distribution of "yes" and "no" responses for the *smashed, hit,* and control subjects. An independence chi-square test on these responses was significant beyond the .025 level, $\chi^2(2) = 7.76$. The important result in Table 2 is that the probability of saying "yes," P(Y), to the question about broken glass is .32 when the verb *smashed* is used, and .14 with *hit.* Thus *smashed* leads both to more "yes" responses and to higher speed estimates. It appears to be the case that the effect of the verb is mediated at least in part by the speed estimate. The question now arises: Is *smashed* doing anything else besides increasing the estimate of speed? To answer this, the function relating P(Y) to speed estimate was calculated separately for *smashed* and *hit.* If the speed estimate is the only way in which effect of verb is mediated, then for a given speed estimate, P(Y)

TABLE 2   Distribution of "Yes" and "No" Responses to the Question, "Did You See Any Broken Glass?"

Response	Verb Condition		
	Smashed	Hit	Control
Yes	16	7	6
No	34	43	44

should be independent of verb. Table 3 shows that this is not the case. P(Y) is lower for *hit* than for *smashed*: the difference between the two verbs ranges from .03 for estimates of 1–5 mph to .18 for estimates of 6–10 mph. The average difference between the two curves is about .12. Whereas the unconditional difference of .18 between the *smashed* and *hit* conditions is attenuated, it is by no means eliminated when estimate of speed is controlled for. It thus appears that the verb *smashed* has other effects besides that of simply increasing the estimate of speed. One possibility will be discussed in the next section.

DISCUSSION

To reiterate, we have first of all provided an additional demonstration of something that has been known for some time, namely, that the way a question is asked can enormously influence the answer that is given. In this instance, the question, "About how fast were the cars going when they smashed into each other?" led to higher estimates of speed than the same question asked with the verb *smashed* replaced by *hit.* Furthermore, this seemingly small change had consequences for how questions are answered a week after the original event occurred.

As a framework for discussing these results, we would like to propose that two kinds of information go into one's memory for some complex occurrence. The first is information gleaned during the perception of the original event;

TABLE 3   Probability of Saying "Yes" to, "Did You See Any Broken Glass?" Conditionalized on Speed Estimates

Verb condition	Speed estimate (mph)			
	1–5	6–10	11–15	16–20
Smashed	.09	.27	.41	.62
Hit	.06	.09	.25	.50

the second is external information supplied after the fact. Over time, information from these two sources may be integrated in such a way that we are unable to tell from which source some specific detail is recalled. All we have is one "memory."

Discussing the present experiments in these terms, we propose that the subject first forms some representation of the accident he has witnessed. The experimenter then, while asking, "About how fast were the cars going when they smashed into each other?" supplies a piece of external information, namely, that the cars did indeed smash into each other. When these two pieces of information are integrated, the subject has a memory of an accident that was more severe than in fact it was. Since broken glass is commensurate with a severe accident, the subject is more likely to think that broken glass was present.

There is some connection between the present work and earlier work on the influence of verbal labels on memory for visually presented form stimuli. A classic study in psychology showed that when subjects are asked to reproduce a visually presented form, their drawings tend to err in the direction of a more familiar object suggested by a verbal label initially associated with the to-be-remembered form (Carmichael, Hogan, & Walter, 1932). More recently, Daniel (1972) showed that recognition memory, as well as reproductive memory, was similarly affected by verbal labels, and he concluded that the verbal label causes a shift in the memory strength of forms which are better representatives of the label.

When the experimenter asks the subject, "About how fast were the cars going when they smashed into each other?", he is effectively labeling the accident a smash. Extrapolating the conclusions of Daniel to this situation, it is natural to conclude that the label, smash, causes a shift in the memory representation of the accident in the direction of being more similar to a representation suggested by the verbal label.

REFERENCES

Bird, C. The influence of the press upon the accuracy of report. *Journal of Abnormal and Social Psychology*, 1927, 22, 123–129.

Block, R. A. Memory and the experience of duration in retrospect. *Memory & Cognition*, 1974, 2, 153–160.

Bransford, J. D., & McCarrrell, N. S. A sketch of a cognitive approach to comprehension. Some thoughts about understanding what it means to comprehend. In D. Palermo & W. Weiner (Eds.), *Cognition and the symbolic processes*. Washington, D.C.: V. H. Winston & Co., in press.

Carmichael, L., Hogan, H. P., & Walter, A. A. An experimental study of the effect of language on the reproduction of visually perceived form. *Journal of Experimental Psychology*, 1932, 15, 73–86.

Clark, H. H. The language-as-fixed-effect fallacy: A critique of language statistics in psychological research. *Journal of Verbal Learning and Verbal Behavior*, 1973, 12, 335–359.

Danill, T. C. Nature of the effect of verbal labels on recognition memory for form. *Journal of Experimental Psychology*, 1972, 96, 152–157.

Fillmore, C. J. Types of lexical information. In D. D. Steinberg and L. A. Jakobovits (Eds.), *Semantics: An interdisciplinary reader in philosophy, linguistics, and psychology*. Cambridge: Cambridge University Press, 1971.

Gardner, D. S. The perception and memory of witnesses. *Cornell Law Quarterly*, 1933, 8, 391–409.

Marshall, J. *Law and psychology in conflict*. New York: Anchor Books, 1969.

Ornstein, R. E. *On the experience of time*. Harmondsworth, Middlesex, England: Penguin, 1969.

Whipple, G. M. The observer as reporter: A survey of the psychology of testimony. *Psychological Bulletin*, 1909, 6, 153–170.

Supreme Court Reporter, 1973, 3: Rules of Evidence for United States Courts and Magistrates.

(Received April 17, 1974)

CRITICAL THINKING QUESTIONS

1. In our introduction to this article, we asked you to consider the debate about whether the wording of the question affects a witness's memory or just his or her response. What do you think Loftus and Palmer believe about this issue? Why do they think this? What is your personal opinion about this issue?

2. What are the implications of the issues raised in this paper? How might the processes described affect various aspects of law? How do the two sides of the debate mentioned in the previous question suggest different implications?

3. In which stage or stages of the three stages of memory discussed in Chapter 12 (acquisition, storage, and retrieval) should reconstructive memory be most relevant? Why?

4. Under what conditions should the effects observed in this article be stronger? Why? Under what conditions should the effects observed in this article be weaker? Why?

5. Apart from the wording of a question, what other postevent information might have a biasing effect on a witness's memory or testimony?
6. In addition to eyewitness testimony, how might reconstructive memory, or similar processes, be relevant to each of the following issues: the hindsight bias (Chapter 2), attribution (Chapter 3), stereotypes and prejudice (Chapter 4), intimate relationships (Chapter 6), and compliance (Chapter 9)?

READING 14

Being rewarded for one's work is critical for maintaining motivation and commitment, but the effects of reward on motivation and behavior can be complex. As Chapter 13 of your textbook explains, the timing and nature of rewards can increase or decrease one's intrinsic motivation for some behavior. Chapter 13 also discusses the role of the perceived fairness of rewards. According to equity theory, one is most satisfied when the ratio between benefits and contributions is the same for oneself and others. This is relevant not only to the workplace, as discussed in Chapter 13, but also to intimate relationships, as discussed in Chapter 6. In the workplace, if you feel you work just as hard and as well as another person, you should be most satisfied if you and this other person are rewarded equally. If you feel you perform better than one person and not as effectively as a second person, you should feel most satisfied if you are rewarded more than the first person but less than the second person.

Is this theory applicable in real-world workplaces? Moreover, can nonmonetary factors (that is, factors other than salary or other financial considerations) influence our perceptions of equity? The article by Greenberg describes a creative test of these questions. In the best tradition of field experiments, Greenberg took advantage of an existing situation in a real workplace to study this issue. When workers in an organization had to be relocated temporarily from their regular offices, they were placed into offices of either higher-, lower-, or equal-status coworkers. Would workers feel a sense of inequity if they were placed into a higher-status or lower-status office than others of their rank? By examining the workers' performance before, during, and after the reassignment, Greenberg was able to answer this question.

In field studies such as this, researchers are often constrained by the situation that exists in the organization or setting, so that they cannot ensure internal validity. As Chapter 1 explains, internal validity is the degree to which there can be reasonable certainty that the independent variable in an experiment caused the effects obtained on the dependent variable. Greenberg was able to increase the internal validity of this study dramatically by using random assignment; that is, the workers in this organization were reassigned offices through a random procedure. This helping to ensure that any differences found in the study would most likely be due to the manipulation rather than some other factor.

Equity and Workplace Status: A Field Experiment

Jerald Greenberg
Faculty of Management and Human Resources
The Ohio State University

In a field experiment, 198 employees in the underwriting department of a large insurance company were randomly reassigned on a temporary basis to the offices of either higher, lower, or equal-status coworkers while their own offices were being refurbished. The present study tested the hypothesis, derived from equity theory, that the status value of the temporary offices would create increases, decreases, or no change in organizational outcome levels. The resulting pattern of performance supported equity theory. Specifi-cally, relative to those workers reassigned to equal-status offices, those reassigned to higher status offices raised their performance (a response to overpayment inequity) and those reassigned to lower status offices lowered their performance (a response to underpayment inequity). As hypothesized, the size of these performance changes was directly related to the magnitude of the status inconsistencies encountered. The value of these findings in extending equity theory to the realm of nonmonetary outcomes is discussed.

SOURCE: Greenberg, Jerald, "Equity and Workplace Status: A Field Experiment," *Journal of Applied Psychology*, 1988, Vol. 73, No. 4, 606–613. Copyright © 1988 by the American Psychological Association. Reprinted with permission.

There can be little doubt about the existence of certain trappings of success in organizations—physical symbols (cf. Goodsell, 1977) reflecting the organizational status of job incumbents (Steele, 1973). Indeed, previous research has confirmed that certain indicators of status demarcation (cf. Konar & Sundstrom, 1985), such as large offices (Langdon, 1966), carpeting (Joiner, 1976), and proximity to windows (Halloran, 1978), are recognized as rewards symbolizing one's high standing in an organizational status hierarchy. Although these environmental rewards typically are associated with relatively high-status individuals, thereby reinforcing the social order of organizations (Edelman, 1978), there are some occasions in which the status of the job incumbent and the physical symbols associated with the status are not matched (Wineman, 1982). Such instances may be recognized as cases of status inconsistency (cf. Stryker & Macke, 1978) and, as such, reactions to them may be explained by equity theory (e.g., Adams, 1965; Walster, Walster, & Berscheid, 1978).

According to equity theory, workers who receive levels of reward (i.e., outcomes) higher or lower than coworkers who make equivalent contributions to their jobs (i.e., inputs) are considered overpaid and underpaid, respectively. Such inequitable states have been shown to result in dissatisfaction and to bring about increases and decreases, respectively, in job performance (for a review, see Greenberg, 1982). As such, the present investigation addresses whether the characteristics of an employee's workspace influence his or her perceptions of equitable treatment on the job. If the characteristics of one's work space are perceived as constituting part of one's work-related rewards, then it follows that receiving work-space-derived rewards greater or less than coworkers of equal status may create conditions of overpayment and underpayment inequity, respectively. The focal question of the present investigation is whether equity theory explains the reactions of persons encountering consistencies and inconsistencies between their job status and the rewards offered by their work space.

Although there is little direct evidence bearing on this question, managers have intuitively believed and long advocated the importance of basing office design decisions on employees' ranks in their organizations' status hierarchies as a mechanism for ensuring equitable treatment (Robichaud, 1958). According to equity theory, an employee's work space may be recognized as an element of equitable treatment insofar as it is perceived as a reward that reflects his or her organizational status. Indeed, previous research (e.g., Konar, Sundstrom, Brady, Mandel, & Rice, 1982) has shown that several elements of work space, such as the nature of the furnishings, amount of space, capacity for

personalization, and the ability to control access by others, have been found to covary with workers' relative status rankings (for reviews, see Becker, 1981, 1982; Davis, 1984; Sundstrom, 1986).

Although previous researchers have not incorporated work-space elements into equity theory-based predictions directly, extrapolations from existing research suggest that reactions to work-space characteristics may be predictable from equity theory. For example, Burt and Sundstrom (1979) found in a field study that workers who were underpaid financially were less dissatisfied with their pay if they worked under conditions that were more environmentally desirable than those who did not receive additional work-space-related benefits. These results suggest that the desirable working conditions constituted an additional reward that offset the dissatisfaction created by inadequate monetary payment. Such a finding is consistent with the possibility that workers' reactions to their work spaces may be explained by equity theory. Inequities created by nonmonetary rewards have also been studied by Greenberg and Ornstein (1983), who found that experimental subjects who were overpaid by receiving an inappropriately high job title responded by increasing their job performance, as predicted by equity theory. Thus, much as an inappropriately high job title resulted in attempts to redress overpayment inequity by raising inputs, similar reactions may result from overpayments created by the introduction of work-space elements that are inappropriately lavish for one's organizational ranking.

On the basis of this logic, the present study tested hypotheses derived from equity theory in an organizational setting in which the refurbishing of offices necessitated the reassignment of employees to temporary offices. Specifically, I hypothesized that employees reassigned to offices of higher status workers (i.e., those who are overpaid in terms of office status) would be more productive than those reassigned to offices of other equal-status workers. Similarly, employees reassigned to offices of lower status worker (i.e., those who are underpaid in terms of office status) would be expected to be less productive than those reassigned to offices of other equal-status workers.

Following from equity theory's proposition that the magnitude of the inequity-resolution efforts will be proportional to the magnitude of the inequity (Adams, 1965; Walster et al., 1978), it was expected that improvements or decrements in performance would be greater the larger the over- or underpayments, respectively. Employees reassigned to offices of workers two levels above them would be expected to perform at a higher level than employees reassigned to offices of more modestly overpaid workers one level above them. Similarly, employees reassigned to offices of workers two levels below them would be expected to perform at a lower level than employees reassigned to offices of more modestly underpaid workers one level below them.

METHOD

Subjects

The 198 participants in the study (123 men and 75 women) were drawn from three groups of salaried employees in the life insurance underwriting department of a large insurance company. There were 91 underwriter trainees (Mdn age = 24 years; Mdn job tenure = 8 months), 60 associate underwriters (Mdn age = 28 years; Mdn job tenure = 1 year, 9 months), and 47 underwriters (Mdn age = 31 years; Mdn job tenure = 3 years, 2 months). All of these employees were charged with the responsibility for reviewing and either approving or disapproving applications for life insurance on the basis of the extent to which information uncovered in their investigations satisfied the company's criteria for risk. The primary difference in responsibility for the three groups was the monetary size of the policies they were permitted to approve.

Design

Because the offices of the underwriting department were being refurbished, an opportunity presented itself for studying the behavior of employees working temporarily (10 consecutive work days) in offices regularly assigned to higher, lower, or equally ranked coworkers in the underwriting department. With the cooperation of the participating organization, assignment to temporary office conditions was made at random.[1] The reassignment made it possible to create conditions of potential overpayment (assignment to a higher status office), underpayment (assignment to a lower status office), or equitable payment (assignment to an equal-status office), as well as the degree of inequitable payment (office assignment either one or two levels above or below the worker's status). To create control groups, some workers in each employee group remained in their own permanent offices during the study period. Table 1 summarizes the experimental design and reports the number of subjects assigned to each condition.

In addition to these between-subjects elements, the design of the present study also included time as a within-subjects element. Repeated measures of the dependent variables were taken at six intervals: the second week before reassignment to a temporary office, the first week before

TABLE 1   Summary of Study Design

Worker group/temporary office	n	Payment condition
Trainee		
Other trainee	42	Equitably paid
Associate	18	One-step overpaid
Underwriter	12	Two-steps overpaid
Own	19	Control
Associate		
Trainee	18	One-step underpaid
Other associate	18	Equitably paid
Underwriter	12	One-step overpaid
Own	12	Control
Underwriter		
Trainee	12	Two-steps underpaid
Associate	12	One-step underpaid
Other underwriter	12	Equitably paid
Own	11	Control

reassignment, the first week during the reassignment period, the second week during reassignment, the first week back in one's permanent office after reassignment, and the second week after reassignment.

Procedure

Office assignment procedure   Before the study began, workers (except those in the control groups) were informed that they would have to work for 2 consecutive 5-day work weeks in other offices while their own offices were being refurbished.[2] So as to not disrupt performance, but allowing ample time for workers to gather their belongings, workers were informed of the impending temporary move 2 workdays in advance. Workers drew lots to determine their temporary office assignments and were not permitted to switch these assignments. This procedure helped safeguard against the possibility that reactions to office assignments could be the result of perceived managerial favoritism or hostility resulting from an undisclosed (and potentially capricious) basis for the office assignments. The procedure also controlled against any possible self-selection bias in office reassignments.

Office characteristics   The offices used in the study were those regularly assigned to either underwriter trainees, associate underwriters, or underwriters. In the organization studied, as in others (e.g., Harris, 1977; Kleinschrod, 1987), the offices of workers of different status-rankings differed along several predetermined, standardized dimensions. Consensual knowledge of such differences helped reinforce the status differences between the offices used in the study.[3] The key physical characteristics of the offices used in the experiment are described in Table 2. Although these dimensions were known within the host organization to reflect status differential, it is instructive to note that they are not idiosyncratic. Indeed, these dimensions are among those found in the survey study by Konar et al. (1982) to be associated with status differences among employees in other organizations.

As shown in Table 2, the offices of associate underwriters were shared by fewer office mates, allowed more space per person, and had larger desks than the offices of underwriter trainees. Underwriters' offices were always completely private (used by only one person), allowed the most space per person, and had the largest desks. In addition, the underwriters' offices had doors, whereas the offices of underwriter trainees and associate underwriters did not. The use of these status markers (cf. Konar & Sundstrom, 1985) is in keeping with previous studies showing that higher status is associated with the use of unshared, private offices (Sundstrom, Burt, & Kamp, 1980), greater floorspace (Harris, 1977), larger desks (Wylie, 1958), and the option to limit access to oneself by the presence of doors (Geran, 1976).

Performance measure   The principal dependent measure was job performance in reviewing applications for life insurance. It was the practice of the company studied to derive corrected performance scores for all underwriters. (Such measures typically were used, in part, as the basis for performance evaluations and pay raises.) Raw performance measures were computed weekly on the basis of the number of cases completed. These were then adjusted by supervisory personnel for decision quality, the complexity of the cases considered (both of which were based on predetermined criteria), and the number of hours spent reviewing application files, resulting in a corrected performance score. So as to provide a basis of comparison for interpreting these scores, the mean corrected performance scores of the workers studied in the 2 months prior to the present investigation was 49.2. Because this score was not significantly different than the two prereassignment scores observed in this investigation, $F < 1.00$, *ns*, there is no reason to believe that the study period was in any way atypical.

Questionnaire measures   To help explain the performance measure, questionnaire data were collected as supplementary measures. These questionnaires were administered at three times: one week before reassignment, one week into the reassignment period, and one week after reassignment.

To measure job satisfaction, the 20-item general satisfaction scale of the Minnesota Satisfaction Questionnaire (MSQ; Weiss, Dawis, England, & Lofquist, 1967) was used. It requires participants to indicate whether they are *very satisfied, satisfied, neither satisfied nor dissatisfied, dissatisfied,* or *very dissatisfied* with respect to a broad range of job dimensions, such as "the feeling of accomplishment I get from the job" and "the freedom to use my own judgment." This scale was chosen because it has excellent psychometric properties (Price & Mueller, 1986) and because its use enhances comparability with other tests of equity theory using the same measure (e.g., Pritchard, Dunnette, & Jorgenson, 1972). For the present sample, coefficient alpha was .88.

An additional set of questions was designed to determine the extent to which workers recognized the outcome value of their office environments. As such, a measure of environmental satisfaction was derived by asking subjects, "How pleased or displeased are you with each of the following aspects of your current work environment?": privacy, desk space, floorspace, noise level, lighting, furnishings, and overall atmosphere. Scale values could range from *extremely*

TABLE 2   Physical Characteristics of Offices

Physical characteristic	Offices		
	Underwriter trainees ($n = 15$)	Associate underwriters ($n = 30$)	Underwriters ($n = 47$)
No. of occupants per office	6[a]	2	1
Presence of door	No	No	Yes
Occupant space (m^2 per occupant)	21.34	29.87	44.81
Desk size (m^2)	1.14	1.32	1.53

Note. Because the host company standardized office characteristics as a function of employee status, there was very little or no variation in the values reported here.
[a] One of the 15 offices that was larger than the others housed seven underwriter trainees; the remaining 14 housed six.

displeased (1) to *extremely pleased* (7). Coefficient alpha was computed to be .82.

Finally, a separate item asked, "How would you characterize the overall level of rewards you are now receiving from your job?" Scale values could range from *extremely low* (1) to *extremely high* (7).

Manipulation checks   As the basis for explaining performance differences in terms of the inequities caused by status differences in office assignments, it was necessary to establish that workers correctly perceived the status differences of their temporary offices and, also, had unaided and unimpaired opportunities to perform in their temporary offices. Accordingly, checklist questions addressing these matters were administered at the end of the first week in the temporary offices (at the same time as the second administration of the questionnaire measures). Because these questions were not applicable to workers in the control group, the checklist was not administered to them.

Specifically, to determine whether subjects recognized the status differences between their regular offices and their temporary offices, they were requested to respond to a checklist item that asked, "Is your temporary office usually assigned to a coworker of: lower status than you, equal status to you, or higher status than you?" An additional checklist item asked subjects, "Relative to your regular office, do the facilities found in your temporary office: help you do your job better, enable you to do your job equally well, or cause you to do your job more poorly?"

RESULTS

Manipulation Checks

Subjects' responses to the questionnaire item asking them to identify the relative status attached to their temporary offices showed that they were, in fact, aware of the similarities or differences between their own offices and their temporary ones. Virtually all of the subjects assigned to the offices of equal-status others recognized those offices as being of equal status. All of the subjects assigned to offices of higher and lower status others (whether one or two steps higher or lower) recognized the hierarchical level of those offices. This evidence supports the claim that subjects were aware of the status similarities or differences they encountered during the course of the study and that the manipulations of status were successful.

Another manipulation check sought to ensure that subjects' performance differences could not be attributed to differential opportunities to perform their jobs while in the temporary offices. In response to a checklist item, virtually all 198 participants reported that the facilities in their temporary offices enabled them to perform their jobs as well as they did in their regularly assigned offices. These data discount the possibility that performance increases or decreases noted while in the temporary offices were the result of opportunities provided by or thwarted by office conditions.

Preliminary Analyses

Prior to testing hypotheses, analyses were conducted on the work performance data to determine whether combining the various cells that composed the identically defined payment conditions shown in Table 1 was justified. This was done by including the identically defined groups (as a between-subjects factor) and the observation time (as a repeated measure) in mixed-design analyses of variance (ANOVAS). Justification for combining the responses of the identically defined groups required finding no significant differences between groups, either as main effects or in interactions with the observation time.

As shown in Table 1, four distinct payment conditions were identified by more than one group of workers. Specifically, three groups of workers (those reassigned to equal-status offices) were identified as equitably paid, three groups of workers (those who remained in their own offices) were identified as control subjects, two groups of workers (those assigned to offices one status level higher) were identified as one-step overpaid, and two groups of workers (those assigned to offices one status level lower) were identified as one-step underpaid. Separate ANOVAS for the groups defining each of these four payment conditions revealed no significant main effects of group membership and no interaction of group membership with time, all values of $F < 1.00$, *ns*. Accordingly, distinct payment conditions were created by combining the data for the identically defined groups.

Performance Measure

To test hypotheses regarding the effects of payment equity on task performance, a $6 \times (6)$ mixed-design ANOVA was used, in which the six payment conditions composed the between-subjects factor and the six observation periods composed the within-subjects factor. A significant interaction effect between these two factors was obtained, $F(25, 950) = 8.41$, $p < .001$; the corresponding means are displayed in Figure 1.

Simple effects tests were performed to compare the six payment groups at each of the time periods. These tests revealed no significant differences between groups during

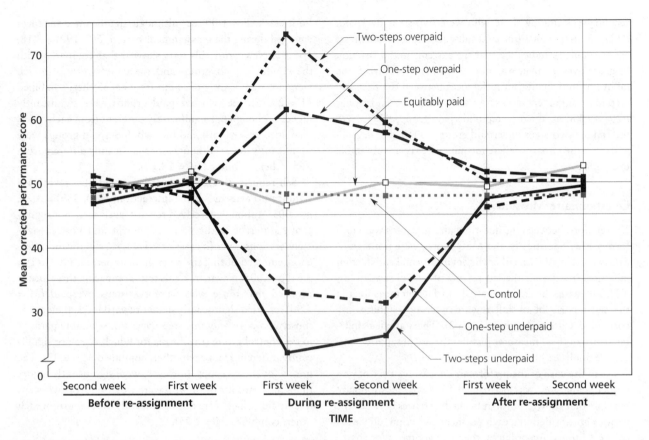

Figure 1   Mean job performance for each payment group over time.

each of the two weeks before reassignment, in both cases, $F < 1.00$ *ns*, and also during the second week after reassignment, $F < 1.00$, *ns*. However, significant differences between groups were found as workers readjusted to their permanent offices during the first week after reassignment, $F(5, 192) = 2.85$, $p < .025$. Newman-Keuls tests (this and all subsequent Newman-Keuls tests are based on an alpha level of .05) revealed that significant differences existed between workers in the one-step overpaid group and the one-step underpaid group, whereas those in the remaining groups were not significantly different from each other.

Significant differences emerged in simple effects tests comparing payment groups during the first week of reassignment, $F(5, 192) = 13.99$, $p < .001$. Newman-Keuls tests revealed that the performance of the equitably paid group and the control group did not differ significantly. However, compared with this base level, the one-step overpaid group was significantly more productive and the one-step underpaid group was significantly less productive. Additional comparisons showed that those who were two-steps overpaid were significantly more productive than those who

were one-step overpaid, and that those who were two-steps underpaid were significantly less productive than those who were one-step underpaid. Thus, for the first week during reassignment, all hypotheses were supported.

During the second week of reassignment, a significant simple effect of payment group was found as well, $F(5, 192) = 11, 60$, $p < .001$. As in the first week of reassignment, Newman-Keuls tests showed the equivalence of the control group and the equitably paid group. Also, as in the first week of reassignment, those who were one-step overpaid and underpaid performed significantly higher and lower than these base levels, respectively. The magnitude of inequity hypothesis was only partially supported during the second week of reassignment: Those who were two-steps underpaid were less productive than those who were one-step underpaid, but those who were two-steps overpaid did not perform at significantly higher levels than those who were one-step overpaid (although the difference between the means was in the predicted direction).

This finding is the result of a significant drop in performance from the first week during reassignment to the second week among those who were two-steps overpaid, $t(11) = 5.56$, $p < .001$ (this and subsequently reported t tests are two-tailed), indicating that the extreme initial reaction to gross overpayment was not sustained. By contrast, the failure to find significant differences between the first and second reassignment weeks for the one-step overpaid group, $t(29) = 1.98$, ns, the one-step underpaid group, $t(29) = .76$, ns, and the two-steps underpaid group, $t(11) = .88$, ns, suggests that the impact of these inequities was relatively stable over time.

Questionnaire Measures

Correlations between the questionnaire measures were uniformly low. Specifically, the MSQ scores were not significantly correlated with either the environmental satisfaction measures ($r = .04$) or the self-reports of overall reward ($r = .07$). Likewise, the environmental satisfaction measure and the self-reports of overall reward were not significantly correlated with each other ($r = .03$). The statistical independence of these measures justifies the use of separate univariate analyses.

As in the case of the performance measure, a set of preliminary analyses was performed for each questionnaire measure that showed nonsignificant differences between the various groups defining each payment condition, all values of $F < 1.00$, ns. Accordingly, the same six payment conditions that were used for the performance measure were created in analyses of the questionnaire measures. However, because there were three questionnaire-administration periods (as opposed to six performance-measurement periods), analyses of the questionnaire items were based on $6 \times (3)$ mixed-design ANOVAS.

A significant Payment × Time interaction was found for responses to the MSQ, $F(10, 389) = 3.01$, $p < .005$. A simple effects test found this interaction to be the result of between-group differences during the reassignment period, $F(5, 192) = 2.59$, $p < .01$, and no significant differences either before or after the reassignment, in both cases $F < 1.00$, ns. Newman-Keuls comparisons of the means within the reassignment period revealed significantly lower levels of satisfaction reported by workers who were two-steps underpaid ($M = 44.15$) compared with any of the other cells (combined $m = 75.50$), none of which were significantly different from each other.

Analyses of the environmental satisfaction questionnaire also revealed a significant interaction effect, $F(10, 389) = 3.65$, $p < .001$. Simple effects tests found that both the prereassignment and the postreassignment levels of satisfaction were not significantly different from each other, in

both cases, $F < 1.00$, ns, although significant differences emerged during the reassignment period, $F(5, 192) = 3.18$, $p < .01$. Newman-Keuls tests showed that compared with the equitably paid group and the control group (which were not significantly different from each other; combined $M = 29.75$), the two overpaid groups were significantly higher (although not significantly different from each other; combined $M = 40.50$) and the two underpaid groups were significantly lower (although not significantly different from each other; combined $M = 18.10$).

Self-reports of overall reward received also revealed a significant Payment × Time interaction, $F(10, 389) = 3.74$, $p < .001$. Although perceived reward levels were not significantly different at the prereassignment and postreassignment sessions, in both cases, $F < 1.00$, ns, significant differences emerged during the reassignment period, $F(5, 192) = 3.61$, $p < .005$. Newman-Keuls tests comparing these means revealed that those who were two-steps overpaid ($M = 5.90$) reported significantly higher reward levels than either those who were only one-step overpaid, equitably paid, or in the control group (the means for which were not significantly different from each other; combined $M = 4.33$). The means for these groups, however, were significantly higher than the means for those who were either one- or two-steps underpaid (which were not significantly different from each other; combined $M = 2.75$).

DISCUSSION

The results of the present study provide strong support for hypotheses concerning the status value of offices (Edelman, 1978; Konar & Sundstrom, 1985) as outcomes amenable to analysis by equity theory (e.g., Adams, 1965). The performance increases demonstrated by overpaid workers and the decreases demonstrated by underpaid workers in the present study take their place among many other studies that successfully support equity theory predictions (see reviews by Greenberg, 1982, 1987). The unique contribution of the present work, however, is the finding that conditions of overpayment and underpayment were able to be created by manipulating nonmonetary outcomes—elements of the work environment associated with organizational status.

Implications

As such, these findings support Adams's (1965) claim that "job status and status symbols" (p. 278) constitute outcomes in the equity equation, a notion that is just beginning to receive empirical support (e.g., Greenberg & Ornstein, 1983). This is in contrast to the well-established impact of monetary outcomes demonstrated in the equity theory literature (Greenberg, 1982, 1987). The specific vehicle of status examined in the present work, the physical environment of offices, although previously recognized by students of office design (e.g., Becker, 1981, 1982; Steele, 1973), heretofore has received scant attention as a possible determinant of workers' equity perceptions (e.g., Burt & Sundstrom, 1979). The present work extends the findings of research by Konar et al. (1982), which demonstrated that certain physical features of offices are related to organizational status by showing that these physical symbols of status demarcation operate as outcomes amenable to equity theory analysis. As such, the present findings provide a useful complement to the accumulated literature on office design (e.g., Davis, 1984; Konar et al., 1982; Sundstrom, 1986) by providing an explanatory mechanism that may account for employees' reactions to their work environments (e.g., Wineman, 1982).

The present investigation also supports equity theory's prediction that the reaction to an inequity will be proportional to the magnitude of the inequity experienced (Adams, 1965, p. 281). Specifically, underpaid workers were found to reduce their performance (i.e., lower their inputs) more when they were extremely underpaid (i.e., assigned offices of others two steps below them) than when they were more moderately underpaid (i.e., assigned offices of others one step below them). Likewise, workers who were more overpaid (i.e., assigned to offices of others two steps above them) raised their performance more than those who were more moderately overpaid (i.e., assigned to offices of others one step above them). This set of findings is particularly noteworthy in that it is one of only a few studies (e.g., Leventhal, Allen, & Kemelgor, 1969) that directly manipulate the magnitude of the inequity encountered. As such, it is notable in attempting to reverse a trend toward the "striking absence of attempts to quantify the magnitude of inputs and outcomes, and thus inequities in the research literature on equity" (Adams & Freedman, 1976, p. 52).

Of particular interest in the present research is observed tendency for overpayment inequity to bring about overall lower levels of performance increments than did underpayments bring about performance decrements. Such a finding is in keeping with Adams's (1965) supposition that the threshold for experiencing overpayment inequity is higher than that for underpayment inequity. Similarly, several studies (see review by Walster et al., 1978) have shown that reactions to underpayment are more pronounced than reactions to overpayment. The overall weaker effects of overpayment demonstrated in the present study appear to be the result of lower performance levels in the second week of overpayment than in the first week. Similar temporary effects of overpayment have been demonstrated in both laboratory (e.g., Greenberg & Ornstein, 1983) and field (e.g., Pritchard et al., 1972) settings. Such findings are in keeping with theoretical assertions that reactions to inequity may be moderated by the passage of time (Cosier & Dalton, 1983). Knowing that their overpayment was only going to be temporary, workers may have had little motivation to redress the inequity they experienced by sustaining high levels of performance (Greenberg, 1984). In contrast to the sustained effects of underpayment, more precise explanations for the diminished effects of overpayment over time are lacking and should be recognized as a topic in need of future research.

Further evidence for the less potent effects of overpayment relative to underpayment are provided by the job satisfaction data. Significantly lower levels of satisfaction were found only for the most extremely underpaid workers, but not for overpaid workers, thereby corroborating the weaker effects of overpayment demonstrated by Pritchard et al. (1972). In this regard, it is essential to note that the failure to find more pronounced differences on the job satisfaction measure does not weaken the equity-theory-based interpretation of the present findings. Although equity theory postulates that behavioral reactions to inequity are driven by attempts to alleviate feelings of dissatisfaction (Walster et al., 1978), it has been argued elsewhere (Greenberg, 1984) that such affective mediation has not been clearly demonstrated in previous research and may not be a necessary precondition for behavioral reactions to inequity.

Indeed, an equity theory analysis of the pattern of observed performance differences is supported by other questionnaire findings. Specifically, during the reassignment period, extremely overpaid workers reported receiving higher rewards and extremely underpaid workers reported receiving lower rewards than equitably paid workers. Apparently the office-assignment manipulation was successful in getting workers to perceive changes in their outcome levels. Specific evidence attesting to the fact that these overall rewards were the result of the work environment is provided by the findings of the environmental satisfaction questionnaire: During the reassignment period, overpaid workers reported greater satisfaction, and underpaid workers reported less satisfaction, compared with equitably paid workers (and compared with their reactions to their permanent offices). Such evidence not only shows that workers were aware of the differences in their work environments, but also that changes in environmental satisfaction levels (outcomes) may account for the observed performance differences (inputs).[4]

Limitations and Future Research Directions

Prompted by the diminished impact of overpayment over time found in the present study, one cannot help but wonder how long the observed effects of status-based inequities would persist. Before managers can be advised to manipulate workplace elements as a tactic for improving subordinates' attitudes or job performance (cf. Goodsell, 1977; Ornstein, in press), future longitudinal investigations need to be conducted to determine the persistence of the presently observed effects (or any reactions to inequity; Cosier & Dalton, 1983). Previous research suggesting that workers suspecting such manipulative intent might actually lower their performance (Greenberg & Ornstein, 1983) would dictate against intentional manipulations of inequity for instrumental purposes (Greenberg, 1982; Greenberg & Cohen, 1982). Clearly, future research is needed to determine the long-term reactions to inequities.

Additional future research is needed to help determine the relative contributions of the specific environmental elements manipulated in the present study. Indeed, the complex set of manipulations that defined relative status in the present study makes it impossible to determine which specific features may have had the greatest impact on the results. For example, we cannot determine from the present study whether the results were due to subjects' knowledge of the status of the office's permanent resident or of the status value of any of the furnishings or design (cf. Davis, 1984; Sundstrom, 1986). Although the inherent confounding of these features was necessary to enhance the validity of this field experiment, it would appear useful to isolate these factors in future laboratory experiments to determine their individual contributions (as outcomes) to inequity effects.

CONCLUSION

Given the importance of the workplace environment as a determinant of workers' job attitudes (Oldham & Fried, 1987; Sundstrom et al., 1980), it should not be surprising to find that workers' assignment to offices was related to their perceived level of job rewards and to their actual job performance. In this regard, equity theory proved to be a useful mechanism for explaining workers' reactions to temporarily encountered environmental conditions. As such, this work broadens the potential horizons of research and theory on organizational justice (Greenberg, 1987), as well as that on workplace environments (Becker, 1981; Sundstrom, 1986). As the rapprochement between these lines of investigation develops, we may well begin to understand the potential of the work environment as a tool for use by practicing managers (cf. Goodsell, 1977; Ornstein, in press; Steele, 1973).

REFERENCES

Adams, J. S. (1965). Inequity in social exchange. In L. Berkowitz (Ed.), *Advances in experimental social psychology* (Vol. 2, pp. 267–299). New York: Academic Press.

Adams, J. S., & Freedman, S. (1976). Equity theory revisited: Comments and annotated bibliography. In L. Berkowitz & E. Walster (Eds.), *Advances in experimental social psychology* (Vol. 9, pp. 43–90). New York: Academic Press.

Becker, F. D. (1981). *Workspace.* New York: Praeger.

Becker, F. D. (1982). *The successful office.* Reading, MA: Addison-Wesley.

Burt, R. E., & Sundstrom, E. (1979, September). Workspace and job satisfaction: Extending equity theory to the physical environment. In H. M. Parsons (Chair), *Physical environments at work.* Symposium presented at the 87th Annual Convention of the American Psychological Association, New York.

Cosier, R. A., & Dalton, D. R. (1983). Equity theory and time: A reformulation. *Academy of Management Reviews, 8,* 311–319.

Davis, T. R. V. (1984). The influence of the physical environment in offices. *Academy of Management Review, 9,* 271–283.

Edelman, M. (1978). *Space and social order.* Madison, WI: University of Wisconsin, Institute for Research on Poverty.

Geran, M. (1976). Does it work? *Interior Design, 47*(2), 114–117.

Goodsell, C. T. (1977). Bureaucratic manipulation of physical symbols: An empirical study. *American Journal of Political Science, 21,* 79–91.

Greenberg, J. (1982). Approaching equity and avoiding inequity in groups and organizations. In J. Greenberg & R. L. Cohen (Eds.), *Equity and justice in social behavior* (pp. 389–435). New York: Academic Press.

Greenberg, J. (1984). On the apocryphal nature of inequity distress. In R. Folger (Ed.), *The sense of injustice: Social psychological perspectives* (pp. 167–186). New York: Plenum Press.

Greenberg, J. (1987). A taxonomy of organizational justice theories. *Academy of Management Review, 12,* 9–22.

Greenberg, J., & Cohen, R. L. (1982). Why justice? Normative and instrumental interpretations. In J. Greenberg & R. L. Cohen (Eds.), *Equity and justice in social behavior* (pp. 437–469). New York: Academic Press.

Greenberg, J., & Ornstein, S. (1983). High status job title as compensation for underpayment: A test of equity theory. *Journal of Applied Psychology, 68,* 285–297.

Halloran, J. (1978). *Applied human relations: An organizational approach.* Englewood Cliffs, NJ: Prentice-Hall.

Harris, T. G. (1977, October 31). Psychology of the New York work space. *New York,* pp. 51–54.

Joiner, D. (1976). Social ritual and architectural space. In H. Proshansky, W. Ittleson, & L. Rivlin (Eds.), *Environmental psychology: People and their physical settings* (2nd ed., pp. 224–241). New York: Holt, Rinehart & Winston.

Kleinschrod, W. A. (1987, July). A balance of forces. *Administrative Management, 48*(7), 18–23.

Konar, E., & Sundstrom, E. (1985). Status demarcation in the office. In J. Wineman (Ed.), *Behavioral issues in office design* (pp. 48–66). New York: Van Nostrand.

Konar, E., Sundstrom, E., Brady, C., Mandel, D., & Rice, R. W. (1982). Status demarcation in the office. *Environment and Behavior, 14,* 561–580.

Langdon, F. J. (1966). *Modern offices: A user survey* (National Building Studies Research Paper No. 41, Ministry of Technology, Building Research Station). London: Her Majesty's Stationery Office.

Leventhal, G. S., Allen, J., & Kemelgor, B. (1969). Reducing inequity by reallocating rewards. *Psychonomic Science, 14,* 295–296.

Louis Harris & Associates, Inc. (1978). *The Steelcase national study of office environments: Do they work?* Grand Rapids, MI: Steelcase.

Oldham, G. R., & Fried, Y. (1987). Employee reactions to workspace characteristics. *Journal of Applied Psychology, 72,* 75–80.

Ornstein, S. (in press). Impression management through office design. In R. Giacolone & P. Rosenfeld (Eds.), *Impression management in organizations.* Hillsdale, NJ: Erlbaum.

Price, J. L., & Mueller, C. W. (1986). *Handbook of organizational measurement.* Marshfield, MA: Pitman.

Pritchard, R. D., Dunnette, M. D., & Jorgenson, D. O. (1972). Effects of perceptions of equity and inequity on worker performance and satisfaction. *Journal of Applied Psychology, 56,* 75–94.

Robichaud, B. (1958). *Selecting, planning, and managing office space.* New York: McGraw-Hill.

Steele, F. (1973). *Physical settings and organizational development.* Reading, MA: Addison-Wesley.

Stryker, S., & Macke, A. S. (1978). Status inconsistency and role conflict. In R. H. Turner, J. Coleman, & R. C. Fox (Eds.), *Annual review of sociology* (Vol. 4, pp. 57–90). Palo Alto, CA: Annual Reviews.

Sundstrom, E. (1986). *Work places.* New York: Cambridge University Press.

Sundstrom, E., Burt, R., & Kamp, D. (1980). Privacy at work: Architectural correlates of job satisfaction and job performance. *Academy of Management Journal, 23,* 101–117.

Walster, E., Walster, G. W., & Berscheid, E. (1978). *Equity: Theory and research.* Boston: Allyn & Bacon.

Weiss, D. J., Dawis, R. V., England, G. W., & Lofquist, L. H. (1967). *Manual for the Minnesota Satisfaction Questionnaire.* Minneapolis: University of Minnesota, Industrial Relations Center.

Wineman, J. D. (1982). Office design and evaluation: An overview. *Environment and Behavior, 14,* 271–298.

Wylie, H. L. (1958). *Office management handbook* (2nd ed.). New York: Ronald Press.

NOTES

1. The number of employees within each worker group assigned to each condition was predetermined by the number of available offices and the number of desks per office. To maintain the characteristics of the permanent offices while they were used as temporary offices, the number of temporary residents assigned to an office was kept equal to the number of its permanent residents. Further stimulating the permanent characteristics of the offices, while also avoiding possible confoundings due to having mixed-status office mates, all multiple-employee offices were shared by equal-status coworkers.

2. To keep constant the amount of time that all of the workers spent in their temporary offices, none were allowed to return to their permanent offices in advance of the 2-week period, even if the work was completed ahead of schedule. The physical separation of the various offices and the placement of construction barriers made it unlikely that workers could learn of any possible early completions. Because the 2 weeks allowed for completion of the offices was liberally budgeted, no delays in returning to permanent offices were necessitated.

3. A preexperimental questionnaire conducted among employees of the host organization indicated strong consensual agreement about the existence and nature of symbols of status demarcation in their organization. In responding to an open-ended question, 222 employees surveyed identified the four dimensions listed in Table 2 most frequently (from 75% to 88%) as reflective of status differences in their organization. Such findings are in keeping with those reported in more broad-based survey research (Louis Harris & Associates, 1978).

4. Unfortunately, however, because these questionnaires were administered only once during the reassignment period, the responses cannot be used to gauge changes in affective reactions within this critical period.

Received September 15, 1987
Revision received December 18, 1987
Accepted February 17, 1988

CRITICAL THINKING QUESTIONS

1. Why did the workers who were placed in offices of higher-status coworkers improve their performance? Why did the workers who were placed in offices of lower-status coworkers perform less well? Why was the effect stronger in the second situation?
2. What other nonmonetary factors affect perceptions of equity in the workplace? What nonmonetary factors affect perceptions of equity in intimate relationships (see Chapter 6)?
3. What would the effects have been like if the reason for the office reassignments had been different? What if the reassignments had been for a much longer period of time?
4. One might speculate that workers who had the chance to get a taste of the high-status office would feel deprived when they returned to their regular office, and that their performance would drop below their original level. But the results show that their performance did not drop below their original level. Why do you think this was the case?

5. What impact would giving everyone wonderful offices have on performance and perception of equity? Do you think randomly assigning people to offices would be effective? Given limited space and resources, how would you try to maintain equity and peak performance from your employees?

6. Is equity important in your life as a student (in team sports, group projects, grades, part-time or full-time jobs, intimate relationships, etc.)? How does your boss, instructor, or coach try to maintain equity, and how do you try to do this with others? Does equity seem more or less important than simply the total amount of rewards you get? Does equity play more or less of a role in social relationships than in working relationships?

READING 15

With the unprecedented amount of media coverage of recent high-profile crimes and trials, such as the trial of O.J. Simpson, the issue of the potential prejudicial effects of pretrial publicity has become more and more relevant. From dawn until late night, television news and talk shows, radio call-in shows, and tabloid newspapers and magazines present to the public a great deal of information concerning the crime and the participants in the trial. In many cases, much of this information is inaccurate, and even more of it would not be admissible in court. And yet impartial individuals must be found who can serve on the jury. Having been exposed to pretrial publicity, can these individuals disregard all that they have heard and base their verdict solely on the evidence presented in the trial itself?

In this article, Dexter, Cutler, and Moran cite a growing body of research that suggests that jurors can be prejudiced by pretrial publicity. Chapter 12 of your textbook also summarizes this literature, such as the extensive 1990 study by Kramer, Kerr, and Carroll. Kramer and colleagues found that instructions to the jury designed to minimize the effects of pretrial publicity did not reduce the impact of pretrial publicity. Delaying the trial so that jurors' memories of the pretrial publicity would have more time to fade was successful for some but not all types of publicity.

In the study described in this article, Dexter, Cutler, and Moran also examined the effectiveness of another possible remedy: the voir dire. As defined in Chapter 12, the voir dire is the pretrial examination of prospective jurors by the judge or opposing lawyers to uncover signs of bias. Many judges and lawyers are confident that they can eliminate the effects of jurors' exposure to pretrial publicity during the voir dire. Dexter and colleagues also designed their study to begin to address this question.

A Test of Voir Dire as a Remedy for the Prejudicial Effects of Pretrial Publicity

Hedy Red Dexter, Brian L. Cutler, and Gary Moran
Florida International University

The present experiment asked two questions: Does prejudicial pretrial publicity produce bias that may impair juror objectivity and, if it does, can extended, defense attorney-conducted voir dire (jury examination procedure) remedy its untoward effects? Subjects were 68 college undergraduates who had or had not read pretrial publicity one week before viewing a mock murder trial. Just prior to viewing the trial, subjects experienced either minimal or extended voir dire. Both pretrial publicity and voir dire produced significant main effects on subjects' perceptions of defendant culpability. Subjects exposed to pretrial publicity perceived the defendant as more culpable than subjects not exposed to pretrial publicity. Subjects who experienced extended voir dire perceived the defendant as less culpable than subjects who experienced minimal voir dire. The interaction between pretrial publicity and voir dire was nonsig-

nificant, indicating that, contrary to our hypothesis, voir dire did not reduce the impact of pretrial publicity.

In their review of the early literature on the effects of pretrial publicity on jury decision making, Carroll et al. (1986) noted that, after two decades of research, the fewer than a dozen studies assessing the prejudicial effects of pretrial publicity and judicial remedies yield little usable knowledge. Since then, however, the body of research addressing these issues has grown in both quality and quantity. Although there are many questions yet to be answered about how pretrial publicity affects jury decision making and which types of publicity are more prejudicial, there is now ample evidence that pretrial publicity can affect the juror's ability to be impartial (Carroll et al., 1986; Greene & Loftus, 1984; Greene & Wade, 1987; Kramer & Kerr, 1989;

SOURCE: Dexter, H. R., Cutler, B. L., & Moran, G. (1992). "A Test of Voir Dire as a Remedy for the Prejudicial Effects of Pretrial Publicity," *Journal of Applied Social Psychology,* 22, 819–832.

Kramer, Kerr, & Carroll, 1990; Moran & Cutler, 1991; Otto, Dexter, & Penrod, 1991; Otto, Penrod, & Hirt, 1991). Much less is known, however, about the effectiveness of various remedies that are believed to offset the prejudicial impact of pretrial publicity. Among the remedies available are judicial admonition, continuance, change of venue, and voir dire (the jury examination procedure).

An early study by Simon (1966) concluded that judicial admonitions cured the potential adverse effects created by either factual or sensational newspaper clippings about a murder case (Simon, 1966). The study, however, suffered methodologically (e.g., a biased subject selection strategy, the state's case was especially weak, and the design lacked conditions without judicial admonition). Other simulated jury studies, where juror verdicts were elicited, yielded effects for news exposure that were not remedied by judicial admonition (e.g., Kline & Jess, 1966; Padawer-Singer & Barton, 1975; Sue, Smith, & Gilbert, 1974; Sue, Smith, & Pedroza, 1975; Thompson, Fong, & Rosenhan, 1981).

The most comprehensive and ambitious study of the effectiveness of judicial remedies was conducted recently by Kramer et al. (1990). Using data from mock trials involving 617 Michigan residents and 174 undergraduates, they tested the remedial effects of judicial admonition and continuation on the impact of two types of pretrial publicity (emotional vs. factual). Judicial admonition had no remedial effect. Continuance (delaying the trial) remedied the effect of factual but not of emotional publicity. In real life, however, the media can usually be relied upon to reinstate the original prejudicial material at the time of the delayed trial.

The current study examines the extent to which voir dire serves as a remedy for publicity-induced prejudice. Previous attempts to offset the untoward effects of pretrial publicity with voir dire have failed (Kerr, Kramer, Carroll, & Alfini, 1991; Padawer-Singer, Singer, & Singer, 1974; Sue et al., 1975). In fact, the Padawer-Singer et al. (1974) study is frequently cited as demonstrating the curative effects of voir dire. Regrettably, this conclusion has been demonstrated to be the consequence of a methodological error (Kerr et al., 1991).

Opinions about the appropriateness and effectiveness of the voir dire examination could hardly be more disparate. Senator Howell Heflin of Alabama, in 1983, introduced bills in the Senate mandating attorney participation in civil and criminal voir dire. In Connecticut, attorney-conducted voir dire is constitutionally guaranteed and other large states (e.g., Florida, New York) also allow extensive voir dire. On the other hand, on June 5, 1990, California voters passed Proposition 115, effectively eliminating attorney-

conducted voir dire. Certain judges strongly favor attorney conducted voir dire (Hittner, 1989), but a researcher at the Federal Judicial Center, speaking for himself, authored a report critical of attorney ethics and effectiveness in voir dire (Bermant, 1985). Civil plaintiffs' attorneys and criminal defense attorneys believe strongly in the value of attorney-conducted voir dire, and civil defense attorneys as well as prosecutors regard it with misgivings (Bermant, 1985). Academicians (e.g., Hastie, 1991) frequently repeat the opinions of prior reviewers without noting that these opinions were not based upon empirical data. An optimal test of the efficacy of voir dire would not be based on a single trial. Rather, extensive voir dire would be compared to limited voir dire in trials where the evidence frequently allows for acquittal (e.g., rape or fraud offenses). In the absence of such data, conclusions about the effectiveness of voir dire remain speculative.

The present study tested the efficacy of an extended voir dire strategy—where the defense attorney sought to educate rather than eliminate prejudice—against a minimal voir dire (the typical procedure in the federal courts). Extended voir dire was used to: (a) provide examples of how pretrial publicity could inappropriately affect a juror's posture; (b) call jurors' attention to the relevant points of law and explain what is meant by them; (c) elicit individual and public commitments to comply with the law; and (d) make jurors accountable (to each other) for their actions. We attempted to create a manipulation with powerful impact by confounding many of the differences between minimal and extended voir dire, including source, content, and style. With respect to source, Jones (1987) found that attorney-conducted voir dire elicited more candid responses from mock-jurors than judge-conducted voir dire. Jones also found that personal style (formal vs. informal) had a significantly greater impact if the voir dire was conducted by an attorney than if conducted by a judge. Attorneys who adopted an informal style elicited more candid statements than attorneys who adopted a more formal style. In an effort to create a powerful manipulation, our minimal voir dire reflected the judge-formal whereas our extended voir dire reflected the attorney-informal conditions. In addition, extended voir dire took advantage of communication and persuasion techniques described by Penrod and Linz (1984) and exemplified in Crump (1980). The strategy of creating a powerful manipulation by deliberately confounding these factors is based on the following rationale. No study has been able to demonstrate that voir dire remedies the effect of pretrial publicity. Our goal was to attempt to demonstrate a remedial effect using a powerful manipulation and, if successful, to unconfound the techniques in subsequent research. By combining insight, public commitment, and juror accountability we hoped to focus jurors' attention on the evidence, convince them to hold the government to its burden of proof, and to set aside any influence of the pretrial publicity.

The following two hypotheses were tested: (I) pretrial publicity will exert a main effect on jurors' perceptions of defendant culpability such that subjects exposed to pretrial publicity will perceive the defendant as more culpable; and (II) voir dire and pretrial publicity will interact such that the effect of pretrial publicity on jurors' perceptions of defendant culpability will be stronger in the minimal voir dire condition than in the extended voir dire condition.

METHOD

Overview

Half of the subjects read newspaper articles containing information prejudicial to the defendant in a murder case. One week later all subjects then met at a courtroom. Subjects experienced either minimal or extended voir dire by a judge and two attorneys and then watched a 2-hour murder trial. Immediately following the trial subjects rendered judgments about the defendant.

Experimental Design

Two factors were manipulated independently, between subjects, in a 2×2 factorial design: (A) Pretrial Publicity (No Publicity vs. Publicity) and (B) Voir Dire (Minimal vs. Extended).

Subjects

Sixty-eight undergraduates at Florida International University were recruited from various psychology courses and were given extra credit for their participation. The cell sizes were as follows: No Publicity/Minimal Voir Dire = 15; Publicity/Minimal Voir Dire = 15; No Publicity/Extended Voir Dire = 15; Publicity/Extended Voir Dire = 23.[1]

Procedure

One week prior to the trial proceedings, subjects completed the Juror Bias Scale and some demographic items. Subjects were then randomly assigned to pretrial publicity condition. Immediately following completion of the preliminary questionnaires, news packets were distributed. This was done in class to ensure that subjects would read and, for those receiving pretrial publicity, rehearse the newspaper information. After reading the publicity subjects reported, in open-ended format, (a) if they had an opinion as to the guilt or innocence of each murder defendant and (b) what evidence they could cite to support their opinion. Subjects also rated the culpability of the defendant.[2] Trial proceedings took place at the University of Miami Law School. Voir dire, trial viewing, and deliberations were conducted in the moot courtroom. Subjects were randomly assigned to one of the two voir dire conditions. Successive voir dire examinations were conducted in the courtroom by the same legal ensemble (i.e., judge, prosecutor, defense attorney) beginning with the minimal voir dire. Experienced local attorneys played the roles of prosecutor and defense counsel in both voir dire conditions.[3] During voir dire, and afterward, subjects (whose turn was either over or not up yet) waited in a common area. Subjects in the extended voir dire condition waited 15 minutes while the other subjects went through the minimal voir dire. Attorneys admonished subjects not to discuss anything relevant to the trial until deliberation.

Contrasts between the minimal voir dire and extended voir dire conditions were sharply defined in terms of presenter length, content, and personal style. The minimal voir dire was conducted primarily by the judge, lasted only 15 minutes, and contained questions that were superficial. The judge's and attorneys' behavior [was] formal and there was little interaction between them and the mock-jurors. The prosecuting and defense attorneys each asked some superficial questions. The extended voir dire was conducted primarily by the defense attorney (following some superficial questions by the judge and prosecuting attorney), lasted approximately 60 minutes, and contained more probing questions. The defense attorney adopted an informal style and attempted to establish rapport with the mock-jurors. The prosecutor's role was minimal and constant across the two conditions.[4] Additional details about the voir dire conditions are provided below.

Minimal voir dire   The minimal voir dire condition was based on the standard voir dire examination used by federal courts (see Krauss & Bonora, 1983). It consisted of 10 questions asked by the judge. These questions, which are intended to probe the jury panel for prejudice, tend to be superficial and give little opportunity for those queried to disclose anything at all.

The following is typical of these questions:

Is there anyone on this jury panel who cannot, or will not, try this case fairly and impartially, based solely on the evidence that is received here in court, and under the instructions on the law as given to you by the court, and render a just and true verdict?

Most standard voir dire questions concern such matters as knowledge of any of the trial principals (e.g., attorneys, defendant, victim, witnesses, law enforcement officers, experts, etc.), occupation, prior jury service, and personal interest in the case at bar. The demand implications of the minimal voir dire are such as to encourage acquiescence with the court's presumption of impartiality. Supreme Court rulings (*Mu'min vs. Virginia*, 1991; *Wainwright vs. Witt*, 1985) clearly state that the mere assertion by a venireperson that (s)he will conscientiously apply the law and find the facts is a legally sufficient standard for impartiality. Despite this, it is important to understand that it is the trial judge who establishes the scope of the voir dire examination and the determination of venireperson excusals for reasons of bias (Hittner, 1989).

Extended voir dire   Following a few perfunctory questions by the judge the defense attorney spent most of the hour lecturing the jury and attempting to establish rapport through a casual and friendly question/response dialogue with individual mock-jurors. Mock-jurors were questioned about their attitudes in general and their exposure to pretrial publicity in particular. Upon ascertaining that many of the jurors had read pretrial publicity,[5] the defense attorney attempted to "debias" the jury. His strategy was to explain that journalists have different goals and standards than courts, that the news might not be true or relevant, and that, legally, it must be ignored. Rather than simply admonishing the jury not to rely on the news (as is typically done), he explained that, given the way people process information, it is natural to expect information learned earlier to affect later judgments and that in most contexts such learning is beneficial. The unnatural task, in contrast, is setting aside information once learned, such as that contained in pretrial publicity. To do so requires a conscious effort to monitor one's thinking and to censor oneself. Further, the attorney asked mock-jurors to hold fellow jurors accountable for not raising issues from the pretrial publicity. The attorney obtained public commitments from many of the jurors to base the verdict solely on the evidence presented in court and to ensure that fellow jurors do the same. The defense counsel elicited public commitments to objectivity from a number of subjects and attempted to make all subjects cognizant of their personal responsibility for their verdicts. It was thought that by (a) stressing accountability, both for one's own judgment and for others' behavior during anticipated deliberations (cf. Tetlock & Kim, 1987), (b) eliciting public commitments (cf. Kiesler, 1971), and (c) establishing rapport through an informal style and interactive dialogue (cf. Jones, 1987), subjects in

the extended voir dire condition would be more persuaded than subjects in the minimal voir dire condition to ignore the pretrial publicity.

After voir dire, all subjects assembled in the courtroom and watched the videotaped trial. Immediately following the trial, subjects completed the dependent measures.[6]

Materials

Juror Bias Scale   Kassin and Wrightsman's (1983) 17-item Juror Bias Scale assesses dispositional conviction-proneness. Sample items are "If a suspect runs from the police, then he probably committed the crime"; "Out of every 100 people brought to trial, at least 75 are guilty of the crime with which they are charged"; and "Too many innocent people are wrongfully imprisoned." In Kassin and Wrightsman's data, the Juror Bias Scale had a split-half reliability coefficient of .81 ($N = 221$) and a test-retest reliability, after 5 weeks, of .67 ($N = 31$; $p < .001$). Responses to each item were recorded on 7-point scales ranging from strongly disagree (1) to strongly agree (7). Possible scale scores therefore range from 17 to 119. The Juror Bias Scale has been found to correlate with the tendency to convict in a variety of criminal cases including murder (Cutler, Moran, & Narby, in press; Gallun & Kassin, 1983). It was included here so that individual differences in conviction-proneness could be covaried from the primary dependent variables.

Pretrial publicity   All media packets contained 7 news accounts of the murder case on which our stimulus trial was based. Articles were from the front page (including headlines) and from elsewhere in the newspaper. The articles were shuffled within each packet to avoid clustering of specific types of information. Subjects within a condition received identical news packets. Included in the publicity packet were 7 fictionalized news articles built on the original media coverage of the stimulus case, a Milwaukee, Wisconsin, murder. Starting with the basic case facts, statements about the defendant's prior criminal record, character, retracted confession, drug use, and physical abusiveness have been added to each article, information that the American Bar Association (1978) has called "highly prejudicial." Otto, Dexter, and Penrod (1991) found that excessive negativity in a news story reduced its prejudicial effect, so care was taken not to overdo the inflammatory tone of each article. All the "fictionalized" articles had the appearance of typical news stories in style, language, and format. Subjects in the no pretrial publicity condition received a publicity packet that contained 10 local interest news stories (not about crime or the law); these were originals and were not modified.

The trial Four 19-inch TV monitors, strategically positioned for easy viewing, were used to show the trial. The original trial was a 6 hour videotaped mock trial obtained from the State Bar of Wisconsin based on an actual criminal case. The state charged the defendant with first degree murder, contending that the victim was murdered after he made a pass at the defendant's girlfriend and that there may have been some involvement with drugs. Witnesses testified that the defendant had been holding the gun at the time of the shooting. The defense, on the other hand, claimed that there were no eyewitnesses to the actual shooting. A forensic expert testified that the bullet traveled at a 45° angle through the head of the deceased and would have to have been fired by a person positioned right next to him. Witnesses, in contrast, testified that the defendant had been standing 8 to 10 feet away from the deceased when the shot was fired. The videotape was filmed in an actual courtroom from a juror's perspective. Playing the roles of judge, prosecutor, and defense counsel in the videotaped reenactment are the individuals who actually tried the case. The witness roles are played by actors, and the reenactment is well done and compelling. In an effort to avoid floor or ceiling effects for verdicts and to reduce trial length, some of the testimony was edited out. Pretesting suggested that the trial was well balanced, $N = 10$; guilty = 60%; not guilty = 40%. The final version of the trial was approximately 2 hours in length.

Dependent measures Each subject rendered a predeliberation verdict (guilty vs. not guilty). In addition, each subject rated the strength of the prosecution's and defense's cases. These ratings were recorded on [a] 9-point scale (1–9) with higher scores indicating stronger cases. These three dependent variables were chosen because previous research has shown that they are highly intercorrelated (e.g., Cutler, Dexter, & Penrod, 1989). We believe that they are indices of defendant culpability.

RESULTS

Descriptive Statistics

Of the 68 subjects, 28 (41%) convicted and 40 (59%) acquitted. Prosecution case strength ratings ranged from 2 to 9 and averaged 5.04 ($sd = 2.33$). Defense case strength ratings ranged from 1 to 9 and averaged 5.43 ($sd = 2.13$). A paired t-test revealed that mean ratings for prosecution and defense case strength did not differ significantly, $t(67) = -.81$, $p > .10$, indicating that the case was well balanced. Juror Bias Scale scores ranged from 34 to 88 and averaged 65.55 ($sd = 11.85$). Two subjects failed to complete some

TABLE 1 Breakdown of Verdict and Case Strength Ratings by Condition

	Minimal VD		Extended VD	
	No PTP	PTP	No PTP	PTP
Juror Bias Scale scores	63.47	64.67	71.71	63.64
Proportion of acquittals	.53	.33	.80	.65
Prosecution case strength	5.27	5.73	4.73	4.65
Defense case strength	5.73	4.60	6.33	5.17

Note: PTP = pretrial publicity; VD = voir dire. Case strength ratings were recorded on 9-point scales (1–9); higher scores indicate stronger cases.

items of the Juror Bias Scale; their data were therefore excluded from the inferential analysis reported below. Cell means are displayed in Table 1.

Relations between dependent variables Table 2 displays the correlations between verdict (scored: 0 = guilty; 1 = not guilty), prosecution case strength, and defense case strength. The three correlations were substantial in magnitude ($rs > .50$) and statistically significant ($p < .01$). As expected, perceived strength of the prosecution's case was inversely related to perceived strength of the defense's case as well as to the tendency to acquit. Perceived strength of the defense's case was positively associated with the tendency to acquit. As mentioned above, we believe that these three variables are common indices of defendant culpability. To further test this contention, the dependent variables were subjected to a principle component analysis using orthogonal rotation. The first factor had an eigenvalue of 2.26 and accounted for 75% of the common variance. The remaining two factors had eigenvalues below .50. A single factor was therefore extracted. The communalities, displayed in Table 2, were .70 or greater. The factor loadings, also displayed in Table 2, were .84 or greater. These data indeed support the contention that verdict, prosecution case strength, and

TABLE 2 Relations Between Dependent Variables

	Correlations		Factor analysis	
	(2)	(3)	CM	FL
(1) Verdict	−.70	.65	.82	.91
(2) Prosecution case strength		−.54	.74	−.86
(3) Defense case strength			.70	.84

Note: CM = communality; FL = factor loading.

defense case strength assess a common underlying dimension. Hereafter we refer to this principle component as *defendant culpability*. For purposes of clarification of further analyses, increases in defendant culpability refer to a tendency to convict and perceptions of a stronger prosecution case and a weaker defense case.

Hypothesis Tests

We hypothesized that the main effect of Publicity and the Publicity × Voir Dire interaction would be statistically significant. The principal component of the dependent variables, defendant culpability, was subjected to analysis of covariance by performing a 2 (Publicity) × 2 (Voir Dire) MANCOVA. The dependent variables in this analysis were verdict, prosecution case strength, and defense case strength. The covariate was Juror Bias Scale score.[7] Results of the univariate analyses (ANCOVAs) are also presented following the results of the multivariate analyses.

Juror Bias Scale   The covariate produced a marginally significant multivariate effect on defendant culpability, $F(3,59) = 2.36$, $p < .10$. Consistent with previous findings, higher scores on the Juror Bias Scale were associated with increased defendant culpability. The univariate tests revealed that the Juror Bias Scale was a significant predictor of defense case strength, $F(1,61) = 7.20$, $p < .01$, $r = .32$, a marginally significant predictor of verdict, $F(1,61) = 3.67$, $p < .10$, $r = .24$, and a nonsignificant predictor of prosecution case strength, $F(1, 61) = 1.90$, $p > .10$, $r = .17$.

Pretrial publicity   In accordance with Hypothesis I, pretrial publicity produced a significant multivariate main effect on defendant culpability, $F(3,59) = 2.82$, $p < .05$. Subjects exposed to pretrial publicity perceived the defendant as more culpable than subjects exposed to no pretrial publicity. The univariate tests showed that pretrial publicity was significantly related to verdict, $F(1,61) = 4.33$, $p < .05$, $\eta^2 = .05$, and to defense case strength, $F(1,61) = 7.73$, $p < .01$, $\eta^2 = .07$, but nonsignificantly related to prosecution case strength, $F(1,61) = .92$, $p > .10$, $\eta^2 = .01$.

Voir dire   Voir dire also produced a statistically significant multivariate main effect on defendant culpability, $F(3,59) = 3.07$, $p < .05$. Subjects exposed to minimal voir dire perceived the defendant as more culpable than subjects exposed to extended voir dire. In the univariate analyses, voir dire was significantly associated with verdict, $F(1,61) = 8.82$, $p < .01$, $\eta^2 = .10$, marginally significantly associated with prosecution case strength, $F(1,61) = 3.09$, $p < .10$, $\eta^2 = .05$, and nonsignificantly associated with defense case strength, $F(1,61) = 1.71$, $p > .10$, $\eta^2 = .02$.

Pretrial Publicity × Voir Dire   Contradicting Hypothesis II, the interaction was nonsignificant in the multivariate analysis of defendant culpability, $F(3,59) = .14$, $p > .10$. The univariate analyses revealed that, for each dependent variable, the interaction was nonsignificant ($p > .10$) and trivial in magnitude ($\eta^2 < .005$). For verdict, $F(1,61) = .22$; for prosecution case strength, $F(1,61) = .04$; and for defense case strength, $F(1,61) = .38$.

DISCUSSION

The present study tested two hypotheses: (I) prejudicial pretrial publicity increases perceptions of defendant culpability; and (II) the impact of pretrial publicity on perceptions of defendant culpability is smaller after extended voir dire than after minimal voir dire. In support of Hypothesis I, subjects exposed to prejudicial pretrial publicity perceived the defendant as significantly more culpable than subjects exposed to no pretrial publicity. Hypothesis II received no support; the interaction between pretrial publicity and voir dire was nonsignificant for each dependent variable.

There are several plausible explanations for the failure of extended voir dire to reduce the impact of pretrial publicity. The first explanation is that the extended versus minimal voir dire manipulation had weak impact. Evidence against this explanation is the significant main effect of voir dire on juror judgments. Subjects exposed to extended voir dire perceived the defendant as significantly less culpable than subjects exposed to minimal voir dire. Although many doubt the efficacy of the voir dire, there is evidence of its effectiveness (e.g., Moran, Cutler, & Loftus, 1990). Because so many factors are deliberately confounded in the voir dire manipulation, future research is necessary to determine what caused the main effect. Regardless, it is clear that the voir dire had some impact on jurors' judgments.

A second plausible explanation for the nonsignificant interaction is that the extended voir dire employed here was insufficient to dislodge prejudice presumably caused by pretrial publicity. Although less frequent, some court systems (e.g., Florida and New York state courts) as well as many individual judges allow attorneys considerably more latitude and time than we afforded the attorney in the current study. Perhaps a longer and more in-depth voir dire would dislodge prejudice. Whether an even more extensive voir dire could neutralize pretrial publicity it seems to some essential to make a good faith effort. U.S. Supreme Court Justice Marshall decried a Virginia court's failure to probe jurors' exposure to pretrial publicity as "going through the motions" on the Sixth Amendment (*Mu'min vs. Virginia*,

1991). Marshall pointed out that a probing voir dire is always necessary because the burden of proving juror prejudice remains with the defendant.

A third plausible explanation is that publicity-induced prejudice cannot be dislodged with voir dire (Kerr et al., 1991).

In summary, this study produced findings consistent with earlier research on remedies in general (e.g., Kramer et al., 1990) and voir dire, in particular (Padawer-Singer & Singer, 1974; Sue et al., 1975). Pretrial publicity increased perceptions of defendant culpability and a proposed remedy, extended voir dire, failed to qualify the effect of pretrial publicity. At the same time, certain limitations associated with this study must be acknowledged, including its use of undergraduates as mock-jurors, a brief trial, no exercising of peremptory or causal challenges, and reliance on juror rather than jury decisions. How these limitations may have affected the results of the current study is unclear. A small sample size prevented us from examining *jury* (as opposed to *juror*) verdict. Kramer et al.'s (1990) data indicates that deliberation, if anything, exaggerates rather than reduces the impact of pretrial publicity. It is unknown how deliberation might interact with voir dire procedure. It is also possible that the main effect of pretrial publicity was affected by demand characteristics although it is consistent with findings of earlier studies that may be less susceptible to demands (e.g., Kramer et al., 1990).

Additional research efforts should be directed toward further revision of the voir dire procedure and tests of its ability to dislodge prejudice produced by pretrial publicity. Although the results of this study cause us to be somewhat pessimistic, we are nevertheless reluctant to throw the baby out with the bath water. Rather than raising questions about whether voir dire, as currently used, serves as an effective remedy, perhaps cognitive and social psychological research can be used to develop more effective voir dire procedures.

REFERENCES

American Bar Association. (1978). *Standards relating to the administration of criminal justice, fair trial and free press.* Chicago: American Bar Association.

Bermant, G. (1985). Issues in trial management. In S. M. Kassin & L. S. Wrightsman (Eds.), *The psychology of trial procedures* (pp. 298–322). Beverly Hills, CA: Sage.

Carroll, J. S., Kerr, N. L., Alfini, J. J., Weaver, F. M., MacCoun, R. J., & Feldman, V. (1986). Free press and fair trial: The role of behavioral research. *Law and Human Behavior, 10,* 187–201.

Crump, D. (1980). Attorney's goals and tactics in voir dire examination. *Texas Bar Journal, 43,* 244–247.

Cutler, B. L., Dexter, H. R., & Penrod, S. D. (1989). Expert testimony and jury decision making: An empirical analysis. *Behavioral Sciences & the Law, 7,* 215–225.

Cutler, B. L., Moran, G., & Narby, D. J. (in press). Jury selection in insanity cases. *Journal of Research in Personality.*

Gallun, E. Z., & Kassin, S. M. (1983). *The effect of the insanity defense and its consequences on jury verdicts.* Unpublished manuscript, Williams College.

Greene, E. L., & Loftus, E. F. (1984). What's new in the news? The influence of well-publicized news events on psychological research and courtroom trials. *Basic and Applied Social Psychology, 5,* 211–221.

Greene, E. L., & Wade, R. (1987). Of private talk and public print: General pre-trial publicity and juror decision-making. *Applied Cognitive Psychology, 1,* 1–13.

Hastie, R. (1991). Is attorney conducted voir dire an effective procedure for the selection of impartial juries? *The American University Law Review, 40,* 703–726.

Hittner, D. (1989, March). Federal voir dire and jury selection. *Trial,* 85–87.

Jones, S. E. (1987). Judge-versus attorney-conducted voir dire: An empirical investigation of juror candor. *Law and Human Behavior, 11,* 131–146.

Kassin, S. M., & Wrightsman, L. S. (1983). The construction and validation of a juror bias scale. *Journal of Research in Personality, 12,* 423–442.

Kerr, N. L., Kramer, G. P., Carroll, J. S., & Alfini, J. J. (1991). On the effectiveness of voir dire in criminal cases with prejudicial pretrial publicity: An empirical study. *The American University Law Review, 40,* 665–701.

Kiesler, C. (1971). *The psychology of commitment.* New York: Academic Press.

Kline, F. G., & Jess, P. H. (1966). Prejudicial publicity: Its effects on law school mock juries. *Journalism Quarterly, 43,* 113–116.

Kramer, G. P., Kerr, N. L. (1989). Laboratory simulation and bias in the study of juror behavior: A methodological note. *Law and Human Behavior, 13,* 89–99.

Kramer, G. P., & Kerr, N. L., & Carroll, J. S. (1990). Pretrial publicity, judicial remedies, and jury bias. *Law and Human Behavior, 14,* 409–438.

Krauss, E., & Bonora, B. (1983). *Jurywork: Systematic techniques* (2nd ed.). New York: Clark Boardman.

Moran, G., & Cutler, B. L. (1991). The prejudicial impact of pretrial publicity. *Journal of Applied Social Psychology, 21,* 345–367.

Moran, G., Cutler, B. L., & Loftus, E. F. (1990). Jury selection in major controlled substance trials: The need for extended voir dire. *Forensic Reports, 3,* 331–348.

Mu'min v. Virginia, 111 S. CT. 1899 (1991).

Otto, A. L., Dexter, H. R., & Penrod, S. D. (1991). *Pretrial publicity and jury decisionmaking: Experimental studies with actual cases.* Unpublished manuscript, University of Minnesota.

Otto, A. L., Penrod, S. D., & Hirt, E. R. (1991). *The influence of pretrial publicity on juror judgments in civil cases.* Unpublished manuscript, University of Minnesota.

Padawer-Singer, A., & Barton, A. H. (1975). Free press, fair trial. In R. J. Simon (Ed.), *The jury system: A critical analysis* (pp. 123–139). Beverly Hills, CA: Sage.

Padawer-Singer, A. M., Singer, A., & Singer, B. (1974). Voir dire by two lawyers: An essential safeguard. *Judicature, 51,* 386–391.

Penrod, S., & Linz, D. (1984). Voir dire: Uses and abuses. In M. F. Kaplan (Ed.), *The impact of social psychology on procedural justice* (pp. 135–163). Springfield, IL: Charles C. Thomas.

Simon, R. J. (1966, May–June). Murder, juries, and the press. *Trans-Action,* 64–65.

Sue, S., Smith, R. E., & Gilbert, R. (1974). Biasing effect of pretrial publicity on judicial decisions. *Journal of Criminal Justice,* 3, 163–171.

Sue, S., Smith, R., & Pedroza, G. (1975). Authoritarianism, pretrial publicity and awareness of bias in simulated jurors. *Psychological Reports,* 37, 1299–1302.

Tetlock, P. E., & Kim, J. I. (1987). Accountability and judgment processes in a personality prediction task. *Journal of Personality and Social Psychology,* 52, 700–709.

Thompson, W. C., Fong, G. T., & Rosenhan, D. C. (1981). Inadmissible evidence and juror verdicts. *Journal of Personality and Social Psychology,* 40, 453–463.

Van Dyke, J. M. (1977). *July selection procedures.* Cambridge, MA: Ballinger.

Wainwright v. Witt, 469 U.S. 412, 423 (1985).

NOTES

1. The unequal cell size was due to the following circumstances. Our organizational procedure required random assignment to experimental condition immediately after pretrial assessments. A substantial number of subjects who completed the pretrial assessments failed to attend the experiment at the University of Miami Law School. Presumably by chance, subjects assigned to the pretrial publicity/extended voir dire condition were more likely to attend the trial.

2. Our reason for having subjects rate the culpability of the defendant at this point was to ensure that they rehearsed the pretrial publicity. Rehearsal should decrease the likelihood that the publicity is forgotten during the subsequent trial (1 week later). The disadvantage to this procedure is that it creates a confound in the publicity manipulation. The manipulation is better characterized as: Publicity Plus Culpability Judgment vs. No Publicity. Further research can determine the impact of this confound.

3. The defense attorney has been practicing criminal defense law for 20 years; the prosecuting attorney has been practicing criminal law for 7 years.

4. Our decision to use extended voir dire only for the defense attorney is justifiable for a number of reasons. First, voir dire is traditionally employed for the benefit of the defendant and less so for the benefit of the government (Van Dyke, 1977, Chap. 6). As Van Dyke noted, it wasn't until this century that the government's right to exercise peremptory challenges was firmly established. It remains quite common in both state and federal courts for the defendant to have more peremptory challenges than the government. Further, the government usually takes less interest in the voir dire procedure, asking fewer questions and exercising fewer challenges. This is due to the fact that most venirepersons evidence a pro-government bias.

5. Half of the mock-jurors had read the pretrial publicity. Regrettably, it did not occur to us, in the planning of this experiment, that conducting the extended voir dire en-masse, during which mock-jurors discussed the publicity that they read, could lead to contamination of mock-jurors not exposed to pretrial publicity. This contamination might have reduced the magnitude of the pretrial publicity effect obtained in this experiment. Still, as noted by a reviewer of this article, extended voir dire (inadvertently exposed) subjects did not make harsher judgments than minimal voir dire/no pretrial publicity subjects. More importantly, in real trials, nonexposed venirepersons are made acquainted with the publicity when attorneys attempt to assess and allay it.

6. After watching the trial, subjects formed groups (within condition), deliberated to a group verdict, and completed a post-deliberation questionnaire. Our purpose for including this procedure is that, in our experience, subjects anticipate deliberation, learn from it, and enjoy it. The post-deliberation data are not reported here because the small number of juries (8) precluded analyses of group decisions and individual post-deliberation data violate the independence assumption. Readers interested in these data may contact the authors.

7. Our reason for using Juror Bias Scale score as a covariate is as follows. First, as mentioned above, Juror Bias Scale scores predict conviction-proneness in previous research and in this experiment. Second, despite our randomization procedure, the groups differ somewhat in mean scale scores (see Table 1). The Juror Bias Scale was administered *before* the manipulations, so scores on the scale cannot be influenced either by publicity or voir dire. Tests of heterogeneity of variance revealed no statistically significant two- or three-way interactions between Juror Bias Scale scores and the independent variables.

CRITICAL THINKING QUESTIONS

1. Why were the jurors' verdicts affected by the pretrial publicity, even when they received such extensive warnings against this? Do you think the jurors were aware that they were influenced by the pretrial publicity?

2. One possible reason why the extensive voir dire did not reduce the effects of pretrial publicity any more than the minimal voir dire is that the difference between the two conditions was not strong enough. What evidence suggests that the extensive voir dire was much stronger than the minimal voir dire?

3. How can the primacy effect and confirmatory hypothesis testing (Chapter 3) contribute to the effects of pretrial publicity?

4. The data reported in this study were from individual subjects' verdicts, not from verdicts reached after deliberations. Do you think the prejudicial effects of pretrial publicity would

have been stronger, weaker, or about the same if the jurors had deliberated before giving their verdicts? Why?

5. If you were a judge or lawyer, how would you try to reduce the effects of pretrial publicity?

6. Chapter 12 indicates that pretrial publicity is often biased in favor of the prosecution because the police and district attorney's office are in a better position to influence the media. Do you think that the same is true for very high profile cases in which the defendant can afford to hire expensive lawyers? Why or why not? Give examples to support your argument.

READING 16

This pair of articles describes a classic field study in health psychology that demonstrates the important effect that psychological changes can have on people's health. These two articles describe the short- and long-term effects of an intervention study of the elderly in a nursing home setting. A simple change in the structure of a nursing home that allowed residents to make more of their own choices, take responsibility for their actions, and care for other people and objects created benefits for general health and well-being and appeared to help residents live longer. These dramatic effects show the positive effects that perceived control of a situation can produce.

Chapter 14 in the textbook discusses this study and describes in more detail the notion of perceived control and its benefits on physical and psychological well-being.

In reading this article, note the care that the authors took in designing their intervention in the nursing home. At each instance they tried to give the residents receiving the intervention a sense of control. The two articles repeat some of the same information, but they are generally clear and easy to understand.

The Effects of Choice and Enhanced Personal Responsibility for the Aged: A Field Experiment in an Institutional Setting

Ellen J. Langer
Graduate Center, City University of New York

Judith Rodin
Yale University

A field experiment was conducted to assess the effects of enhanced personal responsibility and choice on a group of nursing home residents. It was expected that the debilitated condition of many of the aged residing in institutional settings is, at least in part, a result of living in a virtually decision-free environment and consequently is potentially reversible. Residents who were in the experimental group were given a communication emphasizing their responsibility for themselves, whereas the communication given to a second group stressed the staff's responsibility for them. In addition, to bolster the communication, the former group was given the freedom to make choices and the responsibility of caring for a plant rather than having decisions made and the plant taken care of for them by the staff, as was the case for the latter group. Questionnaire ratings and behavioral measures showed a significant improvement for the experimental group over the comparison group on alertness, active participation, and a general sense of well-being.

The transition from adulthood to old age is often perceived as a process of loss, physiologically and psychologically (Birren, 1958; Gould, 1972). However, it is as yet unclear just how much of this change is biologically determined and how much is a function of the environment. The ability to sustain a sense of personal control in old age may be greatly influenced by societal factors, and this in turn may affect one's physical well-being.

Typically the life situation does change in old age. There is some loss of roles, norms, and reference groups, events that negatively influence one's perceived competence and feeling of responsibility (Bengston, 1973). Perception of these changes in addition to actual physical decrements may enhance a sense of aging and lower self-esteem (Lehr & Puschner, Note 1). In response to internal developmental changes, the aging individual may come to see himself in a position of lessened mastery relative to the rest of the world, as a passive object manipulated by the environment (Neugarten & Gutman, 1958). Questioning whether

SOURCE: "The Effects of Choice and Enhanced Personal Responsibility for the Aged: A Field Experiment in an Institutional Setting," by Ellen J. Langer and Judith Rodin, *Journal of Personality and Social Psychology*, 1976, Vol. 34, No. 2, 191–198. Copyright © 1976 by the American Psychological Association. Reprinted with permission.

these factors can be counteracted, some studies have suggested that more successful aging—measured by decreased mortality, morbidity, and psychological disability—occurs when an individual feels a sense of usefulness and purpose (Bengston, 1973; Butler, 1967; Leaf, 1973; Lieberman, 1965).

The notion of competence is indeed central to much of human behavior. Adler (1930) has described the need to control one's personal environment as "an intrinsic necessity of life itself" (p. 398). deCharms (1968) has stated that "man's primary motivation propensity is to be effective in producing changes in his environment. Man strives to be a causal agent, to be the primary locus of, causation for, or the origin of, his behavior; he strives for personal causation" (p. 269).

Several laboratory studies have demonstrated that reduced control over aversive outcomes increases physiological distress and anxiety (Geer, Davison, & Gatchel, 1970; Pervin, 1963) and even a nonveridical perception of control over an impending event reduces the aversiveness of that event (Bowers, 1968; Glass & Singer, 1972; Kanfer & Seidner, 1973). Langer, Janis, and Wolfer (1975) found that by inducing the perception of control over stress in hospital patients by means of a communication that emphasized potential cognitive control, subjects requested fewer pain relievers and sedatives and were seen by nurses as evidencing less anxiety.

Choice is also a crucial variable in enhancing an induced sense of control. Stotland and Blumenthal (1964) studied the effects of choice on anxiety reduction. They told subjects that they were going to take a number of important ability tests. Half of the subjects were allowed to choose the order in which they wanted to take the tests, and half were told that the order was fixed. All subjects were informed that the order of the tests would have no bearing on their scores. They found that subjects not given the choice were more anxious, as measured by palmar sweating. In another study of the effects of choice, Corah and Boffa (1970) told their subjects that there were two conditions in the experiment, each of which would be signaled by a different light. In one condition they were given the choice of whether or not to press a button to escape from an aversive noise, and in the other one they were not given the option of escaping. They found that the choice instructions decreased the aversiveness of the threatening stimulus, apparently by increasing perceived control. Although using a very different paradigm, Langer (1975) also demonstrated the importance of choice. In that study it was found that the exercise of choice in a chance situation, where choice was objectively inconsequential, nevertheless had psycho-

logical consequences manifested in increased confidence and risk taking.

Lefcourt (1973) best summed up the essence of this research in a brief review article dealing with the perception of control in man and animals when he concluded that "the sense of control, the illusion that one can exercise personal choice, has a definite and a positive role in sustaining life" (p. 424). It is not surprising, then, that these important psychological factors should be linked to health and survival. In a series of retrospective studies, Schmale and his associates (Adamson & Schmale, 1965; Schmale, 1958; Schmale & Iker, 1966) found that ulcerative colitis, leukemia, cervical cancer, and heart disease were linked with a feeling of helplessness and loss of hope experienced by the patient prior to the onset of the disease. Seligman and his co-workers have systematically investigated the learning of helplessness and related it to the clinical syndrome of depression (see Seligman, 1975). Even death is apparently related to control-relevant variables. McMahon and Rhudick (1964) found a relationship between depression or hopelessness and death. The most graphic description of this association comes from Bettelheim (1943), who in his analysis of the "Muselmanner," the walking corpses in the concentration camps, described them as:

> Prisoners who came to believe the repeated statements of the guards—that there was no hope for them, that they would never leave the camp except as a corpse—who came to feel that their environment was one over which they could exercise no influence whatsoever. . . . Once his own life and environment were viewed as totally beyond his ability to influence them, the only logical conclusion was to pay no attention to them whatsoever. Only then, all conscious awareness of stimuli coming from the outside was blocked out, and with it all response to anything but inner stimuli.

Death swiftly followed and, according to Bettelheim,

> [survival] depended on one's ability to arrange to preserve some areas of independent action, to keep control of some important aspects of one's life despite an environment that seemed overwhelming and total.

Bettelheim's description reminds us of Richter's (1957) rats, who also "gave up hope" of controlling their environment and subsequently died.

The implications of these studies for research in the area of aging are clear. Objective helplessness as well as feelings of helplessness and hopelessness—both enhanced by the environment and by intrinsic changes that occur with increasing old age—may contribute to psychological withdrawal, physical disease, and death. In contrast, objective control and feelings of mastery may very well contribute to physical health and personal efficacy.

In a study conceived to explore the effects of dissonance, Ferrare (1962; cited in Seligman, 1975; Zimbardo & Ruch, 1975) presented data concerning the effects of the ability of geriatric patients to control their place of residence. Of 17 subjects who answered that they did not have any other alternative but to move to a specific old age home, 8 died after 4 weeks of residence and 16 after 10 weeks of residence. By comparison, among the residents who died during the initial period, only one person had answered that she had the freedom to choose other alternatives. All of these deaths were classified as unexpected because "not even insignificant disturbances had actually given warning of the impending disaster."

As Zimbardo (Zimbardo & Ruch, 1975) suggested, the implications of Ferrare's data are striking and merit further study of old age home settings. There is already evidence that perceived personal control in one's residential environment is important for younger and noninstitutional populations. Rodin (in press), using children as subjects, demonstrated that diminished feelings of control produced by chronic crowding at home led to fewer attempts to control self-reinforcement in the laboratory and to greater likelihood of giving up in the face of failure.

The present study attempted to assess directly the effects of enhanced personal responsibility and choice in a group of nursing home patients. In addition to examining previous results from the control-helplessness literature in a field setting, the present study extended the domain of this conception by considering new response variables. Specifically, if increased control has generalized beneficial effects, then physical and mental alertness, activity, general level of satisfaction, and sociability should all be affected. Also, the manipulation of the independent variables, assigning greater responsibility and decision freedom for relevant behavior, allowed subjects real choices that were not directed toward a single behavior or stimulus condition. This manipulation tested the ability of the subjects to generalize from specific choices enumerated for them to other aspects of their lives, and thus tested the generalizability of feelings of control over certain elements of the situation to more broadly based behavior and attitudes.

METHOD

Subjects

The study was conducted in a nursing home, which was rated by the state of Connecticut as being among the finest

care units and offering quality medical, recreational, and residential facilities. The home was large and modern in design, appearing cheerful and comfortable as well as clean and efficient. Of the four floors in the home, two were selected for study because of similarity in the residents' physical and psychological health and prior socioeconomic status, as determined from evaluations made by the home's director, head nurses, and social worker. Residents were assigned to a particular floor and room simply on the basis of availability, and on the average, residents on the two floors had been at the home about the same length of time. Rather than randomly assigning subjects to experimental treatment, a different floor was randomly selected for each treatment. Since there was not a great deal of communication between floors, this procedure was followed in order to decrease the likelihood that the treatment effects would be contaminated. There were 8 males and 39 females in the responsibility-induced condition (all fourth-floor residents) and 9 males and 35 females in the comparison group (all second-floor residents). Residents who were either completely bedridden or judged by the nursing home staff to be completely noncommunicative (11 on the experimental floor and 9 on the comparison floor) were omitted from the sample. Also omitted was one woman on each floor, one 40 years old and the other 26 years old, due to their age. Thus, 91 ambulatory adults, ranging in age from 65 to 90, served as subjects.

Procedure

To introduce the experimental treatment, the nursing home administrator, an outgoing and friendly 33-year-old male who interacts with the residents daily, called a meeting in the lounge of each floor. He delivered one of the following two communications at that time:

[*Responsibility-induced group*] I brought you together today to give you some information about Arden House. I was surprised to learn that many of you don't know about the things that are available to you and more important, that many of you don't realize the influence you have over your own lives here. Take a minute to think of the decisions you can and should be making. For example, you have the responsibility of caring for yourselves, of deciding whether or not you want to make this a home you can be proud of and happy in. You should be deciding how you want your rooms to be arranged—whether you want it to be as it is or whether you want the staff to help you rearrange the furniture. You should be deciding how you want to spend your time, for example, whether you want to be visiting your friends who live on this floor or on other floors, whether you want to visit in your room or your friends' room, in the lounge, the dining room, etc., or whether you want to be watching television, listening to the radio, writing, reading, or planning social events. In other words, it's your life and you can make of it whatever you want.

This brings me to another point. If you are unsatisfied with anything here, you have the influence to change it. It's your responsibility to make your complaints known, to tell us what you would like to change, to tell us what you would like. These are just a few of the things you could and should be deciding and thinking about now and from time to time everyday. You made these decisions before you came here and you can and should be making them now.

We're thinking of instituting some way for airing complaints, suggestions, etc. Let [nurse's name] know if you think this is a good idea and how you think we should go about doing it. In any case let her know what your complaints or suggestions are.

Also, I wanted to take this opportunity to give you each a present from the Arden House. [A box of small plants was passed around, and patients were given two decisions to make: first, whether or not they wanted a plant at all, and second, to choose which one they wanted. All residents did select a plant.] The plants are yours to keep and take care of as you'd like.

One last thing, I wanted to tell you that we're showing a movie two nights next week, Thursday and Friday. You should decide which night you'd like to go, if you choose to see it at all.

[*Comparison group*] I brought you together today to give you some information about the Arden House. I was surprised to learn that many of you don't know about the things that are available to you; that many of you don't realize all you're allowed to do here. Take a minute to think of all the options that we've provided for you in order for your life to be fuller and more interesting. For example, you're permitted to visit people on the other floors and to use the lounge on this floor for visiting as well as the dining room or your own rooms. We want your rooms to be as nice as they can be, and we've tried to make them that way for you. We want you to be happy here. We feel that it's our responsibility to make this a home you can be proud of and happy in, and we want to do all we can to help you.

This brings me to another point. If you have any complaints or suggestions about anything, let [nurse's name] know what they are. Let us know how we can best help you. You should feel that you have free access to anyone on the staff, and we will do the best we can to provide individualized attention and time for you.

Also, I wanted to take this opportunity to give you each a present from the Arden House. [The nurse walked around with a box of plants and each patient was handed one.] The plants are yours to keep. The nurses will water and care for them for you.

One last thing, I wanted to tell you that we're showing a movie next week on Thursday and Friday. We'll let you know later which day you're scheduled to see it.

The major difference between the two communications was that on one floor, the emphasis was on the residents' responsibility for themselves, whereas on the other floor, the communication stressed the staff's responsibility for them. In addition, several other differences bolstered this treatment: Residents in the responsibility-induced group were asked to give their opinion of the means by which complaints were handled rather than just being told that any complaints would be handled by staff members; they were given the opportunity to select their own plant and to care for it themselves, rather than being given a plant to be taken care of by someone else; and they were given their choice of a movie night, rather than being assigned a particular night, as was typically the case in the old age home. However, there was no difference in the amount of attention paid to the two groups.

Three days after these communications had been delivered, the director visited all of the residents in their rooms or in the corridor and reiterated part of the previous message. To those in the responsibility-induced group he said, "Remember what I said last Thursday. We want you to be happy. Treat this like your own home and make all the decisions you used to make. How's your plant coming along?" To the residents of the comparison floor, he said the same thing omitting the statement about decision making.

Dependent Variables

Questionnaires   Two types of questionnaires were designed to assess the effects of induced responsibility. Each was administered 1 week prior to and 3 weeks after the communication. The first was administered directly to the residents by a female research assistant who was unaware of the experimental hypotheses or of the specific experimental treatment. The questions dealt with how much control they felt over general events in their lives and how happy and active they felt. Questions were responded to along 8-point scales ranging from 0 (none) to 8 (total). After completing each interview, the research assistant rated the resident on an 8-point scale for alertness.

The second questionnaire was responded to by the nurses, who staffed the experimental and comparison floors and who were unaware of the experimental treatments. Nurses on two different shifts completed the questionnaires in order to obtain two ratings for each subject. There were nine 10-point scales that asked for ratings of how happy, alert, dependent, sociable, and active the residents were as well as questions about their eating and sleeping habits. There were also questions evaluating the proportion of weekly time the patient spent engaged in a variety of activities. These included reading, watching television, visiting other patients, visiting outside guests, watching the staff, talking to the staff, sitting alone doing nothing, and others.

Behavioral measures   Since perceived personal control is enhanced by a sense of choice over relevant behaviors, the option to choose which night the experimental group wished to see the movie was expected to have measurable effects on active participation. Attendance records were kept by the occupational therapist, who was unaware that an experiment was being conducted.

Another measure of involvement was obtained by holding a competition in which all participants had to guess the number of jelly beans in a large jar. Each patient wishing to enter the contest simply wrote his or her name and estimate on a piece of paper and deposited it in a box that was next to the jar.[1]

Finally, an unobtrusive measure of activity was taken. The tenth night after the experimental treatment, the right wheels of the wheelchairs belonging to a randomly selected subsample of each patient group were covered with 2 inches (.05 m) of white adhesive tape. The following night, the tape was removed from the chairs and placed on index cards for later evaluation of amount of activity, as indicated by the amount of discoloration.

RESULTS

Questionnaires

Before examining whether or not the experimental treatment was effective, the pretest ratings made by the subjects, the nurses, and the interviewer were compared for both groups. None of the differences approached significance, which indicates comparability between groups prior to the start of the investigation.

The means for responses to the various questionnaires are summarized in Table 1. Statistical tests compared the posttest minus pretest scores of the experimental and comparison groups.

In response to direct questions about how happy they currently were, residents in the responsibility-induced group reported significantly greater increases in happiness after the experimental treatment than did the comparison group, $t(43) = 1.96$, $p < .05$.[2] Although the comparison group heard a communication that had specifically stressed the home's commitment to making them happy, only 25% of

them reported feeling happier by the time of the second interview, whereas 48% of the experimental group did so.

The responsibility-induced group reported themselves to be significantly more active on the second interview than the comparison group, $t(43) = 2.67$, $p < .01$. The interviewer's ratings of alertness also showed significantly greater increase for the experimental group, $t(43) = 2.40$, $p < .025$. However, the questions that were relevant to perceived control showed no significant changes for the experimental group. Since over 20% of the patients indicated that they were unable to understand what we meant by control, these questions were obviously not adequate to discriminate between groups.

The second questionnaire measured nurses' ratings of each patient. The correlation between the two nurses' ratings of the same patient was .68 and .61 ($ps < .005$) on the comparison and responsibility-induced floors, respectively.[3] For each patient, a score was calculated by averaging the two nurses' ratings for each question, summing across questions, and subtracting the total pretreatment score from the total posttreatment score.[4] This yielded a positive average total change score of 3.97 for the responsibility-induced group as compared with an average negative total change of –2.37 for the comparison group. The difference between these means is highly significant, $t(50) = 5.18$, $p < .005$. If one looks at the percentage of people who were judged improved rather than at the amount of judged improvement, the same pattern emerges: 93% of the experimental group (all but one subject) were considered improved, whereas only 21% (six subjects) of the comparison group showed this positive change ($\chi^2 = 19.23$, $p < .005$).

The nurses' evaluation of the proportion of time subjects spent engaged in various interactive and noninteractive activities was analyzed by comparing the average change scores (post-precommunication) for all of the nurses for both groups of subjects on each activity. Several significant differences were found. The experimental group showed increases in the proportion of time spent visiting with other patients (for the experimental group, $\bar{X} = 12.86$ vs. –6.61 for the comparison group), $t(50) = 3.83$, $p < .005$; visiting people from outside of the nursing home (for the experimental group, $\bar{X} = 4.28$ vs. –7.61 for the comparison group), $t(50) = 2.30$, $p < .05$; and talking to the staff (for the experimental group, $\bar{X} = 8.21$ vs. 1.61 for the comparison group), $t(50) = 2.98$, $p < .05$.[5] In addition, they spent less time passively watching the staff (for the experimental group, $\bar{X} = -4.28$ vs. 9.68 for the comparison group), $t(50) = 2.60$, $p < .05$. Thus, it appears that the treatment increased active, interpersonal activity but not passive activity such as watching television or reading.

TABLE 1   Mean Scores for Self-Report, Interviewer Ratings, and Nurses' Ratings for Experimental and Comparison Groups

Questionnaire responses	Responsibility induced (*n* = 24)			Comparison (*n* = 28)			Comparison of change scores (*p* <)
	Pre	Post	Change: Post–Pre	Pre	Post	Change: Post–Pre	
Self-report							
Happy	5.16	5.44	.28	4.90	4.78	−.12	.05
Active	4.07	4.27	.20	3.90	2.62	−1.28	.01
Perceived Control							
Have	3.26	3.42	.16	3.62	4.03	.41	—
Want	3.85	3.80	−.05	4.40	4.57	.17	—
Interviewer rating							
Alertness	5.02	5.31	.29	5.75	5.38	−.37	.025
Nurses' ratings							
General improvement	41.67	45.64	3.97	42.69	40.32	−2.39	.005
Time spent							
Visiting patients	13.03	19.81	6.78	7.94	4.65	−3.30	.005
Visiting others	11.50	13.75	2.14	12.38	8.21	−4.16	.05
Talking to staff	8.21	16.43	8.21	9.11	10.71	1.61	.01
Watching staff	6.78	4.64	−2.14	6.96	11.60	4.64	.05

Behavioral measures

As in the case of the questionnaires, the behavioral measures showed a pattern of differences between groups that was generally consistent with the predicted effects of increased responsibility. The movie attendance was significantly higher in the responsibility-induced group than in the control group after the experimental treatment ($z = 1.71$, $p < .05$, one-tailed), although a similar attendance check taken one month before the communications revealed no group differences.[6]

In the jelly-bean-guessing contest, 10 subjects (21%) in the responsibility-induced group and only 1 subject (2%) from the comparison group participated ($\chi^2 = 7.72$, $p < .01$). finally, very little dirt was found on the tape taken from any of the patients' wheelchairs, and there was no significant difference between the two groups.

DISCUSSION

It appears that inducing a greater sense of personal responsibility in people who may have virtually relinquished decision making, either by choice or necessity, produces improvement. In the present investigation, patients in the comparison group were given a communication stressing the staff's desire to make them happy and were otherwise treated in the sympathetic manner characteristic of this high-quality nursing home. Despite the care provided for these people, 71% were rated as having become more

debilitated over a period of time as short as 3 weeks. In contrast with this group, 93% of the people who were encouraged to make decisions for themselves, given decisions to make, and given responsibility for something outside of themselves, actually showed overall improvement. Based on their own judgments and by the judgments of the nurses with whom they interacted on a daily basis, they became more active and felt happier. Perhaps more important was the judged improvement in their mental alertness and increased behavioral involvement in many different kinds of activities.

The behavioral measures showed greater active participation and involvement for the experimental group. Whether this directly resulted from an increase in perceived choice and decision-making responsibility or from the increase in general activity and happiness occurring after the treatment cannot be assessed from the present results. It should also be clearly noted that although there were significant differences in active involvement, the overall level of participation in the activities that comprised the behavioral measures was low. Perhaps a much more powerful treatment would be one that is individually administered and repeated on several occasions. That so weak a manipulation had any effect suggests how important increased control is for these people, for whom decision making is virtually nonexistent.

The practical implications of this experimental demonstration are straightforward. Mechanisms can and should be established for changing situational factors that reduce real or perceived responsibility in the elderly. Furthermore, this study adds to the body of literature (Bengston, 1973; Butler, 1967; Leaf, 1973; Lieberman, 1965) suggesting that senility and diminished alertness are not an almost inevitable result of aging. In fact, it suggests that some of the negative consequences of aging may be retarded, reversed, or possibly prevented by returning to the aged the right to make decisions and a feeling of competence.

REFERENCE NOTE

1. Lehr, K., & Puschner, I. *Studies in the awareness of aging.* Paper presented at the 6th International Congress on Gerontology, Copenhagen, 1963.

REFERENCES

Adamson, J., & Schmale, A. Object loss, giving up, and the onset of psychiatric disease. *Psychosomatic Medicine*, 1965, 27, 557–576.

Adler, A. Individual psychology. In C. Murchinson (Ed.), *Psychologies of 1930.* Worcester, Mass.: Clark University Press, 1930.

Bengston, V. L. Self determination: A social and psychological perspective on helping the aged. *Geriatrics*, 1973.

Bettelheim, B. Individual and mass behavior in extreme situations. *Journal of Abnormal and Social Psychology*, 1943, 38, 417–452.

Birren, J. Aging and psychological adjustment. *Review of Educational Research*, 1958, 28, 475–490.

Bowers, K. Pain, anxiety, and perceived control. *Journal of Consulting and Clinical Psychology*, 1968, 32, 596–602.

Butler, R. Aspects of survival and adaptation in human aging. *American Journal of Psychiatry*, 1967, 123, 1233–1243.

Corah, N., & Boffa, J. Perceived control, self-observation, and response to aversive stimulation. *Journal of Personality and Social Psychology*, 1970, 16, 1–4.

deCharms, R. *Personal causation.* New York: Academic Press, 1968.

Geer, J., Davison, G., & Gatchel, R. Reduction of stress in humans through nonveridical perceived control of aversive stimulation. *Journal of Personality and Social Psychology*, 1970, 16, 731–738.

Glass, D., & Singer, J. *Urban stress.* New York: Academic Press, 1972.

Gould, R. The phases of adult life: A study in developmental psychology. *American Journal of Psychiatry*, 1972, 129, 521–531.

Kanfer, R., & Seidner, M. Self-Control: Factors enhancing tolerance of noxious stimulation. *Journal of Personality and Social Psychology*, 1973, 25, 381–389.

Langer, E. J. The illusion of control. *Journal of Personality and Social Psychology*, 1975, 32, 311–328.

Langer, E. J., & Abelson, R. P. The semantics of asking a favor: How to succeed in getting help without really dying. *Journal of Personality and Social Psychology*, 1972, 24, 26–32.

Langer, E. J., Janis, I. L., & Wolfer, J. A. Reduction of psychological stress in surgical patients. *Journal of Experimental Social Psychology*, 1975, 11, 155–165.

Leaf, A. Threescore and forty. *Hospital Practice*, 1973, 34, 70–71.

Lefcourt, H. The function of the illusion of control and freedom. *American Psychologist*, 1973, 28, 417–425.

Lieberman, M. Psychological correlates of impending death: Some preliminary observations. *Journal of Gerontology*, 1965, 20, 181–190.

McMahon, A., & Rhudick, P. Reminiscing, adaptational significance in the aged. *Archives of General Psychiatry*, 1964, 10, 292–298.

Neugarten, B., & Gutman, D. Age-sex roles and personality in middle age: A thematic apperception study. *Psychological Monographs*, 1958, 72(17, Whole No. 470).

Pervin, L. The need to predict and control under conditions of threat. *Journal of Personality*, 1963, 31, 570–585.

Richter, C. On the phenomenon of sudden death in animals and man. *Psychosomatic Medicine*, 1957, 19, 191–198.

Rodin, J. Crowding, perceived choice, and response to controllable and uncontrollable outcomes. *Journal of Experimental Social Psychology*, in press.

Schmale, A. Relationships of separation and depression to disease. I.: A report on a hospitalized medical population. *Psychosomatic Medicine*, 1958, 20, 259–277.

Schmale, A., & Iker, H. The psychological setting of uterine cervical cancer. *Annals of the New York Academy of Sciences*, 1966, 125, 807–813.

Seligman, M. E. P. *Helplessness.* San Francisco: Freeman, 1975.

Stotland, E., & Blumenthal, A. The reduction of anxiety as a result of the expectation of making a choice. *Canadian Review of Psychology*, 1964, 18, 139–145.

Zimbardo, P. G., & Ruch, F. L. *Psychology and life* (9th ed.). Glenview, Ill.: Scott, Foresman, 1975.

NOTES

1. We also intended to measure the number of complaints that patients voiced. Since one often does not complain after becoming psychologically helpless, complaints in this context were expected to be a positive indication of perceived personal control. This measure was discarded, however, since the nurses failed to keep a systematic written record.

2. All of the statistics for the self-report data and the interviewers' ratings are based on 45 subjects (25 in the responsibility-induced group and 20 in the comparison group), since these were the only subjects available at the time of the interview.

3. There was also significant agreement between the interviewer's and nurses' ratings of alertness ($r = .65$).

4. Since one nurse on the day shift and one nurse on the night shift gave the ratings, responses to the questions regarding sleeping and eating habits were not included in the total score. Also, in order to reduce rater bias, patients for whom there were ratings by a nurse on only one shift were excluded from this calculation. This left 24 residents from the experimental group and 28 from the comparison group.

5. This statistic is based only on the responses of nurse on duty in the evening.

6. Frequencies were transformed into arc sines and analyzed using the method that is essentially the same as that described by Langer and Abelson (1972).

(Received July 5, 1975)

Long-Term Effects of a Control-Relevant Intervention with the Institutionalized Aged

Judith Rodin
Yale University

Ellen J. Langer
Harvard University

Elderly nursing home residents who were tested as part of an intervention designed to increase feelings of choice and personal responsibility over daily events were reevaluated 18 months later. Nurses' ratings and health and mortality indicators suggest that the experimental treatment and/or the processes that it set in motion had sustained beneficial effects.

In a field study (Langer & Rodin, 1976), we assessed the effects of an intervention designed to encourage elderly nursing home residents to make a greater number of choices and to feel more control and responsibility for day-to-day events. The study was intended to determine whether the decline in health, alertness, and activity that generally occurs in the aged in nursing home settings could be slowed or reversed by choice and control manipulations that have been shown to have beneficial effects in other contexts (Lefcourt, 1973; Seligman, 1975; Zimbardo & Ruch, 1975). This also allowed us to extend the domain of the control conception by using a new population and a new set of response variables.

The hospital administrator gave a talk to residents in the experimental group emphasizing their responsibility for themselves, whereas the communication given to a second, comparison group stressed the staff's responsibility for them as patients. To bolster the communication, residents in the experimental group were offered plants to care for, whereas residents in the comparison group were given plants that were watered by the staff. In reality, the choices and potential for responsibility that we enumerated in the treatment condition were options that were already available; the administrator simply stated them clearly as possibilities. Thus the institutional readiness was already there, and the experimental induction was intended to bolster individual predispositions for increased choice and self-control.

The data indicated that residents in the responsibility-induced group became more active and reported feeling happier than the comparison group of residents, who were encouraged to feel that the staff would care for them and try to make them happy. Patients in the responsibility-induced group also showed a significant improvement in alertness and increased behavioral involvement in many different kinds of activities, such as movie attendance, active socializing with staff and friends, and contest participation. In addition to collecting these multiple questionnaire and behavioral measures at the time, we have now been able to collect long-term follow-up data on several variables, including mortality. As in Langer and Rodin (1976), our intent was to gather as many measures as were accessible for this population with the goal of increasing accuracy with increased heterogeneity of methodology (Campbell & Fiske, 1959).

METHOD

Subjects

There were 91 subjects given the original experimental treatment. The analyses in Langer and Rodin (1976) were based on 52 of these subjects. These were all the people for whom two nurses' ratings (for reliability assessment) were available. Table 1 indicates which subjects are included in

TABLE 1   Number of Subjects in Test Samples

Condition	Responsibility induced	Comparison	Control
Received original induction	47	44	—
Included in Langer & Rodin (1976) analyses	24	28	—
In follow-up and included in Langer & Rodin (1976) analyses	14	12	—
Total in follow-up	20	14	9

SOURCE: "Long-Term Effects of a Control-Relevant Intervention with the Institutionalized Aged," by Ellen J. Langer and Judith Rodin, *Journal of Personality and Social Psychology*, 1977, Vol. 35, No. 12, 879–902. Copyright © 1977 by the American Psychological Association. Reprinted with permission.

the follow-up analyses. Twenty-six of the 52 were still in the nursing home and were retested. Twelve had died, and 14 had been transferred to other facilities or had been discharged. The differences between treatment conditions in mortality are considered in a subsequent section. The groups did not differ in transfer or discharge rate. Only 9 other persons from the original sample of 91 were available for retesting. Since they had incomplete nurses' ratings in the first study, they are only included in follow-up analyses not involving change scores in nurses' evaluations. Almost all of the participants now lived in different rooms, since the facility had completed a more modern addition 13 months after the experimental treatment.[1]

We also evaluated a small control group of patients who had not participated in the first study due to a variety of scheduling problems. Five had previously lived on the same floor as subjects in the responsibility-induced condition, and 4 lived on the same floor as the comparison group. All were now living in the new wing. The average length of time in the nursing home was 3.9 years, which was not reliably different for the three groups.

Measures

Nurses' ratings   Two nurses on different shifts evaluated each patient along 9-point verbally anchored semantic differential scales for mood, awareness, sociability, mental attitude, and physical activity. Nurses were unaware of a relationship between prior experimental treatments and the purpose of these particular ratings.

Physician's ratings   A doctor on the nursing home staff evaluated the medical records of each patient for two periods. The first period represented the 6 months prior to the first study in 1974, and the second period represented the 6 months that immediately preceded the follow-up. On the basis of the medical data reported on the charts, he assigned the person an overall health score (1 = very good to 5 = poor) for each period. The physician's health ratings were independent of the nurses' evaluations, which did not appear on the medical charts that he used. Like the nurses, he was unaware of the nature of the study and how his ratings would be used. Further, the physician was not employed by the nursing home when the original intervention occurred.

Behavioral indices   After all the questionnaire measures had been taken, one of us (JR) gave a talk at the nursing home on psychology and aging. This was advertised widely among the residents, and they were encouraged to come and ask questions. The number of people in each condition who attended and the frequency and type of questions they asked were recorded.

Mortality   A frequency count of deaths occurring during the 18-month period was made, and the cause of death was noted.

RESULTS

Nurses' Ratings

Since the interrater reliability coefficient between nurses who rated the same patient was high ($r = .76$), the ratings were averaged, and the resulting means were used for subsequent analysis.[2] First, a composite score was developed representing the total of the individual evaluative items. A one-way analysis of variance comparing the responsibility-induced ($M = 25.03$), comparison ($M = 18.71$), and no-treatment ($M = 17.60$) groups was significant, $F(2, 40) = 7.04$, $p < .01$. A Scheffé test indicated that the responsibility-induced group was rated reliably higher than the comparison group, $F(1, 40) = 6.31$, $p < .05$.

The means for each individual item are presented in Table 2. On the average, the patients in the responsibility-induced group were judged to be significantly more actively interested in their environment, more sociable and self-initiating, and more vigorous than residents in the comparison group. The mean ratings also show the similarity between the comparison group given the "happiness" induction and the no-treatment group.

Composite scores for all the evaluative items were also available from the questionnaire, which the nurses com-

TABLE 2   Mean Ratings for Residents 18 Months Following Experimental Interventions

Nurses' rating	Responsibility induced (20)[a]	Comparison (14)[a]	No treatment control (9)[b]
Happy	4.35	3.68	3.28
Actively interested	5.15	3.96	3.95
Sociable	5.00	3.78	3.40
Self-initiating	5.15	3.90	4.18
Vigorous	4.75	3.39	3.33

Note: The difference between the responsibility-induced and comparison groups was reliable at $p < .05$ for all ratings but happy. Numbers in parentheses are *n*s.
[a] Received experimental treatment in Langer and Rodin (1976).
[b] Not previously tested.

pleted prior to the original intervention and at the 3-week posttest. The means presented in Table 3 include all residents for whom these two scores and follow-up data were available ($n = 14$ for the responsibility-induced group, and $n = 12$ for the comparison group). Change scores between the preintervention means and the 18-month follow-up data indicate that the decline was significantly smaller for the responsibility-induced group ($M = 58.21$) than for the comparison condition ($M = 175.42$), $t(24) = 2.68, p < .02$. Change scores calculated between the 3-week postintervention ratings and the 18-month follow-up showed marginally, reliable differences in the same direction, $t(24) = 1.82, p < .10$.

Health Ratings

Change scores were calculated between the preintervention (1974) and follow-up (1976) health evaluation ratings. Health ratings were retrospective, based on the medical records, so change scores could be calculated for all 43 follow-up subjects. There was no significant difference among the three groups in the preintervention health evaluations, $F(2, 40) = 1.77$. The responsibility-induced group showed a mean increase in general health of .55 on a 5-point scale, which was reliably greater than means for the comparison group ($M = -.29$) and the no-treatment group ($M = -.33$), $F(2, 40) = 3.73, p < .05$.

Mortality

The most striking data were obtained in death rate differences between the two treatment groups. Taking the 18

months prior to the original intervention as an arbitrary comparison period, we found that the average death rate during that period was 25% for the entire nursing home. In the subsequent 18-month period following the intervention, only 7 of the 47 subjects (15%) in the responsibility-induced group died, whereas 13 of 44 subjects (30%) in the comparison group had died. Using the arcsine transformation for frequencies, this difference is reliable ($z = 3.14$, $p < .01$).

Because these results were so startling, we assessed other factors that might have accounted for the differences. Unfortunately, we simply cannot know everything about the equivalency of these subjects prior to the intervention. We do know that those who died did not differ reliably in the length of time that they had been institutionalized or in their overall health status when the study began. These means are presented in Table 4, which also presents the nurses' evaluations prior to the intervention. From these ratings it is clear that the nurses had given lower evaluations prior to the intervention to those patients who subsequently died than to those who were still living, $F(1, 48) = 7.73, p < .01$. The interaction between treatment group and the life-death variable was not significant, however.

The actual causes of death that appeared on the medical record varied greatly among individuals and did not appear to be systematic within conditions. For example, deaths in the responsibility-induced group were listed as due to factors such as cardiovascular disease, congestive heart failure, gastrointestinal bleeding, lymphoma, and cerebral hemorrhage. Similarly there were patients in the comparison group whose cause of death was also listed as congestive heart failure and cardiac arrest, as well as those dying from problems like gangrene foot and polynephritis.

Behavioral Measures

There were no reliable differences among the three conditions in lecture attendance. Thirty-three percent of the responsibility-induced group attended, as compared to 30% of the comparison group and 20% of the no-treatment group. However, these groups did differ in the number and type of questions that they asked. Of the 14 questions that were asked, 10 came from residents in the responsibility-induced condition. The lecture and questions were taped, and subsequent content analysis by a coder who was blind to the experimental treatments indicated that 4 of the 10 questions had themes of autonomy and independence. For example, one female inquired whether intelligence really did decline with age, and if so, did that necessarily mean

TABLE 3 Mean Composite Nurses' Evaluation Scores Taken at Three Different Time Periods Relative to the Intervention

Time period	Responsibility induced	Comparison
Preintervention	402.38	442.93
Postintervention (3 weeks)	436.50	413.03
Follow-up (18 months)	352.33	262.00

Note: There were seven 10-point items on the scales used by Langer and Rodin (1976), making a total of 70 points possible. There were five items in the follow-up questionnaire, and the ratings were made on 9-point scales making a total of 45 possible points. The Langer and Rodin totals were multiplied by 9 and the follow-up totals by 14 to make the scores comparable.

TABLE 4   Mean Ratings Prior to Intervention Grouped by Subsequent Mortality Outcome

Variable	Responsibility induced		Comparison	
	Dead	Living	Dead	Living
Time institutionalized	2.40 (7)	2.70 (40)	2.80 (13)	2.20 (31)
Health ratings	3.57 (7)	3.85 (40)	3.69 (13)	3.64 (31)
Nurses' evaluations	36.20 (5)	44.79 (19)	31.69 (8)	47.39 (20)

Note: The numbers in parentheses represent the number of residents on whom each mean is based.

that older people should be taken care of? Another asked how to make her children feel less guilty about putting her in the nursing home. No questions from the comparison or no-treatment group dealt with these themes, but 2 of their 4 questions dealt with death. For example, one man asked whether senility could cause death. A woman who had obviously read the self-reported experiences of people who had a close brush with death asked whether this euphoric feeling was a universal experience or whether it differed as one got older. No one in the responsibility-induced group asked a death-relevant question.

DISCUSSION

The intervention described by Langer and Rodin (1976) was stimulated, in part, by our theoretical interest in control. We attempted to capture these theoretical concerns in a manipulation that suggested how elderly residents might increase choice and self-control in the nursing home. The manipulation did indeed produce strong effects that lasted as long as 18 months later. Compared to the staff-support comparison group, and to the no-treatment group where relevant, residents in the responsibility-induced condition showed higher health and activity patterns, mood and sociability which did not decline as greatly, and they had mortality rates that were lower. We would like to interpret these effects as suggesting that decline can be slowed or, with a stronger intervention, perhaps can even be reversed by manipulations that provide an increased sense of effectance in the institutionalized elderly. Krantz (Note 1) and Schulz (1976) also recently found that experimental manipulations involving increased or diminished prediction and control have a significant impact on the elderly. Moreover, adjustment to relocation for older people appears more related to whether or not they have had a choice regarding the new setting than to specific features of the setting itself (Sherman, 1975).

Since the original intervention (Langer & Rodin, 1976) encouraged residents to create or utilize opportunities for control over on-going daily events rather than over momentary, experimentally created tasks, it seemed reasonable to assume that the effects of this induction would continue after the study itself was completed. However, despite our intent in designing this particular set of interventions to extend the domain of the control conception, we have no real way of knowing without direct on-line observation exactly what the process was that generated the obtained improvements. As is often the case in any field study, we were unable to control some important features of the setting due to both ethical and practical constraints.

First, it would certainly have been more desirable to randomly assign residents to conditions within a floor rather than between floors. A manipulation aimed at changing the behavior of any individual resident could have interacted with changes occurring in his or her neighbors, who were also exposed to the same manipulation. However, we believed that at least some of the residents might discuss the administrator's communication if they saw themselves divided into different groups and that we would be unable to know whether and for whom this had occurred. Once having decided to assign by floor, we would also have chosen to have a third floor as a no-treatment control group. Although we simply lacked this option, data from the control group formed for the follow-up suggest that the responsibility group improved, rather than that the comparison group worsened, relative to "no-treatment" controls.

Second, the nurses could undoubtedly have made a great deal of difference in a variety of ways. Although they were unaware of the nature of the original intervention and did not attend the meeting where the communication was given, simply recording data about the residents and perhaps feeling observed themselves may have changed their awareness and behavior. In addition, once the patients began to change, the nurses must have responded favorably to improved behavior, sociability, and self-reliance. We can only take the administrator's word that he did not change his own behavior differentially toward the patients as a result of delivering the communications. The differences in nurses' ratings between conditions were maintained, however, even with changes in the nursing personnel, staff rotations, a move, and relocation of some residents to different floors. Nonetheless, it is striking to note that the nurses' evaluations of the patients and not the overall health ratings were more closely related to subsequent life and death. Either the psychological variables that the nurses were rating are better predictors of later mortality than medical symptom evaluations or the nurses' views of the residents are significant factors in their potential longevity. One clear area for further study is the patient-nurse interaction to assess if and how this factor is related to patient health.

Finally, it is especially true that this particular nursing home was open and primed to be responsive. When the options for increased patient involvement do not already exist, simple interventions of the sort used by Langer and Rodin (1976) may have to be elaborated over repeated trials and bolstered by changing the setting enough to allow the manipulations to have a sustainable outcome.

This is not an exhaustive list; it is simply provided to illustrate some of the most plausible ways in which the results could have been obtained without being due to increased choice and responsibility per se. Whatever the actual mediating process, it seems clear that decline is not inevitable. Indeed, the strength of the data suggests the value of further investigation into the context-specific social-psychological factors that influence aging. In these studies, process measures must now be taken to assess how the manipulations actually produce their effects.

If the improvements are due to greater control; it must surely be the case that potential benefits are nonmonotonically related to increasing control. For example, one can conceive of circumstances in which a great amount of choice and responsibility would have negative effects for both the patients themselves and on the setting too. In addition, it should be clear that interventions that increase control-relevant features of one's life, including increased predictability, decision-making, and outcome control, should be those that are not withdrawn by the termination of the study. The long-term beneficial effects observed in the present study probably were obtained because the original treatment was not directed toward a single behavior or stimulus condition. They instead fostered generalized feel-ings of increased competence in day-to-day decision making where it was potentially available. To the extent that a treatment is successful in providing these kinds of control, its termination could serve to make salient the loss of control and, as such, might lead to even greater debilitation than was first encountered.

REFERENCE NOTE

1. Krantz, D. Data presented at an invited discussion on *New directions in control research.* Presented at the annual meeting of the American Psychological Association, Washington, D.C., September 1976.

REFERENCES

Campbell, D. T., & Fiske, D. W. Convergent and discriminate validation by the multitrait-multimethod matrix. *Psychological Bulletin,* 1959, *56,* 81–105.

Langer, E. J., & Rodin, J. The effects of choice and enhanced personal responsibility for the aged: A field experiment in an institutional setting. *Journal of Personality and Social Psychology,* 1976, *34,* 191–198.

Lefcourt, H. The function of the illusion of control and freedom. *American Psychologist,* 1973, *28,* 417–425.

Schulz, R. Effects of control and predictability on the psychological well-being of the institutionalized aged. *Journal of Personality and Social Psychology,* 1976, *33,* 563–573.

Seligman, M. E. P. *Helplessness.* San Francisco: Freeman, 1975.

Sherman, S. Patterns of contacts for residents of age-segregated and age-integrated housing. *Journal of Gerontology,* 1975, *30,* 103–107.

Zimbardo, P. G., & Ruch, F. L. *Psychology and life* (9th ed.). Glenview, Ill.: Scott, Foresman, 1975.

NOTES

1. All patients were given the option to move, and all did so. Those who wished to remain with their roommates were kept together, although people previously on the same floor were not all moved together to the same floor in the new wing. Interestingly, 33% of the patients in the responsibility-induced group, as compared to 21% in the comparison group, spontaneously requested to move even before they were given the choice.

2. Two nurses on each floor rated all relevant patients on their floor, regardless of condition. Six nurses participated as raters. Since the patients no longer all lived together, residents formerly in the same group and thus rated by the same nurses were now rated by different nurses. Thus it is unlikely that the means for each treatment group were due to differences in the nurses who did the rating rather than to the patients themselves.

Received February 16, 1977

CRITICAL THINKING QUESTIONS

1. This study was conducted in the mid-1970s. Do you think that conditions in nursing homes have changed much since that time? If so, could the results of this study have

influenced those changes? If not, why do you think the results of this study did not help produce change?

2. Langer and Rodin used several different ways to try to give residents a sense of choice and control. How do we know which of these methods actually work? For example, is it enough to just give someone a plant to take care of? What factors do you think were most important?

3. What other groups besides the elderly might benefit from changes in their environment that give them an increased sense of control?

4. Why was it important to follow up the study to examine its long-term effects? How would it have mattered if there had been no long-term effects of the study? Would the study still be valuable?

5. Other than increasing their sense of control, do you think that the procedures used in the intervention group might have had any other effects that contributed to the results of the study? Are there other social psychological factors that you think would also improve the health and well-being of nursing home patients? Would the same social psychological factors help the health of younger patients who are hospitalized for various reasons?

6. Langer and Rodin used residents' own ratings, nurses' ratings, and interviews to assess how residents were responding to the treatment. Why did they select several different measures? Are there other measures they should have collected?